Design and Analysis of Security Protocol for Communication

Scrivener Publishing
100 Cummings Center, Suite 541J
Beverly, MA 01915-6106

Publishers at Scrivener
Martin Scrivener (martin@scrivenerpublishing.com)
Phillip Carmical (pcarmical@scrivenerpublishing.com)

Design and Analysis of Security Protocol for Communication

Edited by

Dinesh Goyal, S. Balamurugan, Sheng-Lung Peng and O.P. Verma

Scrivener Publishing

WILEY

This edition first published 2020 by John Wiley & Sons, Inc., 111 River Street, Hoboken, NJ 07030, USA and Scrivener Publishing LLC, 100 Cummings Center, Suite 541J, Beverly, MA 01915, USA

For more information about Scrivener publications please visit www.scrivenerpublishing.com.

Wiley Global Headquarters
111 River Street, Hoboken, NJ 07030, USA

For details of our global editorial offices, customer services, and more information about Wiley products visit us at www.wiley.com.

Library of Congress Cataloging-in-Publication Data

ISBN 978-1-119-55564-3

Cover image: Pixabay.Com
Cover design by Russell Richardson

Set in size of 11pt and Minion Pro by Manila Typesetting Company, Makati, Philippines

Printed in the USA

10 9 8 7 6 5 4 3 2 1

Contents

Preface

Over the past few decades, digital communication has grown by leaps and bounds. The expanding use of the internet in our day-to-day lives has resulted in a six-fold increase in the number of internet users in the past two decades alone, leading to an evolution of technologies for home use such as Cloud Computing, Artificial Intelligence, Big Data Analytics and Machine Learning.

Today, 30% of the total business worldwide is done online, with approximately 25% of banking transactions being done exclusively from smartphones and laptops at home or the office. Moreover, 50% of the world's population is currently using social media as a platform for connecting with their friends and colleagues; and primary and higher education institutions are using internet-based education as a tool for enriching students' knowledge and at the same time keeping track of their academic performance. Now even Government agencies are moving to internet platforms, with most of their services currently available online.

Although this huge volume of internet usage has made life easier for every individual, insecurity or loss of information continues to be a major concern. There have been many cases across the globe of breach of information or platforms leading to loss of data, money, faith and much more.

Various research scientists have done a lot of work over the past five to six decades to develop security protocols for ensuring minimization of breach of data either being stored or under one network. The history of information security has been quite long and has evolved from the era of its birth to present date. During this period millions of cryptographic algorithms have evolved, some of which have been quite successful for ensuring many secure communications across the World Wide Web.

The application of security has changed as technology has evolved from tube computing to palm (nano) computing. Presently, we have many different security protocols for various types of applications of the internet like email, web browsing, webchat, video streaming, cloud-based communication, closed group communication, banking transactions, e-commerce and many more both at network level and user end.

Security has evolved to counter many kinds of attacks like intrusion, manipulation, spoofing and so on, for which techniques like cryptography, message digest, digital signature, steganography, watermarking, time stamping, access control, etc., have been incorporated into various layers of communication, resulting in protocols like HTTP, SMTP, RTP, RTCP, FTP, UDP and many more.

The issue with these protocols is that they are not being reviewed from time to time, nor are they being compiled and compared in one place. Our aim in publishing this book is to combine the analysis and comparison of various protocols which might act as a Mobile Communication Security Protocol or Multimedia Streaming Security Protocol. Therefore, this book discusses and analyzes some of the security protocols available for communication in various application areas.

The 16 chapters of this book are well placed to illustrate the security protocols for communication. Following is a brief synopsis of each chapter:

- Chapter 1 gives a detailed history of communication and the evolution of its protocols; and relates the evolution of security and the need for it in communication protocols.
- Chapter 2 discusses the evolution of various information security algorithms, from basic models to complex information security algorithms currently in use.
- Chapter 3 digs further into security algorithms by focusing on the philosophy of security by cryptostake schemes, a model for public key cryptographic techniques.
- Chapter 4 introduces a new technique for key management of security algorithms being implemented over a communication channel.
- Chapter 5 introduces a soft computing-based intrusion detection system with reduced false positive rate, which helps in intrusion detection in a communication channel, even if the signature of the intruder is not available.
- Chapter 6 proposes a new simple cipher, namely recursively paired arithmetic technique (RPAT): A field-programmable gate array (FPGA)-based block cipher simulation and its cryptanalysis.

- Chapter 7 reviews security protocols like RTP, RTMP, UDP, etc., for multimedia communication over a channel; it attempts to analyze the performance of these protocols on the basis of delay as parameter.
- Chapter 8 presents the concept of a new dimension in intrusion detection, i.e., a nature-inspired approach, and justifies the approach by comparing the benefits of using the same against that of a host-based intrusion detection system.
- Chapter 9 presents a secure and efficient symmetric key technique that harnesses the readily available social profiling information of the sender for encryption and decryption of the data, blending the social behavior of the sender with the cryptography.
- Chapter 10 introduces the concept of smart grid and the significant role that intrusion detection plays in it. Also addressed are the various threats to security and detection of intrusion frameworks in smart grid.
- Chapter 11 provides a glance into security protocols for cloud-based communication.
- Chapter 12 provides a detailed review of security protocols for mobile communications.
- Chapter 13 introduces a new dimension of advanced technologies in the design of security protocols using machine learning.
- Chapter 14 discusses privacy and authentication of security protocol for mobile communications.
- Chapter 15 discusses cloud communication and the different security measures and cryptographic protocols for secure cloud computing.

Communication has become a lifeline for the current era, and secure communication is blood in the veins of that lifeline. Currently very few books are available on the security protocols of different communication models like wireless communication, cloud-based communication, multimedia communication, MANET (infrastructureless) communication, etc. By providing this book to an audience working in the domains of network security, we have attempted to cover the history of the evolution of communication protocols and also provide some new techniques for security of communication channels with the use of tools like machine learning and nature-inspired algorithms.

We thank all the authors for contributing to our book with their valuable knowledge. We hope this book will prove to be a good resource for the intended audience to access all relevant technologies on one platform!!

Dinesh Goyal
S. Balamurugan
Sheng-Lung Peng
O.P. Verma
March 2020

1

History and Generations of Security Protocols

Bright Keswani[1†], Poonam Keswani[2*] and Rakhi Purohit[3‡]

[1]*Department of Computer Applications, Suresh Gyan Vihar University, Jaipur, India*
[2]*Akashdeep PG College, Jaipur, India*
[3]*Global Institute of Technology, Jaipur, India*

Abstract
For personal computers, organizations and military users, network security has become more important. Due to the recent arrival of the internet in network, and security now a key issue, the safety record maybe availability as well all people understand very good requirements security technologies in communications. Knowing the attack method can generate enough security. Many companies testing protection auto using some techniques of the network internet through download programs firewalls and some mechanisms encryption in itself company origin it has a special internal network known as "Intranet" to maintain in contact internet access from outside also safe from any threatening state. All the security of the network is huge as well in stage specific development for evaluation. It is a theme that consists of date summary for the security that shows in internet assets security, as well development internet current techniques security. To understand the ongoing investigation, understand previous for the internet, and level his from weak points from attacks, and also methods attack different via network internet known, as well security technologies what they are very mission a lot they are need as well to be reviewed and analysis.

***Keywords*:** Network security, security protocols, attacks collective, security techniques

**Corresponding author*: poonamkeswani777@gmail.com
†*Corresponding author*: kbright@rediffmail.com
‡*Corresponding author*: rakhimutha@gmail.com

Dinesh Goyal, S. Balamurugan, Sheng-Lung Peng and O.P. Verma (eds.) Design and Analysis of Security Protocol for Communication, (1–28) © 2020 Scrivener Publishing LLC

1.1 Introduction

Due to advent of the Internet and ever changing network technologies, the world is increasingly interconnected day by day. There are many personal, commercial, military, and government information in the creation of infrastructure networks around the world. Network security has become very important because intellectual property can be easily accessible via the efficient use of Internet and related tools. Although there are various types of networks but two fundamentally different networks, i.e., data networks and synchronous networks consisting of switches. The Internet is seen as a data network. From its current data network, information can be obtained through special procedures by router-based computers such as planting in the router "Trojan Horse". Data is not stored by switches of a synchronous network; therefore it is not compromised by attackers. That is why security is emphasized in data networks such as the Internet, as well as in various aspects of the Internet connection proposed by other networks.

For clear understanding, this chapter is divided into the following Sections. Further, each section is discussed in brief.

1. Network Security
2. The History and Security of the Network
3. Common Methods of Attack
4. Network Security Technology
5. Evolution of Network Security Protocols
6. Network Security Protocol

1.2 Network Security

When thinking about network security, we should know that the network should be a secure place. The network security does not affect the security of the client computers at any of the point of the connection chain [2]. So, when transferring the data from the communications channel which does not be attacked, there will be a potential intruder can indicate to a specific communication channel, which access data and decrypt and also re-encrypt the message, which is falsified. The task of repairing a network is as important as obtaining a computer and encrypting a message.

The system and some network technologies are the key technologies for various applications in network. Network security is critical for the specific network and the applications of network [1]. Network security is a prerequisite for emerging networks; also it is easy to implement a very secure approach for networking.

At time of development of secure network, there are some of the factors considered accordingly, i.e., "Access", which provide authorized users with the methods to communicate with specific network; "Confidentiality", which ensures that information/data flow on the network will remains private; "Authentication", which makes sure that the users of the network are what they call people; "Integrity", which feature makes sure that the message is not modified during transmission, and "Do not repudiate", which makes sure that the user does not refute their use of the network [1].

The crimes committed by Kevin Mitnick have fueled the recent interest in security. Kevin Mitnick committed the greatest cybercrime in the history of the United States [3]. Losses of property and intellectual property of several companies amount to $80 million [3]. Since then, information security has become the focus of attention. The public network is called to provide personal as well as financial information. Security of such information must also evolve due to the development of information which is available online. Due to an attack Kevin Mitnick, The Company emphasizes the security of system. The Internet always works as main part behind data security.

Development of an effective security plan on the Internet require to address primarily to understand security issues, about the potential attackers, the level of security required, and about various factors that make the network insecure and vulnerable. Following are the steps to learn how to configure a secure network, the Internet, or other aspects during the search process.

In order to minimize the weaknesses from one device to another, many products are available which includes various tools for encryption of data and information, effective mechanisms for user authentication, intrusion detection and, security management. Companies around the world use a variety of these tools. The intranet connects and protects The Internet in a reasonable way. The same structure of the Internet may create weaknesses in the network. Internet security has greatly improved the development of new security mechanism and methods for networks including Internet as well as Intranet access.

It is also necessary to study the types of attacks online so that they can detect and prevent these attacks. Intrusion detection systems rely on the most common types of attacks.

Previous Internet protocols were not developed for assurance. In the TCP/IP communication stack, no security protocol is applied. This led to an attack on the Internet. Due to advancement in the Internet architecture information communications became more secure.

1.3 Historical Background of Network Security and Network Timeline

The Internet was first introduced in 1969, when the Department of Defense (ARPANET) conducted a network survey. Since the beginning of the year, ARPANET has been successful. The original design was intended easy access to remote computers so that scientists to share data and, it will become one of the most popular email for ARPANET to become a high-speed digital communication, which can be used to research various topics of interest and discuss. Collaboration in international network work is the first of many rules for entities that operate a growing network. He was the first president of INWG of Winton Joseph and became known as the "father of the Internet."

In the 1980s, TCP/IP was created by Bob Kent and Winton Joseph who were the main members of the TCP/IP team. TCP/IP is the general language for all computers to connect to the Internet. The loose network that makes the ARPANET known as today's "Internet". During 1980s, this kind of boom appeared in the computer industry. Combining low-cost desktops with powerful servers allows companies to communicate with their customers and business partners with the use of Internet.

In 1990, due to advent of World Wide Web [WWW] the Internet made accessible to everyone. Netscape Navigator and Microsoft Internet Explorer like search engines came into existence. Many important events have contributed to the development of computer security and networks. The timetable can be started in advance in 1930 to invent a Polish programmer's jigsaw machine in 1918 to convert simple information into cipher text. In 1930, the shocking mathematician Alan Turing broke the Enigma code. Make sure the connection is very important to the images of World War II. In 1960, it was launched by many students at the Massachusetts Institute of Technology (MIT) and the Department of Defense in the term "piracy", which is a popular electronic data and information exchange pipeline [3]. Telnet protocol was developed in 1970s. This led to the widespread use of data networks, initially limited to government contractors and academic researchers [3]. In the 1980s, online piracy and cybercrime began to emerge. After nine days of carnival, the authorities conducted an accidental search and penetrated into a highly confidential system. The 1986, Act of Fraud and Abuse was created, and computer crime Ian Murphy stole information from military computers. After graduation, Robert Morris was judged to launch more than 6,000 weak computers connected to the Internet. In the 1990s, the Internet became public and security issues increased dramatically. Today, about 950 million people worldwide use the Internet [3]. On any given day, there are approximately 225 important security violations [3]. These security breaches can also result in significant financial losses. For large organizations and the average user, priority should be given to investing in appropriate security.

In 1975, the first malware was invented by two researchers who started the Xerox Company. It is called a "Worm" and looks for a lazy computer processor as an attempt to improve it. The creators of the simple diagnostic tool inadvertently created the first malware and created terms that are commonly used in multiple malware applications.

Many important events have contributed to the birth and development of computer security and networks. The program began in the 1930s, when Polish programmers invented a machine in 1918 to convert simple encrypted text messages. In 1930, the shocking mathematician Alan Turing broke the Enigma code ensuring that contact was crucial during the Second World War.

In 1960, he created the term "hacker" for many students at the Massachusetts Institute of Technology (MIT) and launched the Arpanet Department of Defense, which is popular as a channel for electronic exchange of data and information [3]. This paves the way for today's carrier network called the Internet. In 1970, the Telnet protocol was developed. This led to the widespread use of data networks, initially limited to government contractors and academic researchers [3].

In the 1980s, online piracy and cybercrime began to emerge. After 9 days of carnival, the authorities conducted an accidental search and penetrated into a highly confidential system. The 1986 Act of Fraud and Abuse was created, and computer crime Ian Murphy stole information from military computers. After graduation, Robert Morris was judged to launch more than 6,000 weak computers connected to the Internet. The Emergency Response Team (CERT) alerts computer users to cyber security issues based on concerns that Morris may repeat.

In the 1990s, the Internet became public and security issues increased dramatically. Today, about 950 million people worldwide use the Internet [3]. On 1 day, there were about 225 major security incidents [3]. These security breaches can also result in significant financial losses. For large organizations and the average user, priority should be given to investing in appropriate security.

1.4 Internet Architecture and Security Aspects

Fear of Internet security vulnerabilities has led companies to use private networks or protected internal networks. Security mechanisms in multiple layers of the Internet Protocol suite allow for logical protection of packet data sent over the network [11].

Analyze existing and new versions of the Internet Protocol to determine security risks. Although there may be security in the protocol, some attacks cannot be protected. Analyze these attacks to determine other security mechanisms that may be needed.

The Internet security architecture is called the Internet Safe security standard [19]. IPsec IP security covers next-generation IP (IPv6) (current version) (IPv4) although the development of new technologies such as IPsec does not seem to be sufficient to overcome the most common flaws on the Internet. A visual representation of IPsec provides a secure connection. IPSec is a peer-to-peer protocol that includes partial code and another part of decryption. The two parties share the key or key. IPSec can be used in two modes, transport mode and tunneling.

1.4.1 IPv4 and IPv6 Architecture

IPv4 was designed in 1980 to replace the NCP protocol in ARPANET. Twenty years later, IPv4 has many limitations [6]. IPv6 defect protocol design IPv4 is required. IPv6 is not a complete IPv4 packet protocol; instead, it is a new design. Internet protocols are designed to be very broad and cannot be fully covered. A key part of the security architecture is discussed in detail.

1.4.1.1 Structure of IPv4

The agreement contains several aspects that can cause problems when in use. Not all of these issues are related to security. It is worth noting that there is a full understanding of the Internet Protocol and its shortcomings. The reasons for the protocol issue are:

1. Address space
2. Routing
3. Configuration
4. Security
5. Quality of service

The IPv4 structure contains a 32-bit wide address [6]. This limits the maximum number of computers that can connect to the Internet. A 32-bit address can provide up to 2 billion computers connected to the Internet. No other issues are expected when the protocol is created. It facilitates malicious code distribution in IPv4 address space [5].

Routing is a problem with this protocol because the size of the routing table is constantly increasing. The maximum theoretical size input for the Global Positioning Table is 2 million [6]. Some methods have been used to reduce the number of entries in the routing table. This is useful in a short amount of time, but major changes are required to resolve this issue.

A TCP/IP IPv4-based network is required to provide users with some data to configure the network. Some of the required information is the IP gateway, subnet mask and DNS server [4]. The simplicity of network configuration is not clear in the IPv4 protocol. The user can request the appropriate network configuration from the central server [6]. This is very useful.

For many of today's attacks, insecurity leads to the IPv4 protocol [9]. There is a mechanism to ensure IPv4, but not necessarily. IPsec is a specific protocol protection mechanism. Load the packet with encryption protection space. It provides confidentiality and ipsec integrity and authentication. This protection does not take into account pirate experts who can crack the encryption method and obtain the key.

When creating the Internet, QoS is based on the QoS of information sent over the network. The delivery of the original message is primarily dependent on the text. With the expansion of the Internet and the development of technology, other forms of communication have begun to spread on the Internet. For standard text, the quality of service for transmitting video and music is different. This protocol does not include QoS features. Dynamics vary depending on the type of data being sent [6].

1.4.1.2 IPv6 Architecture

In the development of IPv6, various aspects of the Protocol have been highlighted IPv4 address. It should be improved. Development efforts include the following areas:

1. Routing and addressing
2. Multi-protocol architecture
3. Safety Engineering
4. Traffic control

Extend the IPv6 address space by accepting a 128-bit address. The protocol uses a 128-bit address and supports up to three and four 10^38 devices. In this protocol, the use of address bits is less efficient because it simplifies the addressing configuration. The routing system is more efficient IPv6 and provides a smaller global routing table. The host configuration has also been simplified. The host can be configured automatically. This new design allows users and network administrators to easily configure.

The security architecture of the IPv6 protocol was born. Of great interest is that IPsec is integrated into the IPv6 protocol. IPsec IPv4 and IPv6 have the same function. The only difference is that IPv6 can use security mechanisms along the way [6]. IPv6 addresses the issue of quality of service. IP allows special handling of certain packets with higher quality of service. You must confirm this after verifying IPv6. Its security features are not necessarily more secure than IPv4. Better security, not overall improvement.

1.4.2 Attack Through IPv4

Computer security has four main characteristics. The approach mentioned earlier is slightly different, but he rethinks comfort and attention. These security features are confidential, complete, private, and usable. Confidentiality and integrity remain the same. Availability means that authorized employees have access to computer assets [8]. Privacy is the right to protect personal secrets [8]. There are four attack methods associated with these four security features. Table 1.1 shows the attack methods and solutions.

A brief discussion of common attack techniques and security techniques will be provided. Not all methods are discussed in the table above. The current understanding of the techniques used to handle attacks is to understand the research and development of current secure hardware and software.

1.4.2.1 Internet Attacks Common Methods

There are several common methods of Internet attack. Some attacks gain system knowledge or personal information, such as spyware and phishing.

Table 1.1 Attack methods and security technology.

Computer security attributes	Attack methods	Technology for internet security
Privacy	Email bombing, Spamming, Hacking, Virus, Worms, IP Spoofing and DoS.	IDS, Firewall, anti-malware software, IPSec and SSl.
Integrity	Trojans, Virus, Worms, IP Spoofing and DoS.	IDS, Firewall, Anti-Malware Software, IPSec and SSl
Confidentiality	DoS, Eavesdropping, Phishing and IP Spoofing	IDS, Firewall, Cryptographic Systems, IPSec and SSL
Availability	DoS, Email, Bombing, Spamming and System Boot Record Infectors	IDS, Anti-Malware Software and Firewall.

Attacks can also interfere with the intended function of the system, such as viruses, worms, and Trojan horses. Another form of attack is the consumption of system resources, which may be the result of a denial of service attack. There are other forms of network intrusion, such as ground attacks, bomb attacks, and tear gas attacks. These attacks are not known in the name of two attacks, but they are used in some way even if they are not mentioned.

1.4.2.1.1 Listen Closely

Unauthorized interception of communications is known as illegal listening. Passive listening means that a person secretly listens to only network messages. Active spies, on the other hand, mean that intruders listen to certain content and listen to traffic. This can cause message distortion. Sensitive information can be stolen in this way [8].

1.4.2.1.2 Virus

A virus is a self-replicating program that uses file transfer and transmission [8]. Once the file is opened, the virus will be activated within the system.

1.4.2.1.3 Worm

Worms are considered viruses because they are repeated, but worms do not need files that allow them to spread [8]. There are two main types of worms and network identification worms and worms. A large number of email viruses use email as a means of infecting other computers. Network-sensitive worms are a major problem on the Internet. The target worm identifies the target network and once the worm reaches the target host, it is infected by a Trojan horse or other worm.

1.4.2.1.4 Trojan Horse

Trojan horses seem to be benign to users, but in reality they have some malicious targets. Trojan horses usually carry some goods, just like viruses.

1.4.2.1.5 Phishing

Phishing is an attempt to obtain confidential information from individuals, groups, or organizations. Deceive fraudulent users in detection. Personal information such as credit card numbers, online banking vouchers and other confidential information.

1.4.2.1.6 IP Spoofing Attack IP

It means that the address reflects the trusted address of the computer accessing other computers. The identity of intruders is hidden by a variety of means, making detection and prevention difficult and unable to delete fake IP (IP) packets by the use of current IP technology.

1.4.2.1.7 Denial of Service

A denial of service is considered an attack when a system that receives a large number of requests cannot reconnect with the applicant. The system then consumes resources waiting for the exchange to complete. Finally, the system is unable to respond to other unanswered requests.

1.4.2.2 Internet Security Technology

While information can be accessed and transmitted over the Internet, online threats will remain a major problem in the world. They developed various security and exploration measures to address these attacks.

1.4.2.2.1 Encryption System

Encryption is a useful tool widely used in current security architectures, including the use of code and passwords to transform information into model data to understand it.

1.4.2.2.2 Firewall

A firewall is a mechanism for controlling model boundaries or protecting perimeters. The goal of the firewall is to avoid traffic from outside, but it can also be used to avoid traffic from inside. The firewall is the first line of defense against hackers. It is a system designed to prevent unauthorized access or access from a private network. The firewall can be implemented in hardware or software, or a combination of the two.

1.4.2.2.3 Intrusion Detection System

An intrusion detection system is an additional measure to prevent intrusion into a computer. It can be an IDS system, which is software and hardware that detects attacks. IDS products are used to monitor connections and determine if an attack has been initiated. Some IDS systems only monitor and alert attacks, while others try to block attacks.

1.4.2.2.4 Software Methods and Anti-Malware

Viruses, worms, and Trojan horses are examples of malware or malware. Special anti-software tools are used to detect and process infected systems.

1.4.2.2.5 Secure Sockets Layer (SSL)

Secure Sockets Layer (SSL) is a set of protocols that is a standard way to achieve a high level of security between a web browser and a website. SSL is designed to create a secure tunnel or tunnel between a web browser and a web server to protect any information shared in a secure tunnel. SSL uses a certificate to provide client authentication for the server. The client sends the certificate to the server for identification.

1.4.3 IPv6 IP Security Issues

From a security perspective, IPv6 has made significant progress in IPv4 IP. Although IPv6 has a strong security mechanism, it is still weak. There are still potential security issues with certain aspects of the IPv6 protocol.

The new Internet protocol does not prevent properly configured servers, poorly designed applications, or protected sites.

Security issues may occur for the following reasons:

1. Problems in the management process
2. Flood problem
3. Liquidity issues

Due to the built-in IPsec function, there is a problem with the spindle operation [7]. The extension header avoids some of the common sources of attack caused by head operations. The problem is that the steering guide must be processed through all the stacks, which can result in a long series of steering heads. A large number of attachments may be confused by a knot, which is a form of attack if deliberate. Tradition remains a threat to IPv6 security.

When the entire network portion is resolved while searching for a possible destination with an open service, an attack type called port check [5] occurs. The IPv6 protocol address space is large, but the protocol is not threatened by such attacks.

Navigation is a new feature integrated with IPv6. This feature requires special security measures. Network administrators should be aware of these security requirements when using IPv6 Mobility.

1.5 Different Aspects of Security of the Network

The company currently uses a range of protection, encryption, and authentication mechanisms to create an Internet-connected intranet, but it is also protected.

An intranet is a dedicated computer network that uses the Internet protocol [12]. The difference between an intranet and an "external network" is that the first is usually limited to the employees of the organization, while the external network is usually available to customers, suppliers, or other authorized parties.

The company intranet does not require Internet access. This access is usually done through gateway and user authentication with a secure server, message encryption, usually using a virtual private network (VPN).

Although the intranet can be quickly configured to share data in a controlled environment, this information is still at risk unless there is strict security [12]. The downside of intranet networks is that important data may not reach the people who need it. The intranet has a place in multiple organizations. However, for a wider range of data exchanges, it is best to keep the network open and have the following security measures:

1. Detect and report whether the firewall has an intrusion attempt
2. Check for complex viruses in the firewall
3. Open the rules for additional employee emails
4. Encrypt all communication and data transmission
5. Authenticate by synchronization, password synchronization, or security certificate

If the intranet wants to access the Internet, it typically uses a virtual private network [13, 14]. Interfaces in multiple locations usually work on separate leased lines, or you can use the updated VPN method. The following technologies are different

1. Encryption system
2. Firewall
3. Intrusion detection system
4. Malignant and scanning procedures
5. Secure Sockets Layer (SSL) SSL

The network security zone continues on the same path. Use the same method and add biometric data. Biometric technology provides better authentication than passwords, which can greatly reduce unauthorized access to the security system. New technologies such as smart cards are emerging in the field of Internet security research. The sidebar security network is very dynamic. A new firewall and encryption system is being implemented.

1.6 Evolution of Security Protocols for Network

The evolution of the network security protocol can be divided into three age groups [10]:

1. Filter packaging
2. Check the meeting
3. Application control

Although the development of anything is a continuous process, it is not a matter of cleaning up the next cycle. The spiritual perspective can determine certain characteristics that people lead in time.

This shows how the basic concepts of the Internet have changed the security and analysis of the five most advanced Internet security systems that must work in every network assessment.

1. Next Generation Firewall (NGFW)
2. Secure Web Portal (SWG)
3. Network Access Control (NAC)
4. Malware protection program
5. Secure access to the intermediary (CASB)

There are some network security systems, NGFW, NAC, and SWG, which have been developed for many years to accommodate the latest security threats. Other tools, such as sandbox protection and CASB, have some new concepts in the Public Safety Act.

1.6.1 Understanding the Key Components of Network Security

Traditional firewalls have been the most important and important line of defense for decades. Most corporate structures require secure servers at the edge of the core network to connect to other networks, especially if other networks are managed by a third party or are considered less centralized and secure.

This typically involves using a firewall to partition Internet connections, external networks, and remote WAN sites. The original firewall has no state, which means the firewall has no intelligence to monitor the data flow. As a result, the first wall of the fire was hit by a suicide bomber, and the attackers indicated that they were entering the rules allowed by the firewall.

Powerful firewalls are becoming common because they can monitor and track traffic between two devices that communicate with each other through a firewall. The state table not only controls the correct transport stream, but also ensures that the transmitted and received packets are connected to the original device. This is done by examining the network layer, the packets on OSI Layers 3 and 4, and tracking the IP address data. The TCP serial number and port number are processed. When transmitting a confirmed firewall packet, this information falsifies the hardware firewall to receive more harmful packets in the perimeter.

Although traditional firewalls are only designed to allow certain ports and protocols, they are not sure whether the visited site is harmful or inappropriate. This leaves a big gap, especially in terms of network traffic. The firewall can only allow or deny any traffic; it cannot selectively or see the upper layer protocol. This led to the creation of the SWG.

The first generation of SWGs had only one feature: filtering URLs. In most applications, Web Gateway is used to block access to websites that are included in a predefined blacklist. The company is responsible for maintaining SWG manufacturers, usually a blacklist database that is regularly updated on the gateway's network equipment. The administrator can choose which blacklist category to apply. There are some blacklist categories that include sites that include pornography, gambling, and hate groups, as well as sites that are often referred to as malware.

1.6.2 A Deep Defense Strategy

Over the years, network security systems such as traditional firewalls and secure web portals have run independently and performed different security functions [16]. Although this structure is better than nothing, it only provides a layer of defense for any threat. In order to add some extra layers of protection, there are some concepts of deep defense strategies. Our idea is to implement an interlocking security system to expose risks to multiple security measures designed to prevent malicious behavior.

Firewalls and traditional security gates are used for the Internet, email, and intrusion prevention systems (IPS). Protecting the infrastructure boundaries of an infrastructure company typically involves accessing cloud resources. All data entering and exiting the network is filtered through firewalls and IPS. All traffic and email on the Internet will then be sent to the relevant security portal for further review to identify possible attachments contained in email attachments and malware.

With proper tuning and maintenance, deep defense engineering strategies using these components provide strong security. However, hackers began to discover that the network could find cracks between each system it entered. There are three main reasons for this. First of all, some security systems are difficult to fully implement. Usually, only some of the security features available in production are implemented.

Second, the security system cannot be maintained and updated correctly. For example, you must periodically update your firewall software to fix newly discovered vulnerabilities. Security portals and databases are often reviewed and sometimes require manual intervention updates.

Finally, while these systems overlap and provide multiple layers of protection, they work independently and are not shared and can be used to discover information between systems that have difficulty detecting threats.

1.6.3 How Does the Next Generation Network Security System Work Best

The next generation of security tools not only goes deeper into defense strategies, but goes further with tightly integrated and improved systems. Integrated with next-generation firewall capabilities to monitor and detect legacy firewalls, revealing regular IPS functionality by identifying signatures that contain known attack patterns. It is also known as NGFW for applications that use the firewall feature to check the deep technology package you are using. This allows the firewall to check the package not only by loading the subsidiary but also by the application to which the package belongs. This policy allows NGFW to securely interact with IPS and web portals by providing multiple layers of protection.

The web security gateway uses standard URL filtering for standards and direct protection against malware. The SWG acts as an IPS, focusing on web-based exceptions and virus signatures. When the new company discovers these signatures, it is automatically sent to the SWG device. Another new feature of most WWG groups is the ability to access global threat sensor networks. The threat of these sensors is typically maintained through security, identifying new threats and SWG groups locally and globally to better protect against real-time web threats. This type of security is an effective blow to increase rescue attacks.

Malware protection is a relatively new security tool for security administrators in many organizations. A limited number of malware environments are designed to create an isolated environment simulation test environment that allows the system to perform multiple tests on suspicious packets. This approach sets a serious burden and hinders access to the production environment. The protective case can detect other tools such as NGFW and SWG. You can ignore this threat. Some malware installations require a sandbox filter. All data sandboxes are responsible for repairing suspicious downloads. In other designs, the limited malware environment relies on NGFW and SWG to classify the load as suspicious and then move it to the basement for further testing.

Next-generation networks are also beginning to rely on greater control over network access than their predecessors. I created a BYOD explosion. Concerns about cyber security vulnerabilities, rather than security personnel in the network, are very serious in identifying, evaluating, approving, and monitoring personnel who have access to network resources for production.

The NAC user and the correct device must be properly selected before allowing access to the network. If authenticated, the user or device receives a user access policy. Access policies provide access to resources that are accessible in the production network. In addition, you can access and follow resources. This is used to understand potential theft. In fact suspicious behavior refers to intellectual property or may be another harmful behavior.

The Internet was born in a military and academic environment. In this environment, users are always reliable and work together to make technology mutually beneficial. Therefore, IP and standard IP applications are safe from the start. Today, unsecure IP is still at the heart of Internet operations, with a range of long-term IP services such as:

1. Search Name—DNS Domain Name Service
2. File Transfer—FTP (FTP)
3. Email: SMTP Simple Mail Transfer Protocol (SMTP)
4. Web browsing: Hypertext Transfer Protocol (HTTP)

When the Internet was first developed, the basic technology running on the Internet was more secure than the trust era. However, the Internet has grown tremendously, with millions of people, many of whom are unreliable. Internet crime, corruption, espionage, extortion, etc., are getting bigger and bigger.

Therefore, Internet users must pay attention to managing their data security needs. Various unwelcome people roam the streets of the Internet without protection, so they must have strong defenses, valuable data, and services. Over the years, as the value of data and services on the Internet has grown, so does the current threat and the network industry has developed a range of hardware and security software to address threats for network security in three eras.

1.7 Network Security Protocols

Due to the advancement and continuous growth of Internet, personal as well as business communication has increased the need for "Privacy" and "Information Security" for Eastern digital communication channels [18].

Both are critical to continuing personal communications and e-commerce that thrive in the Internet world Calls, security and privacy have come up with many security protocols and standards. These include Secure Communication Layer SSL Protocol (Transport Layer Security) TLS); IP Security (IPSec); HTTP Security (S-HTTP), Secure Email (PGP and S/MIME), DNDSEC, SSH, etc.

We will discuss these protocols and standards in a network protocol cluster in the following ways:

1.7.1 Application Layer

1. PGP
2. S / MIME
3. S-HTTP
4. HTTPS
5. SET
6. Kerberos

1.7.1.1 Good Privacy (PGP)

The Sensitive communications should not be underestimated. The best way to protect this type of information so far is to encrypt it. Email and any other form of communication encryption are critical to everyone's personal information. This is where you come from PGP, which is why PGP is very popular today. Phil Zimmermann is a public key encryption system for PGP. This feature creates the circle of trust between users. In such circle of trust, the two primary users are the loops of the public key pairs stored by each user and using keys in a person's keychain.

Unlike basic PKI infrastructure keys, such circle contains potential vulnerabilities and it can be exploited by hackers. In PGP there is a digital signature for verifying documents or files. This helps ensure that emails or files that have just been received from the Internet are secure and will not change.

1.7.1.2 *Email/Multipurpose Security (S/MIME)*

Expand Multipurpose Internet Mail Extensions/Security Protocol Multipurpose Internet Mail Extensions (MIME) when adding digital signatures and encryption. MIME is communication protocols for transmission of multimedia data, which includes sound, images, and video. The reader must be interested in RFC protocol. MIME returns RFC 1521. Because web content (files), including hyperlinks to other hypertext links, describe the protocol message as MIME, you must state any type of relationship. This is what the MIME server does every time a client requests a web document. When the web server sends the requested file to the client browser, it adds a MIME header to the document and moves it. So, online email consists of following two parts, i.e., the "address" and the "body". In "address" part, there is information about MIME type and subtype. The MIME type describes the type of file that transfers the content type, such as images, sounds, applications, etc. Subtypes contain certain types of files, such as jpeg/GIF/tiff.

The development of S/MIME is the most lack of security services. Add two encryption elements: Encrypt and Encrypt Digital Encryption S/MIME. It supports three types of encryption algorithms, using common encryption keys for message navigation: Davey–Holman, RSA, and Triple DES. Digital signatures generate summary messages for SHA-1 or MD5 decentralized functions.

1.7.1.3 *HTTP Secure (S-HTTP)*

Secure HTTP (HTTP S-HTTP) is very simple for web development when developing HTTP. I do not have dynamic graphics. I did not need to encrypt the hard drive at the time. From end to end, it was developed for trading.

As the network becomes more popular in the company, users realize that if HTTP Current still represents the backbone of e-commerce, it needs additional improvements in encryption and graphics.

Each encrypted file of S-HTTP contains a digital certificate. A secure connection between the client and the HTTP server, especially business transactions is done through a various mechanisms to provide security when separating policies from mechanisms. It consists of a two-part HTTP message: the message title and text. This address contains a description of how the message text (browser and server) is processed in the transaction, client, and browser. HTTP negotiation will be used to transfer the actual format of the desired information.

It uses other S-HTTP headers to encrypt digital mail, certificates, and HTTP authentication, and provides instructions about how to decrypt the text of the message.

1.7.1.4 Hypertext Transfer Protocol (HTTPS) in Secure Sockets Layer

Secure Sockets Layer (SSL) uses HTTPS as a subset of HTTP commonly used in the application layer. Also known as a protocol that transfers hypertext documents to HTTPS (HTTPS) or HTTP-based HTTP protocols.

A web protocol named HTTPS developed by Netscape. To encrypt and decrypt requests for user/web pages, it is integrated with the browser software. Port 443 in place of HTTP 80 port uses by the HTTPS protocol to interact with lower layer TCP/IP.

1.7.1.5 Secure E-Commerce (SET)

SET is an encryption protocol developed by companies such as Visa, Microsoft, IBM, RSA, Netscape, and MasterCard. These complex specifications are contained in three books on book introduction, a highly specialized system, and a programmer's guide, giving three formal instructions to the Convention. The SET sends services for each transaction, i.e. authentication, confidentiality, message integrity, and SET connection. Use public key cryptography and certificate signing to identify everyone involved in the transaction and allow each communication between them to be private.

1.7.1.6 Kerberos

The Kerberos network authentication protocol is designed to allow users, clients, and servers to authenticate each other. Verification process is accomplished by encrypting the keys because some keys are mutually authenticated over an insecure network connection. After verifying identity with the client and Kerberos server, the connection between both the parties can be secure. From this issue, you can communicate between future encryptions to ensure the privacy and integrity of your data.

Client/Server Authentication requirements are as follows,

1. Security: Kerberos is no longer powerful enough to prevent potential spies from seeing it as a weak link.
2. Reliability: The Kerberos server architecture is distributed in large quantities with the support of other servers. This means that the Kerberos system is secure, which means a slight deterioration.
3. Transparency: In addition to providing a password, the user does not know that the HE will be authenticated.
4. Scalability: Kerberos is accepted. It identifies new clients and servers.

To meet above mentioned requirements, the stylist came to Kerberos. It is a trusted external authentication service for arbitration when mutual authentication occurs between the client and the server.

1.7.2 Transport Layer

These protocols are located below the application layer. The SSET unit IETF is measured after the consortium Netscape, and the IETF Engineering. Engineering Working Group IETF is modified by TLS.

1.7.2.1 Secure Sockets Layer (SSL)

SSL is also an encryption system which is used in Internet search engines like Netscape and Explorer provides an encrypted data path between the endpoint, client, and server. Data encryption, server authentication, message integrity, and authentication over TCP, LDAP, or POP3 clients provide a secure and authenticated service application layer compete with S-HTTP.

These giants have many common networks. First, S-HTTP is only available for the Web protocol. Since the SSL in the network group is smaller than S-HTTP, it can run on many other network protocols. In addition, second, in terms of implementation, because SSL is lower than S-HTTP. Replace applications that require a secure connection, such as a socket interface. On the other hand, it places the S-HTTT in the previous data in the named text field in the HTTP header.

Although SSL was introduced in a wide range of browsers, the Netscape S-HTTP browser was introduced in a smaller, narrower NCSA interface. This unfortunate choice condemns the fate of the S-HTTP SSL handshake.

There must be approximately three contact addresses before creating any TCP connections between the client and the service and working with SSL. This process is also known as a protocol for linking SSL. During the connection agreement, the client and server perform the following tasks: Set the encryption set to use. The server-enforced authentication provides a server that sends the certificate to the client to verify that the server certificate is signed by a trusted certificate authority. If necessary, provide the client with optional client authentication, which sends its own certificate to the server to verify that the client certificate is signed by a trusted certificate authority.

When using public key encryption, the primary information is exchanged after authentication, which causes the client to create a session key (usually a random number) that is used to negotiate all subsequent encryption or decryption. The client encrypts the session key using the commercial server's public key (from the merchant certificate). The server retrieves the session key by decrypting the session key using its private key. Both parties now use this symmetric key for all subsequent connections.

1.7.2.2 Transport Layer Security (TLS)

TLS is the result of the Internet Engineering Task Force (IETF). In 1996, you were trying to unify secure network communication. In 1999, RFC 2246 formed a new protocol named "Transport Layer Security" [TLS]. It is responsible for providing security and data integrity in the transport layer between two applications [4]. "Interoperability" is an additional features which have been added in the basic version means any party exchanges the capability parameter TLS without anyone having to understand the implementation details of TLS to the other party, and "Expandability", i.e., plan for future expansion and adapt to new engagements.

1.7.3 Network Layer

1. IP security
2. VPN

Above mentioned protocols are also address Internet communications security issues. These protocols include IPSec and VPN.

1.7.3.1 Internet Protocol Security (IPSec)

IP Security is the Internet Engineering Task Force Group (IETF) designed and developed to address the lack of inherent security protocols, authentication, and encryption based on Internet protocols [18]. IPSec is a very complex set of protocols described in many documents, including RFC 2401 and 2411. Although designed to run on a new version of Internet Protocol IP Version 6 (IPv6), it is also correctly implemented in the previous IPv4.

Try to provide IPSec protection by providing the following services at the network layer:

1. Access Control: Prevent unauthorized access to resources.
2. Security without connection: Make sure that the traffic is not modified in any way.
3. Confidentiality: Ensure that unauthorized third parties do not investigate Internet traffic. This requires encrypting the data fields of all packets IP, TCP, UDP, ICMP, or any other data field.
4. Verification: Especially the verification of key elements, so when the server receives the target IP for the specific purpose of the data source IP, it can ensure that the IP datagram is indeed created by the server with the source IP address to avoid this fake IP address.
5. Copy protection: Make sure that each package is different between the two.

These goals achieved by the IPSec protocol with dividing it into two protocols: the header AH authentication protocol i.e. the security of the protocol and the protection of the surrounding ESP, which provides the integrity of the source and data authentication protocol AH, but does not provide confidentiality. Provide ESP authentication, data integrity, and confidentiality. Any data unit in the source must be protected with AH or ESP. There are two ways to run IPSec, i.e., Transport and Tunneling. Transport mode provides host-to-host protection for top-level protocols between IPv4 and IPv6 hosts. Tunnel mode provides complete IP data mapping protection in AH and ESP between IPSec gateways because new IP headers have been added to both IPv4 and YIPv6. Between the two ports, the datagram is secure and has an IP address. The original is also very safe.

Data units may not be safe abroad. This protection is created when an IPSec gateway is created. First to encapsulate the data planner (including your IP address) into a new set of compelling data that is titled a new

IP gateway with IP security. At the receiving gateway, the new packet is unpacked and returned to the original data map.

1.7.3.2 Virtual Private Network (VPN)

VPN private networks add security measures through secure communication channels, leveraging public communication infrastructure data such as the Internet. Security measures including encryption are implemented using a tunneling protocol. There are two types of virtual private networks (VPNs) [13, 14]. Remote access allows one user to connect to a protected corporate network and a site that supports connections between two protected network networks. In any case, VPN technology is available. The cost of a private leasing company is much lower when using a public infrastructure such as the Internet.

The two components of a VPN are: These two terms are programs or devices. It implements encryption, decryption and authentication services. It also includes information. Tunnel: The endpoint is connected. A tunnel is a secure connection between an endpoint and a network, such as the Internet. In fact, this tunnel is actually created from the endpoint.

You must do the following:

1. IP packaging: Includes a TCP/IP packet contained in another package that contains the IP address of the firewall or the server acting as a VPN endpoint. This package helps hide host IP address hosts.
2. Encryption: The data portion of the package. Like SSL, encryption can be done in transport mode, which encrypts data as it is created, or encrypts and decrypts data by encrypting data and headers during transmission.
3. Authentication: Includes the creation of an encrypted domain that includes authentication of computers and packets using regular encryption.

Technical security is divided into three types of VPNs: Trust VP N; VPN security and hybrid VPN.

Trusted VPN: In these VPNs, customers rely on VPN providers to protect their privacy and security while maintaining the integrity of their components. This security depends on trust.

Secure VPN: Virtual Private Network (VPN) not only provides virtual security, so there are still security issues in VPN. To solve these problems, any other data encrypted by the Internet source or mobile traffic is similar to the data used to decrypt when accessing the corporate network or host protocol.

In this way, encrypted traffic seems to have passed through the tunnel between the two networks. Initially and destination, although the data is clear, the attacker can see the transfer but still cannot read it. The recipient does not change the traffic that cannot be changed, so you can see a lot and will be rejected. The created network is called Secure VPN Encryption. VPN Secure is more secure than trusted VPN.

Hybrid VPN: Hybrid VPN is the latest Internet VPN technology that can be used as an alternative to a telephone system. Fixed VPN component VPNs do not provide new security, but provide customers with a way to easily create a network chip for the WAN. WAN On the other hand, components can control VPN VPN from one place, and QoS is usually guaranteed by the provider.

1.7.4 Data Link Layer

1. PPP
2. Radio
3. TACACS +

Link layer and LANS security There are several protocols used in the data link layer, such as PPP and RADIO AND TACAS +.

1.7.4.1 Point-to-Point Protocol (PPP)

This is the old agreement for Internet users to use the modem and PPP to dial the Internet. This protocol is limited to a single data link. Each call goes directly to the Remote Access Server (RAS). This feature is used to verify the call when a call is received.

The PPP connection containing the link protocol begins to negotiate between the client and the RAS to send and resolve security issues before the data begins to be sent.

These negotiations are performed using the LCP Link Control Protocol. Negotiations can result in approval or disapproval because purchasing power parity does not require approval.

1.7.4.2 Remote Authentication User Service (RADIO)

RADIO is a server for remote user authentication and accounting. Class-based online class security protocols, including Password Authentication

Protocol (PAP) and Challenge Identification Authentication Protocol (CHAP). It is primarily used by Internet Service Providers (ISPs) to provide authentication. Consider a remote user. It can also be used in private networks for authentication and accounting services in a centralized network to serve all dial-up connections. It has two main components: authentication and accounting.

1.7.4.3 Terminal System Access Control Access Control Equipment (TACACS +)

This protocol is called the "tac-plus" authentication protocol and is a common method. It is a powerful protocol for providing tags: Verifies any changes in authentication and content duration, allowing for many authentication mechanisms. Therefore, auditing: Recording the work done by users in TACASCS + has two purposes: to consider the services used by security auditing equipment.

1.8 Current Evolution of Red Security

The network security zone continues on the same path. Use the same method and add biometric data. Biometric technology provides better authentication than passwords, which can greatly reduce unauthorized access to the security system. New technologies such as smart cards have emerged in cyber security research. The security aspects of network software are very dynamic. A new firewall and encryption system is being implemented. The research carried out helps to understand current developments and predict future developments in the field.

1.8.1 Hardware Development

The development of this device has not developed rapidly. Dynamic systems and smart cards are the only new hardware technologies that have a major impact on security.

The most obvious use of cyber security biometrics is to start recording secure workstations from networked workstations. Each workstation requires some software support to dynamically identify the user and identify some of the biometric devices used. Hardware costs are a cause of widespread use of biometric measurements, especially for companies and institutions that offer low budgets. The next step will be the next device, such as a computer mouse with a built-in fingerprint reader. Because each device requires its own device, deploying it to multiple computers is more expensive. The price of biometric mice and the software they support is about $120 in the United States. UU speech recognition programs are controlled to reduce the cost of implementation per device. At the top of the series, biometric bio packages cost $50,000, but you can manage secure registrations for up to 5,000 devices.

The primary use of biometric network security is to replace existing encryption systems. Keeping passwords safe is an important task even for small businesses. The password must be changed every few months, and people will forget the password or enter the password multiple times to remove the password from the system. People usually type in a password and store it near a computer. Of course, this completely undermines any effort in cyber security. Biometric technology can replace this method for secure identification. By using biometrics to solve this problem, although this is the first time cost-effective, these devices can provide management costs and user assistance.

Smart cards are usually digital electronic media-sized credit cards. The card itself is used to store encryption keys and other authentication and identity information. The main idea behind smart cards is to provide undeniable user identification. From logging in to your network to protect secure network connections and email transactions, smart cards can be used for a variety of purposes.

It seems that the smart card is just a repository for storing passwords. Someone can easily steal someone else's smart card. Fortunately, smart cards include built-in security features that prevent anyone from using stolen cards. Smart cards require anyone to use a PIN before granting access to any level of the system. It looks like the PIN code used by ATM.

When the user inserts the smart card into the card reader, the smart card user is required to enter the PIN code. When the boss card is sent to the user, the administrator sets a password for the user. Because the PIN number is short and the number is pure, the user must not face any problems in the ticket sales, so it is impossible to write the PIN.

But what is interesting is what happens when the user enters a PIN. The PIN code is verified in the smart card. Since the PIN is not transmitted over the network, there is no risk of intercepting the PIN. However, the main benefit is that if there is no smart card, the PIN is inefficient and the smart card is used without code. There are other security issues with PIN smart cards. Smart cards are profitable, but they are not as secure as biometric devices.

1.8.2 Software Development

Every aspect of the cyber security program is very broad including firewall, anti-virus, VPN, intrusion detection, and so on. It is currently not possible to search all security software. The goal is to achieve the goals of the security plan based on current priorities [17].

Improvements to the standard safety plan remain unchanged. Antivirus software is updated to protect against these threats when new viruses appear. The firewall process is the same as the intrusion detection system. Many of the research papers developed are based on an analysis of attack patterns to create smarter security programs [17].

When a security service enters biometrics, the program also needs to be able to use this information appropriately. Study safety procedures using neural networks. The purpose of this study was to use neural network face recognition software.

Many small and complex devices can connect to the Internet. Most security algorithms are currently highly computational and require a lot of processing power. However, this power is not suitable for small devices such as sensors. Therefore, it is necessary to design a lightweight security algorithm. Research in this area is ongoing.

1.9 Future Security Trends

What will improve Internet security is the most important set of applications [15]. The future may be similar to the immune system. The immune system can fight attacks and fight against powerful enemies. Similarly, cyber security can act as an immune system. The trend in biotechnology development may not be long ago, but it seems that it has not been effectively implemented. Many ongoing security developments are part of the same security technology with minor modifications.

References

1. Dowd, P.W. and McHenry, J.T., Network security: It's time to take it seriously. *Computer*, 31, 9, 24–28, 1998.
2. Kartalopoulos, S.V., Differentiating Data Security and Network Security, Communications, ICC '08. *IEEE International Conference on*, 19–23, pp. 1469–1473, 2008.

3. Security Overview, www.redhat.com/docs/manuals/enterprise/RHEL-4- Manual/security-guide/ch-sgs-ov.html, 2011.
4. Molva, R. and Institut Eurecom, Internet Security Architecture. *Computer Networks & ISDN Systems Journal*, 31, 787–804, 1999.
5. Sotillo, S. and East Carolina University, IPv6 security issues, www.infosecwriters.com/text_resources/pdf/IPv6_SSot illo.pdf, 2006.
6. Andress, J., IPv6: The Next Iinternet Protocol, www.usenix.com/publications/login/2005-04/pdfs/andress0504.pdf, 2005.
7. Warfield, M., Security Implications of IPv6, Internet Security Systems White Paper, documents.iss.net/whitepapers/IPv6.pdf, 2003.
8. Adeyinka, O., Internet Attack Methods and Internet Security Technology, Modeling & Simulation, AICMS 08, *Second Asia International Conference on*, 13–15, pp. 77–82, 2008.
9. Marin, G.A., Network security basics, Security & Privacy. *IEEE*, 3, 6, 68–72, 2005.
10. Internet History Timeline, https://www.baylor.edu/cms/index.php?id=93716, 2011.
11. Landwehr, C.E. and Goldschlag, D.M., Security issues in networks with Internet access. *Proc. IEEE*, 85, 12, 2034–2051, 1997.
12. "Intranet" Wikipedia, The Free Encyclopedia. 23 Jun 2008, 10:43 UTC. Wikimedia Foundation, Inc. <http://en.wikipedia.org/w/index.php?title=Intranet&oldid=221174244>, 2008.
13. Virtual private network. Wikipedia, The Free Encyclopedia. 30 Jun 2008, 19:32 UTC. Wikimedia Foundation, Inc. <http://en.wikipedia.org/w/index.php?title=Virtual_private_network&oldid=222715612>, 2008.
14. Tyson, J., How Virtual private networks work, http://www.howstuffworks.com/vpn.htm, 2014.
15. Al-Salqan, Y.Y., Future trends in Internet security, Distributed Computing Systems, *Proceedings of the Sixth IEEE Computer Society Workshop on Future Trends of*, 29–31, pp. 216–217, 1997.
16. Curtin, M., Introduction to Network Security, http://www.interhack.net/pubs/network-security, 1997.
17. Improving Security, http://www.cert.org/tech_tips, 2006.
18. Serpanos, D.N. and Voyiatzis, A.G., Secure network design: A layered approach, Autonomous Decentralized System, *The 2nd International Workshop on*, 6–7, 2002, pp. 95–100, 2002.
19. Ohta, T. and Chikaraishi, T., Network security model, Networks, *International Conference on Information Engineering '93. 'Communications and Networks for the Year 2000', Proceedings of IEEE Singapore International Conference on*, 2, 6–11, pp. 507–511, 1993.

2

Evolution of Information Security Algorithms

Anurag Jagetiya[1*] and C. Rama Krishna[2†]

[1]*Department of Information Technology, MLV Textile and Engineering College, Bhilwara, Rajasthan, India*
[2]*National Institute of Technical Teachers Training and Research, Chandigarh, India*

Abstract
The chapter begins with the classical encryption techniques namely substitution cipher and transposition cipher. It covers popular substitution ciphers like Caesar, mono-alphabetic, Playfair, poly-alphabetic, and vignere cipher. Transposition-based ciphers like Rail Fence and Simple Columnar are also discussed with example.

Modern security algorithms, designed using both substitution and transposition based approaches, are categorized as stream cipher and block cipher. The chapter explores popular stream cipher algorithms like one-time pad (Vernam cipher), RC4, and A5/1. The key concepts of block cipher algorithms like key expansion method, Shannon's theory of confusion and diffusion, and the basic Feistel structure are covered elegantly. Later, the chapter covers block cipher algorithms like DES, 3DES, IDEA, Blowfish, and CAST-128 and analyzes them with respect to their key generation methods, S-box designs, and vulnerabilities, etc.

Keywords: Classical encryption techniques, stream cipher, block cipher, A5/1, 3DES, IDEA, Blowfish, CAST-128

**Corresponding author*: Anurag.mlvtec@gmail.com
†*Corresponding author*: ramakrishna.challa@gmail.com

Dinesh Goyal, S. Balamurugan, Sheng-Lung Peng and O.P. Verma (eds.) Design and Analysis of Security Protocol for Communication, (29–78) © 2020 Scrivener Publishing LLC

2.1 Introduction to Conventional Encryption

Over the decades many protocols and mechanism were invented to achieve information security. Information stored on magnetic disks and transmitted via wired/wireless links can be copied and altered. The need for information security for today's internet-savvy generation requires fast and efficient methods of information security that cannot be penetrated by any intruder. Information security is the study of hiding useful and sensitive information from the illegitimate audience. It is the art of secret writing to thwart unauthorized access to someone's secret information. In Cryptography, word "Cryptos" is taken from Greek that means "hidden" and graphy means "study". Modern Cryptography is better described as the science of using mathematical techniques to scramble the data and transmit through a public network like the Internet in a way that is only readable by its intended recipient. In this chapter, human-readable information is termed as plaintext while scrambled information is termed as ciphertext. Scrambling of human-readable information into unintelligent text using mathematical formula or a well-defined procedure is referred as encipherment or encryption, while the reverse of encryption is termed as decipherment or decryption. Well-defined and proved algorithms are used for encryption and decryption purposes. For example, web traffic is secured by a protocol named Hyper Text Transfer Protocol over Transport Layer Security (HTTPS), wireless traffic is secured by protocol Wireless Protected Access-2 (WPA2), files stored on disk are also encrypted by Encrypting File System (EFS) or TrueCrypt software, and content of DVDs is encrypted with the Content Scramble System (CSS).

The principle of symmetric key cryptography states that two or more legitimate parties involved in the communication share a confidential piece of information termed as secret key among them. The sender encrypts the plaintext using an encryption algorithm and secret key. It, then, transfers the ciphertext to the receiver through a communication channel. Receiver, on the other hand, deciphers the ciphertext to get the plaintext using the same algorithm and the secret key. The key must remain secret to thwart against any kind of attack to reveal the secret key or compromise the information. Symmetric key cryptography involves only a single shared secret key to encrypt and decrypt the message between a pair, therefore, it is also known as a secret key or single key encryption. Generally, the encryption algorithm is having a reversible structure, i.e., the same algorithm is used in the decryption process, given the key in reverse order. A most common form of communication network used to transmit the information is publicly available internet. But, the internet cannot be trusted enough to share

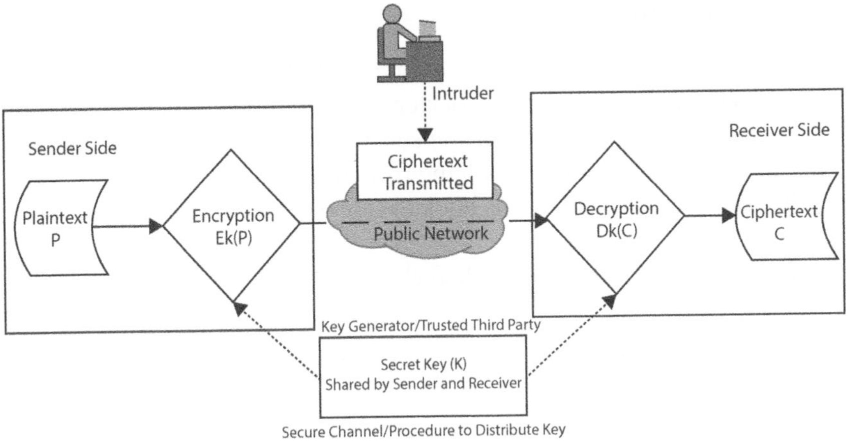

Figure 2.1 Conventional cryptography.

sensitive information. Therefore, this chapter will discuss the algorithms and practices used to protect the sensitive information over insecure networks. Figure 2.1 shows the principle of symmetric encryption between a sender and receiver. Intruder's aim here is to discover the shared secret key. Because, once the key is known, all the ciphertext exchanged between legitimate parties can be decrypted using the same algorithm available publically.

In symmetric key cryptography, encryption algorithms are well known and documented. Therefore, it should be strong that if intruder possesses some pairs of plaintext and corresponding ciphertext, he/she cannot decipher the ciphertext in order to discover the secret key. As shown in Figure 2.1 that symmetric key procedure is safe unless intruder obtains the shared secret key. Therefore, the key distribution must be a secure process. The symmetric key encryption process takes very less time to encrypt/decrypt as there is no heavy mathematics involved. Nevertheless, if opponent obtains the key, it can compromise the message as the algorithm is known already. In fact, a large number of keys will be required if the symmetric key procedure is used among many machines.

2.2 Classical Encryption Techniques

Classical encryption techniques are the elderly ciphers used to protect the information. Most of the classical ciphers are based upon substitution or permutation based approach [1].

2.2.1 Substitution Based

In substitution, each individual element of plaintext is mapped onto some different element of the given set of elements to produce ciphertext. In one of the most basic approaches of the substitution cipher, each alphabet in English is assigned a number ranging from 0 to 25.

The terminology used in this book to represent plaintext and ciphertext is shown below.

Plaintext "*P*" consist of individual elements so

$P->p_1, p_2, p_3 ... p_n$ Similarly Ciphertext $C->c_1, c_2, c_3 .... c_n$ where $c_1 = E_k(p_1)$, ... $c_n = E_k(p_n)$ Here k is a secret key

- Encryption - $C = E_k(P) = (P + k) \; mod \; Z$
- Decryption - $P = D_k(C) = (C - k) \; mod \; Z$

In the case of English alphabets, the value of Z is 26, and k is the secret key (ranging from 1 to 25). For example, a plaintext letter "E" and key value 25 will be substituted to ciphertext letter "D"

C = ("E" + 25) mode 26 ➔ (4+25) mod 26 ➔ 29 mod 26 ➔ 3 ➔ D

2.2.1.1 *Caesar Cipher*

It was the ancient example of substitution based ciphers and it was believed to be applied in practice by ancient king Julius Caesar. In Caesar cipher, the smallest unit of a message is replaced by a unit three position next in its alphabet set. Therefore, plaintext message "How are you" will be transformed into "Kru duh brx".

Caesar cipher is quite easy to implement but prone to brute force attack. Trying all the possible key space to deduce the plaintext from ciphertext is termed as Brute Force attack or exhaustive key search method. The approach is useful only when the key size is smaller otherwise for a larger key size this approach is quite impractical. Therefore, Caesar cipher can be easily decrypted by trying all the 25 keys.

2.2.1.2 *Monoalphabetic Cipher*

The problem of smaller key space of Caesar cipher was rectified in Monoalphabetic cipher. In Monoalphabetic cipher substitution characters are a random permutation of 26 alphabets. It means B can be replaced by alphabets A to Z, other than B. Furthermore there is no relation among replacement of each character. In other words replacement of A by D (i.e., A + 3 = D) does not mandate replacement of B by E.

Generally, the plaintext is written in well-known language therefore its statistical properties are easily available that can lead to statistical analysis attack on the ciphertext. It is not easy to apply brute force method in this case as it will take a lot more time trying 26! possible combinations of keys[1] or even half of them. But, the frequency of occurrence of characters may lead to statistical analysis attack, i.e., same plaintext symbols always map to same ciphertext symbols [2].

Statistical analysis techniques provide good results if the length of the analyzed text is large. Therefore, good ciphers must hide the statistical properties of plaintext i.e., generates a random sequence of ciphertext symbols. Alternatively, plaintext available can be compressed before encryption to thwart against such attacks. Mathematician Carl Friedrich Gauss suggested an idea of using homophones i.e., multiple occurrences of a symbol will be replaced with different symbols. But, the biggest challenge of occurrence of combinations of two letters known as digraph cannot be removed.

An enhancement to the Monoalphabetic cipher is made by Polygram substitution cipher where a group of plaintext letters is encrypted with a group of ciphertext letters. It may be applied to a group of two (termed bigram or digraph) to N letters (N-gram). For example plaintext block "HIJ" may be encrypted to "KTQ" while "HIK" may be encrypted to "CDS". This hides the frequency of individual letters.

2.2.1.3 *Playfair Cipher*

It has been seen that all the previously discussed ciphers were majorly suffering from the occurrence of a digraph in the text. Sir Charles Wheatstone suggested a method to treat diagrams as a single unit. He analyzed that ciphertext generated by one character substitution methods are more likely to preserve much of the plaintext syntax. However, substituting multiple plaintext letters i.e., treating them as a unit will wipe out some of that plaintext. Playfair Cipher is a popular cipher for multiple-letter substitution. This Cipher treats digraphs (i.e., the

---

[1] $26! > 4 * 10^{26}$ that is almost equal to 2^{88} and remember that this keyspace is much larger than the key space of DES algorithm.

combination of two letters) of plaintext syntax as a single unit and substitutes them into equivalent cipher digraphs.

Playfair cipher requires a *5 * 5* matrix of letters of a keyword. For example, if the keyword is: Cryptography then the corresponding matrix will be as per Table 2.1:

This matrix is constructed by filling the alphabets of keyword: Cryptography left to right without writing duplicates (*r and p*). Rest of the matrix is filled by the remaining of the alphabets (*a to z*) in their actual order. Letters *I* and *J* considered as a single letter. Two letters of alphabets are translated at a time as per the following rules:

- A pair of same alphabets will be separated by a filler letter, for example say *Z*. So "Collect" will be treated in digraphs as "Colzlect".
- Plaintext letter that comes in the same row will be replaced by their immediate right letter of the same row in a circular manner. So *PT* will be translated as *TC*.
- Plaintext letter of the same column will be replaced by the letter beneath from top to down in a circular manner of the same column. So *RV* will be translated as *GR*.
- Else, every plaintext character is swapped by the character found at the intersection of its row and remaining plaintext character's column position. E.g., plaintext unit GQ will be changed to HM, similarly, BN will be changed to AS.

Playfair remains robust cipher for a long time and popularly used during World War I and II. But, the cryptanalysis of the Playfair cipher is also aided by the fact that a digraph and its reverse will encrypt in a similar fashion. It means that if the encryption of MN will be AJ,

Table 2.1 Playfair matrix.

C	R	Y	P	T
O	G	A	H	B
D	E	F	I/J	K
L	M	N	Q	S
U	V	W	X	Z

then encryption of NM will be JA. So by looking for words like: receiver, departed, repairer that begin and end in reversed digraphs may lead intruder to apply frequency analysis method to reveal plaintext.

2.2.1.4 *Polyalphabetic Cipher*

Monoalphabetic cipher uses the same substitution rule for each substitution but in Polyalphabetic cipher rule changes with each letter or alphabet according to key value as per Table 2.2.

An early example of Polyalphabetic cipher is Vigenere cipher. Each letter of plaintext substituted into cipher as per the corresponding key value. For example, key: abracadabra and plaintext: "Can you meet me at midnight", then corresponding ciphertext will be as shown in Table 2.3.

Generally, the key string is shorter than the message length like "abracadabra" is the key in the above example, so a same key string is appended and repeated for entire message length, or as an alternate, plaintext may be appended to the key. It is quite difficult to implement a frequency analysis method on Polyalphabetic cipher as the output is having multiple ciphertext letters corresponding to the same plaintext letter. For a key length N;

Table 2.2 Polyalphabetic cipher.

Text \ Key/Keyword	a	b	c	d	……	z
a	a	b	c	d	……	z
b	b	c	d	e	……	a
c	c	d	e	f	……	b
	d	e	f	g	……	c
……	……	……	……	……	……	……
z	z	a	b	c	……	y

Table 2.3 Polyalphabetic cipher example.

Key	**abracadabra**abracadabra
Plaintext	canyoumeetmeatmidnight
Ciphertext	CBEYQUPEFKME.........

Cipher consists of N monoalphabetic substitution cipher and the plaintext letters at positions 1, N, 2N, etc., will be encrypted by same monoalphabetic substitution cipher. This may be useful to decrypt each monoalphabetic cipher. The same cipher will be produced if two same sequence of plaintext appears at a distance that is an integer multiple of keyword length e.g., plaintext "hello to hell" and key "welcome" will produce ciphertext dlqkcfsdlqk.

It is not difficult for the intruder to steal the information for a shorter key length. Therefore, it is recommended that length of key and plaintext should be same, and key should be a random permutation of 26 letters of the alphabet.

2.2.2 Transposition Based

Transposition is a technique to rearrange the order of plaintext elements to produce ciphertext. This technique is based upon permutation of the plaintext, i.e., SECURITY can be transposed to SCRYEIUT. Some popularly used transposition ciphers namely Simple Columnar and Rail Fence are discussed for better understanding of the approaches.

2.2.2.1 Simple Columnar

In this approach plaintext message is written in the rows of a certain size matrix and cipher is produced by reading its contents column-wise. The order to read the column is determined by the secret keyword shared among the communicating parties. If the keyword is given in alphabets, then, it is to be first converted into numbers according to their alphabetic order. For example, if the keyword is "BASH", then the corresponding key will be 2143. For example, to encipher the plaintext "*I AM SENDING YOU A MESSAGE*" with keyword "*SECRET, a two-dimensional matrix of 4 rows and 6 (keyword length) column is required.* Number of rows (M) can be calculated as $\lceil$Length (plaintext)/*Length (keyword)* $\rceil$[2].

Thus, the final matrix is as per Table 2.4.

Three places of the matrix left vacant after filling the matrix with plaintext. These vacant places should be filled with random letters instead of filling with a single padding character (for example "X"). The ciphertext will be written in the blocks of five to avoid guessing of keyword length. Thus, the cipher text is MNMEA IAGEY SPSGE QIDUA NOSJ.

---

[2] $\lceil\ \rceil$ is a ceiling operator.

Table 2.4 Simple columnar example.

Keyword	S	E	C	R	E	T
Key	5	2	1	4	3	6
Plaintext	I	A	M	S	E	N
	D	I	N	G	Y	O
	U	A	M	E	S	S
	A	G	E	Q	*P*	*J*

Double Columnar:
The cipher produced by simple columnar can be made more secure by applying another round of the same permutation where ciphertext of above example is treated as intermediate plaintext to produce final ciphertext that is more secure.

2.2.2.2 *Rail Fence Cipher*

In Rail Fence transposition technique, plaintext characters are arranged diagonally and processed row by row to produce ciphertext. The number of rows is termed as the depth of the cipher. For example, plaintext "this is secret" will be arranged in depth of 2 as shown in Table 2.5. Depth is also known as 'rail' justifying its name as 'Rail Fence'.

The corresponding ciphertext is produced by reading the characters row by row, therefore ciphertext is:

tiisce (row1) hssert(row2) => tiisce hssert

The number of rows (rails) can be more than two to enhance the robustness of the cipher. The strength of the cipher can be judged on the basis that the intruder can simply start assuming that there are two rows hence letters 1, 3, 5, ... of the message are from the same row and 2,4,6, ... are from another. If this is not the case then intruder will assume three rows

Table 2.5 Rail fence cipher example.

Row1:	t		i		i		s		c		e	
Row2:		h		s		s		E		r		T

hence letters 1,5,9, ... are in the first row, letters 2,4,6,8, ... are in second and 3,7,11 are in row number three.

Generally, many modern security algorithms achieve information security by applying multiple rounds of substitution and transportation in a combined fashion [3].

2.3 Evolutions of Modern Security Techniques

As discussed in earlier chapters that there are two methods to convert plaintext into ciphertext namely block cipher and stream cipher. Block cipher works upon a chunk of plaintext bytes at a time and convert it into ciphertext. The size of the block depends upon the underlying algorithm used for encryption. A generally acceptable size of a block is 64-bit. Contrary to this, in stream cipher mode, a symbol is encrypted at a time; symbol can be a character or a bit. The below sections discuss both the modes in detail.

2.3.1 Stream Cipher Algorithms

Stream cipher encrypts symbols of plain text one at a time into corresponding ciphertext symbol with the help of a pseudo-random key value. Generally, stream cipher works on byte level i.e., it encrypts one byte at a time. The pseudo-random key in stream cipher is generated from an initial random secret key. The generator function is described as:

$$G: \{0, 1\}^S \rightarrow \{0, 1\}^N$$

$$N >> S$$

It indicates that generator function G maps initial seed value in seed space S to a pseudo-random value in space N. Here the value of N is very large than S, i.e., a seed value of around hundreds of bit might be mapped to a Gigabyte long pseudo-random value. Here, generator G should be efficiently computable through a deterministic function. The only randomness lies in the initial seed value. However, the output of generator G must look random. Figure 2.2 show that the generator produces a large value from a fixed length small seed value. In stream ciphers, this large value acts as an internal state for the generator from which it can produce a 1-byte key value per iteration. This key value is XOR'd with plain text byte to produce ciphertext byte.

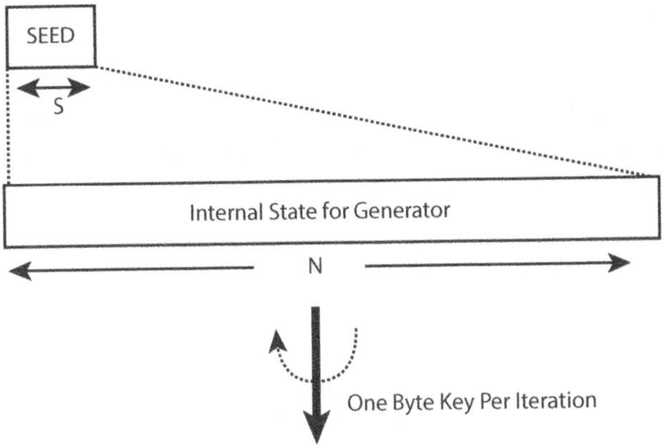

Figure 2.2 Generator function in stream cipher.

Most of the stream ciphers are based upon Linear Feedback Shift Register (LFSR). It is a shift register in which input is determined by XORing some of its existing bit-values called 'taps'. LFSR is used to produce pseudo-random numbers; therefore, it can act as a generator in stream ciphers. It is chosen for this purpose due to ease of its development in both software and hardware. Figure 2.3 shows a LFSR, whose rightmost bit is taken as output and an initial bit is XOR'd to feedback into the register as input after every clock cycle. LFSR operation starts from an initial state determined by a seed value.

The length of LFSR is fixed. It means it has a limited number of input values which will be feedback to the register. Therefore, ultimately, LFSR will be stuck in a repeating cycle of output bit which makes it vulnerable to attacks. However, if the feedback function is chosen carefully, this cycle can be extended to some more time. There are many stream ciphers based upon LFSR viz. Content Scrambling System (CSS) used to encrypt DVD data uses two LFSRs, A5 (1/2) algorithm used in GSM system uses four LFSRs, E0 algorithm used to secure Bluetooth communication uses five LFSRs. Following subsections discusses popular stream ciphers One-Time Pad, RC-4, and A5/1.

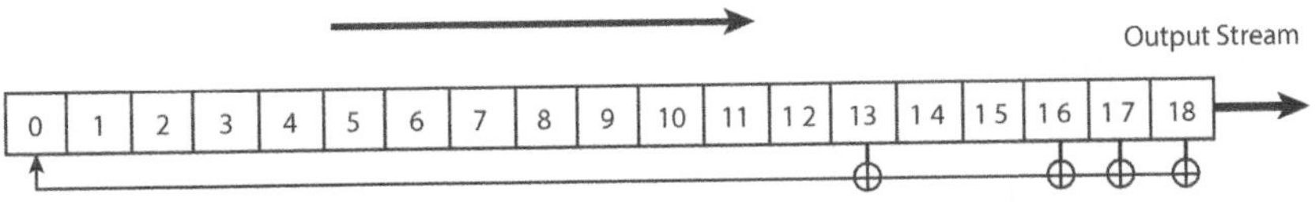

Figure 2.3 Linear feedback shift register.

2.3.1.1 *One Time Pad (OTP)*

To begin with the simplest approach of a stream cipher, we illustrate the One Time Pad (OTP) invented by Vernam in 1917. The OTP cipher considered to be first secured stream cipher. In OTP, plaintext, ciphertext, and key value consist of binary numbers:

Plaintext := Ciphertext := $\{0,1\}^n$
Key value :=.$\{0,1\}^n$

Key value is a random stream of bits whose length is equal to the length of plaintext message and the cipher is defined as:

$$C = E_K(P)$$

In OTP, the encryption process is simply XOR[3] of key and plaintext message, so

$$C = P \oplus K$$

XOR operation is also termed as modulo two additions as the results of modulo-two additions are exactly same as of XOR operations.

Based upon the properties of XOR, decryption of the ciphertext is:

$$P = D_K(C)$$

$$P = D_K(E(_K(P)) \quad => \quad D_K(P \oplus K)$$

$$(K \oplus P) \oplus K = (K \oplus K) \oplus P = P \text{ // Addition operator is associative}$$

OTP approach is efficient and fast to encrypt and decrypt plaintext. However, it requires a large key size to thwart against attacks. If plaintext P and its OTP encryption C are given, it is possible to find out the OTP key K.

$$C = P \oplus K$$

Now, XOR both the side by P

[3] XOR operation outputs 1 on dissimilar inputs and 0 otherwise.

$$P \oplus C = P \oplus P \oplus K \Rightarrow P \oplus C = 0 \oplus K$$

$$\Rightarrow P \oplus C = K$$

Readers must note that encryption process is often randomized while decryption process is always deterministic.

2.3.1.2 RC-4

RC-4 (Rivest Cipher) is a stream cipher algorithm that uses variable length secret key ranging from 1 to 256-bytes. It was developed in 1987 by Ron Rivest. RC-4 generates a keystream in the form of a bit which is XOR'd with the plaintext to produce ciphertext.

Working of RC-4 is divided into two parts namely: initialization of state vector and key generation. Initialization phase uses a key K as a seed value to populate state vector (array) S, and the key generation phase produces key in the form of pseudo-random bit streams. The idea of the key generation phase is to use a key value as a seed to generate a look-up table that can be used to produce pseudo-random bit streams, which act as key values. Array S is basically a 256-byte long state vector, which is populated using the small pseudo-code given below:

```
j := 0
for i from 0 to 255, do        //Initialization
S[i] = i;
T[i] = key [i mod keylen]
for i from 0 to 255, do                 // Initial Permutation
j = (j + S[i] + T[i]) mod 256;
swap (S[i], S[j]); // swap the values at ith and jth location of state vector S
```

As the key length is variable, it can be less than 256 bytes, therefore, a temporary array T of size 256 bytes is used to copy the key value. If key length is less than 256 bytes, key values will be repeated to fill the array T.

The code is permuting the initial values of state vector S which were initialized from 0 to 255 in the beginning. The second loop which takes key values to produce the value of index j indicates that the values of state vector S are dependent upon key K. Once this code is over, the second phase, i.e., key generation starts. The pseudo code of the key generation phase is shown below:

```
i = j= 0;
for k = 0 to N-1, do
   i = (i + 1) mod 256;
   j = (j + S[i]) mod 256;
   swap (S[i], S[j])
   tmp= (S[i] + S[j]) mod 256
   PRK = S[tmp];
   output P[k] XOR PRK;
```

In the pseudo code, PRK stands for Pseudo-Random Key and P [0: N-1] denotes to plaintext. The code suggests that the value of index *i* is incremented in each iteration, and the value at that index is used to compute next index value *j*. Then, values at both the indexes in the state vector S are swapped. It means every iteration will make changes in the state look-up table. Values of S[i] and S[j] are added and 'modulo 256' operator is used to limit the result in the range of 0 to 255. Finally, the value at this index which is shown as tmp" in the code is used to fetch the value from state vector S. This value is the key for this iteration. The key value is XOR'd with the plaintext and this process is repeated for next byte of plaintext and so on. RC-4 generates pseudo-random bytes of the key at a time, which can be XOR'd with the byte of plaintext to produce ciphertext byte, i.e., operations of RC-4 are byte oriented. Figure 2.4 illustrates the operations of RC-4 graphically.

RC-4 is a simple and easy to implement encryption algorithm that works fast in software. HTTPS and WEP (Wired Equivalence Privacy) incorporates RC-4. However, WEP protocol is no longer considered secure due to

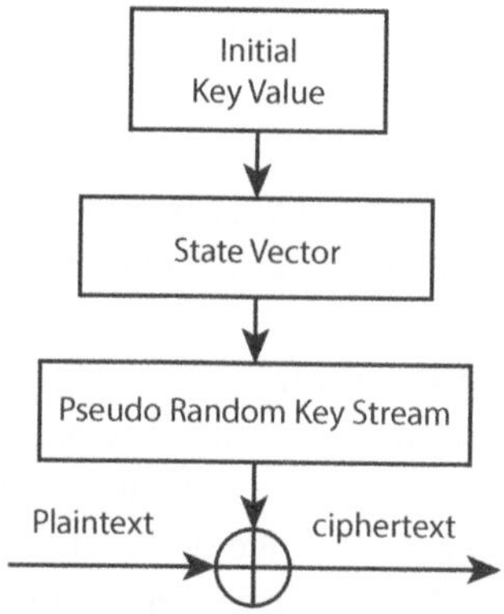

Figure 2.4 RC-4 operations.

the way of implementing RC-4 in it. Nevertheless, the problem is not with RC-4, but the way it is implemented.

2.3.1.3 A5/1

A5/1 is a stream cipher algorithm used to encrypt the telephonic conversations. It was first used by the Global System of Mobile (GSM) based mobiles as a built-in support to provide confidentiality to their users. Initially, A5/1 remained secret by GSM service providers, but, later, it was reverse engineered and analyzed by cryptanalysts.

A5/1 uses a secret key of size 64-bit and an initialization vector (IV) of size 22-bit. IV is obtained from a publically known frame number of 22-bit. The key component of A5/1 stream encryption is a linear feedback shift register (LFSR). It incorporates three LFSRs namely R1, R2, and R3 of size 19-bit, 22-bit, and 23-bit, respectively. LFSRs uses their bit number 8, 10, and 10, respectively, as clocking bit, i.e., LFSRs are clocked regularly as per the value of their corresponding clocking bit. Clocking decision involves all the three registers. Clocking bit of all the three LFSRs are used to compute majority value using the following formula:

$$MAJORITY: MAJ\ (X,Y,Z) = XY + XZ + YZ$$

In Figure 2.5, a clock controlling unit is indicated that controls the clocking decision of A5/1. LFSRs whose clocking bit agrees with the computed majority are clocked i.e., LFSR R1 will be clocked if its 8th bit (clocking bit) agrees with the majority. In every clock cycle, LFSRs updates according to their primitive polynomial as shown in Table 2.6, Only last bit of LFSRs contributes to the output which is calculated by XORing the values of Most

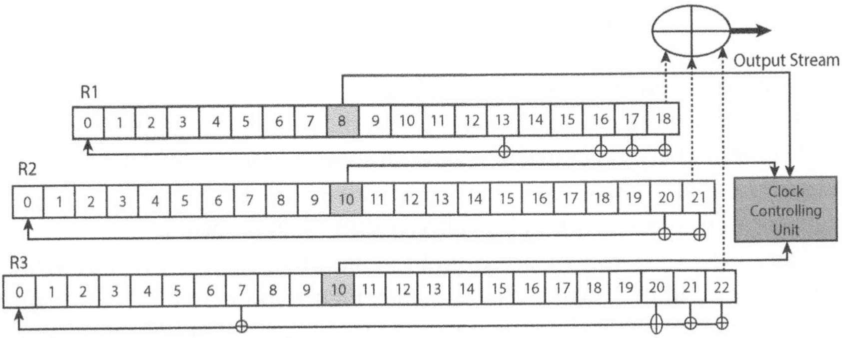

Figure 2.5 A5/1 structure.

Table 2.6 A5/1 parameters.

Register	Length	Primitive Polynomial	Clock Bit	Bits XOR'd
R1	19	$X^{19} + X^5 + X^2 + X + 1$	8	18,17,16,13
R2	22	$X^{22} + X + 1$	10	20,21
R3	23	$X^{23} + X^{15} + X^2 + X + 1$	10	22,21,20,7

Significant Bit (MSB) of R1, R2, and R3. Following expression summarizes the output:

$$\textit{Output Stream} = XOR\ (R1\ [18],\ R1\ [21],\ R1\ [22])$$

Using one bit per clock cycle, A5/1 produces a 228-bit output stream. The first half of the output stream is used to encrypt uplink data while the remaining half is used to encrypt downlink data.

With only 64-bit of key size, A5/1 seems weak using today's modern day computer systems. However, A5/1 is used in many countries to protect their GSM networks. Many countries also use A5/2 which is also a similar kind of stream cipher but it is designed to be weaker than A5/1 [4].

2.3.2 Block Cipher Algorithms

Unlike stream cipher, block cipher coverts a chunk of plaintext byte at a time into ciphertext. Most commonly used size of a block is 64-bits, but it is not fixed and depends upon the nature of the security algorithm used. Block cipher is based upon the fact that entire plaintext message is partitioned into blocks of similar size to be encrypted using a secret key. It is clear that every block of plaintext is encrypted individually, moreover, inside in a single block; every smallest element of a block is encrypted with keystream. So it gives a glimpse of stream cipher inside block cipher. Popular block cipher algorithms are Advanced Encryption Standard (AES), Triple Data Encryption Standard (TDES or 3DES), etc.

Block ciphers are built by iterations, i.e., the plaintext is supplied as input and ciphertext are generated after several rounds of iterations. As shown in Figure 2.6 that a single secret key is expanded to produce multiple unique keys for multiple iterations also called rounds of encryption.

Here R(K, P) is known as a round function that accepts two arguments namely key and the current message state. Figure shows that initially plaintext P is fed into first round function and then the output of this round function is fed as input to another round function with a different key value. The

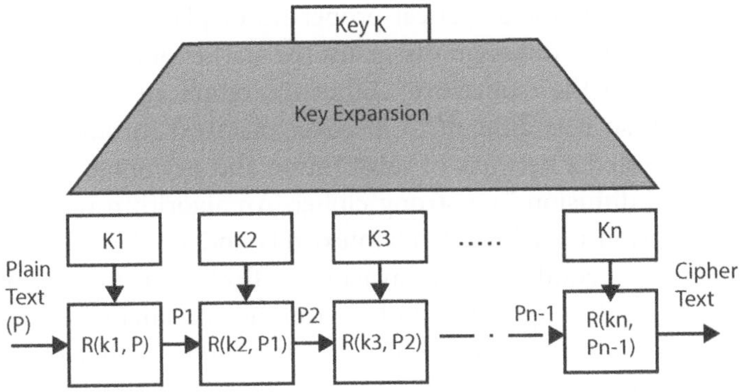

Figure 2.6 Key expansion method in a block cipher.

ultimate output of all the round functions is the ciphertext. The reader might be thinking that is there any generally accepted number of round functions. Actually, it depends upon the algorithm, for example, 1 DES uses 16 rounds, 3DES uses 48 rounds, and AES uses 10 rounds. The idea behind using multiple rounds of encryption is to generate a strong cipher that will not exhibit any relationship between plaintext and secret key. More details of rounds will be discussed in subsequent sections of this chapter. It is found that block cipher may generate same ciphertext block for repeating plaintext block if the key is same, hence cryptanalyst can make a guess of part or pattern of plaintext. With some more efforts, cryptanalyst may also reveal much part of the plaintext which leads to harmful consequences.

Claude Shannon in one of his research publication suggested two primitive operations namely confusion and diffusion in order to perform strong encryption and decryption. The idea was to make a strong cipher such that cryptanalyst cannot deduce key easily from ciphertext and plaintext pair. He also thought of a strong cipher that fulfills the strict avalanche effect, i.e., a single bit change in plaintext will affect several bits in the ciphertext. Shannon suggested that these properties of a strong cipher can be achieved with the help of confusion and diffusion methods [4].

Confusion: Confusion is intended to conceal the relationship between plaintext and ciphertext. In easier words, it is a technique to make sure that ciphertext does not reveal the pattern of plaintext. The process of confusion uses the key in a complex manner that even when an intruder knows the statistics; it is still difficult to infer the key. Confusion means that every bit of ciphertext depends upon many bits of the key. Therefore, changing a single bit in the key will drastically change the cipher.

Diffusion: It spreads the statistical properties of plaintext while producing ciphertext. Thus, diffusion dissipates the statistical structure of plaintext over most of the ciphertext. Diffusion complicates the statistics of the ciphertext, so it is difficult to discover plaintext through ciphertext. Shannon suggested a network of substitution and permutation to achieve confusion and diffusion in a strong cipher. An algorithm will be known for good diffusion if each of its plaintext bits and key bits affects half of the output bits. A good degree of avalanche effect is a major requirement of any cryptographic algorithm. Otherwise, the cryptanalyst can find out plaintext given some ciphertext or cryptanalyst can figure out key having a pair of plaintext and ciphertext. In order to illustrate the avalanche effect, an example of hash algorithm SHA-1 is shown in Table 2.7.

So, it is clear that in the second string only "hello" word is replaced with "hell" but there is a significant change in their corresponding hash value. This is a good example of the avalanche effect in the hash function. In order to achieve a strong avalanche effect most of the modern cryptographic algorithms combine both confusion and diffusion methods.

2.3.2.1 Feistel Cipher Structure

In the early 1970s, IBM realized that the customers are demanding some form of encryption to protect their information stored or transferred digitally. Therefore, IBM formed a group called crypto group and the head of the group was German-born physicist and cryptographer Horst Feistel. His first designed algorithm called Lucifer that accepts a secret key length and block length of 128 bit.

The design of Horst Feistel is popularly known as Feistel network. Feistel network is a symmetric structure used to design most of the block cipher algorithms (except AES). The goal behind building the Feistel network was to develop an invertible function, i.e., a structure that can be used in both encryption and decryption with the change in parameters only. In Feistel network, plaintext passes through a sequence of N-iterations of a round function whose working will be more precisely

Table 2.7 SHA-1 avalanche effect in hash function SHA-1.

Input text	The hash value of SHA-1
hello how are you	BA6A9C00C87E2AA5F02C2085214383FE256529BA
hell how are you	3490BB27F976D61A6EDD5CF799D2519D0AB1DB3E

discussed successively. In each round, 2w-bit plaintext is divided into two equal halves and transformed with the help of secret key and round function. Working of round function remains the same in every iteration and every round produces 2w-bit output. It is worth mention here that the structure of each round is exactly identical, but, input parameters like intermediate ciphertext, secret key value, etc., are quite different. In each round, a unique key value is produced with the help of a key generating function. Finally, the ciphertext is generated after performing final permutation to the output of the last round.

For example, plaintext of size 2w-bit is divided into two equal halves portions termed left and right. As shown in Figure 2.7, right half of first round (R0) is fed directly into the left half of second round (L1) and processed with a secret key (K) in round function (F). Whereas, left half of first round (L0) is XOR'd with the processed output of round function. This procedure is repeated up to a total number of rounds (N) and the final combined value of left and right portions is treated as ciphertext.

Transformations made at each round are summarized through the following equations

$$R_i := L_{i-1}\ XOR\ F(R_{i-1}, key_{[i]}) \tag{2.1}$$

$$L_i := R_{i-1} \tag{2.2}$$

Value of $i = 1, 2.....n$

In the Feistel network, encryption and decryption process are structurally identical. Therefore, in decryption process, ciphertext is used as input and the sub-key K_i is used in reverse sequence of encryption, i.e., K_n will be used in the first round, K_{n-1} in the next and so on.

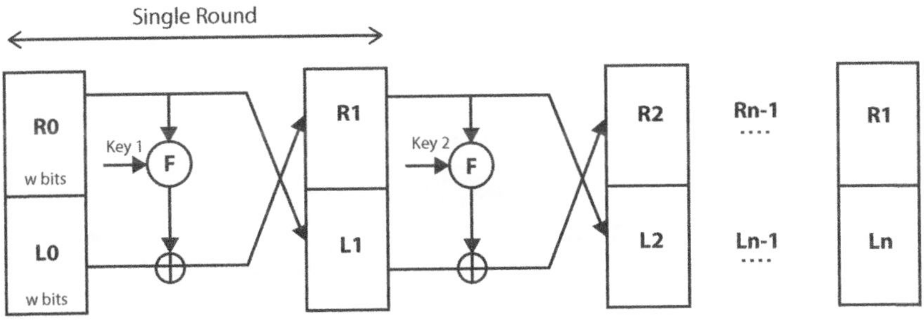

Figure 2.7 Feistel cipher structure.

In order to prove the Feistel network is really reversible, let's construct inverse of Feistel network's round, i.e., if we are given Ri + 1 and Li + 1, we need to find out Ri and Li and so on. With the help of Figure 2.8, it can be said that: Ri = Li + 1 and Li = Ri+1 XOR F (Li + 1). The inverse of a round function in Feistel structure is shown in Figure 2.9.

It is clear that the inverse of a Feistel round is much similar to its original round or it can be said that they are the mirror image of each other. Thus, putting together the inverse of all these rounds, the inverse of the entire Feistel structure can be obtained.

2.3.2.2 Data Encryption Standard (DES)

Data Encryption Standard used to be the most popularly used symmetric block cipher algorithm. The purpose of DES was to provide a standard method for protecting sensitive commercial information. Feistel's suggestion was to keep the key length to 128-bit. But, NBS decided to reduce the key length to be 56-bit. Reduction in size of key length proved as a fatal decision and in the year 1997, DES was broken by exhaustive search method. In the year 2000 Advanced Encryption Standard (AES) was finalized as the next-generation encryption algorithm. Nevertheless,

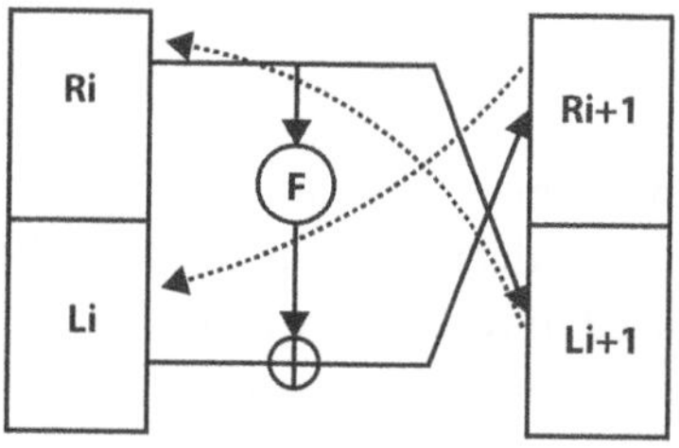

Figure 2.8 Reversibility of Feistel cipher structure.

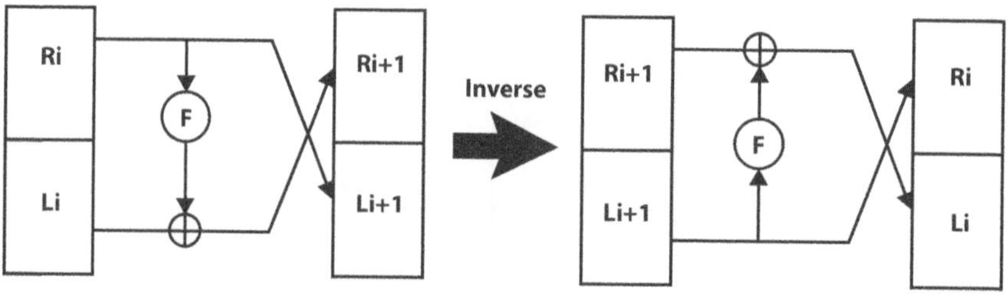

Figure 2.9 Inverse of Feistel cipher structure.

DES was widely deployed in banking and commerce industry before being replaced by AES. These days, the successor of DES known as Triple Data Encryption Standard (TDES) is widely used conventional encryption algorithms. DES operates on a block of 64-bit plaintext and uses a 56-bit key. As shown macroscopically in Figure 2.10, DES has 16 Feistel rounds of encryption. Each round requires a different key (K1-K16) of 48-bit produced through a key generator. Key generation mechanism accepts the initial 56-bit key and subsequently generates unique keys of 48-bit for all the iterations of round function by performing some transformations. Due to reversible design, decryption in DES uses the same structure and key (reverse order).

DES is based upon Feistel network; therefore, its working is similar to Feistel network. The output of an ith iteration in a round can be summarized as:

$$\text{Left part output} \quad Li = Ri\text{-}1 \tag{2.3}$$

$$\text{Right part output } Ri = Li\text{-}1 \text{ XOR } F(Ri\text{-}1, Ki) \tag{2.4}$$

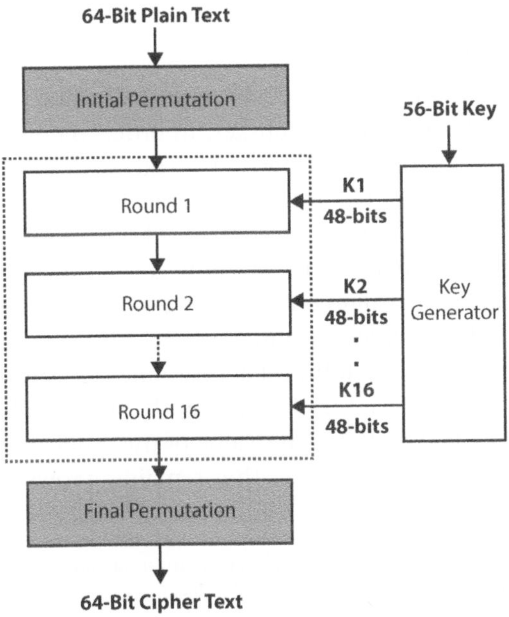

Figure 2.10 General model of DES.

An initial and final permutation is used to add permutations in DES. Working of each portion of DES is discussed subsequently.

Initial and final permutation:
Initial Permutation (IP) and final permutation (IP^{-1}) are used to permute the input plaintext according to a predetermined rule[4]. This is achieved with the help of Permutation (P)-box in DES.

Round Function:
Figure 2.11 illustrates the accurate working of a single round function (left) with key generator (right) used in the DES algorithm. In DES, plaintext block is divided into two equal halves of 32-bit each namely left and right. Right value is entered into a core function F whose working is as follows:

a. The input 32-bit value is expanded into 48-bit through Expansion Permutation and XOR'd with the 48-bit key value produced by the key generator.
b. The resultant 48-bit value is feed into Substitution Box (S-Box) that again converts it into 32-bit and passed into Permutation function P.

Expansion Permutation:
Expansion permutation expands 32-bit right half value (R_{i-1}) to 48-bit so that it can be XOR'd with 48-bit sub-key. In order to do so, R_{i-1} is divided into 8 equal parts of 4-bit each. Now every 4-bit part will be expanded into 6-bit to make it a total 48-bit. This will be done by simply copying certain values of 4-bit input using a predetermined rule of expansion permutation table (Appendix). Numbers in the table indicate bit positions and each row in the table is having six values out of which border values are highlighted, and these highlighted values are added in each row of 4-bit to convert to 6-bit. The first row shows that the bit at positions 1, 2, 3, and 4 in the input will be copied at positions 2, 3, 4, and 5 in the output. The first position of output will be filled by the 32-bit value of the input and 6th position of output will be filled by 5th-bit value. Thus remaining rows of 4-bit will also

[4] However, it is argued that initial and final permutation has no significance in DES, and the actual reason behind the use of them by the designers of DES is unknown. However, it is believed that these operations are very computation intensive while implementing in software and reduces the chances of software simulation of DES.

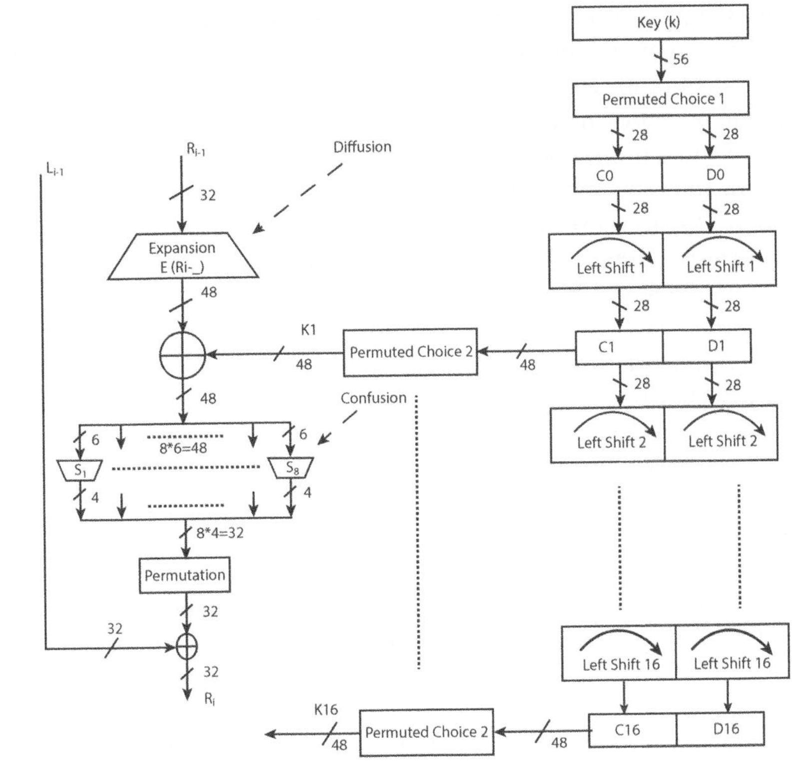

Figure 2.11 DES round structure (left) and key generator (right).

be transformed into 6-bit. Figure 2.12 further demystify the approach used to convert the 32-bit value of the right half into 48-bit.

Substitution (S) Boxes:
This is a very important part of DES and adds the Shannon's suggested confusion phenomena into it. S-boxes again convert the 48-bit value to 32-bit.

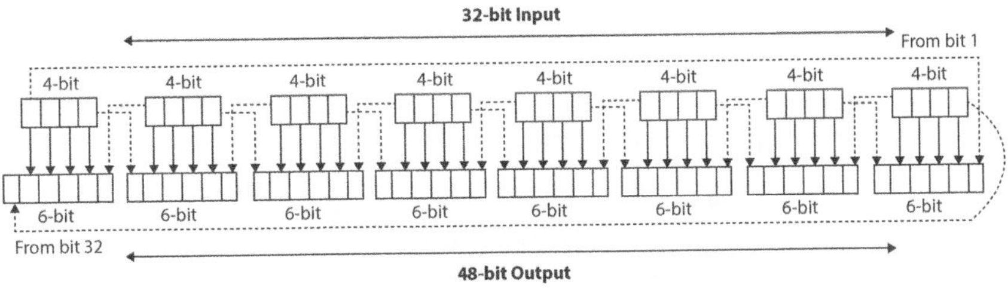

Figure 2.12 DES 32-bit to 48-bit expansion.

DES uses eight S-boxes having 6-bit input and 4-bit output. The substitution is based upon the predetermined table of 4 rows and 16 columns. This table is different for every S-box and contained 64 (4 * 16) random values which can be represented with 4-bit, i.e., 0 to 15. In order to choose a value from 64 values, 6-bit input is used. As shown in Figure 2.13 that first and last bit of the 6-bit input determines the particular row and bit ranging from 2 to 5 (4 bit) is used to find the column number of the table. Thus, the entry corresponding to the given row and column is taken as a 4-bit value corresponding to the given 6-bit value.

To further clarify the working of S-box, take an example whose graphical representation is shown in Figure 2.14. Suppose the 6-bit input for S-box-1 is: **101010**, it means an entry in the table of S-box 1 corresponding to row 10 (2 in decimal) and column 0101 (5 in decimal) is-06 (binary equivalent 0110). Thus string 101010 will be converted to 0110. Each S-box is having a different Table that is shown in the Appendix 2.8.

P-box permutation table:

The 32-bit output of eight S-boxes is fed into a permutation box that again permutes the bit according to the predetermined table shown in Appendix 2.7.

Key Generator:

Actual key size in DES is 64-bit, but before the process starts, every 8th bit of key, i.e., 8, 16, 24, 32, 40, 48, 56, 64, is discarded. These bits can be used

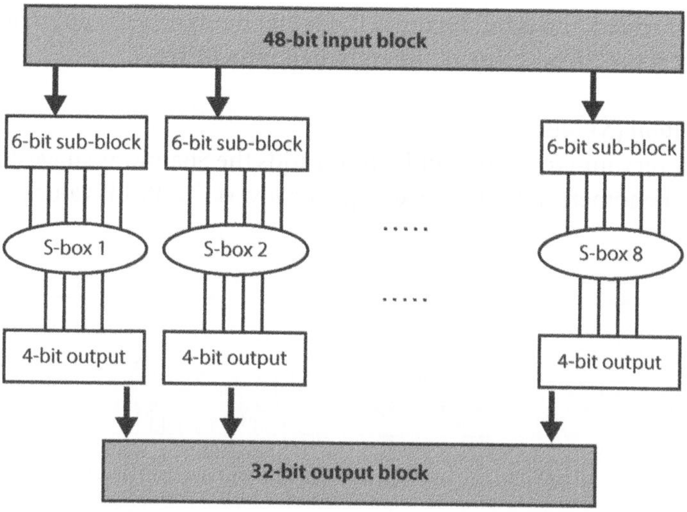

Figure 2.13 DES 48-bit to 32-bit substitution.

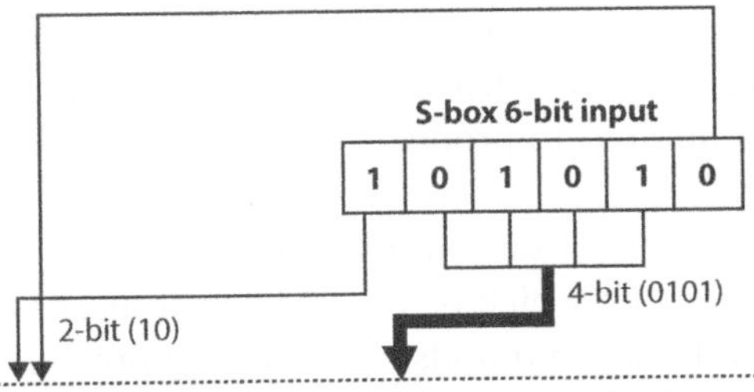

Input bits 1 and 6 / Input bits 2 thru 5

↓	0000	0001	0010	0011	0100	0101	0110	0111	1000	1001	1010	1011	1100	1101	1110	1111
00	1110	0100	1101	0001	0010	1111	1011	1000	0011	1010	0110	1100	0101	1001	0000	0111
01	0000	1111	0111	0100	1110	0010	1101	0001	1010	0110	1100	1011	1001	0101	0011	1000
10	0100	0001	1110	1000	1101	0110	0010	1011	1111	1100	1001	0111	0011	1010	0101	0000
11	1111	1100	1000	0010	0100	1001	0001	0111	0101	1011	0011	1110	1010	0000	0110	1101

S-box-1 Table

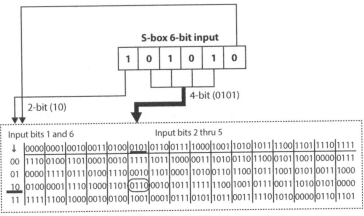

Figure 2.14 DES S-box substitution.

for parity checking to ensure that the key does not contain any error. Key generator as shown in Figure 2.11, divides input 56-bit key into two equal halves of 28-bit each, namely, C_0 and D_0 and then pass through Permutation Choice-1 (PC-1) function for permutation. Every iteration performs Left Circular Shift on these 28-bit values. Schedule of left circular shift is also fixed in every round and is shown in Appendix 2.5. These shifted values fulfill the following two purposes:

I. Serve as input for the next iteration, i.e., C_1 and D_1
II. Serve as input to Permutation Choice-2 (PC-2) function resulting in a 48-bit key K_i. Permutation choice-2 function is basically a compression permutation as it compresses 56-bit key into 48-bit. This 48-bit key is used as the key for round function and process continued for remaining 15 rounds. Tables of PC-1 and PC-2 are predefined and shown in Appendix 2.3 and 2.4 respectively.

It is to be mentioned again that in the very beginning, 64-bit plaintext is divided into two equal halves namely left and right halves. All the transformations discussed so far are applicable to the only the right half. As depicted in Eq. (2.4), 32-bit output of function F mentioned above is XOR'd with 32-bit left half and produces the 32-bit right half for next round. 32-bit right half portion of previous round is copied directly into 32-bit left half of next round as per Eq. (2.3). The process is repeated for 16 iterations of round structure. The right and left output of 16th round are swapped and it is termed as pre-output. Pre-output is delivered to Final Permutation (also called Inverse Initial Permutation) to produces the final 64-bit ciphertext output.

The decryption process in DES is same as of encryption. The difference is only in the sequence of the key, which is reversed key. It means key will be used as K_{16}, K_{15}, K_{14},...K_1 for all 16 rounds of decryption process respectively [1].

Analysis of DES:
DES is robust against analytical attacks as it is based upon avalanche effect i.e., small changes in plaintext or key bit results into drastic changes in ciphertext and changes increase with the number of round functions. DES is very fast in computation, compact in hardware, and easy to adapt in diverse applications. However, as mentioned earlier, DES is vulnerable to brute-force method. But, there are two more methods namely differential and linear cryptanalysis discovered to break DES in less than 2^{56} times, i.e., lesser than brute-force attack on DES.

Differential cryptanalysis: Differential cryptanalysis is a chosen plaintext attack. In chosen plaintext attack, an intruder is able to obtain some ciphertext corresponding to some chosen-plaintext by him. Differential cryptanalysis is the method to measure the differences in the output ciphertext when corresponding input plaintext is changed. The idea is that the cipher of any plaintext may look random but this is not true on a differential basis. This method uses plaintext pairs with a constant difference and the attacker compares the differences in the corresponding ciphertext with the purpose to find out statistical patterns in the cipher to discover the key. Therefore it is termed as differential cryptanalysis. Readers must note that statistical properties depend upon the S-box used for encryption. Input difference of two plaintexts M1 and M2 is wisely chosen such that the difference of their corresponding ciphers C1 and C2 will provide an idea about the statistical properties of some of the key bit. Differential cryptanalysis has become a design concern of modern algorithm as its knowledge is increasing; as a result, Advanced Encryption Standard (AES) has proven secure against this attack.

Linear Cryptanalysis: Linear cryptanalysis is a known plaintext attach based upon the linear calculations of parity bit of all the three entities namely plaintext, ciphertext, and key. It requires 2^{43} known plaintexts and ciphertext pairs to discover the key. The goal of linear cryptanalysis is to find out the secret key in less than 2^{56} time, i.e., less time than the brute force attack. It is assumed that during linear cryptanalysis attacker possess many input and output pairs of plaintext and corresponding ciphertext.

Let C= DES (K, M), suppose for random K, M, there is dependence among message, ciphertext and plaintext such that if we XOR a subset of plaintext with a subset of ciphertext, it produces a subset of the key bit with a probability of ½.

$$Pr\ [p[i_1]\ XOR\ .....p[i_r]\ XOR\ c[j_1]\ XOR....c[j_v]] = k[l_1]XOR...k[l_u] = 1/2$$

If this probability is ½, it means both the sides are completely independent, i.e., given many pairs of message and cipher, an attacker cannot figure out the key bit. But, due to a bug in the design of 5th S-box of DES, this probability is actually ½ + epsilon (ε), not exactly ½. Tiny linearity in the 5th S-box generates liner equations as given below through entire circuit:

$$Pr\ [p[i_1]\ XOR\ .....p[i_r]\ XOR\ c[j_1]\ XOR....c[j_v]] = k[l_1]XOR...k[l_u] = 1/2 + \varepsilon$$

For, DES, this ε is very low (i.e., $1/2^{21} \sim 0.0000000477$), but there is a bias that leads to a linear attack on DES. A theorem suggests that given $1/\varepsilon^2$ random pair of plaintext and corresponding ciphertext, the probability that the above relationship will be correct for more than ½ of the time is more than 97.7%. It is mentioned that for DES, $\varepsilon = 1/2^{21}$, so with 2^{42} (i.e., $1/\varepsilon^2$) pairs of plaintext and ciphertext, an attacker can find out XOR of some of the key bit. Therefore, around 14 key bit can be predicted using this relationship once by going through a backward direction and once by going through forwarding direction. When 14 bits are predicted, the brute force method can be applied to remaining 42 bits (56 – 14 = 42). Brute force on 42 bits will take 2^{42} time or roughly 2^{43}, which is very less than 2^{56}

$$2^{43} << 2^{56}$$

Therefore, in linear cryptanalysis total attack time is 2^{43} with 2^{42} random plaintext and ciphertext pairs [6].

2.3.2.3 *Triple Data Encryption Standard (TDES)*

As the computational capacity of modern machines is increasing tremendously, it is not difficult to brute force a 56-bit long key. Therefore to achieve more security a variation of DES named Triple DES (TDES) is in use. The term variation is used because TDES is not a new algorithm and is based upon DES algorithm differing only in key length.

As per its name, it applies DES algorithm three times on a single block of plaintext with a different key each time. Parameters of 3DES are 64-bit block size, 48 rounds (3 * 16), and key size 3 * 56 = 168-bit. TDES was standardized in 1999 and is in use of the electronic payment industry. The layout of 3DES is shown in Figure 2.15.

TDES uses three keys each of 56 bit length and follow the sequence of Encryption-Decryption-Encryption that is summarized as:

$$3E((k_1, k_2, k_3), m) = \text{Ciphertext} = E(k_1,(D(k_2,(E(k_3, m)))$$

Where Ek denotes encryption of plaintext using key *k* and Dk denotes decryption using key *k*.

Readers might be wondering why its Encryption, Decryption, Encryption instead of Encryption, Encryption, Encryption. So, to justify this, suppose all three keys are the same, i.e., $k_1 = k_2 = k_3 = k$, then the above-stated formula becomes:

$$E(k,(D(k,(E(k, m))) \rightarrow E(k, m)$$, i.e., it becomes normal DES and remains backward compatible.

Key options in TDES:
TDES algorithm uses three consecutive keys viz. k_1, k_2, k_3 so keying option can be described in Table 2.8. Option 1 is TDES with total key size 168-bit.

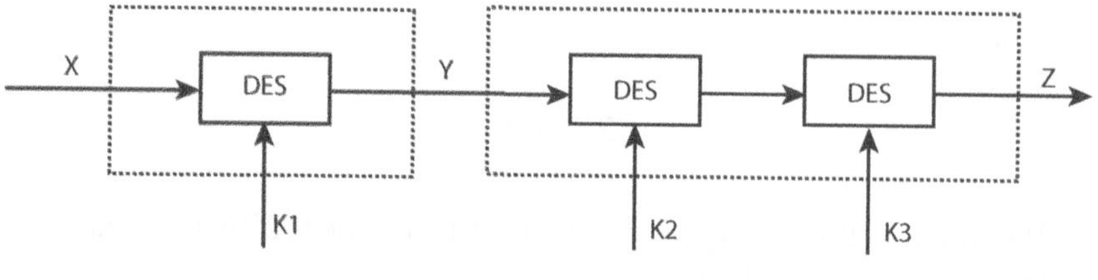

Figure 2.15 Block diagram of 3DES.

Table 2.8 TDES key option.

Option	Description	Key size	Security level
1.	All keys are independent	56 * 3 = 168	High
2.	k1, k2 are independent while k3=k1	56 * 2 = 112	More than DES
3.	All three keys are same	56	Equal to DES

Option 2 uses two keys with key size 112 also known as double DES and option 3 is simple DES.

Analysis of 3DES:
As the key size is 168, any exhaustive search has to try 2^{168} possible keys, that is really a very huge number and practically impossible. But, the number of rounds will definitely slow down the performance of 3DES. It is almost three times slower than DES. Then, Why not use double DES if triple DES is slower?

Defining double DES as 2E((k1,k2),m) = E(k1, E(k2,m)), and key length is: 2 * 56 = 112 that is sufficiently large and its speed will be two times slower than DES. Then, it should be a good choice, but this structure can't be used due to its vulnerability of meet-in-the-middle attack.

Meet-In-The-Middle attack (MITM) on 2DES:
Suppose, given a pair of message $M = \{m_1, m_2,\ldots.m_{10}\}$ and corresponding ciphertext $C = \{c_1,c_2\ldots c_{10}\}$, and the goal is to find out key pairs $\{k_1, k_2\}$ such that

$$E\,(k_1, E\,(k_2, M)) = C$$

If we apply decryption with key *k1* on both the side of this equation, then:

$$D(k_1, E\,(k_1, E(k_2,M))) = D(k_1,C)$$

$$\Rightarrow \ \sout{D(k1, E\,(k1}, E(k2,M))) = D(k_1,C)$$

$$\Rightarrow E(k_2,M) = D(k_1,C)$$

This final equation says that key k_2 encrypts plaintext M to a value, which is same to the decryption of cipher C by key k_1. As shown in Figure

2.16, this attack is called "meet in the middle" and it will take time lesser than exhaustive search.

Total time taken by "meet-in-the-middle" attack on 2DES is around 2^{63} that is very less than 2^{112} of exhaustive search. 2^{63} is really very less time and approximately equal to the time taken by an exhaustive search on DES. Therefore, 2DES is not a recommended block cipher. What if the same attack is applied to 3DES? Figure 2.17 indicates the point where "meet-in-the-middle" attack can be applied to 3DES.

In the forward direction, a table of 2^{56} entries of encryptions of plaintext is to be created, and then try to decrypt cipher with all 2^{112} possible key values until a collision in the encryption table is found. But, this leads to an approximate 2^{112} time that is still much-much larger to brute force. Therefore, 3DES is the NIST standard and DES is no more used in its original form.

2.3.2.4 *International Data Encryption Algorithm (IDEA)*

IDEA is eight rounds, 64-bit symmetric block cipher using 128-bit key size. This algorithm provides full protection of information from unauthorized access by intruders. IDEA is far better in security than 56-bit key based widely used Data Encryption Standard (DES). Instead of look-up tables or S-Box used in DES, IDEA uses a complex transform

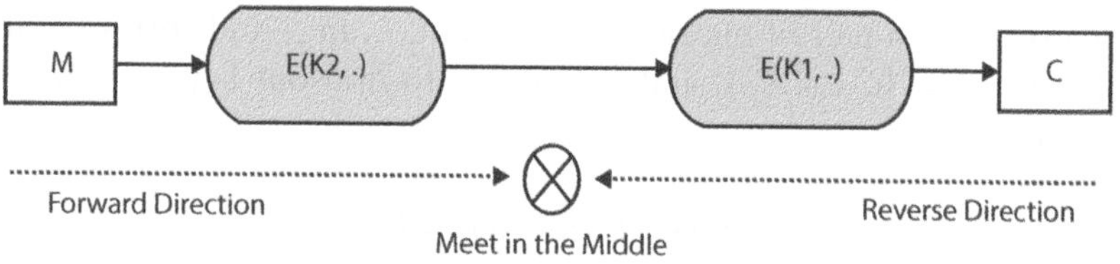

Figure 2.16 Meet in the middle attack in double DES.

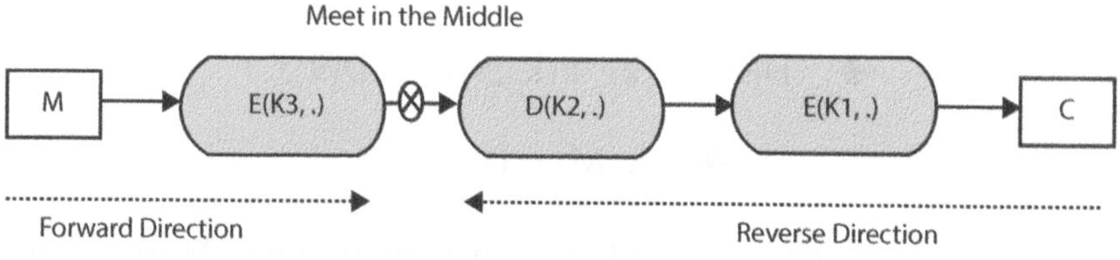

Figure 2.17 Meet in the middle attack in triple DES.

by the combination of XOR, binary addition and multiplication of 16-bit integers.

The IDEA algorithm depicted graphically in Figure 2.18 begins by dividing 64-bit Input block into four equal words of 16-bit each, namely A, B, C, and D. IDEA uses eight rounds of computation and each requires six subkeys (16-bit each). After eight rounds of computations, the output transformation process uses four subkeys. Thus, entire IDEA encryption process uses 52 number of (i.e., 8 * 6 + 4) 16-bit subkeys that are generated by an initial 128-bit master key.

Key Management:
Master key (128-bit) is initially divided into eight 16-bit words and is used as first eight subkeys out of 52 sub keys as mentioned above. Subsequent subkeys (52 – 8 = 44) for the next rounds are generated by rotating 25-bit left to an initial 128-bit master key. The starting process of dividing master key into eight sub keys is again repeated for the next rounds.

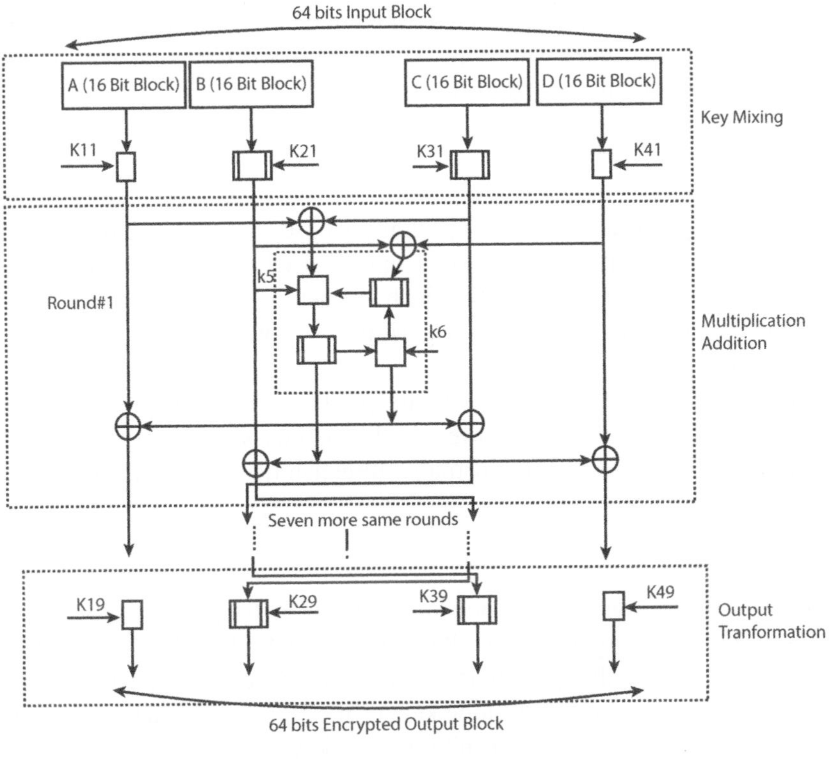

Figure 2.18 IDEA encryption process.

Encryption:
Each round of IDEA encryption is divided into two parts viz. key mixing layer and a multiplication-addition structure.

- *Key mixing layer* performs parall el operations (multiplication and addition) to combine each input word (A, B, C, and D) with first four subkeys (K1, K2, K3, and K4).
- *The multiplication-addition (MA) structure* takes the output of the key mixing layer as input and combines with two next subkeys (K5 and K6). Finally MA structure exchanges two middle words (B and C).

The last step consists of output transformation which uses last four subkeys (e.g., K19, K29, K39, K49) and generates four blocks (each of 16-bit) of ciphertext, these blocks are combined to produce 64-bit ciphertext. The process of decryption remains the same while the inverse of sub keys used during encryption is used. IDEA has several advantages like worldwide presence and fast algorithm, provides high-level security with a 128-bit key (Double of DES), cost effective implement IDEA in hardware chips, etc. IDEA was first used with Pretty Good Privacy (PGP) and later used in various areas like finance, telecom, etc.

2.3.2.5 Blowfish

Blowfish is publically available general-purpose symmetric block cipher encryption algorithm which is based upon Feistel structure. Blowfish was proposed as a replacement to DES which was getting older and slower. It was proposed as a software encryption algorithm that could work easily on 32-bit machines.

The similarity of Blowfish with its predecessor is the use of 64-bit block size of the plain text. However, Blowfish uses a variable key length ranging from 32 to 448-bit. Normally, Blowfish uses 16 rounds of Feistel structure.

Key Management:
Blowfish uses a large 448-bit long key that is used to generate sub-keys of 576-bit. Due to a larger key size, Blowfish calculates keys before performing encryption and decryption. It uses 14 K arrays each of capacity to store 32-bit resulting in the 448-bit long key. While 18 P arrays each of capacity to stores 32-bit resulting in 576-bit long sub-key.

Encryption:
The 64-bit input plaintext is divided into two equal halves, namely, RE and LE. Then, following operations are repeated for each round function, i.e., repeated 16 times.

$$LE_1 = RE_0 \oplus F(LE_0, P_1)$$

$$RE_1 = LE_0 \oplus P_1$$

The above expressions can be generalized as:

$$LE_{i+1} = RE_i \oplus F(LE_i, P_{i+1})$$

$$RE_{i+1} = LE_i \oplus P_{i+1}$$

Here $\oplus$ denotes bitwise exclusive-OR, F is the function used in each round, and P denotes that array holding sub-keys.

As shown in Figure 2.19 the output of the 16th round is to generate final encryption in the following way:

$$LE_{17} = LE_{16} \oplus P_{18}$$

$$RE_{17} = RE_{16} \oplus P_{17}$$

Basically, the output of the 16th round is swapped again to produce LE_{17} and RE_{17}, which are merged to produce final 64-bit ciphertext. Figure 2.19 indicates that function F in a round is having four S-boxes and each S-box takes 8-bit input and produces a 32-bit output which is XOR'd and added to produce 32-bit output.

Decryption process in Blowfish uses encryption structure with reverse oder key. But, first P_{17} and P_{18} are XOR'd with ciphertext, then, remaining sub-keys are used in reverse order.

Blowfish uses a very large key which makes it more robust toward any security attack. Generation of a key in advance makes it suitable for applications, which do not need new key often. Blowfish was designed to run in software-based encryption so its encryption speed is fast. Moreover, it is not patented that makes it more easy to use in many applications.

However, producing key is a slow and intensive task in Blowfish that might be a limitation of the same in many areas. It is also found that the first four rounds of Blowfish can be compromised by second order differential attack. Therefore, the creator of Blowfish proposed its successor Twofish encryption algorithm.

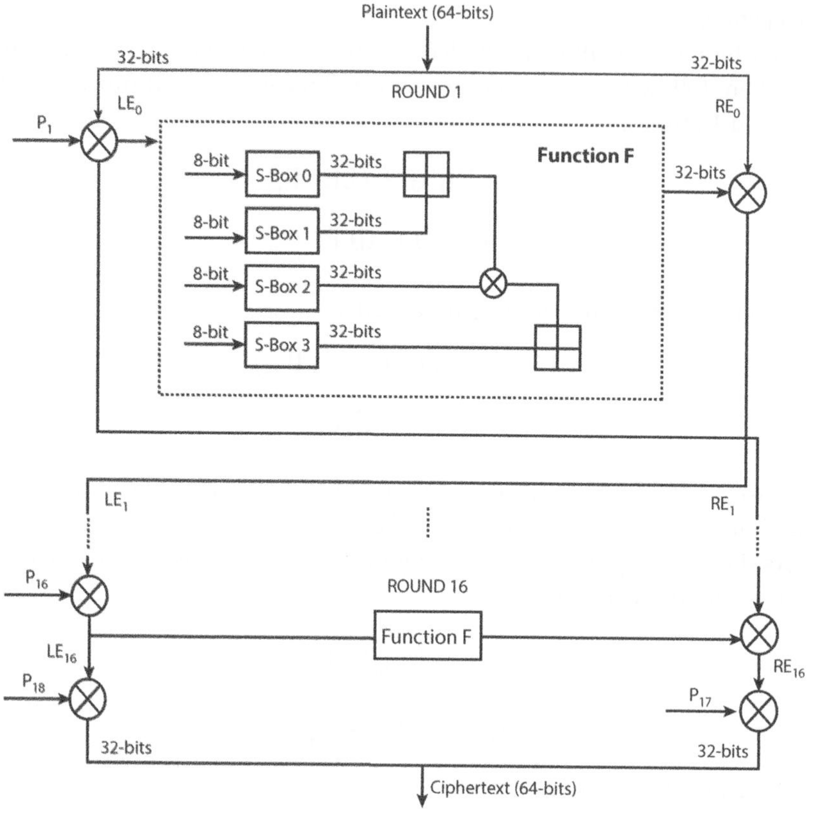

Figure 2.19 Blowfish encryption.

2.3.2.6 *CAST-128*

In order to thwart against linear and differential cryptanalysis, Carlise Adams and Stafford Tavares proposed CAST encryption algorithms in 1996. CAST is a basically a family of symmetric key encryption/decryption algorithms and CAST-128 is a prevalent algorithm of this family that uses a 128-bit long key. Like DES, CAST-128 is also based upon the well-proven design principles of Feistel structure, but, it provides strict avalanche criteria which was absent in DES. Interestingly, it provides better performance by using lesser rounds than DES. CAST incorporates certain changes in round function and key schedule that makes it more suitable for software implementation too. The main idea of CAST algorithm is to use large S-box to thwart against linear and differential cryptanalysis, i.e., it uses 8 × 32 size S-box rather than 6 × 4 size of DES. It uses exclusive OR, addition and subtraction modulo 2^{32} operations. It uses eight S-boxes from which four are used in key scheduling while four are used in round function.

CAST-128 seems structurally identical to Blowfish. But, CAST-128 uses fixed length S-boxes while Blowfish uses key-dependent S-boxes unlike.

The similarity of CAST-128 with its predecessor is the use of 64-bit block size of plaintext. However, CAST-128 uses a variable key length ranging from 40 to 128-bit (128-bit key size is recommended). Key range increments in octets, i.e., 48-bit will be the next possible key size after 40-bit. Normally, CAST-128 uses 12 rounds of Feistel structure if key length is lesser than 80-bit, otherwise, CAST-128 uses all 16 rounds. In case of shorter key lengths than 128-bit, the key is padded with zero bytes. Example shown in Table 2.9 illustrates the padding of key and sample plaintexts (in octets).

Key Management:
Like Feistel structure, CAST-128 uses a primary key to generate sub-keys for subsequent rounds. But, it has been found and proved by many researchers that key generation procedure of DES suffers from certain issues like lack of strict avalanche, bit independent criteria, etc. Therefore, in order to overcome such issues, CAST-128 uses special substitution boxes for the creation of sub-keys from the primary key. This feature of CAST is different from the sub-keys generation method of DES. It uses two 32-bit sub-keys, namely, K_{mi} and K_{ri} per round, where K_{ri} is responsible for rotation, i.e., rotations in CAST-128 are dependent upon the key and K_{mi} performs masking in each round.

Encryption:
Input plaintext block of 64-bit is divided into two equal halves of 32-bit each, namely, L_0 and R_0. Following iterations are calculated for all the 16 rounds of CAST encryption:

$$L_i = R_{i-1}$$

$$R_i = L_{i-1} \oplus F(R_{i-1}, K_{mi}, K_{ri})$$

Table 2.9 Example of key-padding in CAST-128.

40-bit key	12 32 26 89 67
Padded 128-bit key	12 32 26 89 67 00 00 00 00 00 00 00 00 00 00
64-bit plain text	AB EF 24 01 34 13

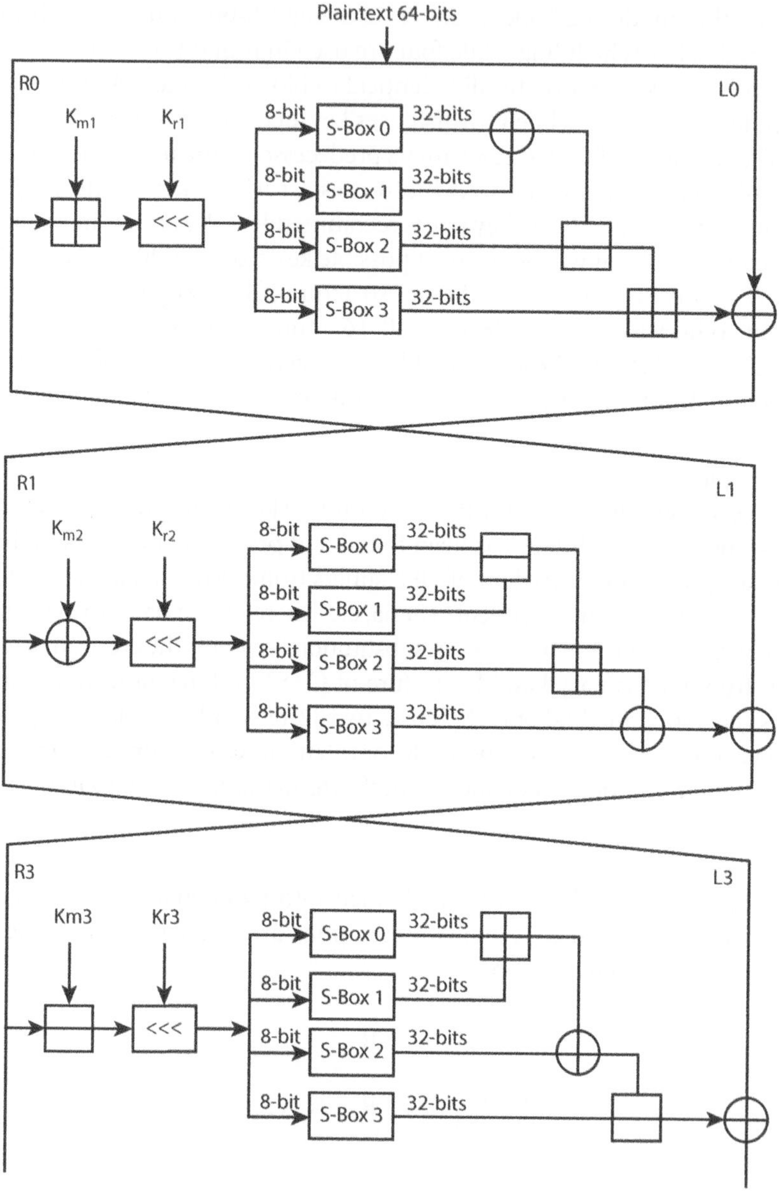

Figure 2.20 CAST-128 encryption (NOTE: right and left halves of plaintext are drawn on opposite sides in Figure 2.20 to indicate the similarity of CAST-128 with Blowfish algorithm).

Here F is the round function and CAST-128 uses three structurally identical round functions having a basic difference in the choice of operations as shown in Figure 2.20. The major difference in round functions is the change in the position of basic operations viz. addition modulo 2^{32}, subtraction modulo 2^{32}, and exclusive OR. Figure 2.20 shows only the first three rounds of CAST-128 to indicate that three types of functions are used one after another. Then, this pattern is repeated for remaining rounds of CAST-128.

Function F consists of four S-boxes having 8-bit input and 32-bit output. To understand the working of function F in a round function, an intermediate variable X is used to store the result of keys masking and rotations with the right half of plaintext/intermediate ciphertext. Thus, the value of X for the first round is:

$$X = [(R3 + Km3) <<< Kr3]$$

This intermediate value X is divided into four equal parts each of 8-bit and fed into four S-boxes respectively to add non-linearity. The output of S-boxes is combined using three different ways in all the three types of functions in the round. The final output of the function in round 1 in the form of intermediate value X is as follows:

$$F(R_{i-1}, K_{mi}, K_{ri}) = ((S_0(X) \oplus S_1(X)) - S_2(X)) + S_3(X)$$

Here S_0, S_1, S_2, and S_3 are the 32-bit output of four S-boxes used in the function and $\oplus$ is eXclusive OR, – is subtraction modulo 2^{32}, and, + is addition modulo 2^{32}.

Similarly, a reader can derive the expressions for rounds 2 and 3. After the end of the 16th round, both halves are swapped and merged to produce 64-bit ciphertext.

Decryption process in CAST-128 uses the same encryption structure with key in reverse sequence.

Although CAST-128, which is also known as CAST5 is patented by Entrust, it can be used for profitable and non-profitable use without any royalty. Mostly 3DES is used to secure the communication of multimedia objects in an e-mail through Secure/Multipurpose Internet Mail Extensions (S/MIME). But, 3DES is found slow in many cases; therefore, according to internet drafts, use of CAST-128 in securing S/MIME provides good speed with security. E-mail encryption standard Pretty Good

Privacy (PGP) and open source based GNU Public Guard (BPG) also makes use of CAST-128.

CAST-128 is vulnerable to linear cryptanalysis through known plaintext attack. Therefore, CAST-256 is proposed as a robust successor of CAST-128 in RFC 2612. Table 2.10 summarizes the differences between CAST-128 and Blowfish encryption algorithm [7].

2.4 Conclusion

Internet is a dominant medium of transmitting information in today's era. But, it is a public network that cannot be relied upon. Therefore, scientists and researchers have been discovering many approaches, methods, and algorithms to protect our sensitive information from illegitimate audience. Elderly encryption algorithm based upon either substitution or transposition approaches cannot withstand the robust cyber attacks. Therefore, modern encryption algorithms intelligently use the combination of both substitution and transposition approaches. Claude Shannon's theory of confusion and diffusion further assisted cryptographers to design robust algorithms. Horst Feistel's initial design "lucifer" paved the path for block cipher designers and many modern day algorithms are based upon it. Increasing computational capabilities indicates that more insights are required to develop futuristic encryption algorithm. Vulnerabilities in DES encouraged for the development of 3DES and AES kind of algorithms. Developments in the field of VLSI and ULSI made the fabrication of algorithms easy and cost-effective. Growing usage of mobile devices encouraged the development of stream cipher based algorithms which are fast and secure. It can be undoubtedly stated

Table 2.10 Differences between CAST-128 and Blowfish algorithms.

Factors	**CAST-128**	**Blowfish**
Key length	128-bit	448-bit
Security	Moderate	Secure Enough
No. of rounds	12–16	16
No. of S-boxes	8	4

that the there is a great scope for new algorithms for ever-changing world of technology.

References

1. Stallings, W., *Cryptography and Network Security: Principles and Practice, 6e*, Prentice Hall Press Upper Saddle River, NJ, USA, 2013.
2. Paar, Christof, Lecture Notes *Applied Crytography and Data Security*, Chair for Communication Security, Department of Electrical Engineering and Information Sciences, Ruhr-Universit¨at Bochum, Germany, version 2.5, January 2005.
3. Kahate, A., *Cryptography and Network Security*, Tata McGraw-Hill Education, India, 2013.
4. Eli Biham, O.D., Cryptanalysis of the A5/1 GSM Stream Cipher. *Indocrypt 2000*, 2000.
5. Shannon, C., A Mathematical Theory of Communication. *Bell Syst. Tech. J.*, 28, 4, 656–715, 1948.
6. Matsui, M., A new method for known plaintext attack of FEAL cipher. *Advances in Cryptology*. EUROCRYPT, 1992.
7. Adams, C.M., *Constructing Symmetric Ciphers Using the CAST Design Procedure*, Kluwer Academic Publishers, Boston, 1997.

Practice Set

Summary

- ✓ Block Cipher encrypts a block of plaintext at a time
- ✓ Block cipher approach is quite faster than its counterpart stream cipher and used in computer-based cryptographic algorithms.
- ✓ Shannon suggested two primitive operations namely confusion and diffusion perform strong encryption and decryption.
- ✓ Confusion makes the relationship of key and ciphertext more complex so that the ciphertext does not reveal the pattern of plaintext
- ✓ Diffusion refers to rearranging or spreading out the bit in the message so that any repetition in the plaintext is spread out over the ciphertext.

- ✓ Block cipher has three modes of operations namely electronic code book, cipher block chaining, and cipher feedback mode to process blocks of plaintext into ciphertext.
- ✓ Electronics codebook mode produces unique ciphertext for every 64-bit block of plaintext given the same key.
- ✓ In cipher block, chaining encryption is performed in 64-bit blocks with the ciphertext output of encrypting block n being XORed with the plaintext input of block n + 1.
- ✓ Bit Padding is a technique to add some extra bit to the original message to make it a positive multiple of the block length.
- ✓ Cipher feedback makes block cipher into stream cipher Like CBC, but do XOR after encryption.
- ✓ Feistel Cipher is a symmetric structure that used in the development of block cipher. This Feistel Network works as the basic building block of DES algorithm.
- ✓ Feistel Cipher structure is affected by parameters like block size, key length, number of rounds, etc. There is a trade-off between security level and encryption speed with the increase in these parameters.
- ✓ Data Encryption Standard is widely used, symmetric block cipher technique, it uses 64-bit block length and 56-bit key with 16 rounds of a cryptographic function.
- ✓ Expansion creates diffusion and Substitution box provides confusion in DES.
- ✓ Avalanche effect causes small changes in the plaintext to lead to significant changes in the cipher.
- ✓ DES with 56-bit key is more prone to be broken by brute-force approach.
- ✓ Differential cryptanalysis is the method to measure the differences in the output ciphertext when corresponding input plaintext is changed.
- ✓ In Liner cryptanalysis, some linear equations are derived relating plaintext, Ciphertext and the key bit. Then these linear equations are used in conjunction with known plaintext-ciphertext pairs to derive key bit.
- ✓ Triple Data Encryption Standard uses three keys each of 56-bit length and follows the sequence of Encryption-Decryption-Encryption.

- ✓ IDEA is eight rounds, 64-bit symmetric block cipher using 128-bit key size.
- ✓ IDEA is far better in security than 56-bit key based widely used DES.
- ✓ IDEA produces a complex transform by the combination of XOR, Binary addition and multiplication of 16-bit integers Instead of look-up tables or S-Box used in DES.
- ✓ In link, encryption data is encrypted just before the system places it on the physical communication links. Either Physical or data link layer in OSI or TCP/IP protocol suites are responsible for link encryption.
- ✓ Link encryption is faster, easier for the user. It also eliminates traffic analysis by the attacker as the entire message is encrypted.
- ✓ Encryption is performed by the Application or presentation layer opposite to link encryption.
- ✓ Traffic flow analysis is based upon the variation of a load of traffic to determine the type of communication.
- ✓ A padding approach is used to insert spurious data into the network to balance the traffic load thus prevent traffic flow analysis.
- ✓ A trusted server symmetric Key-Distribution Center (KDC) is used to provide temporary session-keys to its authorized hosts.
- ✓ Front End Processor (FEP) also known as communication processor is responsible for end to end encryption and asks the KDC to release the session key.
- ✓ Denial of Service is a threat to the entire key distribution system.
- ✓ The secrecy of the cryptographic algorithm is determined by the pure random and unpredictable key values generated by a random number generator.
- ✓ Random bit generator is a system whose output consists of the completely unpredictable bit.
- ✓ Hardware-based random value generator is preferred over software-based because they are having a clearer model of the source and its possible interaction with the outside world.

Review Questions and Exercises

A. Multiple Choice Questions

Q.1 3DES uses ________________ rounds

A. 48
B. 10
C. 15
E. 46

Q.2 AES uses ________________ rounds

a. 10
b. 12
c. 13
d. 48

Q.3 In ECB data is divided into ________ bit blocks

a. 64
b. 32
c. 68
d. 48

Q.4 Bit padding is done in

a. CFB
b. ECB
c. BCE
d. All of above

Q.5 Key length used in Feistel cipher

a. 128
b. 64
c. 32
d. 56

Q.6 Key length in DES

A. 56
B. 64
C. 128
D. 32

Q.7 Plaintext passes through a sequence of ____ iterations of a round function in DES

A. 16
B. 8
C. 10
D. 12

Q.8 S-boxes again convert the ____ value to ____ bit in DES

A. 48 to 32
B. 32 to 48
C. 48 to 46
D. None of the above

Q.9 IDEA uses 8 rounds of computation and each requires ____ subkeys

A. 6
B. 8
C. 4
D. 3

Q.10 Master key in IDEA __bit

A. 128
B. 32
C. 64

Q.11 Link encryption is performed in

A. Layer 1
B. Layer 2
C. TCP
D. DLL

Q.12N users require ____keys in asymmetric cryptography.

A. N*(N-1)/ 2
B. N*(N-1)
C. N
D. N^2

Q.13 Bit-values which are XOR'd in a Linear Feedback Shift Register to produce an output are called:

A. Bit-values
B. Special Bit
C. Taps
D. Tokens

Q.14 What limitation of LFSR makes it vulnerable to security attacks?

A. Feedback Function
B. Fixed Length of LFSR
C. Design of LFSR
D. All of the above

Q.15 Which of these protocol incorporates RC-4

A. HTTPS
B. WEP
C. Both (A) and (B)
D. None of the above

Q.16 Size of secret key and initialization vector (IV) in A5/1 are

A. 128-bit, 22-bit
B. 64-bit, 22-bit
C. 128-bit, 64-bit
D. 64-bit, 64-bit

B. Subjective Questions

Q.1 Discuss Claude Shannon's principles of Confusion and Diffusion.

Q.2 Explain block cipher modes of operations in details.

Q.3 Discuss Feistel cipher structure, parameters affecting its performance, and reversibility of the structure.

Q.4 Describe the DES algorithm in details. Discuss the strength and limitation of the DES algorithm.

Q.5 Explain the parameters affecting the realization of Feistel Cipher architecture.

Q.6 Which operations of DES provide confusion and diffusion?

Q.7 Explain Differential cryptanalysis and Liner cryptanalysis attack on DES.
Q.8 Elaborate TDES algorithm with reference to DES algorithm.
Q.9 Explain International Data Encryption Standard algorithm.
Q.10 State the differences between DES and IDEA.
Q.11 List the differences between link encryption and an end to end encryption.
Q.12 Explain the key distribution process.
Q.13 What is the use of a random number in cryptography? Explain the Random Number Generator.
Q.14 What will be the result of Denial of Service attack on a KDC?
Q.15 If a plain message P and its OTP encryption C is given, is it possible to figure out the OTP key K using P and C?
Q.16 Is Feistel network is really reversible?
Q.17 Draw the inverse diagram of entire Feistel structure.
Q.18 Why not use fewer rounds than 16 in DES?
Q.19 Is there any attack possible on 3DES that takes time lesser than 2168?
Q.20 Why not use double DES if triple DES is slower?

C. Numerical Problems

Q.1 Given a plaintext, P = 1001001 and key K is: 0101101 then find the value of ciphertext C using One Time Pad approach. Decrypt cipher using the same key and confirm your answer.
Q.2 What will be the 4-bit output of S-box-1 when the 6-bit input is: 101010.

D. Lab/Programming Assignments

Q.1 Implement 1-DES algorithm using any of your favorite programming languages.
Q.2 Explain the working of rand() and srand()function of C language.
Q.3 Write a program to generate random numbers between 0 to N numbers.

APPENDIX A: Tables of Data Encryption Standard [1]

Table 2.1 Initial permutation.

58,	50,	42,	34,	26,	18,	10,	2,	60,	52,	44,	36,	28,	20,	12,	4
62,	54,	46,	38,	30,	22,	14,	6,	64,	56,	48,	40,	32,	24,	16,	8
57,	49,	41,	33,	25,	17,	9,	1,	59,	51,	43,	35,	27,	19,	11,	3
61,	53,	45,	37,	29,	21,	13,	5,	63,	55,	47,	39,	31,	23,	15,	7

Table 2.2 Final permutation or IP inverse.

40,	8,	48,	16,	56,	24,	64,	32,	39,	7,	47,	15,	55,	23,	63,	31
38,	6,	46,	14,	54,	22,	62,	30,	37,	5,	45,	13,	53,	21,	61,	29
36,	4,	44,	12,	52,	20,	60,	28,	35,	3,	43,	11,	51,	19,	59,	27
34,	2,	42,	10,	50,	18,	58,	26,	33,	1,	41,	9,	49,	17,	57,	25

Table 2.3 Permutation choice-1.

57	49	41	33	25	17	9
1	58	50	42	34	26	18
10	2	59	51	43	35	27
19	11	3	60	52	44	36
63	55	47	39	31	23	15
7	62	54	46	38	30	22
14	6	61	53	45	37	29
21	13	5	28	20	12	4

Table 2.4 Permutation choice-2.

14	17	11	24	1	5	3	28
15	6	21	10	23	19	12	4
26	8	16	7	27	20	13	2
41	52	31	37	47	55	30	40
51	45	33	48	44	49	39	56
34	53	46	42	50	36	29	32

Table 2.5 Key schedule of left shifts.

Round number	1	2	3	4	5	6	7	8	9	10	11	12	13	14	15	16
Bits rotated	1	1	2	2	2	2	2	2	1	2	2	2	2	2	2	1

Table 2.6 Expansion table.

32	1	2	3	4	5
4	5	6	7	8	9
8	9	10	11	12	13
12	13	14	15	16	17
16	17	18	19	20	21
20	21	22	23	24	25
24	25	26	27	28	29
28	29	30	31	32	1

Table 2.7 P-box permutation.

16	7	20	21	29	12	28	17	1	15	23	26	5	18	31	10
2	8	24	14	32	27	3	9	19	13	30	6	22	11	4	25

Table 2.8 S-box table (1–8).

S-Box 1:															
14,	4,	13,	1,	2,	15,	11,	8,	3,	10,	6,	12,	5,	9,	0,	7
0,	15,	7,	4,	14,	2,	13,	1,	10,	6,	12,	11,	9,	5,	3,	8
4,	1,	14,	8,	13,	6,	2,	11,	15,	12,	9,	7,	3,	10,	5,	0
15,	12,	8,	2,	4,	9,	1,	7,	5,	11,	3,	14,	10,	0,	6,	13
S-Box 2:															
15,	1,	8,	14,	6,	11,	3,	4,	9,	7,	2,	13,	12,	0,	5,	10
3,	13,	4,	7,	15,	2,	8,	14,	12,	0,	1,	10,	6,	9,	11,	5
0,	14,	7,	11,	10,	4,	13,	1,	5,	8,	12,	6,	9,	3,	2,	15
13,	8,	10,	1,	3,	15,	4,	2,	11,	6,	7,	12,	0,	5,	14,	9
S-Box 3:															
10,	0,	9,	14,	6,	3,	15,	5,	1,	13,	12,	7,	11,	4,	2,	8
13,	7,	0,	9,	3,	4,	6,	10,	2,	8,	5,	14,	12,	11,	15,	1
13,	6,	4,	9,	8,	15,	3,	0,	11,	1,	2,	12,	5,	10,	14,	7
1,	10,	13,	0,	6,	9,	8,	7,	4,	15,	14,	3,	11,	5,	2,	12
S-Box 4:															
7,	13,	14,	3,	0,	6,	9,	10,	1,	2,	8,	5,	11,	12,	4,	15
13,	8,	11,	5,	6,	15,	0,	3,	4,	7,	2,	12,	1,	10,	14,	9
10,	6,	9,	0,	12,	11,	7,	13,	15,	1,	3,	14,	5,	2,	8,	4
3,	15,	0,	6,	10,	1,	13,	8,	9,	4,	5,	11,	12,	7,	2,	14
S-Box 5:															
2,	12,	4,	1,	7,	10,	11,	6,	8,	5,	3,	15,	13,	0,	14,	9
14,	11,	2,	12,	4,	7,	13,	1,	5,	0,	15,	10,	3,	9,	8,	6
4,	2,	1,	11,	10,	13,	7,	8,	15,	9,	12,	5,	6,	3,	0,	14
11,	8,	12,	7,	1,	14,	2,	13,	6,	15,	0,	9,	10,	4,	5,	3

(*Continued*)

Table 2.8 S-box table (1–8). (*Continued*)

S-Box 6:															
12,	1,	10,	15,	9,	2,	6,	8,	0,	13,	3,	4,	14,	7,	5,	11
10,	15,	4,	2,	7,	12,	9,	5,	6,	1,	13,	14,	0,	11,	3,	8
9,	14,	15,	5,	2,	8,	12,	3,	7,	0,	4,	10,	1,	13,	11,	6
4,	3,	2,	12,	9,	5,	15,	10,	11,	14,	1,	7,	6,	0,	8,	13
S-Box 7:															
4,	11,	2,	14,	15,	0,	8,	13,	3,	12,	9,	7,	5,	10,	6,	1
13,	0,	11,	7,	4,	9,	1,	10,	14,	3,	5,	12,	2,	15,	8,	6
1,	4,	11,	13,	12,	3,	7,	14,	10,	15,	6,	8,	0,	5,	9,	2
6,	11,	13,	8,	1,	4,	10,	7,	9,	5,	0,	15,	14,	2,	3,	12
S-Box 8:															
13,	2,	8,	4,	6,	15,	11,	1,	10,	9,	3,	14,	5,	0,	12,	7
1,	15,	13,	8,	10,	3,	7,	4,	12,	5,	6,	11,	0,	14,	9,	2
7,	11,	4,	1,	9,	12,	14,	2,	0,	6,	10,	13,	15,	3,	5,	8
2,	1,	14,	7,	4,	10,	8,	13,	15,	12,	9,	0,	3,	5,	6,	11

3

Philosophy of Security by Cryptostakes Schemes

Hemant Kumar Saini

Rajasthan Technical University, Kota, Rajasthan, India

Abstract

The study of asymmetric cryptosystem is done depicting the public key and private key pairing to get the best technique. Also the RSA proofing and modular arithmetic resolve the computation complexity to solve the p-k system. On the other hand, to get sharing Diffie–Helman proved the algorithm with its own color symmetry.

Keywords: P-K system, RSA, trapdoor, SSL, CRT, man in middle attack, DH key, DES key

3.1 Philosophy of Public Key Cryptosystems (p-k Cryptography)

Public-key cryptography is a fundamental disappearance beginning the entire that has vanished by. From the ancient beginning 1960s to today's complete cryptography is based on substitution and permutation [1]. It is also known by its other name asymmetric cryptography since it uses individual encryption key and another diverse except connected decryption key as shown in Figure 3.1.

Characteristics:

1. It is impracticable to decide the decryption key just get merely information procedure and the encryption key.

Email: hemantrhce@rediffmail.com

Dinesh Goyal, S. Balamurugan, Sheng-Lung Peng and O.P. Verma (eds.) Design and Analysis of Security Protocol for Communication, (79–94) © 2020 Scrivener Publishing LLC

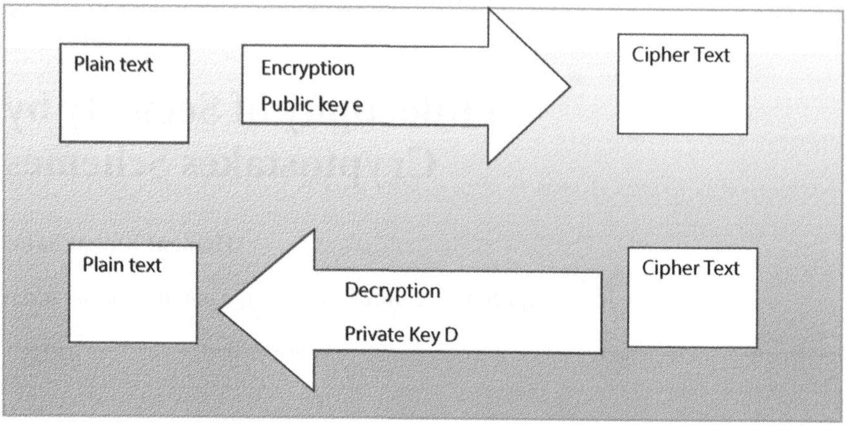

Figure 3.1 Principle of P-k cryptography.

2. Among associated keys would be utilized for encryption, if one for encryption then other will be automatically decrypts it.

For any p-k process, the following are the basic main requirements.

1. Plain text: any readable information, i.e., provide for enter.
2. Encryption algorithm: for converting the plaintext.
3. Encryption and decryption keys: pairs of keys if one intended for making cipher, the further is for re-originating plain text. The precise changes executed by the procedure rely on keys offered like participation.
4. Cipher text: it is output in mess up form which relies on the puretext and key in support of same communication, with two dissimilar keys two disparate ciphers can be created.
5. Decryption algorithm: production of original message with the decryption key and cipher.

Note: Each key used has significance in p-k processing. Since Public key of a user A is available for world then it is used in encryption for secrecy and the same is used for decryption for authentication purposes. Whilst the private key seeded in decryption with both reasons: secrecy plus authentication as private hold only by owner.

In this, if only one of the authentication/confidentiality is considered then there would be chances to breach. Hence the pk process with aggregation of both gives the better unbreakable way. With the deeper into details consider Figure 3.2(a) in which we can see the opponent can easily determine message with the private key of receiver B. Also Figure 3.2(b) gives us the idea of beaching the authenticity as the text was arranged using A's private key where A's public key known by everyone so opponent can easily determine the private key of sender A. There it is decided in modern cryptography that p-k inbuilt both and secure the message by first encrypting by senders private key then again encrypt second time by the receivers public key, which brings confidentiality as seen in Figure 3.2(c). But this produces the complexity as the same algorithm processed four times [2, 3].

3.2 RSA Algorithm

It was given by Ron Rivest, Adi Shamir, and Len Adleman at MIT in 1978. The RSA is a chunk where the message and cipher are numbers from 0 to n – 1. RSA uses exponentials to encrypt the plain text into blocks having a binary value < n.

From ancient times, messages are encrypted using specific key to cipher text message. To regaining the message we need same key toward the mapping. Hence to communicate securely both sender and receiver both need to share the identical keys. On the way, sender has to share each identical key with each receiver and hence it has to manage the ring of identical keys to manage and also there would an extra overhead communication to share those keys. In 1970, James Alice gives a clever concept based on lock and unlocks which is inverse operation of each other. He said sender purchase a lock open it and send to receiver. On receiving the lock now the receiver lock it and send the message to sender where the sender can unlock it and read message, no keys were exchanged as seen in Figure 3.3(a). But in this opponent may also become a recipient and get the key. So it extended the concept by developing the keys inverse of each other [4]. The idea of inverse keys can be simplified by explaining with color mixing. The inverse of some color is the complementary color which one added to it produces white. Sender must randomly select an private key say red, next using the complementary color of red, i.e., cyan sends as an public key on non secured communication channel if an intruder traps then it gets cyan as shown in Figure 3.3(b). Let us say now receiver wants to send secret yellow so he mix it with cyan and form a new green which is sent back to sender, where intruders traps this green also. Now sender adds private color

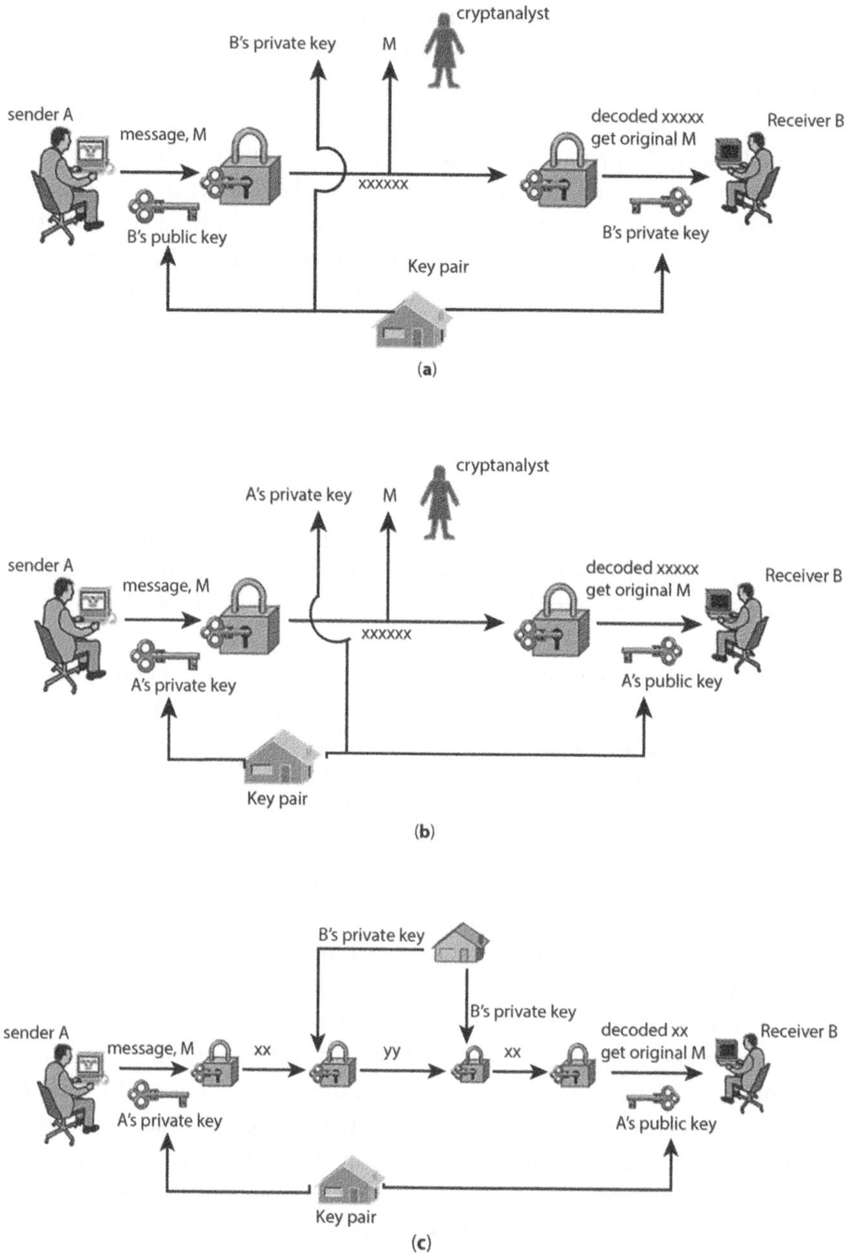

Figure 3.2 (a) p-k secrecy, (b) p-k authentication, (c) p-k confidential + authentication.

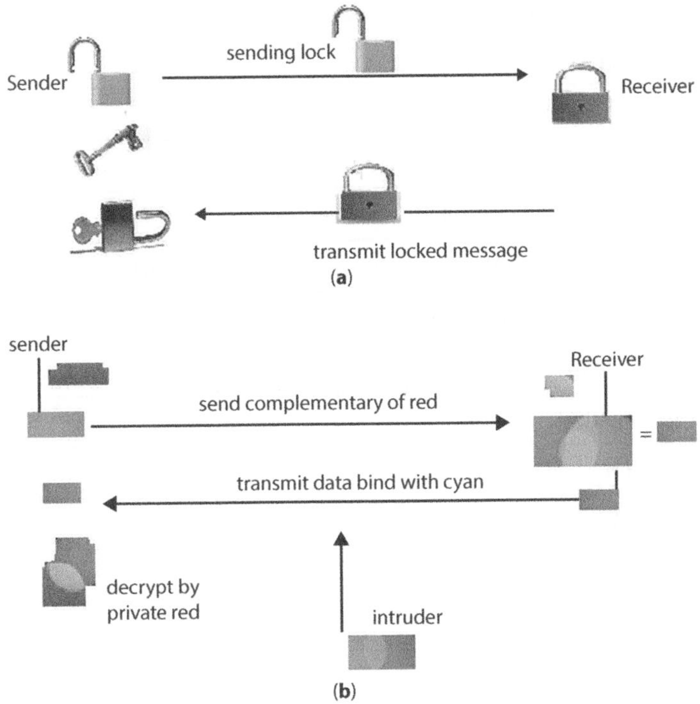

Figure 3.3 (a) Way of locking and unlocking in RSA, (b) RSA analogy to inverse color.

red to green and gets yellow which the receiver sent. So with the more advances Ron Rivest, Adi Shamir, and Len Adleman together gives an algorithm which is given in Table 3.1 fundamentally uses the prime factorization one way function which is quite hard to reverse and it takes hundreds of years to break. As such sender after computing all the x, y, n, Φ(n), e, and d sends only the n and e as a public key acting as an open lock where intruder traps n, e [5]. At receiver side, receiver locks by C, and sent back to sender so now the intruder trapped n, e, and C. But it must be notified that none can find the M without f(n) which requires prime factorization of n and which cannot be solved long years [6]. Illustration:

a) choose $x = 11, y = 19$
b) compute $n = xy = 11 \times 19 = 209$
c) compute $f(n) = (x - 1)(y - 1) = 180$.
d) decide on e, relatively prime to and less than f(n), say $e = 17$.

Table 3.1 Algorithm for RSA stepwise.

Key generation
choose prime x and y
compute n = x y
Compute f(n) = (x−1)(y−1)
choose integer e such that HCF(Φ(n),e) =1 but $1<e< f(n)$
Compute $d = e^{-1}$ mod f(n) or we say de = f(n)
Public key {e,n}
Private key {d,n}
Encryption
Message M
Cipher C = Me mod f(n)
Decryption
Cipher C = Me mod f(n)
Original message M = Cd mod f(n)

e) establish d such that de = 1 (mod 180) and $d < 180$.
f) The accurate assessment for d is 77 as 77 × 17 = 1309 = 7 × 180 + 49 (using the extended version of Euclid's algorithm)

3.3 Security Analysis of RSA

RSA obtains security by the complexity of factoring large numbers. Recuperating the message with single key and the cipher is two prime product factors. Therefore RSA can be break by the following attacks of determining the d while considering e and n.

1. Swine Force: Attempt finally probable keys. Typical protection is a bulky key to get better higher encryption key and decryption key.
2. Arithmetical attacks (trapdoor): Bifurgate the number n into two so permit computation of f(n) and the encryption key

$e = d^{-1} \pmod{f(n)}$. The most excellent RSA algorithm is utilized to ratio n into:

$$O(n) = e^{\sqrt{\ln(n).\ln(\ln(n))}}$$

This take much large years to break but new factorization methods also eases to this.

3. Time attacks: Kocher explained a novel assault on RSA where intruder know sender A hardware in enough feature moreover intelligent to determine the decryption period for frequent known ciphers, A can infer the d rapidly. This bother be functional beside the RSA. During Boneh and Brumley attacks over 2003 revealed a more sensible attack competent of recuperating RSA used in a system, e.g., by a Secure Socket Layer (SSL)-enabled web server. Such information is gained escaped by the CRT principle optimization taken by countless RSA accomplishments.

But new method of choosing r with sightless technique, the decryption period is nix lengthy correlated to the inputted cipher and so the timing attack is unsuccessful.

3.4 Exponentiation in Modular Arithmetic

In modular arithmetic, digits are by no means larger than the "modulus". For instance, for "mod 12" digits are in no way superior than 11. The easiest technique to adapt digits in modular arithmetic is by separating at pleasing the remainder. Obtain 17/3. That is 5 with a remainder of 2, while it said "mod 17" that way that the intact phrase is modular, not presently the preceding number. Like is there would be an large multiplicative expression in modular arithmetic then before multiplication reduce into mod reduction and then solve this is the loveliness of modular arithmetic that the digits stay convenient.

Example: 12 * 29 * 408 mod 13
12 mod 13 = 12
29 mod 13 = 3
408 mod 13 = 5
Solution: 12 * **3** = 36, but "mod 13" it is 10

Then 10 * 5 = 50 but "mod 13" that is 11, which is our answer.
→12 * 29 = 348 348 * 408 = 141,984 mod 13 = 11 so we get in above.

This is how a mod reduction can be applied.

However the exponentiation function and the logarithm function are reverse of each other which is a modular arithmetic. As we already discussed about the modular arithmetic in unit first so we do not repeat its details. The logarithm of any number is significant (except 1) that have to be lift so as to the same the integer. explicitly, for p and for q,

$$q = p\log_{p}^{(q)}$$

If we consider k = l (mod s) for some *l*, where 0 <l < (*s* – 1) then with the properties of logarithm we can discover a sole exponent as $k = a^i \pmod s$ where 0 < i < (s – 1). So the discrete logarithm for the base a (mod s), which is $\text{dlog}_{a,s}(k)$[10].

This can be seen as $\text{dlog}_{a,s}(a) = 1$ because $a^1 \bmod s = a$.

Fortunately with the previous example of 12 * 29 * 408 mod 13 it is already clear that proviso the exponentiation is ended above the integers plus next it must be condensed to modulo n, which is deducted as:

$$[(a \bmod n) * (k \bmod n)] \bmod n = (a * k) \bmod n$$

Example: watch $M^{11} = M^{1+2+8} = (M)(M^2)(M^8)$. First calculate M mod n, M^2 mod n, M^4 mod n, and M^8 mod n and get $[(M \bmod n) \times (M^2 \bmod n) \times (M^8 \bmod n)] \bmod n$.

In general, a^b would found with m positive integers where b is a binary number such that

$$b = \sum_{bi \neq 0} 2i$$

$$a^b = a\left(\sum_{b_i \neq 0} 2^i\right) = \prod_{b_i \neq 0} a(2^i)$$

Therefore

We can follow the algorithm to find for computing a^b mod n.

```
x ← 0; y ← 1
   for i ← k down to 0
   do x ← 2 * x
         y ← (y*y)mod n
   if b_i = 1
   then x ← x + 1
         y ← (y * a) mod n
return y
```

Solve itself: $37 * 10 \bmod 53$; $5^6 \bmod 23$

3.5 Distribution of Public Keys

There are numerous method have been planned for the sharing of public keys in the history. Those proposals can be grouped into four.

A. Public announcement
Public key since announced publicly and it is an uncontrolled way of sending and sharing the key publicly. This can be easily forged, namely, various consumer might imagine user A to send a encryption key to a new member or transmit such a encryption key.

B. Publicly available directory.
More security is provided by upholding a publicly accessible active index keys though preservation with the sharing of the community directory would contain to be liable of have confident organization. The authority maintains each entry by {name, public key} which is registered to the participant in a secure way. It is much secure but still fails when an opponent thrive in attain or calculate the confidential key of the index influence, the opponent might confidently passing the imitation public keys and snoop

Example: Modular Exponentiation Algorithm for ab mod n, where a = 7, b = 560 = 1000110000, and n = 561.

i	9	8	7	6	5	4	3	2	1	0
B_i	1	0	0	0	1	1	0	0	0	0
x	1	2	4	8	17	35	70	140	280	560
y	7	49	157	526	160	241	298	166	67	1

on post propel to any member an additional approach to reach the similar ending at challenger tampering influencing with account.

C. Public-key authority

Since every contributor consistently knows a public key for the authority, by means of merely the authority meaningful the matching private key, the sharing of public keys commencing the directory is strongly controlled. However it is not safe as a user have to plea to the authority for a public key for each further user so as to it needs to call. Moreover the index of names in addition to public keys preserve by the authority is susceptible to tampering.

D. Public-key certificates

An unconventional loom where the participants uses certificates to swap keys devoid of drop a line to a public-key authority demonstrated in Figure 3.4. Certification authority (CA) attach public key to picky participant P, i.e., P (person, router) list its public key with CA by only if "proof of identity" to CA and CA generate certificate attaching P to its public key. This credential hold P's public key digitally marked by CA or CA says "this is E's public key".

Thereafter, certificate authority generated the certificates, which are known by the applicant with the corresponding confidential key. A

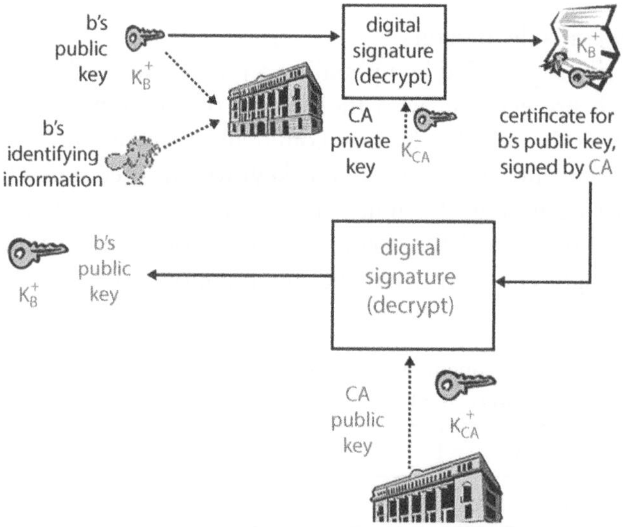

Figure 3.4 Mark verification by CA {source: http://image.slidesharecdn.com/cryptography-130612222853-phpapp01/95/stallings-kurose-and-ross-59-638.jpg?cb=1371094157}.

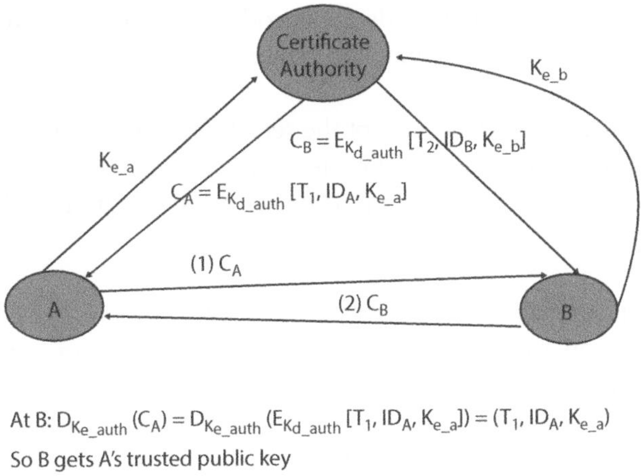

Figure 3.5 Mathematical Exchange of PK certificates {source: http://flylib.com/books/3/190/1/html/2/images/10fig04.jpg}.

contributor broadcasts its credential to express its entered information and other participants can validate that the certificate was shaped by the ability. Here certificate authority (CA) configures the entire nodes. When participant A wants participant B's public key it gets B's certificate and apply CA's public key to B's certificate, so what verifying B's public key which has been demonstrated mathematically in Figure 3.5.

3.6 Distribution of Secret Keys Using Public Key Cryptosystems

Since the public-key are incompetent intended for huge post because secret keys used conventionally are attribute ally small. But if conservative confidential keys are considered like a message, the encryption of the input by means of a pk scheme will not be an overhead at the dispensation for a processor. Therefore, their combined employ a predictable and public-key cryptography be worn that offer verification, veracity, and privacy in a competent way [6].

Suppose sender sending a marked, secret message to a recipient. Sender primary add a digital signature as a purpose of the sender's confidential input and message digest. With this, sender also breeds a predictable surreptitious key, and uses it to convert the message into miscible form. Successively, the sender converts the confidential key via the receiver's public key. The sender lastly adds the encode the secret key and the digital signature to the miscible format, and put on the air the data to the receiver as shown in Figure 3.6.

On receiving, recipient's decrypt the secret key with its private key. Now this secret key is worn dto decrypt the cipher. Hence the receivers authenticate the message signature as a purpose of the signature and the originator's public key.

- So it surefire confidentiality as the receivers private key is the only way to decrypt the secret key which is further required to decrypt the message.
- It also guaranteed veracity as the digital signature was produced by a digest of the inventive plaintext message.
- Last, verification proved since digital signature proves that pain text comes is from original sender only and not being forged.

But with this some disadvantages are also held:

- public-key encryption shared might corrupt network since it comparatively lofty computational weight of public-key encryption and decryption. This can be minimizing, since a predictable scheme (e.g., DES) is worn to convert the plain text. Merely the encoding the confidential key (e.g., the DES key) entails a public-key algorithm.
- incapability to propel a message to many recipients. Proviso the message is spread to numerous receivers, the inventor

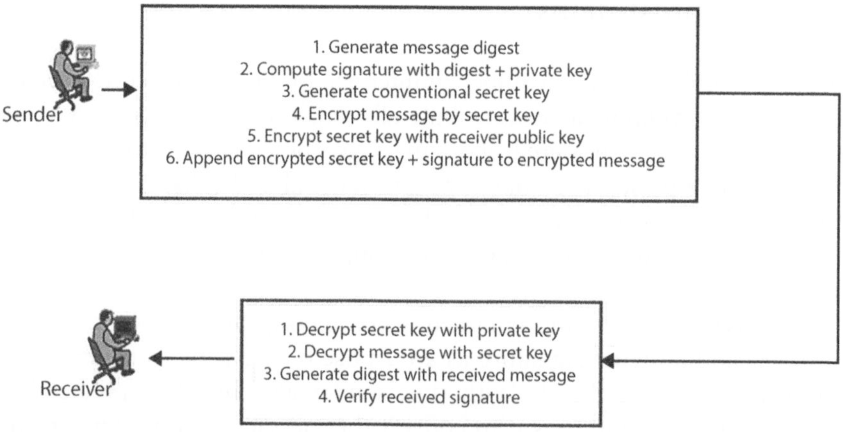

Figure 3.6 Circulation of confidential keys using Public Key phenomenon.

encoding the confidential key one instant per receiver, by means of that recipient's public-key such as, if a text is propel to five participants, five unusual encodings of the private key might be affixed to the plain text.

3.7 Discrete Logarithms

These are the basis of the asymmetric key including Diffie–Hellman key swap with the digital signature algorithm (DSA). Recalling from Euler's theorem, for each prime a and n.

$$a^{\Phi(n)} = 1 \ (\text{mod } n)$$

where $\Phi(n)$ is Euler's totient function < n.

In general, $a^m = 1$ (mod n) means that there is no less than one integer m that satisfies it $M = \Phi(n)$.

For example, 7 mod 19.
$7^1 = 7$ (mod 19)
$7^2 = 49 = 11$ (mod 19)
$7^3 = 343 = 1$ (mod 19)
$7^4 = 2401 = 7$ (mod 19)
$7^5 = 16807 = 11$ (mod 19).

Here is no point in enduring for the reason that the progression is recurring.

This can be proven by noting $7^3 = 343 = 1$ (mod 19) whichever $7^{3+j} = 7^3 7^j = 7^j$ (mod 19) so, any two powers of 7 whose exponents vary by 3 are congruent to each other. So sequence is periodic with $7^m = 1$ mod 19.

With this problem of finding Φ such that $a^{\Phi} \equiv b$ (mod p) is called the discrete logarithm problem. Suppose that n is the smallest integer such that $a^n \equiv 1$ (mod p), i.e., $n = \text{ord}_p(a)$. By assuming $0 \leq \Phi < n$, we denote $\Phi = L_a(b)$, and call it the discrete log of b w.r.t. a (mod p).

Ex: p = 11, a = 2, b = 9, then $\Phi = L_2(9) = 6$.

3.8 Diffie–Hellman Key Exchange

From the ancient soviet union and north America who were made the NORAD to communicate over the space shuttles and make the communication between computers. This way since the 1958s Internet had became worldwide and new problem of secrecy came that is how can the secrecy could be achieved by sharing the key. This was proposed by Diffie and Hellman by giving an short trick. Let it be explored with colors to easy understanding. The trick was based on two facts first is it is easy to mix two color to make a new and second cleansing mix color to get exact original color which is basis for an lock where two colors mix and form an lock but the inverse of its to get colors from a mixed is hard which is one way function.

So the solution works as follows, Say both sender S and recipient R agreed on standing color i.e. yellow, both s and R chooses their private color red and green respectively and mix separately either in order to disguise the original color. Now both exchange their mixtures keeping their private colors themselves only. So in this intruder without having their private colors cannot deduce the exact color. To more elaboration for hardness of one way function of mod algorithm consider Figure 3.7.

Diffie and Hellman proposed public key cryptosystem in 1976. The algorithm is for exchanging secret key (not for secrecy of data) based on discrete logarithms. Since it is infeasible to calculate inverse so to ease computation calculate exponentials modulo a prime [7].

This provide a secure way for two communicating parties to share a symmetric key (so called a session key) which is then used to provide privacy and authentication for subsequent message flow. The algorithm follows [8, 9]:

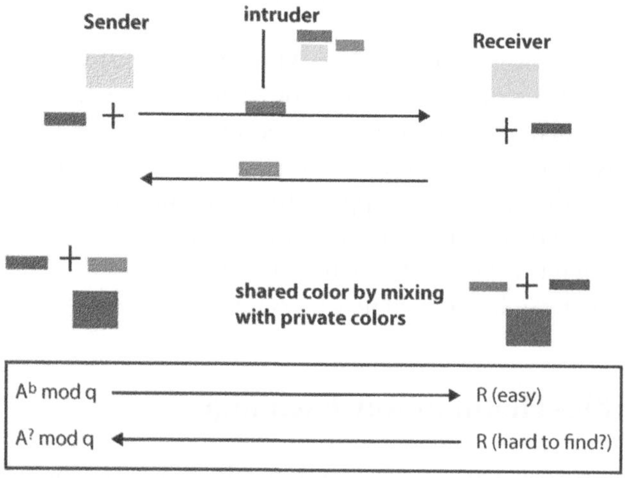

Figure 3.7 DH exchange.

1. Global public elements—Large prime integer q, i.e., 1024 long, α a primitive root/generator of Zq* (i.e., the multiplicative group modulo q, $\alpha < q$)
2. Sender key generation—select private $X_s < q$ and compute public $Ys = \alpha^{X_s} \bmod q$
3. Receiver key generation—select private $X_r < q$ and compute public $Yr = \alpha^{X_r} \bmod q$
4. Secret key by sender—$K = (Y_r)^{X_s} \bmod q$
5. Secret key by receiver—$K = (X_r)^{Y_s} \bmod q$

To attack in this an attacker needs to compute K from Y_s and Y_r but this is difficult to solve. The genuine key swap for any party consists of lifting the others "public key" to control of their private key. The ensuing digit (or as much of as is necessary) is worn as the key for a block cipher or additional private key method. For an attacker to gain the equivalent value they require no less than single of the secret numbers, which way solving a discrete log, that is computationally impractical set bulky adequate numbers [10].

Let it be understood by an example:

A and B want to carry out DH Key Exchange:

1. concur on prime p = 353 and $\alpha = 3$
2. choose random secret keys:
   A decide $X_s = 97$
   B decides $X_r = 233$
3. calculate session key contributions
   $Y_s = 397 \bmod 353 = 40$ (A)
   $Y_r = 3233 \bmod 353 = 248$ (B)
4. calculate shared session key as:

$$K = Y_r^{Xs} \bmod 353 = 24897 \bmod 353 = 160(A)$$

$$K = Y_s^{Xr} \bmod 353 = 40233 \bmod 353 = 160(B)$$

Disadvantage: Insecure against man-in-the-middle-attack.

3.9 Review Exercise

Elaborative:

1. What is a prime number?
2. What is Euler's totient function?

3. Distinguish index with discrete logarithm?
4. Briefly explain Diffie–Hellman key exchange.
5. What are the two approaches of encryption/decryption technique?
6. For n no. of users, how many keys needed in private key cryptography and public key cryptography?
7. Explain how RSA works.
8. Computer the primary essentials of a public-key cryptosystem?
9. Explain the trap-door one-way function?

References

1. Blake, I., Seroussi, G., Smart, N., *Elliptic Curves in Cryptography*, Cambridge University Press, Cambridge, 1999.
2. Enge, A., *Elliptic Curves and Their Applications to Cryptography*, Kluwer Academic Publishers, Norwell, MA, 1999.
3. Diffie, W., The First Ten Years of Public-Key Cryptography. *Proc. IEEE*, Vol. 76, pp. 560–577, 1988.
4. Rosen, K., *Elementary Number Theory and its Applications*, Addison-Wesley, Reading, MA, 2000.
5. Kumanduri, R. and Romero, C., *Number Theory with Computer Applications*, Prentice Hall, Upper Saddle River, NJ, 1998.
6. Boneh, D., Twenty Years of Attacks on the RSA Cryptosystem. *Not. Am. Math. Soc.*, vol. 46, 2, pp. 203–213, 1999.
7. Cormen, T., Leiserson, C., Rivest, R., Stein, C., *Introduction to Algorithms*, MIT Press, Cambridge, index MA, 2004.
8. Shamir, A. and Tromer, E., On the Cost of Factoring RSA-1024. Crypto RSA-1024, RSA CryptoBytes, Vol. 6, pp. 10–19, 2003. http://www.rsasecurity.com/rsalabs.
9. Stallings, W., *Cryptography and network security principles and practice*, fifth edition, Pearson Education, Inc., publishing as Prentice Hall, Upper SaddleRver, NJ, 2006.
10. Diffie, W., Hellman, M.E., New Directions in Cryptography, *IEEE Transactions on Information Theory*, Vol. 22, 6, pp. 644–654, 1976.

4

Zero-Share Key Management for Secure Communication Across a Channel

Mahalingam P. R.* **and Fasila K. A.**

Department of Computer Science and Engineering, Muthoot Institute of Technology and Science, Kochi, India

Abstract

Symmetric ciphers require transmission of a shared key over a seemingly insecure channel. In order to secure the channel, key transmission should be secured as much as possible. Here, we use the power of reversible matrix operations to implement key transmission in symmetric cryptosystems. The concept is based on reversible overlapping operations to add and remove layers of cipher on a plaintext. The advantage of this model is that the operations are independent of the key chosen, and do not require any components of the cipher system to be sent across the channel without protection. But this involves multiple transactions for sending each piece of information, and the same method can be implemented as a handshake. The keys at the host can be random, or based on the data to be sent across the channel. But at the same time handshakes can overload the channel if used over large data items. Hence, this method is adaptable for key transfers.

Keywords: Symmetric ciphers, handshake mechanism, matrix cipher, channel security, random keys

4.1 Introduction

The word cryptography refers to transforming meaningful information to unintelligible format, to facilitate secure transmission. Process of converting the plain message to a mangled form is termed as encryption

**Corresponding author*: mahalingampr@mgits.ac.in

Dinesh Goyal, S. Balamurugan, Sheng-Lung Peng and O.P. Verma (eds.) Design and Analysis of Security Protocol for Communication, (95–108) © 2020 Scrivener Publishing LLC

or enciphering. Resulting message is called cipher text. Deciphering or decryption refers to the process of retrieving original message from the cipher text. The primary aim of incorporating an enciphering technique is to share information between intended participants preventing others from reading it. Based on the type of operation used, encryption techniques can be classified generally into substitution ciphers and transposition ciphers. Substitution ciphers perform replacement of letters in plain text with other contents whereas, transposition ciphers does only rearrangement of plain text letters. Another classification of encryption algorithms is based on the number of keys used. The encryption is said to be symmetric if single key is used for encryption as well as decryption. If the algorithm is using different keys for encryption and decryption, that kind is called asymmetric cipher. Symmetric systems are sometimes known as private key systems and asymmetric systems are known as public key systems.

Symmetric ciphers rely on shared keys. The algorithms are designed such that the operation is dependent on the key itself, and independent on whether the attacker knows the process. But they involve blocks of data, and unless there is enough overlap, they can be vulnerable to statistical cryptanalysis. If we increase the overlap too much, we end up with stream ciphers, which have their own set of limitations. All these are avoided using public cryptosystems, but they have their share of complex mathematical operations.

4.2 Background

A public key cryptosystem relies on mathematical operations to increase the complexity of processing. Most public key systems are based either on the Discrete Logarithm Problem or the Integer Factorization Problem. Both problems are known to be really hard to solve, especially when applied on modular arithmetic. Public key systems are also known as asymmetric ciphers since they work on two different keys. Encryption is done by one key, called the public key, while decryption is done using another key, called the private key. While public key is available in the open, private key is available only with the recipients. The keys are such that they are non-reversible. It means that once encrypted using the public key, only the private key can recover it. The public key will have no role (and cannot be used) to decrypt the data.

Public Key Cryptosystems gained interest with the introduction of two schemes—RSA, and El Gamal Scheme. RSA works on the Integer Factorization Problem with the help of Euler's Totient Function. But it requires selection of large prime numbers even though no critical information is shared across the channel. In contrast, El Gamal Scheme is based on the Discrete Logarithm Problem. It can use smaller values to perform operations, but requires sharing of a common value to both sender and recipient. This was further improved upon by Diffie and Hellman in 1976 to get the Diffie–Hellman key exchange protocol, which was easier to implement. But it also suffered from the drawback that a common value had to be shared between the sender and recipient, which is a large prime number. The problem came to be known as Computational Diffie Hellman problem (CDH Problem), which involves sharing a common large prime number, and using two local secrets to perform processing on that.

Here, we start off by applying the background of CDH Problem to select local secret values. The problem faced there was that the shared value can be potentially insecure because of trustiness of third parties, or security of the sharing channel. One-Time Pad is a cryptosystem based on the reversible XOR operation. The main logic behind the system is that for any given numbers A and B,

$$(A \text{ xor } B) \text{ xor } B = A$$

It implies that if A is a plaintext, and B is a key, we can retrieve the plaintext by performing XOR operation twice with the key at different points of time. The result of first XOR operation will form the ciphertext.

One-time pad proved to be impossible to break if used correctly [2, 3]. Here the plaintext is XOR'ed with a Pad (which is a random key) which is of the same length as the plaintext, and discarded after a single instance of use. That is why the name "One-time Pad". The following are the reasons why One-time pad is not used widely:

1. Since XOR is a bitwise operation, we need correspondence on number of bits used for encoding. For each bit of plaintext, we need one bit of pad. This makes the key excessively long for large plaintexts. A repeated, shorter key can be used, but they can make the system vulnerable to cryptanalysis.
2. Key Transfer is another issue. The reason is that once the key is compromised, any person with the basic knowledge about XOR operation can decrypt it.
3. It is difficult to generate a perfect random key every time, since most generators use timestamps.

So, the same key has to be used for encryption and decryption. This means that even for OTP, key transfer is essential.

Zero-share management model is based on an old puzzle, which involves sending a locked case from one person to another without sending the key. The puzzle is solved in four steps:

4.3 Zero-Share Key Management System

We have seen how the One-Time Pad can be an easy operation for symmetric cryptography. But the main disadvantage was that this needed the common key to be shared among the sender and recipient. In order to avoid this, the model in Figure 4.1 was proposed in Refs. [1–15]. In that method, the sender (S) and recipient (R) choose their own keys—K1 and K2, respectively. Then the following sequence of handshakes happens for a text P:

1. T1 = P xor K1 (at S).
2. Send T1 to R.
3. T2 = T1 xor K2 (at R). Hence T2 = P xor K1 xor K2.
4. Send T2 back to S.
5. T3 = T2 xor K1 (at S), which gives P xor K1 xor K2 xor K1 = P xor K2.
6. Send T3 to R.
7. T4 = T3 xor K2 (at R), which given P xor K2 xor K2 = P.

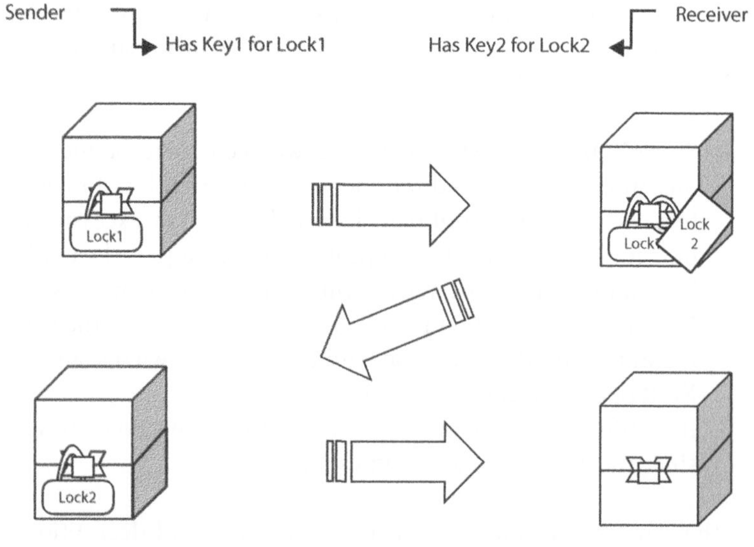

Figure 4.1 The box puzzle.

Hence, at the end of step 7, P is received at the recipient. The method is highly convenient, but the pad has to be as long as the plaintext. So, it can be used for key transfers.

But this method suffers from one major flaw because of the self-cancelling feature of XOR itself. An eavesdropper will be able to capture the values of T1, T2, and T3. Considering the values in them, the following operation can be done:

T1 xor T2 xor T3 =	`(P xor K1) xor (P xor K1 xor K2) xor (P xor K2)`
Rearrange into	`(P xor P xor P) xor (K1 xor K1) xor (K2 xor K2)`
After all cancellations, we get	`P`

Thus, by processing just the handshakes, the eavesdropper can acquire the plaintext. We need an alternate method that can preserve the simplicity of the method, while avoiding this weakness.

Matrix operations have been long considered as a set of complex computations on numbers. Matrices are difficult to process since the operations are mostly non-commutative (like multiplication), and in order to cancel out the effect of a matrix, the inverse of that matrix is needed, which by itself is a time consuming task. In addition, once we initiate matrix product, we are restricting the order of participant matrices. Inverse of matrices impose another constraint since they exist only for non-singular square matrices. Hence, the method may be able to stand up to a good level of brute force attacks.

We are proposing a method of managing keys in a symmetric cryptosystem which does not involve any sharing of information. Conventional methods including Diffie-Hellman key exchange requires sharing a common secret between the sender and receiver. The shared secret is important to generate a common key between both parties. The One-Time Pad method can be extended because the method is simple enough. But at the same time, the peculiarity of XOR enables data to be exposed easily. The model involves a handshake-based method to transfer the key.

Sharing requires either a secure channel for transferring the information to both parties or some method to synchronize the secret between both parties. This may generate overhead and potential for errors in real time systems. In order to serve the purpose of locks, we use matrices (which make mathematical operations harder to perform). The method is as follows:

1. Key K is selected by sender. It is converted to a 4 × 4 matrix. Sender also selects a 4 × 4 private key matrix A.
2. Sender performs multiplication A × K (let it be denoted as M1) and sends it to the recipient.
3. Recipient selects its own 4 × 4 private key matrix B.
4. Recipient performs M1xB (called M2 which, in essence, is A × K × B), and sends it to sender.
5. Sender performs A^{-1} × M2 (called M3 which is actually $A^{-1} \times A \times K \times B = K \times B$), and sends it to recipient.
6. Receiver finally performs M3 × B^{-1} to get K (since $K \times B \times B^{-1} = K$).

Hence, even if the channel is insecure, the value of K cannot be ascertained. This can be proven to be mathematically difficult.

4.4 Simulation

A simple simulation was run on Matlab (educational license number 40525315). The simulation was used to verify the algorithm, and whether it exhibits any pattern in its working. The script contained 8 statements, each for one step of the process. "k" represents the key matrix. Matrices "a" and "b" represent the local secrets chosen by the sender and recipient respectively. They are assigned as random matrices (which can be followed in practice also). HS1, HS2, HS3, and HS4 represent intermediate matrices at each handshake. Finally, "res" matrix is used to check if there are any anomalies. If the operations go well, the result of HS4 will equal the original key matrix, and Step 8 will return the result as a zero matrix. The script which was executed is as follows:

```
1.a=round(rand(4,4)*1000)
2.k=[-a(1,2),-a(1,3),-a(1,4),-a(1,3);
  a(1,1),-a(1,4),-a(1,3),-a(1,4);
  -a(1,4),a(1,1),a(1,2),a(1,1);a(1,3),
  a(1,2), a(1,1), a(1,2)]
3.b=round(rand(4,4)*1000)
4.HS1=round(a*k)
5.HS2=round(HS1*b)
6.HS3=round(inv(a)*HS2)
7.HS4=round(HS3*inv(b))
8.res=HS4-k
```

In practice, the key matrix "k" can be generated at random. But then there is a chance that one of the handshake matrices can be inverted and used to uncover a local secret. An example is:

Handshake 1: HS1 = A × K
Handshake 2: HS2 = A × K × B

If we take the inverse of HS1 (which can be taken by an eavesdropper since the channel is assumed to be insecure) and calculate $HS1^{-1} \times HS2$, we get the result as matrix B, which is the local secret of the recipient. Further, we also see that:

Handshake 3: HS3 = K × B

If the eavesdropper is able to uncover B from HS1 and HS2, and is able to invert it to get B^{-1}, he can easily uncover the original key matrix using $HS3 \times B^{-1}$. Hence, the key matrix K is generated from local secret A such that HS1 will not be invertible. We do that by setting elements of K in such a way that the first row of HS1 becomes zero. This is done by creating the following matrix for K.

```
-A[1][2]    -A[1][3]    -A[1][4]    -A[1][3]
 A[1][1]    -A[1][4]    -A[1][3]    -A[1][4]
-A[1][4]     A[1][1]     A[1][2]     A[1][1]
 A[1][3]     A[1][2]     A[1][1]     A[1][2]
```

The script generated the following outputs.

```
a =

     352        917        380        531
     831        286        568        779
     585        757         76        934
     550        754         54        130


k =

    -917       -380       -531       -380
     352       -531       -380       -531
    -531        352        917        352
     380        917        352        917
```

```
b =
     569         162         166         689
     469         794         602         748
      12         311         263         451
     337         529         654          84

HS1 =
           0           0           0           0
     -666943      446633      245123      446633
       44583      258963     -199835      258963
     -218216     -471156     -483292     -471156

HS2 =
           0           0           0           0
   -16562893   559083946   514725859    22625402
   231693885   287681810   280101701   156049318
  -509716144  -808994192  -755101588  -760317308

HS3 =
     -834425     -816435     -769155    -1187454
     -232258     -763669     -708444     -370644
       -7423      664861      595137      340572
      959546     1384223     1307408     1183516

HS4 =
    -917        -380        -531        -380
     352        -531        -380        -531
    -531         352         917         352
     380         917         352         917

res =
     0           0           0           0
     0           0           0           0
     0           0           0           0
     0           0           0           0
```

We can see that no patterns are exhibited in any handshake, and the final result becomes a zero matrix. Hence, the algorithm has been verified to work on any random input. The only requirement is that matrices "a" and "b" should be invertible, and there is negligible chance that a random matrix will be non-invertible.

4.5 Complexity and Analysis

Mathematical complexity is contributed by the processes of inverting private keys of sender and receiver, and four sets of multiplications of 4 × 4 matrices. Considering the overall system, both stages happen only once. In addition, it is quite difficult to break the cipher since any combination of the information across the channel will not be able to reconstruct the original key (since matrix multiplication is not commutative). Irrespective of the size, the key is currently designed to be broken into 16 parts, and processed in the matrix. (For example, if we consider a 128-bit cryptosystem, the key is broken into 16 parts of 8 bits each, and the matrix K is filled). Brute force attack primarily depends on the size of key being used. Hence, selection of right key length is critical.

The security of the system can be proven by considering the data and operations we consider for the algorithm.

1. Local secrets can be chosen at random since the security of the system does not depend on the key or the secrets (acceptable, as long as no specific information has to be shared).
2. Processing involves matrix multiplication, which is non-commutative. Hence any combination of handshake data will not extract the original data.

Considering 16-bit values in the matrices, a comparative evaluation can be done for different matrix orders, and the result is as in Table 4.1 and Figure 4.2. Step counts for each step are taken as follows.

1. Steps 1, 2, 3: (Taking a number + Multiplication with 1000) × $N^2 = 2 \times N^2$ steps
2. Steps 4, 5: Cost of matrix multiplication = N^3 steps for matrices of order N
3. Steps 6, 7: Cost of inversion + Cost of multiplication = $2 \times N^3$ steps for matrices of order N
4. Step 8: Subtraction of matrices = N^2 steps

As the matrix size increases, the complexity of operations increase, and brute force attacks become more difficult (because of rapidly increasing key lengths). Currently, analysis has been done on 4 × 4 matrix since it was easy for manual verification. Once we plot the variation in Figure 4.2, we can see that as the order of matrix increases, the key size also increases, and more steps are needed to encrypt each bit of the key. Hence, the operations

Table 4.1 Comparison of performance for different matrix sizes.

Order	Number of elements	Key length in bits	Step count									Steps per bit
			Step 1	Step 2	Step 3	Step 4	Step 5	Step 6	Step 7	Step 8	Total	
1	1	16	2	2	2	1	1	2	2	1	13	0.8125
2	4	64	8	8	8	8	8	16	16	4	76	1.1875
3	9	144	18	18	18	27	27	54	54	9	225	1.5625
4	16	256	32	32	32	64	64	128	128	16	496	1.9375
5	25	400	50	50	50	125	125	250	250	25	925	2.3125
6	36	576	72	72	72	216	216	432	432	36	1548	2.6875
7	49	784	98	98	98	343	343	686	686	49	2401	3.0625
8	64	1024	128	128	128	512	512	1024	1024	64	3520	3.4375
9	81	1296	162	162	162	729	729	1458	1458	81	4941	3.8125
10	100	1600	200	200	200	1000	1000	2000	2000	100	6700	4.1875

(Continued)

Table 4.1 Comparison of performance for different matrix sizes. (*Continued*)

Order	Number of elements	Key length in bits	Step count									Steps per bit
			Step 1	Step 2	Step 3	Step 4	Step 5	Step 6	Step 7	Step 8	Total	
11	121	1936	242	242	242	1331	1331	2662	2662	121	8833	4.5625
12	144	2304	288	288	288	1728	1728	3456	3456	144	11376	4.9375
13	169	2704	338	338	338	2197	2197	4394	4394	169	14365	5.3125
14	196	3136	392	392	392	2744	2744	5488	5488	196	17836	5.6875
15	225	3600	450	450	450	3375	3375	6750	6750	225	21825	6.0625
16	256	4096	512	512	512	4096	4096	8192	8192	256	26368	6.4375
17	289	4624	578	578	578	4913	4913	9826	9826	289	31501	6.8125
18	324	5184	648	648	648	5832	5832	11664	11664	324	37260	7.1875
19	361	5776	722	722	722	6859	6859	13718	13718	361	43681	7.5625
20	400	6400	800	800	800	8000	8000	16000	16000	400	50800	7.9375

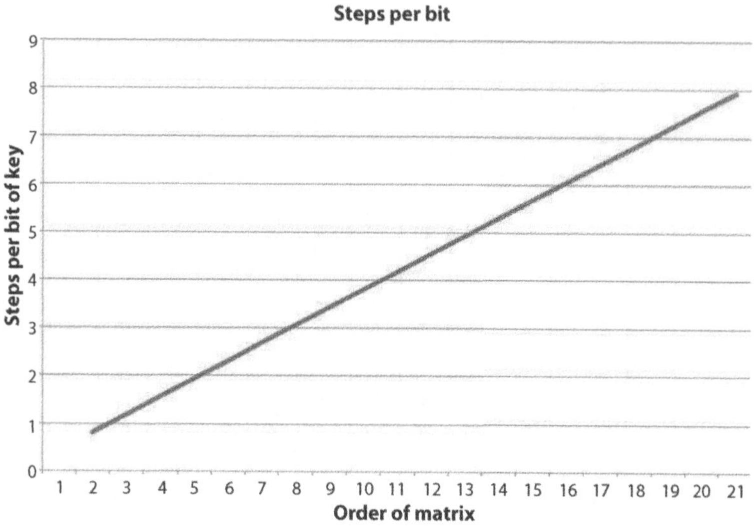

Figure 4.2 Order of matrix vs steps per bit of key.

are complex enough to thwart off most attacks. If the application demands a higher level of safety, and there is enough time, power, and bandwidth for a one-time zero-share transfer, we can afford to pick larger matrices to incorporate larger keys, and consequently larger data items. We can also observe that if the data size is very large, the key size should be increased accordingly. From the table, as key size increases, steps required per key also increases, making it efficient to break bulky data down into smaller blocks and process them.

4.6 Conclusion and Future Trends

Channel security has been a subject of research for decades. Even as new algorithms came up, the computational power in the background has multiplied by larger factors, resulting in most of them being broken. We explored opportunities where symmetric and asymmetric cryptosystems were used to enforce security, and saw that most of them needed some information to be shared across the channel between sender and recipient. We also explored a case of using one-time pad as an alternative for insecure data sharing, using handshakes to transfer coded data between the participants and decrypting them in parts. But we were able to observe a fatal flaw in the operation, and it was improved upon by replacing XOR operations with more complex matrix operations. Mathematical analysis shows that the system can sustain the security to a provably secure extent. But the operations are complex and time consuming, which makes it suitable for smaller data items and key shares in symmetric cryptosystems. For larger data sizes, we may have to fragment it to smaller blocks and send them as parts.

The entire system described here is modeled on top of the end-to-end encryption concept, which gained rapid popularity with messaging systems like WhatsApp implementing it. When a channel is secured using end-to-end encryption, only the communicating parties can decrypt the message. In conventional systems, encryption is limited to the channel and the message is stored in a third party storage in the plaintext form [4]. Using the handshake method enables the channel to be secured without sharing any information across the communicating entities, and implement end-to-end encryption.

Currently the runtime has been monitored for a 4 × 4 matrix. But we have to estimate the performance for larger square matrices, and reach an optimum matrix order that maintains the security, as well as keep the operations fast.

In future, we may also implement it on top of parallel architectures that can perform multiplications faster. Currently, the matrix size is fixed at 4 × 4 due to expensive multiplication algorithms in matrices. If we can implement the algorithm in parallel, we can take larger keys, split them into suitable 4 × 4 matrices and serialize the results on each handshake. In addition, to make the system further secure, we can make calculated modifications on the handshakes (which can be restored in subsequent runs) so that the handshakes also become non-invertible and the transfer becomes entirely foolproof. Attempts may also be made to shuffle rows while transmitting serialized matrices so that confusion is improved.

References

1. Mahalingam, P.R., Three-way handshake-based OTP using random host-side keys for effective key transfer in symmetric cryptosystems. *Recent Trends in Computer Networks and Distributed Systems Security. SNDS 2012*, Communications in Computer and Information Science, 335, Springer, Berlin, Heidelberg, p. 264, 2012.
2. Dodis, Y. and Spencer, J., On the (non)universality of the one-time pad. *Proceedings of the 43rd Annual IEEE Symposium on Foundations of Computer Science*, p. 376, 2002.

3. Yadav, D. and Sardana, A., Enhanced 3-way handshake protocol for key exchange in IEEE 802.11i. *3rd International Conference on Electronics Computer Technology (ICECT)*, p. 132, 2011.
4. Shiyang, D., Compare of New Security Strategy With Several Others in WLAN. *2nd International Conference on Computer Engineering and Technology (ICCET)*, 2010.
5. Rittera, T., Substitution Cipher with pseudorandom Shuffling: The Dynamic Substitution Combiner. *Cryptologia*, 14, 4, 289, 1990.
6. Longjun, Z., Wei, H., Dong, Z., Kefei, C., A Security Solution of WLAN Based on Public Key Cryptosystem. *Proceedings of the 2005 11th International Conference on Parallel and Distributed Systems (ICPADS'05)*, p. 123, 2005.
7. Zeynep Gurkas, G., Halim Zaim, A., Ali Aydin, M., Security Mechanisms And Their Performance Impacts On Wireless Local Area Networks. *Proceedings of the Seventh IEEE International Symposium on Computer Networks (ISCN'06)*, p. 14, 2006.
8. Raub, D., Steinwandt, R., Müller-Quade, J., On the Security and Composability of the One Time Pad. *SOFSEM 2005: Theory and Practice of Computer Science, LNCS 3381*, p. 288, 2005.
9. Harris, B. and Hunt, R., TCP/IP security threats and attack methods. *Comput. Commun.*, 22, 10, 885, 1999.
10. Lindquist, T.E., Diarra, M., Millard, B.R., A Java cryptography service provider implementing one-time pad. *Proceedings of the 37th Annual Hawaii International Conference on System Sciences*, 2004.
11. Apostolopoulos, G., Peris, V., Saha, D., Transport layer security: How much does it really cost? *INFOCOM '99*, vol. 2, p. 717, 1999.
12. Parthasarathy, M., Analysis of network management of remote network elements. *International Conference on Systems and International Conference on Mobile Communications and Learning Technologies*, 2006.
13. A. Shefi, System and method for synchronizing one time pad encryption keys for secure communication and access control. US Patent 6445794, 2002.
14. J.J. Glover, One-time pad Encryption key Distribution. US Patent 6868495, 2005.
15. W.S. Hammersmith, One-time-pad encryption with central key service and key management. US Patent App. 10/254754, 2002.

5

Soft Computing-Based Intrusion Detection System With Reduced False Positive Rate

Dharmendra G. Bhatti[1]* and Paresh V. Virparia[2]

[1]*Uka Tarsadia University, Bardoli, Gujarat, India*
[2]*Sardar Patel University, Vallabh Vidyanagar, Gujarat, India*

Abstract

Intrusion Detection System is one of the important security mechanisms in today's information era. Two different approaches are used for intrusion detection: signature based and anomaly based. Signature based Intrusion Detection System is able to identify known attacks only whose signatures are available. While anomaly based Intrusion Detection System suffers from problem of high false alarms. Intrusion detection analyst need to address all alerts generated by Intrusion Detection System. If most of these alerts are false, then it is difficult for Intrusion detection analyst to identify real attack and act on it. In our research work we have designed solution to reduce false alerts generated by anomaly based Intrusion Detection System.

Keywords: Network security, intrusion detection system, false positive, soft computing, neural network, genetic algorithm

5.1 Introduction

Intrusion detection is defined as the process of monitoring computer system or network, analyzing them for security breaches. The objective of Intrusion Detection System (IDS) is to protect the availability, confidentiality, and integrity of critical networked information systems as per security policy. Intrusion Detection Systems are an important component of defense in depth protecting computer systems and networks from misuse.

**Corresponding author*: dgbhatti@yahoo.com

Dinesh Goyal, S. Balamurugan, Sheng-Lung Peng and O.P. Verma (eds.) Design and Analysis of Security Protocol for Communication, (109–140) © 2020 Scrivener Publishing LLC

When IDS is properly deployed it provides alerts indicating that a system is under attack. Intrusion Detection Systems are characterized based on different aspects:

- host-based or network-based
- on-line or off-line intrusion detection
- signature-based or anomaly-based

Intrusion detection attempts to detect computer attacks by examining data records observed by processes on the same network. These attacks are typically split into two categories, host-based attacks, and network-based attacks. Host based attacks exploits vulnerabilities found in operating system or processes running on the host (i.e., a disgruntle employee is having normal user account on the system but she tries to get root privileges by exploiting vulnerability in one of the running process). Host-based intrusion detection systems are limited to specific host and network data received/sent for the host. This is one of the early intrusion detection systems developed to protect a computing device (typically a server), serving critical information. One of the techniques used by host-based attack detection routines is to use system call data from an audit process that tracks all system calls made on behalf of each user on a particular machine. These audit processes usually run on each monitored machine. Some examples of host-based IDS are: Verisys, OSSEC (a multi-platform open source HIDS), ISS RealSecure Server Sensor (Generic); Tripwire, AIDE (Check host file system), BlackICE, PortSentry (Check host network connections); LogSentry, Swatch (Check host's log files). Network-based attack detection routines typically use network traffic data from a network sniffer like tcpdump/libpcap.

Second aspect is online versus offline intrusion detection. Intrusion Detection System uses various information sources like application log, operating system audit data, and packets received/transmitted over the network. Collectively all these require complex and huge processing for attack identification. Specifically in the high speed networks, huge number of packets passes through per second. If Intrusion Detection System processes this volume in real time it is called Online Intrusion Detection System. Complex intrusion detection algorithm requires more time so alternative approach is, Offline Intrusion Detection System. It needs to store such huge amount of data for subsequent offline processing.

Third aspect is anomaly detection or misuse detection. Nature of traditional pattern or signature matching intrusion detection methods is static. Signature of well known attacks are prepared and subsequently used for evaluating existing traffic. If current traffic is matching any of the attack, signature alert is raised by the Intrusion Detection System. Typically, intrusions are detected by looking for activities that correspond to known signatures of intrusions or vulnerabilities. This is just like anti-virus system which identify virus based on the virus signature database. Signatures generally target widely used applications or systems for which security vulnerabilities are widely advertised. Just like to anti-virus system, which cannot identify new viruses because no matching signature, a signature-based intrusion detection system cannot detect new attacks. If attacker modifies an existing attack slightly and it results in signature mismatch, signature-based intrusion detection system can be easily fooled. So they are limited to known attack identification but not suitable for providing protection against unknown attack. As a result anomaly based anomaly detection technique is gaining increasing attention.

On the contrary, an anomaly based Intrusion Detection System detects intrusions by searching for abnormal behavior. While anomaly-based intrusion detection systems are more capable of identifying new types of attacks than misuse-based system, they also tend to have higher false alarm rates. In this research work we have only considered anomaly-based approach. Many IDS uses hybrid approach—having pattern matching as well as anomaly detection capabilities.

We can describe Intrusion Detection System as a system which processes information travelling through the system/network to be protected. This detector system can also launch investigations to trigger the audit process, such as requesting version numbers for applications. Typically it uses three kinds of information: long-term information related to the technique used to detect intrusions, configuration information about the system's current state, and audit information like the events that are happening to the system. One of the roles of the detector is to eliminate unwanted information from the audit trail. It then presents either a synthetic view of the actions related to security, taken during normal usage of the system, or a synthetic view of the current security state of the system. Based on these actions or this state, decision is then taken to evaluate the probability of an intrusion or vulnerabilities.

5.1.1 Soft Computing for Intrusion Detection

Intrusion detection has become an integral part of the security process with the advent of soft computing for it. Soft Computing is characterized by the use of inexact solutions to computationally hard tasks such as the solutions of NP-complete problems, for which an exact solution cannot be derived in polynomial time. Traditional, hard computing requires huge amount of practically unavailable resources to such scaled problems. Soft computing addresses NP-complete problems by providing inexact answers which is otherwise not possible for practically available resources. Another similar approach is data mining. Here, focus is on extracting hidden patterns from available data. Data mining can address scalability issues but cannot find patterns which are not available in the existing data.

Many researchers have identified potential and suggested use of soft computing techniques for intrusion detection [2, 9, 10, 14]. For intrusion detection some soft computing techniques are used extensively: Genetic Algorithm [1, 18, 20, 22], Neural Network [3, 23, 25, 29], Fuzzy techniques [22], and Support Vector Machine [17, 31, 39].

5.1.2 False Positive

Role of the Intrusion Detection System is to separate attack traffic and normal traffic. Good mixture of attack within normal traffic is provided to Intrusion Detection System and efficient attack identification is expected. When Intrusion Detection System analyzes input traffic, four outcomes are possible:

Case-1. Normal traffic is rightly identified as normal traffic
Case-2. Normal traffic is incorrectly identified as attack traffic
Case-3. Attack traffic is incorrectly identified as normal traffic
Case-4. Attack traffic is rightly identified as attack traffic

Here, case-1 and case-4 correctly classifies the input traffic while remaining two cases are setback. Case-1 is also referred as "True Negative" or TN while case-2 is referred as "False Positive" or FP. Case-3 is referred as "False Negative" or FN while case-4 is referred as "True Positive" or TP. One of the challenges for Intrusion Detection System is false positive where deviated normal traffic behavior is identified as an attack. As a result, alert raise tagging benign user traffic or in worst case genuine traffic is dropped. Rate at which normal traffic is identified as attack is often known as "False Positive Rate". Similarly rate of correctly identified attack traffic is known as "Detection Rate". We can write these in equation as:

False Positive Rate FPR = incorrectly identified normal traffic/total normal traffic

$$\text{False Positive Rate FPR} = FP/(FP + TN) \tag{5.1}$$

Detection Rate DR = correctly identified attacks/total attacks

$$\text{Detection Rate DR} = TP/(TP + FN) \tag{5.2}$$

In theory, zero false positive is desirable but practically false positives are difficult to curb. Researchers are working since long to increase the detection rate and decrease the false positive rate.

5.1.3 Reasons of False Positive

Declaring innocent network traffic as attack leads to negative reputation of Intrusion Detection System. Reduced false positive rate is desirable characteristic for any Intrusion Detection system. Understanding of reasons responsible for birth of false positive gives increased opportunity to curb it. Why an Intrusion Detection System raises false positive? Following are some of the causes responsible for false positives [11]:

- Soft computing based Intrusion Detection System trained with insufficient or biased data

  Efficient training is the main requirement for the success of soft computing based Intrusion Detection System. If the training data is insufficient, Intrusion Detection System did not get exact picture of normal behavior. Similarly biased training data give biased understanding to Intrusion Detection System. In both cases, Intrusion Detection System observes major deviations even if the traffic is normal and raises large number of false positives.
- Low probability of attack occurrence within huge volume of network traffic

  This challenge is faced in many areas like intrusion detection, chemical reaction, cyber forensic. Here, comparison of error rate and probability of attack occurrence is vital. Significantly low possibility of attack occurrence compare to test error rate is responsible for false positives.
- Noise and corrupt network packets

  In this Internet era, networks are connected to Internet in one or other way. Large number corrupted network packets and noise are running over the Internet. What will happen if router forwards packet despite of TTL value is lower than permissible value? Hardware or software bug increases unexpected or corrupted network packets. These noise and corrupt network packets may lead the Intrusion Detection System on wrong path.

- Quality of input packets

  Intrusion Detection Systems performance also depends on quality of input network traffic. Generally, first component of Intrusion Detection System is preprocessing which improves quality of input. Unprocessed and filthy input data is another critical reason behind the increasing false positive rate.
- Different types of networks, networking protocols, network applications

  Quirky nature of computer networks is another challenge for Intrusion Detection System. Some network like LAN expects NetBIOS over TCP/IP while prohibited on network like Internet. Similarly, applications and protocols not exactly following Internet standards are also reasons behind false positives.
- Abnormal traffic due to network incident

  Internet is huge and universally connects large number of diversified computer networks. In such universal network, probability of failure of one or more components is also high. These failures may raise ICMP error messages. These ICMP messages are generated in response to some event and sharply changes network traffic. Such abnormal traffic may also lead the Intrusion Detection System to raise false positive.
- Obsolete, old peculiar devices

  Often obsolete or old peculiar devices are observed in computer network. These devices may generate odd packets for which Intrusion Detection System is not trained and results in false positive.
- New experiments, tests

  In this Internet era, regularly we encounter new devices, applications, and protocols. Intrusion Detection System quickly needs to learn about such new but genuine network traffic to curb the false positives.
- Side effect of Intrusion Detection System optimization efforts

  Intrusion Detection System administrator always strive to improve the overall quality of the security solution. Side effect of such optimization effort may also result in increase of false positive rate. A hardware or software bug in Intrusion Detection System may also raise the false positive.

This is simplified and limited list of reasons behind false positives generated by Intrusion Detection Systems. Practical scenarios are far more complex and beyond the scope of this chapter. Good understanding of such root causes is base of designing Intrusion Detection System with lower false positive rate.

5.2 Existing Technology and Its Review

To understand how researchers have tried to overcome problem of false positive in intrusion detection, we have carried out exhaustive literature review. In the alphabetic order of researcher name, different approached are discussed.

Ahmed *et al.* [1] suggested optimization using Genetic Algorithms for the Security Audit Trail Analysis Problem, which was proposed by L. Mé in 1995 and improved by Pedro A. Diaz-Gomez and Dean F. Hougen in 2005. To classify attacks in "Certainly not existing attacks class", "Certainly existing attacks class", and "Uncertainly existing attacks class". The proposed idea is to divide the 3rd class to independent sub-problems easier to solve.

Dewan *et al.* [10] tried to scale up detection rate and reduce false positive using NBTree. They argued that combination of Decision Tree algorithm and Naïve Bayesian will provide advantage of both. Naïve Bayesian is supervised learning based probabilistic classifier. Decision Tree is another popular algorithm used for prediction and classification. By using the hybrid approach they tried to balance scalability (large number of different types of attack detection) and keep the false positive at acceptable level. To prove the idea researchers used the popular KDD Cup 99 dataset. Their proposed Improved Self Adaptive Naïve Bayesian Algorithm (ISANBT) compared with Naïve Bayesian (NB) classifier and C4.5. In first experiment they used all 41 attributes of KDD Cup 99 while in subsequent experiment they used 12, 17, 19 attributes of KDD Cup 99 dataset. The improved performance of proposed algorithm observed compared to other algorithms.

Fatin *et al.* [14] designed intrusion detection algorithm based on the data mining. They used software tool iDA analyzer for data mining. The reason behind using this tool iDA analyzer is it is GUI based and easy to use. During data mining they used "Data", "Modeling", and "Evaluation" process. For verification Fatin *et al.* also used KDD Cup 99 dataset. They carried out five experiments with different number training and testing data. Five thousand six hundred training data and 1400 testing data resulted better compare to other combinations. They also experimented with different attack class and tabulated the detection rate and false positive rate.

Another aspect of false alert is operation issues. G. Jacob *et al.* [15] proposed a model to reduce the false positive rate considering operational issues. They discussed types of Intrusion Detection System, architecture of Intrusion Detection System, false positive and false negative. They prepare a list of instances which need to be analyzed to monitor false positive rate. This includes design level and operational level instances. They evaluated their approach using gigabit campus network including multiple buildings with online real-time data of one department VLAN's traffic. Their proposed "suppress module" is mainly responsible for reducing the false alerts. They carried experiments with four different protocols: IP, TCP, UDP, and ICMP. They user Windows 2003 as operating system and MySQL database installed on the same server. The alerts generated by Snort are submitted to their application. This application raises first alert generated by Snort and store remaining alert for further analysis. They used Derek Woolverton adaptive algorithm for label duplicates. Based on the network environment they selected five signatures for analysis. Finally they discussed results in the form of "IDS without tuning" and "IDS after tuning".

Georgios and Sokratis [16] have proposed a post-processing filter to reduce false positive. In their proposal three components are suggested: Neighboring Related Alerts component, High Alert Frequency component, and Usual False Positives component. Neighboring Related Alerts component expected related alerts in a time window. While false positive alerts distributed throughout all alerts. High Alert Frequency component is based on fact that attack appears in high frequency compare to the mean frequency of the alert for a particular attack. Usual False Positives component tries to remove false positive which were generated due to topology of the network, incorrectly configured hosts, etc. Such false positive patterns can be identified and subsequently alerts can be filtered.

M. Sadiq [24] demonstrated that Genetic Algorithm can be effectively used for formulation of decision rules. They argued that more common attack detection is having higher accuracy than the less prevailing one. In their solution, rule based attack classification is proposed for network monitoring effectively. They compared expert based knowledge with GA applications and fount it more suitable.

El Mostapha *et al.* [26] discussed data mining and alert correlation approach for reducing false positive rate in intrusion detection. With the help of equation they established various terms like false positive rate, false negative rate, true positive rate, true negative rate, accuracy, and precision. Authors compared various intrusion detection classifiers and data mining techniques. They also discussed about four alert correlations: similarity based, pre-defined attack scenario, prerequisites and consequences of individual attack, and statistical casual analysis. Authors study these four approaches and discussed advantages and limitations of each.

Manish *et al.* [27] reviewed various approaches for reducing false positive rate in Intrusion Detection System. They discussed two different stages for reducing false positives: sensor level, and detection level. Process data at sensor level: based on Fuzzy Cognitive Map to reduce the false positives. Use Intrusion Alert Quality Framework at detection level to achieve same. They have defined various equations and proposed model for reduction of false positive rate in Intrusion Detection System.

Ramesh, S. and Elango, K. [32] have suggested vulnerability assessment for reducing false positive rate. They have argued that for efficient signature generation security staff needs to understand network topology and the hosts in the network. In the paper they have suggested vulnerability assessment based Intrusion Detection System tuning for reduction of false positive rate. This solution remove false positive resulted from incorrect Intrusion Detection System configuration.

Ritu *et al.* [33] reviewed the reduction of false positive rate in Self Organizing Map based Intrusion Detection System. They discussed about various soft computing techniques like Fuzzy Logic (FL), Artificial Neural Network (ANN), Probabilistic Reasoning (PR), and Genetic Algorithm (GA). They have also reviewed the flow chart of signature based intrusion detection and anomaly based intrusion detection. Traditional techniques used for intrusion detection are categorized as "clustering techniques", "hard partitioning", and "soft partitioning". Authors formulated Self Organizing Map based Intrusion Detection System and briefly discussed evaluation measures.

S. Selvakani [35] proposed Intrusion Detection System based on Genetic Algorithm. For evolving and testing new rules for intrusion detection system they have used KDD99 Cup training and testing dataset. In their approach Genetic algorithm was used to obtain classification rules for intrusion detection while correlation technique was used to identify the most important features of network connections.

Tadeusz Pietraszek [44] suggested human intervention based classification for reduction of false positive. They have presented how anomaly based Intrusion Detection System generates large number of alerts constantly. All these alerts are sent to intrusion detection analyst. Thus it is not practical for security analyst to identify the true positive and false positive. Researchers proposed Adaptive Learner for Alert Classifier for reducing false positive rate in Intrusion Detection System. By observing the intrusion detection analyst, ALAC learns to identify true positive and false positive from alerts. Proposed model is validated with two datasets and proven helpful for security analyst. Certain alerts are classified by autonomous alert classification mode with high reliability.

Thomas, A. [46] has proposed architecture based on IP reputation along with signature levels to reduce false positive. In this solution Intrusion

Detection System signatures are classified and grouped into different levels. This grouping is based on false positive rate and IP address reputation. Reputation is build considering alerts from IP address and network traffic heuristics. With each successful alert reputation of the IP address decreases. Consistent absence of alert from a particular IP address increases its reputation.

Researchers have also proposed various other solutions based on Soft Computing, Data Mining, Post processing filter, Alert flooding suppression (post-processing), and Procedure Analysis in HTTP. Many researchers have shown potential results using soft computing techniques like Genetic Algorithm, Neural Network, Fuzzy, and Ant Colony Optimization. Data mining based algorithms are also useful for improving classification.

5.3 Research Design

We have identified various reasons of false alerts based on the thorough literature review, study of various attacks, and experiments. Based on the understanding of why false positives are generated, we have designed the framework for intrusion detection.

5.3.1 Conceptual Framework

In our proposed Intrusion Detection model, we have considered three major sections: input, processing, and output. First section captures the network traffic, second one looks for deviated behavior, and final section, raises alert if deviation found [11].

These three sections are addressed with following major components:

a. As we have discussed in reasons behind false positives, poor quality of network traffic leads to false positives. To improve the quality of network traffic, preprocessing component is used. Responsibility of preprocessing module is to accept the raw network traffic, address the challenges, and provide processed, good quality network traffic to next component. One of the critical requirements is configuration data provided by Intrusion Detection System administrator according to their network characteristics, hosts, available services, and other parameters. Using network scanning tools, administrator can collect such data and effectively configure preprocessing unit to improve input traffic quality.

b. Second section is responsible for the intrusion detection. Detection engine is the component which performs this job of intrusion detection. It accepts processed, good quality network traffic from preprocessing unit. Genetic Algorithm and Neural Network are the proposed techniques for detection engine to achieve the objective of reduced false positive rate. Many researchers have used these techniques intrusion detection and other areas as well. We observed that, ensemble use of Genetic Algorithm and Neural Network results in false positive rate reduction.
c. The component designed in third section is called response unit. It receives input from detection engine and submits outcome to another component called alert monitoring module. Response unit may send outcome to Intrusion Detection Analyst for verification if inconsistency observed. It is responsibility of Intrusion Detection Analyst to verify the inconsistent observations and reply to alert monitoring module. Intrusion Detection Analyst may reconfigure the some configuration parameters.

In our proposed intrusion detection model, we have addressed false positive rate in above mentioned three different sections. In initial preprocessing component, spurious and muddy traffic is corrected to reduce false positive. In the detection engine component, Genetic Algorithm and Neural Network identify attacks in ensemble way and further process to reduce false positives. In the final section, human intervention is recommended. Intrusion Detection analyst addresses inconsistent observations of response unit adjust parameter accordingly [11].

Unique strengths and weaknesses are observed in anomaly based and signature based Intrusion Detection Systems. Signature based approach cannot identify the unseen attack while anomaly based approach suffers from detection efficiency. One of the critical parameter for any anomaly based Intrusion Detection System is training. For training feed forward neural network heuristic algorithms fond better. Poorly trained classification algorithm cannot provide good results. Traditionally gradient descent technique like back propagation is used to train neural network. But from literature review and our experiments we found that back propagation is having two basic limitations. First is low convergence rate and second is local optima problem. To overcome these limitations we have proposed genetic algorithm to train neural network.

Since long, genetic algorithm and neural network are two most prominent techniques used in intrusion detection. Each is having its peculiar advantages. Neural network is good classifier. So we have used it as main part in proposed detection engine. Neural network captures the intrusion evidence from the network traffic provided to it. It puts together all intrusion evidences together and infers the attack.

To achieve the objective of reducing false positive rate, we have divided alerts generated by neural network in two categories: "certain attack", and "probable attack". The input traffic resulted in the second category of alerts "probable attack" are send to genetic algorithm for further processing. For such limited cases genetic algorithm is also used for attack detection. Alerts generated by neural network and opinion from genetic algorithm are forwarded to combiner module. Based on the opinion of neural network and genetic algorithm, combiner decides whether the probable attack is real attack or false positive. If it is false positive, record it for later fine tuning. If attack is confirmed by both neural network and genetic algorithm, it is sent to alert monitoring module. Combiner module uses configurable weights of both classifiers. Initially both classifiers are having equal weight. Intrusion detection analyst can change the default weight depending on the network environment and other parameters.

We can represent the summarized detection logic in following algorithm:

- Step-1. Receive the clean, preprocessed data from preprocessing module and provide it to neural network.
- Step-2. Well trained neural network identifies the deviated behavior and categorized it as "certain attack" or "probable attack". Send "certain attack" to alert monitoring module, while send "probable attack" to genetic algorithm for verification.
- Step-3. Genetic algorithm verifies the network traffic resulted in "probable attack" and gives its opinion.
- Step-4. Combiner module takes decision about "probable attack" based on the opinion of genetic algorithm. If genetic algorithm also confirms it as an attack alert is send to alert monitoring module.
- Step-5. If opinion of genetic algorithm is normal traffic, combiner module uses the weight of both classifiers. Depending on the weight, combiner will decide it as either normal traffic or attack. Alert is sent to alert monitoring module if it identifies as an attack. In any case, combiner module activities are recorded, and further used for fine tuning.

5.3.2 Preprocessing Module

Preprocessing module is designed with the prime objective of reducing false positive rate. We have tried to address major causes of false positive as follows:

- noise, incomplete data
- spurious and duplicate data
- missing network knowledge
- multiple log formats

Four major subcomponents are proposed in the preprocessing module [11]. The first subcomponent is responsible for removing noise and discard spurious packets. Noise and other susceptible traffic are part of the modern Internet. As discussed earlier in this chapter, unwanted traffic like noise and incomplete data makes the intrusion detection challenging by overlapping attack and normal traffic. Soft computing based Intrusion Detection Systems uses data preprocessing to provide quality data to detection engine. Often Intrusion Detection System plagued with huge amount of data to be processed. Processing this huge amount of data in real-time is another challenge faced by most Intrusion Detection Systems. Many researchers have worked for increasing performance to give timely intrusion alerts. Once noise and muddy input data is removed from input traffic, detection engine can significantly focus on its primary role.

The raw network data cannot be used directly by detection engine. Intrusion Detection System needs to extract features out of raw network data to distinguish between attack and normal traffic. Effective and more complex algorithms can be used for intrusion detection if sufficient time and resources available. To accomplish this, Intrusion Detection Systems use feature selection and extraction. Raw input data for intrusion detection consists of spurious and duplicate data. Not all the items available in raw input data are useful for intrusion detection. So we need to remove such spurious data which is not related to the purpose of intrusion detection. Another possible improvement used by modern Intrusion Detection Systems is removing duplicate content and generating summarized data which is directly useful for intrusion detection. Second functionality in our preprocessing module is feature selection and extraction. Removal of spurious and duplicate data will help in reducing false positive rate.

One of the cause behind false positive is missing configuration information like network topology, available hosts and running services. Another subcomponent in preprocessing unit is configuration based processing. A configuration repository is filled with knowledge of existing network, hosts, and services. Vulnerability assessment tools can also provide significant information about the network devices, hosts, and running services. Let us consider the typical attack scenario. Specifically masquerader type of intrusion begins with IP scanning. Here ICMP ECHO request, ARP and other packets are used for live host detection. During the scanning process, attacker sends the packets to non existing IP address. With the help of configuration database, Intrusion Detection System can identify such host is not available and provides this information to detection engine for further processing. After identifying live host, masquerader needs to identify services running. So she starts the port scanning. Once again any single attempt to establish connection on closed port of a server is identified using configuration data and sent to the detection engine for further processing. Finally attacker uses exploitation scripts to exploit vulnerability. So our argument is attacks can be effectively extracted from normal traffic if additional network environment knowledge is configured.

This additional information from configuration database can further help in some scheduled behavior. For example, many organizations use periodic vulnerability assessment to cross check the security of their network. It can be carried out in a special case when some vulnerability is reported. This vulnerability assessment can be carried out by internal team or external agency. This vulnerability assessment activity can result in large number of alerts. In the proposed model this can be overcome by using the configuration database. Information about the scheduled vulnerability assessment or a specific one is stored in configuration database. Now, Intrusion Detection System understands that vulnerability assessment is going on from specific IP address(s) and do not raise unnecessary alerts.

To reduce the false positives raised due to unrecognized traffic generated by outdated/odd devices, we have proposed exception list. Configuration database also includes exception list. For example, intrusion detection analyst has given the normal feedback about an incident of unrecognized traffic. Such devices or non standard applications can be added to the exception list. Counter argument can be this type of exception list may reduce the detection rate. We have designed two solutions to avoid misuse of the exception list. First solution is exception list is more restricted in design. A specific application/protocol bound with particular device for the specific attack can be added in the exception list. Second solution is each exception list item is expired after stipulated time period.

All Intrusion Detection Systems can easily identify certain data as normal while some other as attack. Intrusion Detection Systems remains unanswered in overlapping behavior where it is challenging to differentiate attack from normal traffic. Normal data can be marked as attack or attack can be treated as normal traffic in this overlapping behavior area. From additional network configuration details provided by intrusion detection administrator, we can reduce ambiguous area. But this raises another challenge of dealing with multiple data formats. So in our proposed preprocessing module fourth functionality is to generate unified format from different data formats generated by different data sources. Using this unified log, detection engine increase trust and can identify normal traffic. It will reduce chances of detecting as attack even though behavior is deviated from normal one. This again helps in reducing false positive rate in Intrusion Detection System.

5.3.3 Alert Monitoring Module

In our proposed model [11], alerts generated by detection engine are submitted to alert monitoring module for further processing. For reducing large number of alerts generated by Intrusion Detection System, researchers have suggested alert aggregation approach. In place of raising large number of alerts related to an attack, we can represent unified view of that attack. With the objective of keeping our alert monitoring module simple and lightweight, we have proposed a simple solution for alert aggregation. Group multiple alerts with a particular incident. Attack name, source IP address, and destination IP address are minimum required for grouping. Optionally protocol, source port number, destination port number can be used for alert aggregation.

To reduce the false positive rate, aggregated probable alerts can be divided in three different categories. Once again configuration database and audit records of other sources are used here. Verify the aggregated alert with other sources and configuration parameters. First possibility is the attack is also confirmed by other audits and logs. In this case, raise the alert. Intrusion Detection System is sure that the alert is actual attack not a false positive.

Second possibility in the verification process is alert raised due to abnormal behavior which is not malicious. So the alert is logged as false positive. For example, Intrusion Detection System has raised an alert related to an operating system or application which is not available. Another example is Intrusion Detection System has raised an alert for the known attack but patch for the vulnerability is already in place. From the configuration database Intrusion Detection System gets such confirmation that the alert is false positive.

The third possibility is Intrusion Detection System not getting any confirmation or help from verification process. In this scenario, Intrusion Detection System has to wait. The alert can be false positive or the very first alert indicating begging of an attack. If during this waiting period Intrusion Detection System gets attack confirmation from other sources, alert is raised. At the end of the waiting period if no other supporting confirmation received, alert is processed further considering the reputation parameter.

In the proposed model, reputation is calculated in configuration database. We have considered IP address, MAC address, and application for reputation calculation. Configuration database consists of up to date information about all the network devices, hosts, and applications present. Initially reputation value is neutral (zero). Reputation value decreases with each successful attack identification. Reputation increases if no attack observed for long duration. Based on the reputation parameter, probable attack will be converted in to "normal traffic" or "certain attack" or remain as it is. If positive reputation value changes the "probable attack" to "normal traffic" its reputation value is neutralized to zero. If the result is still "probable attack", it is submitted to intrusion detection analyst for final decision.

This gives a clearer picture to intrusion detection analyst. She knows about these alert categories. In the case of attack she can take corrective measures without worrying about false positive. While in the case of probable alerts, intrusion detection analyst has to further carry out diagnosis and provide the feedback. Such input may affect configuration, post processing filter, and database.

5.4 Results With Implications

Genetic Algorithm and Neural Network are selected for study of Intrusion Detection. For evaluation of these algorithms we have used KDD Cup 99 dataset. It is popularly used as a benchmark dataset in several major Intrusion Detection research works. The KDD Cup 99 intrusion detection Data Set, which is based on DARPA 98 Data Set, provides labeled data for researchers working in the field of intrusion detection and is the only labeled dataset publicly available. We have downloaded KDD Cup 99 dataset from http://kdd.ics.uci.edu/databases/kddcup99/kddcup99.html. This dataset includes audit data of the military environment. It includes a wide variety of intrusion simulations. The dataset was originally used in the thirds international knowledge discovery and data mining tools competition held in 1999.

Following is the Class Distributions of 10% KDD99 Data Set:

Table 5.1 to 5.8 represents data used in experiments and results received.

IDS have three common issues: speed, accuracy. and adaptability. For better understanding, in experiments [11], we have focused on detection rate which is computed as the ratio between the number of correctly detected attacks and the total number of attacks.

Table 5.1 Class distributions of 10% KDD99.

Class	Number of connections
Normal	97277
DoS	391458
U2R	52
R2L	1126
Probe	4107
Total	494021

Detection Rate DR = correctly identified attacks / total attacks

$$\text{Detection Rate DR} = TP / (TP + FN) \qquad (5.1)$$

These experimental results indicate that both soft computing techniques performed well for specific attack class [11]. But in absence of adequate training, both are performing poor for U2R and R2L attack classes. Compare to statistical approach soft computing techniques are capable of identifying unknown attacks. Genetic Algorithm has good learning capability while Neural Network is a good classifier. Comparison of different approaches is given below:

Based on this experimental result, we found both soft computing techniques prominent. These results encouraged us to study more on it and finally designed ensemble approach in the detection engine.

Table 5.2 GA and NN detection rate.

	GA detection rate	NN detection rate
Normal	98.22%	98.82%
DoS	97.46%	97.24%
U2R	82.54%	88.54%
R2L	84.85%	89.16%
Probe	97.57%	97.23%

Table 5.3 Comparison of different algorithms.

	Advantages	Disadvantages
Statistical approach	Higher detection accuracy	Not applicable to NP-complete (non-deterministic polynomial-time complete)
Genetic algorithm	Good learning ability	Early constringency and parameter selection
Neural network	Good classifier	Poor knowledge representation and explanation

5.4.1 Preprocessing Module Benchmark

We have already discussed about the overall architecture of our proposed model [11]. Based on the conceptual framework, we have developed preprocessing module. Four major components are designed as part of the preprocessing module [11]. Here the basic objective is to provide the good quality input data to detection engine. Noisy and spurious data may increase overlapping behavior of normal and attack traffic. After development of preprocessing module, various experiments are carried out to identify effect of it on false positive rate.

Once again we have used KDD Cup 99 dataset to benchmark preprocessing module. Four different attack classes consist of following attacks which we have used for training.

Table 5.4 Attack types used in training.

Attack category	Name of attack
DoS	back, land, neptune, pod, smurf, teardrop
Probe	ipsweep, nmap, portsweep, satan
U2R	buffer_overflow, loadmodule, perl, rootkit
R2L	ftp_write, guess_passwd, imap, multihop, phf, spy, warezclient, warezmaster

First attack category is Denial of Service (DoS). This category of attacks floods the network with useless packets or consumes critical resources extensively. Due to which legitimate user's request does not reach to the server. Effectively server cannot provide services to their legitimate users.

The second attack category probe is just inquiry attack. The attacker would like to know how many servers and hosts are live in the network. Once target server is found she is interested in the services provided by the server. To identify the open port, typically port scanning is used.

The third category of attacks is mostly performed by one of the legitimate users. A normal user tries to exploit some vulnerability to acquire

Table 5.5 Number of examples used.

	Number of examples
Normal	97227
Dos	229853
Probe	4107
U2R	1126
R2L	52

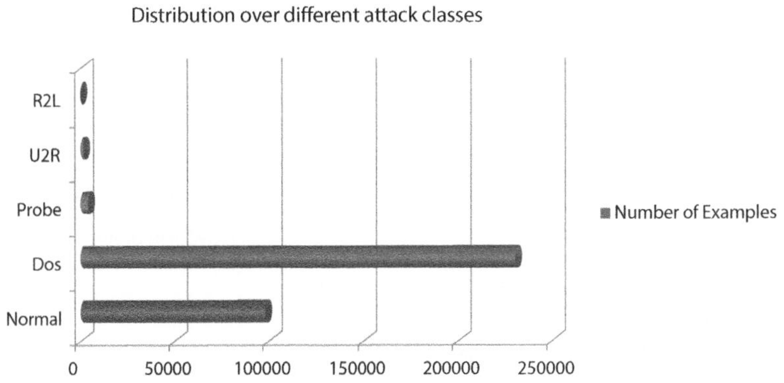

Figure 5.1 Attack distribution over different attack classes.

the root privileges. The last attack category represents remote to local attacks.

In the experimental setup, data includes following frequency of attacks: In the experiment, majority of example data belongs to denial of service attack category while very few belongs to remote to local and user to root category [11]. Figure 5.1 is graphical representation of data used.

Table 5.6 FPR reduction in preprocessed data.

	FPR in raw data	DR in raw data	FPR in pre-processed data	DR in pre-processed data
Experiment 1	0.245579932	0.890591908	0.21226614	0.88308993
Experiment 2	0.243903442	0.893704973	0.216657924	0.914084495
Experiment 3	0.247276991	0.867209894	0.220031473	0.885833
Experiment 4	0.244407418	0.893343483	0.210486799	0.897064702
Experiment 5	0.251936191	0.857177487	0.240643031	0.907977443

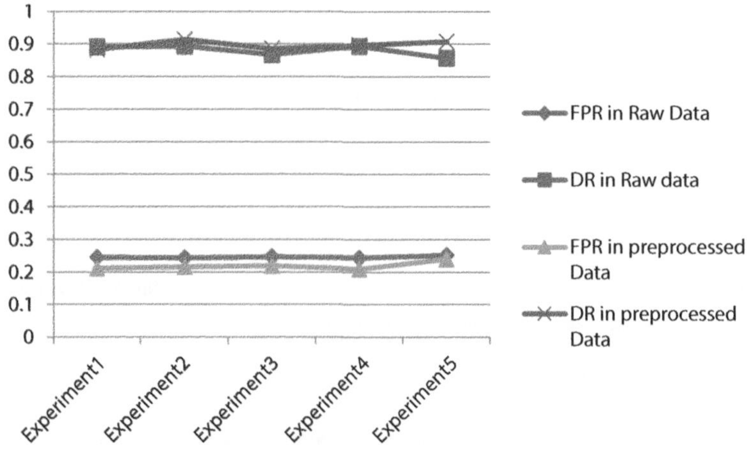

Figure 5.2 Raw data and pre-processed data comparison.

To identify effect of preprocessing experiment is carried out and repeated five times.

These experiments proved that preprocessing has reduced false positive rate while maintaining detection rate.

In the Figure 5.2, effect of preprocessing module is clearly visible. Consistently lower false positive rate is observed with preprocessing module compare to same Intrusion Detection System but without preprocessing module [11].

5.4.2 Alert Monitoring Module Benchmark

Just like preprocessing module, we have also verified effect of alert monitoring module on false positive rate. In our proposed alert monitoring module, we have incorporated alert aggregation, correlation, and classification. We have also heavily used our configuration database to further support false positive reduction. To identify effect of alert monitoring experiment is repeated five times.

These experiments proved that false positive rate is reduced and almost similar detection rate is maintained due to alert monitoring module [11].

Table 5.7 FPR reduction with alert monitoring.

	FPR in IDS	DR in IDS	FPR with alert monitoring	DR with alert monitoring
Experiment 1	0.245453704	0.93803813	0.199666931	0.952281572
Experiment 2	0.255980345	0.930516908	0.212825231	0.939711754
Experiment 3	0.231565529	0.917228742	0.188091738	0.928641643
Experiment 4	0.267524698	0.932878632	0.222837875	0.951583389
Experiment 5	0.226394728	0.920263444	0.182879817	0.932432501

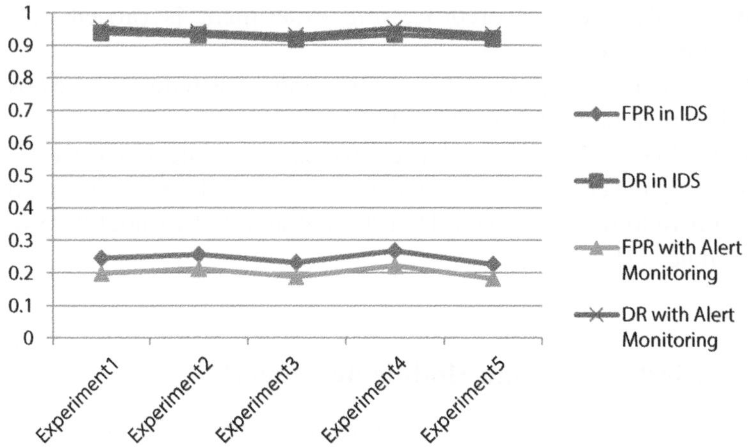

Figure 5.3 Effect of alert monitoring module on FPR.

In the Figure 5.3, effect of alert processing module is clearly visible. Consistently lower false positive rate is observed compare to same Intrusion Detection System but without alert processing module.

5.4.3 Overall Benchmark

Finally after successful implementation of proposed model, experiments are carried out to see effect on false positive rate. Proposed model is compared with Genetic Algorithm based IDS and Neural Network based IDS.

False Positive Rate (FPR) is one of the critical parameter for any Intrusion Detection System. Significant reduction in false positive rate is observed in proposed model with almost similar detection rate [11]. Figure 5.4 represents result while Figure 5.5 represents network design used in experiment.

Table 5.8 Reduced FPR in proposed model.

	GA	NN	Proposed model
FPR	0.24558	0.246917	0.190095652
DR	0.905892	0.948449	0.95816193

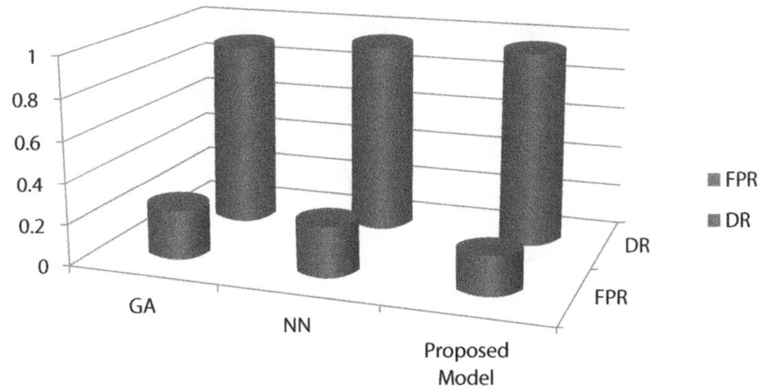

Figure 5.4 FPR comparison.

5.4.4 Test Bed Network Benchmark

Since more than a decade, KDD Cup 99 dataset is used by researchers. Over the period various limitations of this dataset is found. One of the major limitations of KDD Cup 99 dataset is it does not reflect the modern attack scenario. The dataset is developed almost 16 years before and Internet is drastically changed since then. Second argument against KDD Cup 99 dataset is problem of over-fitting. We are training our algorithm with same set of training data. This may result in poor learning quality [11].

There are different alternatives available of KDD Cup 99 dataset. First approach is test the Intrusion Detection System in test environment without background traffic. Such experiment is meaningless for validating false positive rate. Second approach is test the Intrusion Detection System with real traffic. This is good alternative but it raises privacy concern. Third approach is to test the Intrusion Detection System with synthesized traffic in test bed network. We have selected this third approach to validate our proposed algorithm and compare it with open source Intrusion Detection Systems: Snort and Suricata [11].

The overall design of the test network is given in following diagram:

In the test environment two Ubuntu 14.04 LTS servers are installed. One server is configured as database server running MySQL while the second server is configured as Web server running Apache. Ten different clients with different operating systems are connected to test network. Proposed Intrusion Detection System is connected to the network in promiscuous mode. Special client software is developed and installed

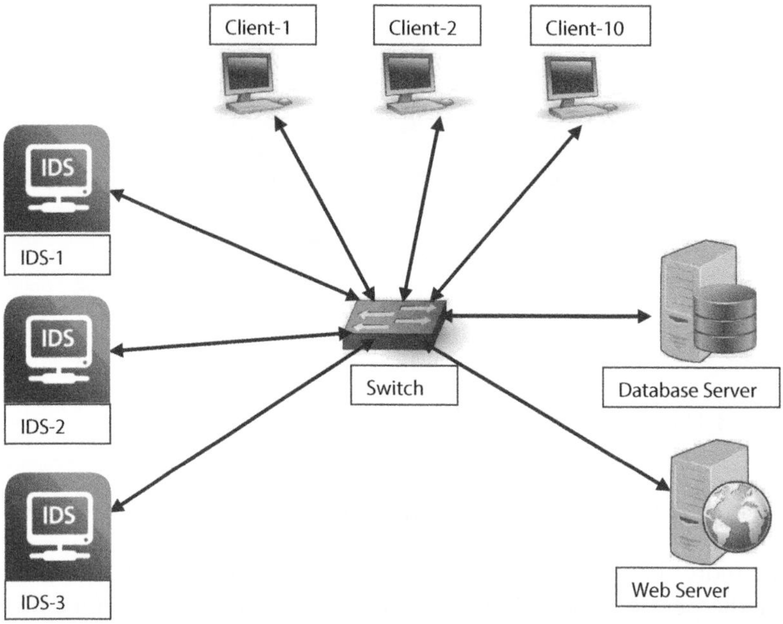

Figure 5.5 Test network design.

on each client. The client software randomly generates requests to Web server and database server. Total 20 tables are created in MySQL database with sample records. Total 43 Web pages are developed and installed on Web server. Client software is configured to open database connection and execute multiple select and/or update queries against randomly selected table. Similarly client software is also configured to randomly access Web pages.

During the test, manually carefully crafted attacks are executed from randomly selected clients. BackTrack Linux operating system, number of open source tools, free tools, and scripts are used for attack generation. How many percentages of attacks are detected by each Intrusion Detection System is recorded. Alerts generated by Intrusion Detection Systems are manually verified and noted false positives [11].

To mimic the real traffic few meaningless spurious IP packets are also generated. Each alert generated by Intrusion Detection System is carefully matched with attacks generated at that time. The Web pages installed on the Web server are designed with various vulnerabilities left behind. Specially crafted attacks are used to validate each concept of the proposed algorithm. In addition to probe and denial of service attacks, modern Web attacks are designed for these experiments. Following OWASP Top 10 – 2013 attacks are considered:

A1 – Injection
A2 – Broken Authentication and Session Management
A3 – Cross-Site Scripting (XSS)
A4 – Insecure Direct Object References
A5 – Security Misconfiguration
A6 – Sensitive Data Exposure
A7 – Missing Function Level Access Control
A8 – Cross-Site Request Forgery (CSRF)
A9 – Using Known Vulnerable Components
A10 – Unvalidated Redirects and Forwards

Random attack pattern and random client pattern is selected for executing these attacks. Attacks generated from each client are recorded with time for alert verification.

This experiment is repeatedly executed and finally average values are considered. The following table represents the summarized outcome of these experiments.

Results from Table 5.9 clearly indicate that compared to open source Intrusion Detection Systems Snort and Suricata, proposed model generates less false positives.

Also we can verify from Figure 5.6 that false positives are reduced in proposed algorithm with similar or better detection percentage.

5.5 Future Research and Conclusion

In the beginning of this chapter we have started with problem formulation. We have asked following question:

Table 5.9 Comparison with open source IDS.

	Snort	**Suricata**	**Proposed model**
Number of false alerts	34	31	14
Detection %	98.76	99.04	99.72

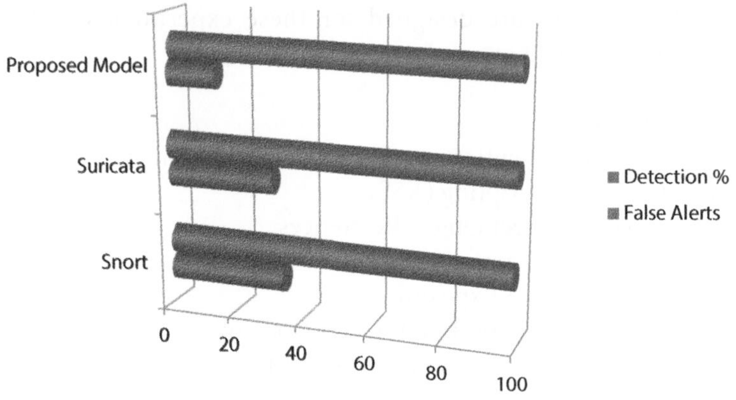

Figure 5.6 False alarm comparison.

"How to make anomaly based Network Intrusion Detection System usable while maintaining efficiency?"

We argued that anomaly based Network Intrusion Detection System can detect unknown attacks but suffers from false positive problem. Intrusion detection analyst cannot process such large number of alerts out of which most are false alert. Thus despite of several advantages anomaly based Network Intrusion Detection System is not usable. Today majority of popular open source and commercial Intrusion Detection Systems are signature based.

We have designed anomaly based Intrusion Detection System with the objective of reducing false positive rate. Three major components are designed in proposed model. The first component is preprocessing unit. Various functionalities incorporated in preprocessing unit to provide quality input to detection engine. The second component, detection engine is also designed considering reduction in false positive rate. Two most prominent soft computing techniques are ensemble to curb false alerts. The third component alert processing module also consists of various techniques to reduce false alerts. Alert aggregation, correlation, and categorization are used within alert processing module. Network devices, host, and application status is stored in configuration database. Intrusion detection analyst supported configuration database helps in reducing false positives.

We improve the standard genetic algorithm and neural network algorithm based Intrusion Detection System by reducing 10% false positives.

Based on the experimental results we can say that this research work is one step further toward making anomaly based Network Intrusion Detection System usable.

The research work and its encouraging results open several new directions. All these open questions will provide new research opportunities to the research community.

- In the detection engine we have used ensemble soft computing techniques. Genetic algorithm and neural network has performed as per our expectation. This opens research questions like Can we use fusion of other soft computing techniques? Can we fuse genetic algorithm and neural network in different way?
- One of the important factors in our proposed model is configuration database. It consists of current status of network devices, host, and applications. Creating and maintaining such configuration database is another challenge. It opens research question Can we have some algorithm which automatically creates and maintains the database?
- Our proposed module is heavily dependent on skill of intrusion detection analyst. In future researcher can work to reduce human dependency and takes most decision automatically.

Another research question raised by our work is related to testing and evaluation of anomaly based Network Intrusion Detection System. KDD Cup 99 is really out dated (more than 16 years old) labeled dataset. This opens another research problem, Can we develop some dataset which represents modern attack and to evaluate anomaly based Network Intrusion System more effectively?

References

1. Ahmim, A., Ghoualmi, N., Kahya, N., Improved Off-Line Intrusion Detection Using A Genetic Algorithm And RMI. *(IJACSA) Int. J. Adv. Comput. Sci. Appl.*, 2, 1, 2011.
2. Azimi, A., Ahrabi, A., Navin, A.H., Bahrbegi, H., Mirnia, M.K., Bahrbegi, M., Safarzadeh, E., Ebrahimi, A., A New System for Clustering and Classification

of Intrusion Detection System Alerts Using Self-Organizing Maps. *Int. J. Comput. Sci. Secur. (IJCSS)*, 4, 6, 2011.

3. Shrivastava, A. and Hardikar, S., Performance Evaluation of BPNN and Genetic Algorithm. *VSRD Int. J. Comput. Sci. Inf. Technol.*, 2, 7, 621–628, 2012.
4. Anusha, K., *An Ontology Based Multi Agent Framework For Network Intrusion Detection*, Ph.D. Thesis, VIT University, India, 2017, http://hdl.handle.net/10603/207041.
5. Hofmann, A. and Sick, B., Online Intrusion Alert Aggregation with Generative Data Stream Modeling. *IEEE Trans. Dependable Secure Comput.*, 8, 2, 282–294, 2011.
6. Bahl, S., *Performance enhancement of intrusion detection system using correlation feature selection*, Ph.D. Thesis, Ansal University, India, 2017, http://hdl.handle.net/10603/176015.
7. Dimitrakakis, C. and Mitrokotsa, A., Statistical decision making for authentication and intrusion detection, IAS technical report IAS-UVA-09-03, http://www.science.uva.nl/research/isla/MetisReports.php, Retrieved December 2013.
8. Weller-Fahy, D.J., Borghetti, B.J., Sodemann, A.A., A Survey of Distance and Similarity Measures Used Within Network Intrusion Anomaly Detection. *IEEE Commun. Surv. Tutor.*, 17, 1, First Quarter 2015.
9. Deepa, A.J., *Performance analysis of efficient intrusion detection systems using evolutionary algorithms*, Ph.D. Thesis, Anna University, India, 2015, Retrieved from http://hdl.handle.net/10603/140288.
10. Md. Farid, D., Hoa, N.H., Darmont, J., Harbi, N., Rahman, M.Z., Scaling up Detection Rates and Reducing False Positives in Intrusion Detection using NBTree, *International Conference on Data Mining and Knowledge Engineering (ICDMKE 2010)*, Rome, Italy, 2010.
11. Bhatti, D.G. and Virparia, P.V., *Soft computing based intelligent intrusion detection algorithm development for reduction of false positive rate*, Ph.D. Thesis, Kadi Sarva Vishwavidyalaya, India, Retrieved from http://hdl.handle.net/10603/96974, 2015.
12. Open Web Application Security Project Top 10 2013, http://owasptop10.googlecode.com/files/OWASP%20Top%2010%20-%202013.pdf, Retrieved June 2015.
13. Bhatti, D., Virparia, P.V., Patel, B., Conceptual Framework for Soft Computing based Intrusion Detection to Reduce False Positive Rate. *Int. J. Comput. Appl.*, 44, 13, 2012.
14. Sabri, F.N.M., Md. Norwawi, N., Seman, K., Identifying False Alarm Rates for Intrusion Detection System with Data Mining. *IJCSNS Int. J. Comput. Sci. Netw. Secur.*, 11, 4, 2011.
15. Jacob Victor, G., Rao, M.S., Venkaiah, V.C., Intrusion Detection Systems - Analysis and Containment of False Positives Alerts. *Int. J. Comput. Appl. (0975–8887)*, 5, 8, 2010.
16. Spathoulas, G.P. and Katsikas, S.K., Reducing false positives in intrusion detection systems. *Comput. Secur.*, 29, 1, 35–44, 2010.

17. Dubey, G.P., Gupta, N., Bhujade, R.K., A Novel Approach to Intrusion Detection System using Rough Set Theory and Incremental SVM. *Int. J. Soft Comput. Eng. (IJSCE)*, 1, 1, 2011.
18. Lavender, B.E., *Implementation of Genetic Algorithms into a Network Intrusion Detection System (netGA), and Integration into nProbe*, M.S. Project, California State University, Sacramento, 2010.
19. Farshchi, J., Statistical-Based Intrusion Detection, http://www.securityfocus.com/print/infocus/1686, Retrieved December 2010.
20. Xiao-Pei, J. and Hou-Xiang, W., A new Immunity Intrusion Detection Model Based on Genetic Algorithm and Vaccine Mechanism. *I.J. Comput. Netw. Inf. Secur.*, 2, 33–39, 2010.
21. Timm, K., Strategies to Reduce False Positives and False Negatives in NIDS, Retrieved Feb2012 from http://www.symantec.com/connect/articles/strategies-reduce-false-positives-and-false-negatives-nids.
22. Mankad, K., Sajja, P.S., Akerkar, R., Evolving Rules Using Genetic Fuzzy Approach—An Educational Case Study. *Int. J. Soft Comput. (IJSC)*, 2, 1, 2011.
23. Khan, K. and Sahai, A., A Comparison of BA, GA, PSO, BP and LM for Training Feed forward Neural Networks in e-Learning Context. *Int. J. Intell. Syst. Appl.*, 7, 23–29, 2012.
24. Sadiq Ali Khan, M., Rule based Network Intrusion Detection using Genetic Algorithm. *Int. J. Comput. Appl. (0975–8887)*, 18, 8, 2011.
25. Siva Prasad, M.V., Vinay Babu, A., Babu Rao, K., An Intrusion Detection System Architecture Based on Neural Networks and Genetic Algorithms. *Int. J. Comput. Sci. Manage. Res.*, 2, 1, 2013.
26. Chakir, E.M., Codjovi, C., Khamlichi, Y.I., Moughit, M., False Positives Reduction in Intrusion Detection Systems Using Alert Correlation and Data mining Techniques. *Int. J. Adv. Res. Comput. Sci. Softw. Eng.*, 5, 4, 2015.
27. Kumar, M., Hanumanthappa, M., Suresh Kumar, T.V., Intrusion Detection System - False Positive Alert Reduction Technique, *Proc. of Int. Conf. on Advances in Computer Engineering*, 2011.
28. Wilkison, M., How to Evaluate Network Intrusion Detection Systems? http://www.sans.org/resources/idfaq/index.php, Retrieved December 2013.
29. Al-Jarrah, O. and Arafat, A., Network Intrusion Detection System Using Neural Network Classification of Attack Behavior. *J. Adv. Inf. Technol.*, 6, 1, 2015.
30. Krishna Kumar, P., *Efficient techniques to detect and mitigate the effects of intrusion over communication networks*, Ph.D. Thesis, Anna University, India, 2017, http://hdl.handle.net/10603/181426.
31. Ramesh Babu, I., *Feature selection techniques for enhancing intrusion detection system using support vector machines*, Ph.D. Thesis, Acharya Nagarjuna University, India, 2014, http://hdl.handle.net/10603/71391.
32. Ramesh, S. and Elango, K., Reducing False Positives using Vulnerability Assessment, Retrieved Feb 2012 from http://www.packetsource.com/article/

nessus/40035/reducing-false-positives-using-vulnerability-assessment, 2011.
33. Singh, R.R., Gupta, N., Kumar, S., To Reduce the False Alarm in Intrusion Detection System using self Organizing Map. *Int. J. Soft Comput. Eng. (IJSCE)*, 1, 2, 2011.
34. Meyer, R. *Challenges of Managing an Intrusion Detection System (IDS) in the Enterprise*, As part of Information Security Reading Room, SANS Institute, http://www.sans.org, June 2011.
35. Selvakani Kandeeban, S. and Rajesh, R.S., Integrated Intrusion Detection System Using Soft Computing. *Int. J. Netw. Secur.*, 10, 2, 87–92, 2010.
36. Selvakani Kandeeban, S. and Rajesh, R.S., A Mutual Construction for IDS Using GA. *Int. J. Adv. Sci. Technol.*, 29, 2011.
37. Aneetha, A.S., *An intelligent and multivariate statistical approach for hybrid network intrusion detection system*, Ph.D. Thesis, Anna University, India, 2016, http://hdl.handle.net/10603/181516.
38. Hasani, S.R., Othman, Z.A., Kahaki, S.M.M., Hybrid Feature Selection Algorithm for Intrusion Detection System. *J. Comput. Sci.*, 10, 6, 1015–1025, 2014.
39. Shrivastava, S.K. and Jain, P., Effective Anomaly based Intrusion Detection using Rough Set Theory and Support Vector Machine. *Int. J. Comput. Appl. (0975–8887)*, 18, 3, 2011.
40. Shilpa, L., Sini, J., Bhupendra, V., Feature Reduction using Principal Component Analysis for Effective Anomaly-Based Intrusion Detection on NSL-KDD. *Int. J. Eng. Sci. Technol.*, 2, 6, 1790–1799, 2010.
41. Streisand, D. and Dove, R., Basic genetic-algorithm-neural-network (GANN) pattern with a self-organizing security example. *2012 IEEE International Carnahan Conference Publication*, 312–318, 15–18, 2012.
42. Khandelwal, S.A., Ade, S.A., Bhosle, A.A., Shirbhate, R.S., A Simplified Approach to Identify Intrusion in Network with Anti Attacking Using.net Tool. *Int. J. Comput. Electr. Eng.*, 3, 3, 2011.
43. Burney, S.M.A., Sadiq Ali Khan, M., Jilani, T.A., Feature Deduction and Ensemble Design of Parallel Neural Networks for Intrusion Detection System. *IJCSNS Int. J. Comput. Sci. Netw. Secur.*, 10, 10, 2010.
44. Pietraszek, T., Using Adaptive Alert Classification to Reduce False Positives in Intrusion Detection, http://citeseerx.ist.psu.edu/viewdoc/summary? 2012.
45. Chou, T.-S., Cyber Security Threats Detection Using Ensemble Architecture. *Int. J. Secur. Appl.*, 5, 2, 2011.
46. Thomas, A., RAPID: Reputation based approach for improving intrusion detection effectiveness, Information Assurance and Security IAS, *2010 Sixth International Conference*, 118–124. 2010.
47. Vogel, V., Network and Host Security Implementation, Retrieved June 2013 from https://wiki.internet2.edu/confluence/display/secguide/Network+and+Host+Security+Implementation+(Stage+1).

48. Engen, V., *Machine Learning for Network Based Intrusion Detection*, PhD thesis, Bournemouth University, United Kingdom, 2010.
49. Dong, Y., Qi, B., Zhu, W., Gao, W., A New Intrusion Detection Model Based on Data Mining and Neural Network. *Prz. Elektrotech.*, Vol. 1b/2013, 88–90, 2013.
50. Muda, Z., Yassin, W., Sulaiman, M.N., Udzir, N.I., A K-Means and Naive Bayes Learning Approach for Better Intrusion Detection. *Inf. Technol. J.*, 10, 3, 648–655, 2011.

6

Recursively Paired Arithmetic Technique (RPAT): An FPGA-Based Block Cipher Simulation and Its Cryptanalysis

Rajdeep Chakraborty[1]* and J.K. Mandal[2]†

[1]Department of CSE, Netaji Subhash Engineering College, Kolkata, India
[2]Department of CSE, FETM, University of Kalyani, Kalyani, India

Abstract
In this chapter a novel and yet simple cipher is proposed, which is fit for track Cryptography and Computer Science and Statistics Journal. Recursively Paired Arithmetic Technique (RPAT), which is an FPGA-based block cipher simulation and its cryptanalysis, is being done with Pearsonian Chi-Square test for non-homogeneity between plaintext with ciphertext and Avalanche ratio test. This cipher is a bit level cryptography where a source stream is considered into a block and RPAT is applied to get the target stream, this cipher has four different types of encryption/decryption processes. So, TB = RPAT (SB, OP), Target Block (TB) is the output of the function Recursively Paired Arithmetic Technique (RPAT) with input parameters, Source Block (SB) and encryption/decryption Options (OP). This cipher has been implemented in IEEE VHDL and simulated for FPGA in Xilinx ISE 8.1i. A good and comparable cryptanalysis result has been found against widely used RSA and TDES.

Keywords: Avalanche ratio test, pearsonian chi-square test, IEEE VHDL, FPGA, XilinX ISE 8.1i

6.1 Introduction

In this era of information and communication technology the digital security has become inevitable [1, 2, 6]. This proposed cipher provides the

**Corresponding author*: rajdeep_chak@yahoo.co.in
†*Corresponding author*: jkm.cse@gmail.com

Dinesh Goyal, S. Balamurugan, Sheng-Lung Peng and O.P. Verma (eds.) Design and Analysis of Security Protocol for Communication, (141–154) © 2020 Scrivener Publishing LLC

primary goal of confidentiality [1, 2], though it is a simple scheme but a good result found against widely used RSA and TDES [1, 2]. Cryptography [1, 2] is of two types, symmetric cipher and asymmetric cipher. Symmetric cipher are those types of cipher where key used is same for both encrypting and decrypting the plaintext and cipher-text, if there are two keys then one can be easily derived from the other. Symmetric cipher has the following advantages over asymmetric:

- Symmetric ciphers are as good as asymmetric ciphers in terms of cryptographic strength.
- Symmetric ciphers have much less encryption/decryption throughput time than that of asymmetric ciphers.
- Symmetric ciphers can be easily embedded in small hardware devices, like mobile phones.

This proposed cipher has been designed for the implementation in FPGA-based simulation [3, 4] and for this it has been coded in IEEE VHDL [5, 6]. Philosophies behind FPGA-based design are:

- Creating new products and lowering the cost of existing "successful" products with fewer people and resources in less time.
- Creating power-less component yet optimal computing for "green" environment.
- Less throughput time and fewer design area.

So, driven by the motivation to work in this new technology, RPAT, which is an FPGA-based symmetric cryptography [1, 2], has been proposed.

Section 6.2 describes RPAT and Session Key generation, Section 6.3 illustrates the implementation details, Section 6.4 does the cryptanalysis, Section 6.5 illustrates simulation based results, Section 6.6 points out some application issues, and Section 6.7 draws the conclusion.

6.2 Recursively Paired Arithmetic Technique (RPAT)

The plaintext to be transmitted is divided and mapped into blocks and RPAT is used to get cipher-text after encryption, same RPAT is used in ciphertext-text for decryption. Figure 6.1 shows the RPAT encryption and decryption, for encryption xor and modulo $2^{n/2}$ are the operations and for decryption xor and modulo $2^{n/2}$ subtraction are the operations. In the

$S^0 0 \oplus S^0 1 \oplus S^0 2 \oplus S^0 3 \oplus S^0 4 \ldots S^0 n\text{-}2 \oplus S^0 n\text{-}1$

$S^1 0 \oplus S^1 1 \oplus S^1 2 \oplus S^1 3 \oplus S^1 4 \ldots S^1 n\text{-}2 \oplus S^1 n\text{-}1$

....

....

$S^{m-1} 0 \oplus S^{m-1} 1 \oplus S^{m-1} 2 \oplus S^{m-1} n\text{-}3 \oplus S^{m-1} n\text{-}2 \oplus S^{m-1} n\text{-}1$

$S^m 0\ S^m 1 \ldots S^m n/2$ (Modn/2-bit Addition)..... $S^m n\text{-}2\ S^m n\text{-}1$

$S^{m+1} 0\ S^{m+1} 1 \ldots S^{m+1} n/2$ (Modn/2-bit Addition)..... $S^{m+1} n\text{-}1$

....

$S^{1-1} 0\ S^{1-1} 1 \ldots S^{1-1} n/2$ (Modn/2-bit Addition)..$S^{1-1} n\text{-}3\ S^{1-1} n\text{-}2\ S^{1-1} n\text{-}1$

Figure 6.1 Block diagram of recursively paired arithmetic technique (RPAT).

following paragraphs we will discuss the RPAT encryption process. The RPAT has two types of iterations, first is the xor iterations and then the modulo $2^{n/2}$ addition iterations.

Consider a block, which is source [7, 8],

$$SB = S^0 0\ S^0 1\ S^0 2\ S^0 3 \ldots S^0 i \ldots S^0 n - 2\ S^0 n - 1$$

Now, $S^0 0$ is exored with $S^0 1$ and the resultant will be $S^1 1$, then $S^1 1$ is exored with $S^0 2$ and the resultant will be $S^1 2$. Similarly this process will be performed for all the bits of n-bit block (0 to n – 1). This whole process is the first iteration. Here it will be noted that Sij is the representation, where "i" is the resultant bit-number after "ith" operation of the whole RPAT encryption/decryption processes, where "j" is the "jth" number of bit in the n-bit block of stream and it is from 0 to n – 1.

This same xor operation is performed "m" number of times, by observing the figure these xor operations are performed from 0 to m – 1.

After that the whole n-bits are broken down into two parts of n/2 bits each. These two blocks are now added with modulo $2^{n/2}$ add operation. The resultant is replacing the second block. This is the iteration number "m".

These addition operations are now performed "l – m" number of times. Moreover, the total iteration of this proposed cipher, RPAT, is "l". So, by observing the figure we can see that the encryption iterations are from 0 to l – 1. Therefore we can say that the total iterations of this cipher, RPAT, is "l" times and where first "m" times are of xor operations and the remaining times are of modulo $2^{n/2}$ addition. The following paragraphs will describe the decryption operation.

The decryption operation will follow these points:

- The number of xor operations needed for decryption is (block length) – (number of iterations required to do encryption). If the block length is 64-bits and the number of iterations required to do encryption is 30, then, number of xor iterations required for decryption is 64 – 30 = 34.
- Then, n-bits are divided into two parts and modulo $2^{n/2}$ subtractions are performed. Here, the number of iterations required in decryption is the same number of iterations that are performed during encryption. Suppose, during encryption the number of modulo $2^{n/2}$ additions are 25 then during decryption the number of modulo $2^{n/2}$ subtraction will also be 25.

Section 6.2.1 will illustrate an example, Section 6.2.2 will give the four types of options available in this proposed cipher, RPAT, and Section 6.2.3 discuss session key generation process.

6.2.1 An Example of RPAT

Figure 6.2 illustrates RPAT encryption process. In this example the Source Block, SB = 10011010, an 8-bit block is considered. Then three iterations of XOR is performed, we get the sub-stream as, S = 11011010. Then two iterations of modulo 16 addition is performed. So, we get the encrypted block, that is Target block, TB = 11010000.

For decryption following points are to be considered:

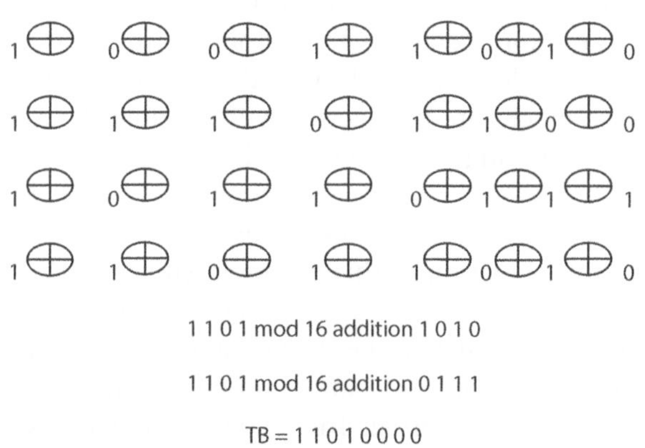

Figure 6.2 RPAT encryption process of SB = 10011010.

- The number of xor operations needed for decryption is (block length) – (number of iterations required to do encryption). The block length is 8-bits and the number of iterations required to do encryption is 3, then, number of xor iterations required for decryption is 8 – 3 = 5.
- Then, n-bits are divided into two parts and modulo $2^{n/2}$ subtractions are performed. Here, the number of iterations required in decryption is the same number of iterations that are performed during encryption. Suppose, during encryption the number of modulo 2^4 additions are two then during decryption the number of modulo 2^4 subtractions will also be two.

6.2.2 Options of RPAT

This technique has four options. These options are given pictorially in Figure 6.3. The options are discussed as follows:

- Option 00: XOR are performed in forward direction and MOD Additions are performed in forward direction. This is already illustrated in Section 6.2.1.

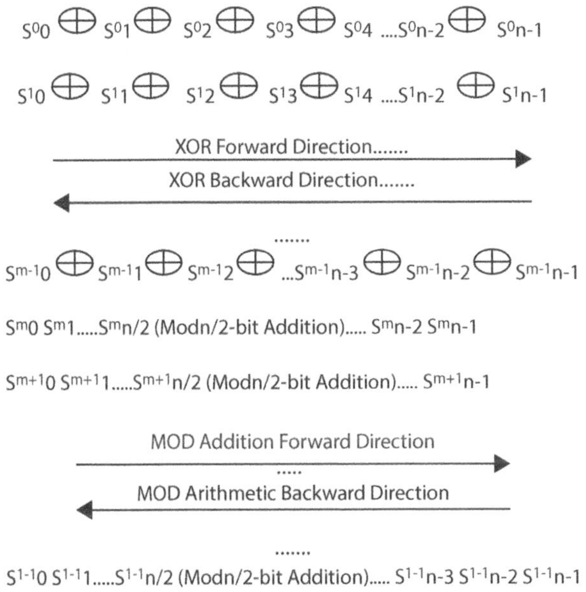

Figure 6.3 Four options of RPAT encryption and decryption.

- Option 01: XOR are performed in forward direction and MOD Additions are performed in backward direction.
- Option 10: XOR are performed in backward direction and MOD Additions are performed in forward direction.
- Option 11: XOR are performed in backward direction and MOD Additions are performed in backward direction.

6.2.3 Session Key Generation

An 130-bit secret/session [1, 2] key is proposed, the key generation is one of the important part of any cipher, symmetric and asymmetric key cipher. In symmetric cipher keys are used for encryption and decrypting, in fact the same.

Table 6.1 illustrates the generation of 130-bit key [1, 2]. Here the plain-text file is encrypted using some block sizes 13-times. Say, in the first

Table 6.1 Generation of secret key.

	Formation of 130-bit secret key			
	Decimal		**Binary**	
Iteration number	**Block size**	**Option**	**Block size**	**Option**
01	128	1st	10000000	00
02	120	3rd	01111000	10
03	112	2nd	01110000	01
04	100	2nd	01100100	01
05	64	1st	01000000	00
06	60	4th	00111100	11
07	32	2nd	00100000	01
08	30	3rd	00011110	10
09	16	4th	00010000	11
10	10	1st	00001010	00
11	8	3rd	00001000	10
12	4	2nd	00000100	01
13	2	1st	00000010	00

iteration block size is 128-bit and encrypted using the first option, in the second iteration block size is 112-bit and encrypted using the third option and so on. In the table this block sizes are considered in 8-bit length and options are coded in 2-bit length.

So, in each iteration we get 10-bit code. Assembling all these 13 iterations we will get 130-bit secret/session key. All these values, block sizes and chosen options, are absolutely random.

These values may change from session to session and therefore in each session we will get unique 130-bit secret key for each session. Here, from this table we get the 130-bit session key as:

K=1000000000011110001001110000010110010001010000000001111 0011001000000100011110100001000011000010100000001000100000010 0010000001000.

6.3 Implementation and Simulation

This proposed cipher has been implemented in IEEE VHDL using 64-bit block size. The block-size can be increased just by increasing the size of bit_vector type [5] variables, signals, and ports from 63 down to 0 to n − 1 down to 0 where "n" is the block size. The modular design approach is taken while coding this cipher. Figure 6.4 shows the top-level simulation of RPAT. The main features of the implementation are given below:

- Triangular Encryption and Decryption using all options.
- Coded using Behavioral model.
- This program is implemented for text file input and output and also for RTL design and simulation for FPGA-chip.
- All the four options are available for encryption/decryption, 00 → 1st option, 01 → 2nd option, 10 → 3rd option, and 11 → 4th option.
- This top-level module has four ports, in_data, out_data, option_data, and EN_DN.
- EN_DN = 0, means encryption is being done, EN_DN = 1, means decryption is being done.
- The chip entity, in_data is the input bit stream; out_data is the output bit stream.
- option_data selects encryption to be performed or decryption to be performed.

```
library IEEE, STD;
use IEEE.STD_LOGIC_1164.ALL;
use IEEE.STD_LOGIC_ARITH.ALL;
use IEEE.STD_LOGIC_UNSIGNED.ALL;
use IEEE.numeric_std.all;
use work.rajdeep_rpac.all;
use std.textio.all;
use std.standard.all;
use IEEE.std_logic_textio.all;
entity RPAC is
   Port ( in_port : in  BIT_VECTOR (64 downto 1); out_port : out  BIT_VECTOR (64 downto 1);
 option_port : in BIT_VECTOR (8 downto 1); EN_DN_port : inout  BIT);
end RPAC;
architecture Behavioral of RPAC is
file IN_FILE1:TEXT open READ_MODE is "C:\Xilinx\Recursive_Parity_Arithmetic_cipher\in.txt";
file IN_FILE2:TEXT open READ_MODE is "C:\Xilinx\Recursive_Parity_Arithmetic_cipher\option.txt";
file OUT_FILE:TEXT open WRITE_MODE is "C:\Xilinx\Recursive_Parity_Arithmetic_cipher\out.txt";
begin
process(EN_DN_port)
                variable BUF_IN, BUF_OUT: LINE;
                variable source_bit, destination_bit, buffer_bit: bit_vector(64 downto 1);
                variable option_bit: bit_vector(8 downto 1);
                variable EN_DN_bit: bit;
                begin
                while not ENDFILE(IN_FILE1) loop
                        READLINE(IN_FILE2,BUF_IN);
                        READ(BUF_IN,option_bit);
                        READLINE(IN_FILE1,BUF_IN);
                        READ(BUF_IN,source_bit);
                EN_DN_port <= option_port(2);
                out_port <= RPAC_enpdep(in_port, option_port, EN_DN_port);
                EN_DN_bit := option_bit(2);
                destination_bit := RPAC_enpdep(source_bit, option_bit, EN_DN_bit);
                        WRITE(BUF_OUT,destination_bit);
                        WRITELINE(OUT_FILE,BUF_OUT);
                end loop;
                file_close(IN_FILE1);
                file_close(IN_FILE2);
                file_close(OUT_FILE);
                end process;
end Behavioral;
```

Figure 6.4 Top level architecture of RPAT.

- option_data also selects which of the four types of encryption/decryption is to be performed.
- EN_DN will tell the receiver side that encryption or decryption is being done.
- There three types of TEXT files used in this implementation, "in.txt" for Source block (SB), "out.txt" for Target Block (TB) and "option.txt" for dual purpose of selecting option and encryption/decryption choice.
- "option.txt" also contains the session key of the encryption and decryption.

The rest of the coding is done by defining the package which contains functions and procedures. The functions and procedures which are used to realize and simulate RPAT are noted below:

- Function RPAC_enpdep: This is the main function which performs encryption/decryption using all options.
- Function RPPT: This is the function which performs encryption and decryption using recursive xor operation and type of encryption and decryption from four alternatives.
- Function mod32_bit_addition: Since this is a 64-bit block cipher implementation so, this is the function which performs modulo 32-bit addition.
- Function mod32_bit_subtraction: This is a modulo 32-bit subtraction used in decryption.
- Function binary_to_decimal: This function converts the binary bits to its equivalent decimal to perform required task as needed by RPPT.
- Function power_of_two: This function calculates 2^n, where "n" is the number of bits of a block.
- Function twos complement: This function calculated twos complement as required by encryption and decryption simulation of RPAT.

Therefore, by using the modular design approach and behavioral approach this proposed cipher has been successfully realized and simulated in IEEE VHDL using XilinX ISE 8.1i. To perform the cryptanalysis, RPAT has also been coded in C-programming language through Cipher Block Chaining (CBC) mode [1, 2].

6.4 Cryptanalysis

Recursively Paired Arithmetic Technique (RPAT) is simple bit-level cryptography. So, all the cryptographic parameters may not be incorporated. In this section emphasis is given on Chi-Square test based cryptanalysis. It is a statistical measure that how far plaintext differs with ciphertext, in another word it is a test for heterogeneity or non-homogeneity.

Pearsonian Chi-Square generation test [7, 8], also known as the Chi-Square fitness test or Chi-Square independence.

$$\chi^2 = (O - E)^2 \tag{6.1}$$

where O is the Observed Frequency in groups of category
E is the Expected Frequency in groups of category
df is the "degree of freedom" (n − 1).
χ^2 is Chi-Square.

The steps in calculating the Chi-Square test value, summarized as below:

- Tabulate the observed frequencies in column O.
- Tabulate the expected frequencies in column E.
- Use the above formula to calculate the Chi-Square value.
- Find the degree of freedom as $df.$ $(N - 1)$.
- Find the table entry value.
- If your Chi-Square value is being found equal to or being found greater than the table calculated value then null hypothesis can be rejected: differences in these data are not appears to chance alone.

To perform Chi-Square test ten different files are selected, then these source files are encrypted with Conical Cipher, RSA and TDES, respectively. Then using Chi-Square test program these values are noted.

Text files (TXT), data file (XLS), image file (JPG), and video file (WMV) have been chosen for cryptanalysis as people used to send data/information using these files and our primary aim is to provide confidentiality.

Moreover, these source files are chosen in increasing file sizes, in categories of tiny (0–10 kilobytes), small (10–100 kilobytes), medium (100 kilo–bytes to 1 megabytes), large (1–16 megabytes), and huge (>16 megabytes) file types.

Table 6.2 gives the Chi-Square values of RPAT, RSA, and TDES. Figure 6.5 illustrates the same graphically in logarithm base 10 scale. Therefore, by observing table and graph we can say that Chi-Square values

Table 6.2 Cryptanalysis of RPAT.

File name	Size in KB	Chi-Square values		
		RPAT	RSA	TDES
Version.txt	1	66	55	62
Ukraine.txt	5	99994	75194	118879
Content.txt	10	483321	454996	460630
Removdrv.txt	21	681325	662409	797476
PropList.txt	53	633312	633725	640814
Python_25_License.txt	101	6841343	6711218	7428782
Result_analysis_ IT_ODD_2011.xls	286	1066115	608316	984520
Metconv.txt	1156	2831418	2786042	2817232
Photo0139.jpg	1272	87889	83015	84719
Wildlife.wmv	25631	956816	951329	953431

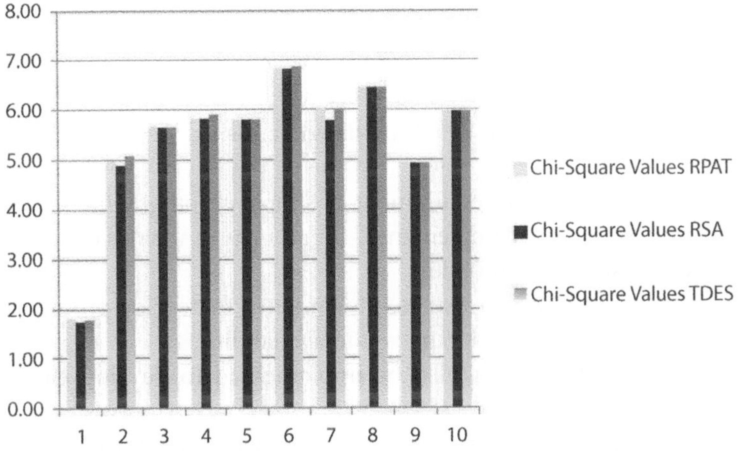

Figure 6.5 Graphical data of Chi-Square value of RPAT in logarithmic scale.

Table 6.3 Simulation based results.

Calculated device utilization summary (estimated values)			
Logic utilization	**Used**	**Available**	**Utilization**
Number of slices	782	960	81%
Number of 4 input LUTs	1369	1920	71%
Number of bonded IOBs	131	66	198%

of this proposed cipher, RPAT, is greater than that of RSA, but, with respect to TDES, 50% of the source files encrypted with RPAT have greater Chi-Square values.

6.5 Simulation-Based Results

Table 6.3 illustrates the simulation based results. Number of slices used in this proposed cipher, RPAT, is 782 out of 960 which 81%. Number of 4-input Look-Up-Tables used is 1369 out of 1920 and it is 71%. Number of Input Output Blocks is 131 that means two IOBs are required for the implementation of this proposed cipher, RPAT. Therefore, it is proved in this section that this proposed cipher, RPAT, is successfully simulated for FPGA-based systems.

6.6 Applications

Some of the applications of RPAT are listed below:

- Since, we get the requirement of simple cryptographic solution, so, it can be implemented for security in various embedded systems like mobiles.
- This technique can also be implemented to develop protocol for confidentiality, integrity and availability.
- This technique can also be implemented to develop electronic code books.
- It can also be implemented to develop a private network system and using master-key-based application security.
- This can also be implemented in hardware applications security such as switches, gateways and routers.

6.7 Conclusion

Therefore in this chapter we have successfully proposed and simulated a 64-bit block cipher. Its cryptanalysis with RSA and TDES using Chi-Square values yields good and comparable result. This cipher, RPAT, is more heterogeneous than that of RSA and TDES. Moreover, by simulation based results we got this cipher occupying almost all resources than that of available resources, thus we can say here that RPAT will have effective throughput time and design area. Keeping in view of these outcomes we can now use RPAT in various applications.

Acknowledgment

The authors express their deepest gratitude toward the Department of Computer Science and Engineering (CSE), Netaji Subhash Engineering College, Kolkata, India, and the Department of Computer Science and Engineering (CSE), University of Kalyani, Kalyani, India.

References

1. Stallings, W., *Cryptography and Network Security: Principle and Practice*, Second Edition, Sixth Indian Reprint, Pearson Education Asia, India, 2002.
2. Forouzan, B.A., *Cryptography and Network Security*, Special Indian Edition, Tata Mc-Graw-Hill, India, 2007.
3. Wolf, W., *FPGA-Based System Design*, First Impression, Pearson Education, India, 2009.
4. Navabi, Z., *Embedded Core Design with FPGA(s)*, Edition, Tata Mc-Graw Hill, India, 2008.
5. Bhasker, J., *A VHDL Primer*, Thirteen Indian Reprint, Pearson Education, India, 2004.
6. Kaur, K., *Digital System Design*, Scitech Publications (India) Pvt. Ltd., India, Copyright © 2009.
7. Chakraborty, R. and Mandal, J.K., A Microprocessor-Based Block Cipher through Rotational Addition Technique (RAT), *9th International Conference on Information Technology (ICIT 2006)*, 18–21 December 2006, IEEE Computer Society, IEEE, Orissa Information Technology Society (OITS), Institute of Technical Education and Research (ITER), New Jersey Institute of Technology (NJIT), Satyam Computers Ltd. and IEEE New Jersey Section,

and published by IEEE Computer Society Conference Publishing Services, Bhubaneswar, India, pp. 155–159, 2006.

8. Chakraborty, R. and Mandal, J.K., FPGA Based Cipher Design & Implementation of Recursive Oriented Block Arithmetic and Substitution Technique (ROBAST). *(IJACSA) Int. J. Adv. Comput. Sci. Appl.*, 2, 4, 54–59, April 2011.

7

Security Protocol for Multimedia Streaming

Dr. N. Brindha[1]*, S. Deepa1 and S. Balamurugan[2]

[1]Department of Applied Mathematics and Computational Sciences, PSG College of Technology, Coimbatore, India
[2]Quants IS & CS, Coimbatore, India

Abstract

In current era the most used transmission system is interactive media streaming, where the multimedia content is compressed and shared across the cyberspace. Streaming media is used to transmit the recorded media content and deploy from a data transmitting system to the consumer. Web based services suffer from multiple problems such as bandwidth obstruction, network traffic, power capabilities, price, safety, and connectivity. Therefore, mediocre quality of service and performance degeneration is the two significant problems that are taken into account for communication. This chapter gives a detailed comparative study on security protocols used for multimedia transmission. As media streaming develops, various security streaming protocols were designed for the above problems.

Streaming protocols are the guidelines for data communication, and also determines elements like file header syntax, verification, and failure handling. Selecting a streaming technology involves various elements like real-time flow control, intelligent stream conversion, and multimedia exploration. Security streaming protocol finds a solution for all the issues mentioned. In multimedia streaming, multiple protocols are used to protect the media which plays an important role in the present and future. This chapter is discussed with a complete study of video classification and retrieval using HLS security protocols to interact streaming media. HLS protocol with Live Streaming encryption and decryption is developed to provide secured method of transmitting multimedia files over the web in not so distant future. HLS gives best administrations to all clients as indicated by their necessities and is a brilliant decision to optimize the activities.

**Corresponding author*: brindhacsepsgtech@gmail.com

Dinesh Goyal, S. Balamurugan, Sheng-Lung Peng and O.P. Verma (eds.) Design and Analysis of Security Protocol for Communication, (155–170) © 2020 Scrivener Publishing LLC

Keywords: Real-time streaming protocol (RTSP), universal datagram protocol (UDP), transmission control protocol (TCP), real-time transport protocol (RTP), real-time transport control protocol (RTCP), real-time messaging protocol (RTMP), motion picture expert group-dynamic adaptive streaming over HTTP (MPEG-DASH)

7.1 Introduction

Video is a visual media source that joins a succession of pictures to frame. The video transmits a frame and the procedures based on the request in which the frame catches should be appeared. Sound segments are compared with the frame being appeared on the screen. Streaming means sending either audio or video data, which enables to begin its processing before it is totally received. Video streaming is a sort of media streaming in which the information from a video document is constantly conveyed by means of the Internet to a remote client [2]. It permits a video streaming to be seen online without being downloaded on a host PC or gadget. Video streaming takes a shot at information streaming standards, where all video streaming recorded information is compacted and sent to a gadget in little lumps. Video streaming normally requires a good video player that connects with a remote server, which has a pre-recorded media document or live feed [10]. The server uses specific calculations to pack the media record or data for exchange over the system or Internet federation.

7.1.1 Significance of Video Streaming

- Corporate correspondences.
- Utilizing streaming media, a webcast can be produced using the CEO's office direct to all the staff, over the corporate WAN/LAN.
- Distance Learning: Often called as e-learning, steps forward when one can include sound and video content.
- Advertising: Many studies have demonstrated that streaming media clients invest more energy, so they are appropriate focuses for Internet-Delivered publicizing.
- Entertainment: Online news, TV shows and films use the concept of video streaming which is more accessible by online viewers [12].

- Does not require a continuous encoding limitation, which can empower more proficient encoding, for example, the multi-pass encoding that is commonly performed for DVD content.
- It gives constrained adaptability—the pre-encoded video cannot be altogether adjusted to channels that help diverse piece rates or to customers that help distinctive showcase abilities than that utilized in the first encoding.
- No sitting tight for downloads (well, hardly any pausing).
- No physical duplicates of the substance are put away locally.
- Diminishing the likelihood of copyright infringement (assuming any).
- No capacity (or constrained stockpiling) prerequisites at the customer side.
- Support of live occasions.

Conventions are utilized in streaming for sending the fitting information (video) to the clients from the principle server. Likewise, the end client may connect with the streaming server utilizing control conventions like MMS or RTSP [9]. All video streaming conventions depend on transport conventions used to anchor the media. The most every now and again utilized are User Datagram Protocol (UDP), HTTP, HDS, HLS, MPEG-DASH, RTSP, RTP, RTCP, and RTMP. UDP is utilized fundamentally to set up low-inertness and misfortune enduring associations between applications on the web. HTTP Streaming is a push-style information exchange method that enables a web server to persistently send information to a customer over a solitary HTTP association that remaining parts open inconclusively. Streaming can be comprehensively split into on-demand and real-time categories. With on-demand streaming, the client appeals a recording or movie and receives it; typically no one else gets the recording at equivalent time. With real-time streaming, the sender figures what to send, and the receiver plays it back as it is sent, with a meager and persistent lag. On-demand does not automatically suggest an appeal by human; if a web page starts playing a movie or song when it is opened, it is on-demand in spite of being troublesome and undesirable. If it takes up a broadcast in process, that is real time. Real-time does not indicate "simultaneous with the source"; at a minimum, there is always a speed-of-light delay. Buffering helps aid to preserve a real-time transmission from skipping, and a delay of a notable fraction of a minute may be an adequate price for this. Each classification has its own confusion. With on-demand streaming, the duty is to open files since they are requested and keep streams going for every client. If the system load is huge, it has to shuffle a lot of separate streams. It may trail, so that the clients are occasionally compelled to pause. This is troublesome but satisfactory, as long as it will not appear too much. With real-time streaming, the service is usually administering a known number of channels, but it has to keep them moving at a rate which they are played back. If it cannot hold on, it is usually exceptional to hop rather than pause [3]. Real-time streaming can be point-to-point (one sender, one receiver) or broadcast (one sender, many receivers). A VOIP communication is an illustration of two-way point-to-point streaming [7]. Streaming servers generally aids more than one protocol, receding on substitutes if the first choice does not work. Streaming and encoding are two individual concerns. Streaming handles how bytes get from one place to another; encoding handles how sounds and images are transformed to bytes and retract.

Streaming comprises protocols at various layers of the OSI Reference Model. The bottom level (physical, data link, and network) are usually taken as given. Streaming protocols contains:

- The transport layer, which is subjected for getting data from one end to other.
- The session layer, which systematize streaming action into current units such as movies and broadcasts.
- The presentation layer, which administers the link between information as seen by the application and information as sent through the network.
- The application layer, the level at which an application interacts to the network.

The initial protocol of the pack is Real Time Streaming Protocol (RTSP), which is a network control protocol created by Real Networks of Netscape. RTSP is used as an application level protocol which supports to the use of numerous protocols in transport layer to carry its packets, including Universal Datagram Protocol (UDP) and Transmission Control Protocol (TCP). RTSP is utilized for implementing and regulating media periods between the end points. It is likewise utilized in entertainment and transmission systems to manage streaming media servers.

The application-level protocols are produced using a specific transport protocol, like Real Time Transport Protocol (RTP), that is generally constructed on UDP transport. RTP is developed by the Audio-Video Transport Working Association of the Internet Engineering Task Force that is a network protocol for transporting sound and video files via IP networks [6]. RTP is broadly used in transmission and entertainment systems that engage streaming media like telephony, video communication applications including WebRTC, television services and internet-related push-to-talk highlights.

The Real Time Transport control protocol (RTCP) is an associate protocol of RTP. In RTP, a new session begins by exchanging information between entities of a given layer through the service provided by the next bottom layer. It does not carry any media data instead it merges with RTP for delivery and packaging of media data. The foremost task of RTCP is to supply quality of service (QoS) in media handling by regularly sending data knowledge like transmitted octet, packet counts, packet loss, packet delay variation, and round trip delay time to associates of streaming media sessions. Quality of service parameters are used to authorize the services of RTCP.

Next streaming protocol is Real-Time Messaging protocol (RTMP) is refined by Macromedia for the purpose of streaming audio, video and data on the internet. It grants very low latency for absorbing live streams. It still precedes the roost because of being robustious and sustained cosmically. Microsoft's Smooth streaming protocol was made current to guide adaptive bit rate streaming and have healthy tools for digital rights management (DRM). Most of the users adopt using adaptive bit rate protocol which is an approach of video streaming over HTTP where the source content is ciphered at multiple bit rates, then individual of different bit rate streams are disjointed into small multi-second parts. The wealth of this technology is to give the best quality of service.

The forthcoming protocol is adaptive streaming over HTTP (MPEG-DASH) which supports adaptive bit rate streaming that obligates Encrypted Media Extensions (EME) and Media Source Extensions (MSE). MPEG-DASH is regular-based API's for browser-based digital rights management (DRM) [8]. It uses transmission control protocol (TCP) to transship the media files and EME to cipher the streaming files. It is codec-agnostic is a content concealed with any coding format like H.264, H.264 and VP9 etc.

Apple established HTTP Dynamic Streaming (HDS) which is a flash-based streaming protocol that holds adaptive streaming and ranks for higher-quality. When latency is deliberated, HDS is another better choice among protocols. This kind of streaming is used in sports ceremonies where time seconds are measured. It is a procedure of productively conveying video to the clients by progressively exchanging among various streams of differing quality and size amid playback.

HTTP Live Streaming (HLS) protocol is an upcoming video streaming protocol proposed by Apple. HLS classic supports flexible bit rate streaming and dynamically provide the best possible video quality at any moment.

It supports less quality live video streaming on personal website with the help of simple embed code. Presently it uses H.265 codec, which delivers 2xtimes the video quality with same file size. HLS is compatible on desktop browsers, smart TV's and both Android and iOS mobile devices. Because of its splendid features like robustness, adaptively, compatibility from error and delivery of high quality, Today HLS is most commonly used. Multiple servers provide high quality media files sequentially even if one server fails to transmit. HLS is used for reliable and dynamically accommodate to the network conditions by inflation playback based on the available speed of wired and wireless connections. HTTP Live streaming supports working for adapting to the unstable network conditions without causing user-visible playback stalling. For instance, on an unstable wireless network, HLS allows a lesser quality video and decrease bandwidth usage.

HTTP Dynamic Streaming (HDS) is Adobe's strategy for versatile bitrate streaming used in Flash Video. This strategy empowers on request and lives versatile bitrate video conveyance of MP4 media over general HTTP associations [3]. HTTP Live Streaming (HLS) convention is a rising video streaming convention created by Apple. HLS standard backings versatile piece rate streaming and progressively conveying the most ideal video quality at any minute. Dynamic Adaptive Streaming over HTTP (DASH), otherwise called MPEG-DASH, is a versatile bitrate streaming procedure that empowers top notch streaming of media content over the Internet conveyed from traditional HTTP web servers [11]. Like Apple's HTTP Live Streaming (HLS) arrangement, MPEG-DASH works by breaking the substance into a succession of HTTP-based document portions, each section containing a short intervening of playback time of substance that is possibly numerous hours in span, for example, a film or the live communicate of a games occasion.

Real Time Streaming Protocol (RTSP) is utilized for setting up and controlling media sessions between end focuses. It is likewise utilized in stimulation and correspondence frameworks to control streaming media servers. Real-time Transfer Protocol (RTP) is produced by the Audio-Video Transport Working Group of the Internet Engineering Task Force which is a system convention for conveying sound and video over IP systems. RTP control protocol (RTCP) is a sister protocol of the RTP. The essential capacity of RTCP is to give nature of administration (QoS) in media conveyance by intermittently sending insights data, for example, transmitted octet and bundle tallies, parcel misfortune, parcel defer variety and round-trip postpone time to members in a streaming mixed media session. Real–Time Messaging protocol (RTMP) is produced by Macromedia for streaming sound, video, and information over the web.

It gives low dormancy to ingesting live streams. Despite everything it governs the perch due to its hearty and generally bolstered.

Smooth Streaming is an IIS Media Services expansion, empowers versatile streaming of media to Silver light and different customers over HTTP. Smooth Streaming gives a brilliant review encounter that scales greatly on content dispersion systems, making genuine HD. Progressive streaming or Progressive downloading implies accepting a customary file and beginning to process it before it is totally downloaded. It requires no uncommon protocols, but it requires a format that can be processed dependent on partial content. This has been around for quite a while; interleaved images, where the odd-numbered pixel lines are accepted and displayed before any of the even ones, are a recognizable example. They are displayed at half resolution previously the rest of the rows fill in the full resolution. Dynamic streaming does not have the adaptability of true streaming since the information rate cannot be changed on the fly and the transmission can't be isolated into various streams. On the off chance that it conveys an entire file rapidly and the user tunes in to or observes only the beginning, it squanders data transmission. The user is given the entire record and duplicate it with no exertion.

"True" streaming utilizes a streaming protocol to control the transfer. The packets got do not add up to a file. Do not confuse streaming for duplicate protection, though; unless there is server-to-application encryption, it is not difficult to remake a file from data. True streaming might be versatile. This implies the rate of transfer will consequently change in light of transfer conditions. If the receiver cannot stay aware of a higher data rate, the sender will drop to a lower data rate and quality. This might be finished by changes inside the server, or by changing the client to an alternate stream, perhaps from another server.

Video streaming aims transmitting media data on network while allowing users to operate it without accomplishing the process of transmission. Every video streaming depends on transport protocols. The most intermittently used are Transmission Control Protocol (TCP), User Datagram Protocol (UDP), HTTP, HDS, MPEG-DASH, RTSP, RTP, RTCP, and RTMP. Above all the listed protocols, Real Time Messaging Protocol is the best and widely used video streaming technology. This video streaming protocol, developed by Adobe systems, desires at live streaming and on demand to Adobe Flash Player. The Microsoft Research (MSR) dataset is selected which is publicly available and contains pairs of actions performed by different humans.

HLS protocol is malleable and facilitates streaming of audio and video and even text data in numerous formats to various devices. The essential thought is to classify video into frames and yield the output of the event occurred and to exchange recordings remotely. HLS protocol is utilized which is a security convention that exchanges recordings securely and secretly, due to its low latency, rate of transmission of video bit rate is quicker.

7.2 Existing Technology and Its Review

In past decades, some ongoing video streaming conventions and mechanisms have actualized like the Real Time Streaming Protocol (RTSP) and Real Time Messaging Protocol (RTMP). These protocols cause it workable to the clients to distribute sound and video streams up the network and perform them frequently. The RTSP is an organized governing protocol proposed to use in amusement and correspondence frameworks to organize streaming media servers. This convention is utilized for implementing and governing media sessions across endpoints. It has been actualized in QuickTime Streaming Server like Apple's shut source streaming server. Continuous Messaging Protocol (RTMP) is a protocol created by Macromedia (now claimed by Adobe) for streaming sound, video, and information over the internet. This convention is utilized for communication between a Flash Player and Adobe Flash Media Server. RTMP sessions might be scrambled utilizing SSL or using RTMPE, however do not give adequate security. Adobe Flash Player can be downloaded for nothing on the client side. Adobe likewise gives engineer rendition of Flash Media Server for non-business purposes for secure streaming which utilizes SSS (Secure Scalable Streaming) which fragments the video outlines into tiles and afterward codes the tiles into header and versatile information arrange, then packetize the header and encode information.

For continuous media streaming on cell phones, RTMP has a couple of problems, RTMP is a TCP-based convention, which underpins retransmission for lossless data correspondence. This implies framework architects need to combine a good missing information retransmission procedure to dodge sound and video delay, jitter, and asynchronization on account of the information parcel misfortune. Besides, RTMP uses distinctive conventions/ports from HTTP that causes helpless in receiving hindered by firewalls and works with Flash.

RTSP is a content based application-layer convention. It assumes the job of "network remote control" in sight and sound administrations, for example, sound and video progressively. In the media streaming transmission, RTSP includes a couple of essential protocols for information communication, media control, and media size depiction. Most RTSP servers exploit Real-time Transport Protocol (RTP) as a distributing technique to broadcast the information streamed by developing a Transmission Control Protocol

(TCP) or User Datagram Protocol (UDP) association as a media streaming conveyance channel [4]. RTSP portrays the advancement of guidance for communication of clients and streaming servers containing OPTIONS, DESCRIBE, ANNOUNCE SETUP, PAUSE, PLAY, RECORD, REDIRECT, and TEAR-DOWN. At the circumstance when a client commences a media streaming session to a streaming server through RTSP directions, they exploit the Session Description Protocol (SDP) to trade multimedia subtle elements, ship addresses and other session confession metadata.

TCP is a federation arranged and strong byte-stream tradition. The sender and beneficiary should fabricate a TCP relationship before data transmission. TCP is a vehicle layer protocol. It has course of action instruments to ensure the transmission trustworthiness. Three-way handshake, moreover insinuated as "SYN-SYN-ACK", is required before transmitting data. In the midst of data transmission, every datum segment should be perceived by the beneficiary. If the sender does not get the perceived information from the authority in a predestined time, TCP will use a retransmission timeout part to qualify non-adversity data an utilize course of action assertion numbers to guarantee the data divide is in the right demand. With an explicit true objective to control the surge of data and to upgrade transmission proficiency, TCP has a sliding window part and uses moderate start calculation to keep up a key separation from organize stop up.

UDP is a connectionless and flawed protocol. Like TCP, UDP is in like manner a vehicle layer tradition. UDP is only in charge of sending and tolerating the datagram, anyway it does not guarantee the datagram is gotten by the objective in the wake of sending the datagram. As needs be, the data can be gotten out of demand, or even lost. Diverged from TCP, UDP is speedier on the grounds that UDP has no stream control, no screw up checking and no datagram recognized systems. Thus, UDP is much of the time used by sight and sound applications for transmitting the data stream, for instance, sound and video streaming data in light of the fact that these applications are asking for on nonstop response and can't be conceded.

RTP is an internet transport protocol which handles real-time multimedia information streams communication. It is determined as functioning in the transport layer, constructed above UDP. The use of RTP is to provide time information and to synchronize several streams. RTP only assures real-time data communication but does not assist a trustable transport mechanism for transmitting data packets in a sequence [4]. Also, it does not give flow control and traffic control, which depends on Real-Time Transport Control Protocol (RTCP). RTP gives a timestamp, serial number, and other structures to handle the real-time streaming data. After getting data packets, the client retrieves the data packets in the actual sequence as per the

RTP header information that conveys the customers how to retrieve the data packets and how the codec bit streams are unloaded. RTP header information contains timing information, sequence number, payload recognition, frame indication, source recognition, intra media synchronization, etc.

RTCP is a control protocol which is subject for handling transmission standard between applications to interchange control details on vast networks, mostly for streaming media, phone and video conferencing. In the course of an RTP session, an application utilizes two ports such as RTP and RTCP, respectively. RTCP packets are sent systematically to monitor the standard of the service and change of user's session details and other functions. RTCP packet comprises the number of packets sent, lost and other data via receiver report (RR), sender report (SR), source description items (SDES), shows the end of participation (BYE) and application specific functions (APP) packets formats. Therefore, the server can utilize these details to dynamically modify the transmission rate, and also modify the payload type. RTP and RTCP work together to reduce transmission above and improve efficiency.

SDP is used to illustrate multimedia sessions. It serves for session statement, request and other forms. SDP does not help the settlement operation of SDP session information or media encoding. When commencing audio/video streaming, video call, or other sessions, there is a need to deliver media information, transport addresses and other session information metadata to the participants. SDP gives a standard portrayal for such details such as session name and objectives, session time, media time and more.

Extensible Messaging and Presence Protocol (XMPP), also known as Jabber convention was planned for IM and online presence detection. XMPP depends on Extensible Markup Language (XML) streaming technology. XMPP makes informing over the web possible, independent of working frameworks and programs. XMPP is intended to support IM undertakings, for example, confirmation, get to control, end-to-end encryption and compatibility with different conventions. Moreover, the XMPP Standards Foundation (XSF) creates numerous ex-strains (XEPs) which make XMPP all the more intense such as roster, client and server elements or traits whose broadened namespaces are "jabber:iq:roster", "jabber:client", and "jabber:-server", separately. Due to the fast evolution of wireless networks and smart technologies, mobile video streaming and social networks have become an important part of the lives in various areas (social connections, education, entertainment, scrutiny, etc.). There have been many video streaming technologies on mobile devices over the web, from the client to streaming server side, from video compression to streaming protocols.

Most of the studies and applications made on video streaming are concentrated on video-clip distribution and currently popular videos streaming. Some are concentrated on video-clip or real-time notations as available in video sharing. Cheng and Liu submitted a NetTube, for small video sharing application. They created a model to minimize the server workload to optimize the playback standard and scalability.

Jia and Ma submitted MoviShare, a video distributing stage that can give the mobile users with video searching and posting services. MoviShare targets a logical combination of area-based mobile social connecting and multimedia distribution. It can likewise create a GIF (Graphics Interchange Format) record of accessible video cuts as video abstraction to take care of transmission capacity and power restriction issues [5]. However, MoviShare is certainly not a live streaming framework yet an on-demand streaming. Clients can only share their videos once they are recorded and the same is sent to a server.

Silva *et al.* portrayed a technique for explaining objects on a live video streaming on Tablets. They planned two ways to deal with enable clients to include comments when the object is moving in the video streaming. They utilize object tracking techniques, for example, Kinect sensor to make stays on those explanations to maintain a strategic distance from the comments lost when overlaid. Yamamoto *et al.* proposed an approach to create explanations dependent on social movements in association with video cuts, for example, client remarks and weblog.

They built up a framework called Synvie to separate profitable data from those social and network exercises as video streaming explanations. El-Saban *et al.* displayed a framework for constant video explanation of captured recordings on cell phones to encourage perusing and seeking. A client can utilize this framework to capture a video using cell phone. The video is sent, continuously, to a brought together server which breaks down video key casings to create explanations by utilizing MSERs (Maximally Stable External Regions) detector with SIFT (Scale-Invariant Feature Transform) highlights. At that point these explanations are returned back to the client's cell phone. Their work is centered on producing explanations from constant recordings.

H. Sun *et al.* displayed a review of video streaming systems which incorporate scalable video coding, video transcoding, network protocols, and streaming techniques that have been produced as of late. Walker *et al.* gave a design of mobile video streaming under 3G and GPRS systems and some standard methods for sound/video streaming, for example, sound/video compression and streaming protocols. In their framework, they utilized customer buffering for packet loss and stream switch-down choice for lower bit rate. In any case, their framework has a consistent postponement of many seconds when streaming live occasions. They tried it with just a single client.

Meyer tended to an examination take a shot at video streaming with Client/Server design. He broadened the SpyDroid 2 project and utilized the VLC Player 3 as a customer streaming player, although his center is advancing encoding principles as per the nature of association for transmission and limiting utilization of energy. It has no social exercises or touch display communications.

7.3 Methodology and Research Design

Video is a visual multimedia basis that associates a series of pictures to form a motion picture. The video spreads a signal to a screen and processes the sequence in which the screen captures should be displayed. Videos usually have audio elements that match with the pictures being presented on the screen.

Video Retrieval is wide area that incorporates features from numerous features and fields including artificial intelligence, machine learning, data base management systems, etc. There have been huge numbers of algorithms fixed in these fields to achieve various video retrieval responsibilities. In our Proposed System video retrieval is nearly a subdivision of Internet Multimedia Subsystems (IMS).

Frames are individual pictures in a sequence of images (video). A keyframe or a unique frame is a frame used to indicate the beginning or end of a change made to a parameter. An arrangement of keyframes describes which movement the spectator will see, while the location of the keyframes on the video expresses the timing of the movement.

Feature extraction normally refers to the process of extracting features from a frame in a video, independently of past or future frames. Feature extraction includes decreasing the amount of resources needed to define a huge set of data.

Feature extraction is a significant part of the system. From the key frame, feature extraction is done. The features of the key frames are extracted according to the requirement from the video. Classification is performed using classifier from the extracted features. In this system, Support Vector Machine (SVM) classifier can be used. SVMs are binary classifiers, yet, they can be accepted to handle the various classification tasks common in remote sensing. SVM is used in information retrieval. The extracted features of the keyframes undergo SVM, where, the classifier classifies various features like behavior, color, shape, etc., of the required data.

This system is preliminarily to detect a person who once had been identified as a victim in any previous cases. For this the video footage of the incidental scenario is partitioned into frames, and from all the frames of the footage the one containing a perfect shot of the complainant is identified. The identified frame is used as a key frame and any frame matching with key frame could be used to determine the complainant in future. The environment returns back to normal situation in a short period of time. Since there exists live video streaming, whenever the victim enters again into the environment where the incident have occurred, he/she could be found by matching the current frame with the key frame and can be intimated to the respective people belonging to that environment. A real-time application and prototype for the system is discussed below:

Consider a robbery has happened in bank. From the video footage during the incident a shot of the victim can be identified. The identified frame can be set as the key frame. The bank returns back to a normal situation within few days. Whenever the victim enters the bank after the recovery of bank, he could be identified with the help of key frames found in prior. When the frame of a live video matches with the key frame, the bank employees can be alerted that the identified victim has entered the bank which helps to capture easily. HLS protocol is used to identify the victim.

7.4 Findings

The transmission delay of various protocols are shown in Figure 7.1. The TCP transmission delay is between 500 ms and 620 ms. The RTP transmission delay is between 20 ms and 70 ms. The HLS transmission delay is between 10 ms and 30 ms. The RTMP transmission delay is between 60 ms and 80 ms. The UDP transmission delay is between 50ms and 65ms. Therefore, using HLS protocol to transmit can effectively reduce the transmission delay, and improve the streaming efficiency as shown in Table 7.1.

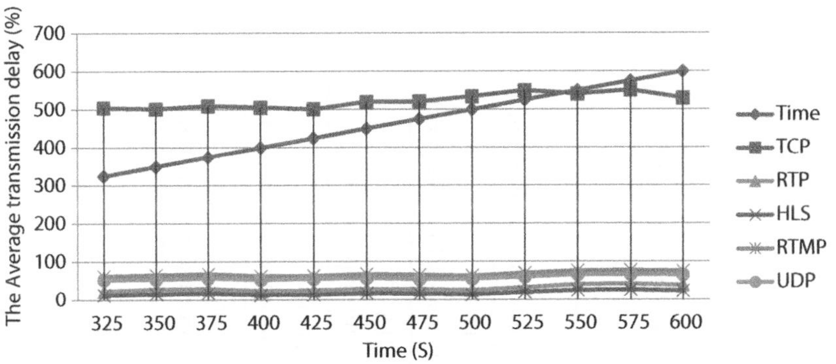

Figure 7.1 Comparison of protocols transmission delay.

Table 7.1 Comparison of protocols with the transmission delay.

Time (S)	325	350	375	400	425	450	475	500	525	550	575	600
TCP transmission delay (ms)	505	502	510	506	501	520	521	534	550	541	551	530
RTP transmission delay (ms)	23	28	29	23	25	28	27	25	32	40	41	38
HLS transmission delay (ms)	13	16	18	13	14	17	16	14	20	25	26	23
RTMP transmission delay (ms)	62	65	68	62	63	67	65	63	70	76	77	75
UDP transmission delay (ms)	53	54	57	53	55	57	54	55	60	66	66	65

7.5 Future Research and Conclusion

The crime rate happening in day to day life and with secured protocol of HLS to overcome with such event is discussed. The adopted system is an implementation of video classification method with HLS security protocol, discussion in the previous sections provides encouraging results and comparatively higher efficiency is achieved by using multiple frames instead of single frame or key frames representing a shot. HTTP based live streaming has the better traversal of NAT and firewalls, ease of deployment, and built-in friendly bandwidth sharing which is used for transfer of videos easily with high transmission bit rate remotely to other places [11]. This is a study for identification of crime and criminals and in the society and also for providing a better future to live in.

References

1. Amir, E. and McCanne, S., Katz, R., Receiver-driven Band width Adaptation for Light-weight Sessions, In the *Proceedings of ACM Multimedia*, Seattle, WA, 1997.
2. Belda, A., Pajares, A., Guerri, J.C., Palau, C.E., Esteve, M., JMFVoD: Design and Implementation in Java of a Media Streaming on Demand System, In the *Proceedings of SCS Euromedia*, Modena, Italy, 2002.
3. Brett, P., Using Multimedia: An Investigation of Learners' Attitudes. *Comput. Assist. Lang. L.*, 1, 2–3, 191–212, 1996.
4. Baier, C. and Katoen, J.P., *Principles of Model Checking*, The MIT Press, 2008, http://www.worldcat.org/isbn/026202649X.
5. Baugher, M, McGrew, D., Naslund, M., Carrara, E., Norrman, K., *The secure real-time transport protocol (SRTP)*, United States, 2004.
6. Busse, I., Deffner, B., Schulzrinne, H., Dynamic QoS Control of Multimedia Applications based on RTP, *Computer Communications* 19, No. 1, 1996.
7. Bilien, J., Eliasson, E., Orrblad, J., Olov Vatn, J., Secure VOIP: Call establishment and media protection, In *2nd Workshop on Securing Voice over IP*, 2005.
8. Chakraborty, P., Dev, S., Naganur, R.H., Dynamic HTTP Live Streaming Method for Live Feeds, 2016.
9. Dutta, A. and Schulzrinne, H., A Streaming Architecture for Next Generation Internet, In the *Proceedings of ACM Multimedia*, 2001.
10. Rathod, N. and Dongre, N., MANET routing protocol performance for video streaming, *2017 International Conference on Nascent Technologies in Engineering (ICNTE)*, 2017.

11. Sidhu, R.S. and Sharad, M., Smart Surveillance System for Detecting Interpersonal Crime, 2016.
12. Zaidi, S., Bitam, S., Mellouk, A., Enhanced user datagram protocol for video streaming in VANET, *IEEE International Conference on Communications (ICC)*, 2017.

8

Nature Inspired Approach for Intrusion Detection Systems

Mohd Shahid Husain

Information Technology Department, Ibri College of Applied Sciences, Ministry of Higher Education, MoHE, Oman

Abstract
Unauthorized access of network resources is one of the major security issues in communication network. Intrusion detection systems are used to identify any intruder in a network by monitoring the activities over a communication network. When these Intruder detection systems find any abnormal activity in a network, it sends signals to administrators alarming the possible presence of intruder in the network system. This chapter deals with the concept of intrusion detection, approaches for detecting intrusion including passive as well active approaches, and how nature inspired approaches can be incorporated effectively for the purpose. The chapter also provide a brief about some top intrusion detection softwares available in the market.

Keywords: Intrusion detection, IDS, malicious nodes, network security, intrusion detection & prevention system, HIDS, NIDS, network intrusion detection, host based intrusion detection

8.1 Introduction

To make your communication over a network secure has been always a major concern. This issue of making your network secure is becomes more vital as the communication network has grown from traditional communication networks to *ad hoc* networks and now in Cloud computing environment.

One of the major security issues in communication network is unauthorized access of network resources to perform some malicious activity.

Email: siddiquisahil@gmail.com; mshahid.ibr@cas.edu.om

Dinesh Goyal, S. Balamurugan, Sheng-Lung Peng and O.P. Verma (eds.) Design and Analysis of Security Protocol for Communication, (171–182) © 2020 Scrivener Publishing LLC

Intrusion detection systems are used to identify any intruder in a network by monitoring the activities over a communication network. When this Intruder detection system finds any abnormal activity in a network, it sends signals to administrators alarming the possible presence of intruder in the network system.

Traditionally various security techniques have been used to protect the communication systems like firewalls, user identification and authorization, antivirus software, etc.; however, nowadays hackers uses sophisticated new techniques every day to attack networks for gaining unauthorized access. Due to these latest sophisticated attacks, traditional systems implemented for security are not capable of protecting the communication network effectively.

So, there is an emerging need of intrusion detection system (IDS), which can effectively monitor and analyze the traffics over the network to spots the threat of intrusions before they damage the network by doing any malicious activity.

8.1.1 Types of Intrusion Detection Systems

Based on the implementation approach, the intrusion detection systems can be categorized in two types, NIDS and HIDS.

1. NIDS: Network based Intrusion Detection Systems.
2. HIDS: Host based Intrusion Detection Systems.

Network based IDS or NIDS are basically hardware systems placed at various key places in a communication network system like routers, switches, gateways etc, where these NIDS keep monitoring and analyzing all the traffic that is moving inward and outward across the network to detect activities which are abnormal. A Network Intrusion Detection System analyze all outbound and inbound data packets and look for any activity/event which is abnormal that is it identifies the patterns which are deviated from normal/routine behavior. These patterns are considered as suspicious patterns. When NIDS finds any such pattern it treats as threat and based on its severity, the Intrusion Detection system opt for various actions like notifying administrators about the activity or block the IP addresses of sources which are suspicious from accessing the network.

Host based IDS or HIDS are software components that are implemented on host machines in a communication network. Host based intrusion detection systems are more effective compare to network-based IDS in cases where host machines are infected with malicious codes and they tried to spread it in the whole network system.

8.2 Approaches Used for Intrusion Detection Systems

The objective of any Intrusion Detection System is to detect malicious activities in a network. The Intrusion Detection Systems, based on the methods implemented for intruder detection, can be broadly categorized as:

1. Signature-Based Intrusion Detection Systems.
2. Anomaly-Based Intrusion Detection System.
3. Specification-Based Intrusion Detection System.

Signature-Based Intrusion Detection Systems make use of pattern recognition approaches based on already stored patterns. These systems analyze the traffic passing by the network and search for some specific network patterns for example bit sequences, set of malicious codes etc known as signatures. As the technique is based on stored patterns/signatures, this technique performs well in case of detecting known attacks but in case of new attacks the technique fails because they have different signatures having pattern not stored in the available database.

Anomaly-Based Intrusion Detection Systems are based on the established baseline activities. The nature of activities and functions of components in any communication network are generally fixed. In this approach IDS analyses each event and activity in a network. If any event or activity is found to be deviated from the normal baseline activities the intrusion detection system informs this behavior to the administrator for actions, considering it a malicious event.

Specification-Based Intrusion Detection System are like anomaly-based intrusion detection system i.e. they also monitor the network traffic for abnormal behavior. Here the normal behavior of the network is defined manually instead of analyzing the network operations.

8.2.1 Intrusion Detection and Prevention Systems

Most of the Intrusion Detection Systems were passive in nature. When these systems find any unwanted activity in the communication network, they do not take any counter action against it by themselves instead they just inform it to the network administrators and then the administrator take counter measures against such activity.

The Intrusion Detection and Prevention Systems (IDPS) are active Intrusion Detection System. On finding any unwanted activity in the network, along with sending alarm to the network administrator these IDS also try to counter the threats from succeeding.

8.2.2 Performance Criteria of Intrusion Detection Systems

There are different parameters which are used to evaluate how effective the implemented Intrusion Detection Systems is. These parameters include:

1. *Accuracy:* there are chances that the implemented intrusion detection system may misinterpret an activity. So, the IDS should be capable of monitoring and analyzing the activities/traffic in such a way that they can detect any threat with high accuracy. The main components used to evaluate this parameter are
   a. True positive rate
   b. False positive rate
2. *Timeliness:* in case of any attack, it is required that system can detect it in quick time. Timeliness defines the amount of time the IDS take in detecting any attack. As the common action of IDS after detecting a threat is to inform it to the administrators. So, this is a very important factor for evaluating the performance of an IDS.
3. *Performance:* the IDS have to monitor and analyze the traffic over the network continuously. The good IDS system should have capability of handling large inbound and outbound traffic for analysis and detection of intrusion.
4. *Robustness:* the resistance capability of the system against attacks. As the technology enhances day by day, the IDS system should be capable of handling various threats including the latest ones.

In addition to the above parameters, it is recommended that the users should also pay attention to the following factors:

1. *Memory usage*: the IDS should consume less memory for intrusion detection and warning.
2. *Ease of use*: the IDS system to be installed should be user friendly so that even users who are not expert in system security can also operate it with ease.

3. *Security*: many hackers nowadays try to attack on the IDS itself to break the system. The IDS to be installed should be secure that is it has capability to defend itself from attacks.
4. *Interoperability*: the IDS should be capable of interoperating with other IDSs also. This enhances the threat detection rate significantly.
5. *Collaboration*: the security system works better if we use combination of different security mechanisms. As firewalls and other security approaches alone cannot make a system hundred percent secure. To enhance the security of the system the IDS should be capable of collaborating with other security measures.

8.3 Intrusion Detection Tools

There are various tools available for detecting intrusion in your communication network. Some of the popular open source Intrusion Detection tools are:

1. *Snort [1]:* Martin Roesch who developed a tool for detecting and preventing intrusions in a communication network in 1998 called Snort. This is an open source tool having benefits of both the signature based inspection as well as anomaly-based inspection of the traffic. It is a rule-based system which checks for malicious data packets travelling in the network and alerts to the administrators when it finds any threats. It effectively analyses all the data packets transmitting through the network without missing any.
2. *OpenWIPS-NG [2]:* OpenWIPS-ng is a modular Wireless tool for preventing Intrusion in a network System. It is an open source IPS which uses variety of sensors to capture traffic in wireless environment and sends the data to the server. These sensors are also responsible to react against the attacks. The server aggregates the data captured by all the sensors and do analysis for detecting the threats. In case of any threat, it responds against the attack and also make a log for future reference. OpenWIPS-ng provides a graphical user interface for server management. It also displays the information regarding threats.

3. *Suricata [3]:* Suricata is a high-performance Network Intrusion Detection and Prevention System. This rule based open source security monitoring system was developed by Open Information Security Foundation (OISF) and its associates in 2009.
4. *OSSEC [4]:* OSSEC is a Host-based Intrusion Detection System (HIDS). It is an open source tool having key characteristics like scalability and multi-platform. The main features of OSSEC are active response with real-time warning by Windows registry monitoring, correlation and analysis engine, checking integrity of files, integrating log analysis, rootkit detection, and centralized enforcement of policies.
5. *BroIDS [5]:* the focus of this IDS is on network analysis which makes it different from other intrusion detection systems. Unlike rules-based systems which are designed to spot an exception, BroIDS are used to detect specific threats in the network and trigger alerts by recording detailed network behavior. Zeek Network security monitor is the new name for this.

8.4 Use of Machine Learning to Build Dynamic IDS/IPS

The objective of an intrusion detection system (IDS) is to monitor and analyze the traffic passing by a communication network in search of any malicious activity, which could be any unwanted activity or event that is not normal. Systems that were used traditionally can detect only known attacks but cannot identify threats which are new and unknown to the system. They work basically on pre-defined rules or behavioral analysis through baselining the network.

Nowadays attackers can evade the security systems based on these methods using sophisticated techniques, so there is an urgent need of intrusion detection systems which intelligent enough to counter unknown attacks actively. Researchers are focusing toward machine learning techniques to make IDS intelligent enough so that they can detect new threats also.

To make Intrusion Detection Systems more effective in detecting unknown attacks having patterns which are not available in the databases, a variety of machine learning algorithms have been incorporated in IDS for example deep learning, Bayesian networks, decision trees, ANN, fuzzy logic, Support Vector machine, etc.

In recent years, various nature inspired methods have been proposed by different researchers. These methods, based on Swarm intelligence, evolutionary algorithms and Artificial Immune System etc have been proved to be quite effective in optimization of intrusion detection and prevention.

Based on the learning and experience these ML enabled Intrusion Detection and Prevention Systems can effectively identify any attack on the system by classifying normal behavior and abnormal behavior.

Machine learning techniques for building efficient IDS can be broadly categorized as:

a. *Supervised learning Techniques:* these approaches are based on training of the system using set of examples. These techniques make use of labeled historical data patterns to categorize any data packet passing through the network as legitimate or malicious. Researchers have used various supervised machine learning techniques for this purpose. The most commonly supervised approaches are Support Vector Machine, Bayesian Network, Artificial Neural Network, Decision Tree, and k-Nearest Neighbor.

   The main advantage of supervised learning approaches is that they are significantly efficient in recognizing already known threats with high accuracy and low false alarm rate. The drawback of these algorithms is that they are not effective against new threats and have a weak recognize capability of 0-Day attacks.

b. *Unsupervised learning Techniques:* In unsupervised algorithms, we do not have any labeled dataset. These approaches are based on two main assumptions. First, the user profile cannot change drastically in a short span of time. Second, malicious activity causes an unexpected variation in the network flow. The working of these algorithms is based on clustering all the activity/event data in the network. This results in creation of certain clusters. Some of these clusters have a huge number of events, whereas others have a very less number of events. Now based on the earlier defined assumptions, the system concludes that the clusters with huge event count represents normal user activity while the clusters having less number of events represent abnormal events and alarm the administrators that these are malicious activities which have produced by attackers.

c. *Hybrid Approach:* Both supervised and unsupervised techniques have some advantages and disadvantages, to make system more efficient by combining advantages of both the approaches and eliminating disadvantages completely, some hybrid approaches are developed. In hybrid systems a part of intrusion detection mechanism works on the supervised algorithm techniques and another part is works on the unsupervised algorithm.

Various researchers have done Noteworthy work in applying machine learning techniques to optimize intrusion detection systems. Some of the prominent works are W. Hu *et al.* [6] uses support vector machine to detect anomalies in a communication network. G. Xiaoqing *et al.* [7] proposed a method for intrusion detection in network with the help of SVM. F. Haddadi *et al.* [8] implemented an intrusion detection system and provided a classification of attacks using feed forward neural network. S. Paliwal and R. Gupta [9] developed a genetic algorithm-based approach for attack detections like probing & remote user attack and denial of service. W. Alsharafat *et al.* [10] applied ANN and extended classifiers for detecting intrusion. W. C. Lin *et al.* [11] implemented nearest neighbors clustering technique for intrusion detection. S. Elhag *et al.* [12], optimize the IDS by applying combination of genetic fuzzy systems with pairwise learning. Ahmad Javaid *et al.* [13] proposed a deep learning model to detect distributed denial of service. Wang, G *et al.* [14] have developed an artificial neural network and fuzzy clustering based system for detecting intrusion in a network.

Results of these works reflect that machine learning techniques can optimize active IDS to detect the unknown attacks by effectively identifying malicious behavior in the network to predict the intrusion.

8.5 Bio-Inspired Approaches for IDS

There are striking similarities between the natural world and fast-growing communication network systems like enormous size, dynamic nature, highly diverse, and complex. Despite having these inherent challenges, biological organisms evolve, self-organize, self-repair and flourish without any centralized control. Many Bio-Inspired Optimization approaches have been implemented as classification techniques for Intrusion Detection Systems, like the genetic algorithm, artificial immune system, Artificial Neural Networks, Artificial Bee Colony, particle swarm optimization and many others. Bio-inspired network intrusion detection can adapt to varying environmental conditions, providing in-built resiliency to failures and damages, collaborative, survivable, self-organizing, and self-healing.

In recent years a lot of work has been done by researchers in this direction like Farhoud Hosseinpour *et al.* [15], implemented Artificial Immune System for optimizing intrusion detection system based on anomaly. Kolias, C *et al.* [16] has developed an intrusion detection system based on swarm intelligence. Yu Sheng Chen *et al.* [17] proposed an intrusion detection system in wireless sensor network based on artificial immune system and SVM. Osama Alomari *et al.* [18] proposed a feature selection method based on Bees algorithm for anomaly detection. Yuk Ying Chung and Noorhaniza Wahid [19] developed an effective system for intrusion detection using simplified swarm optimization. Maoguo Gong *et al.* [20] implemented an artificial immune system based anomaly detection system. Their approach was based on negative selection algorithm, S. Nishanthi [21] has proposed an intrusion detection system in wireless sensor networks using watchdog based clonal selection algorithm. Omar S. Soliman and Aliaa Rassem [22] have applied quantum bioinspired algorithm for efficient detection of intrusion.

Analysis of these works shows that bio-inspired approaches can play a very effective role in increasing the performance of intrusion detection systems.

8.6 Conclusion

As the technology enhances everyday, the traditional security measures like firewalls and authentication system are not able to provide complete security against sophisticated attackers. In addition with these systems we also need Intrusion Detection and Prevention Systems, which can effectively and timely detect any threat and can respond to it.

1. *Capabilities of IDS:* the intrusion detection system can help in following ways:
   a. Monitoring the operation of different network components like routers, firewalls, key management servers and files that can be used by other security systems aimed at detecting, preventing or recovering from cyber attacks.
   b. Providing a user-friendly graphical user interface so that users who are not security experts can also assist with managing system security.

c. Intrusion detection systems can also help the enterprise attain regulatory compliance.
d. Intrusion detection systems can also improve security response.
e. An IDS can be used to analyze the quantity and types of attacks. This information can be very useful to the organizations in updating their security systems or implementing more effective controls.

2. *NIDS vs. HIDS:* the intrusion detection systems can be implemented in two ways, Network based intrusion detection system (NIDS) and Host based intrusion detection system (HIDS).

Features of NIDS	**Features of HIDS**
Ownership cost is low	Lower entry cost
Deployment is easy	Monitors System Activities
Detect network-based attacks	Capable of detecting attacks that are not noticed by network-based IDS
Retaining evidence	Verifies success or failure of an attack
Can detect attacks in real time with low response time	Near real time detection and response
Can also detect attacks that are not successful	Does not require additional hardware

3. *Optimal Solution:* Ideally, a communication network should have features of both the Host based Intrusion Detection and a Network based Intrusion Detection system. The Host based Intrusion detection system will protect local machines and act as a last line of defense, while the Network based Intrusion Detection system will keep the actual network safe and secure. Both can provide more security than any single firewall or anti-virus suite, but each lacks certain features that the other contains. Thus, combining the two is the only way to create a truly robust defensive network.
4. *Challenges of IDS:* although a lot of research work has been done, still there exists a lot of challenges in efficiently detecting the malicious activity or intrusion.

References

1. https://snort.org/
2. http://openwips-ng.org
3. https://suricata-ids.org/
4. https://www.ossec.net/about.html
5. https://www.zeek.org/
6. Hu, W., Liao, Y., Vemuri, V.R., Robust anomaly detection using support vector machines. *Proc. Int. Conf. Mach. Learn.*, pp. 282–289, 2003.
7. Xiaoqing, G., Hebin, G., Luyi, C., Network intrusion detection method based on Agent and SVM. *2010 2nd IEEE Int. Conf. Inf. Manag. Eng.*, pp. 399–402, 2010.
8. Haddadi, F., Khanchi, S., Shetabi, M., Derhami, V., Intrusion detection and attack classification using feed-forward neural network, in Computer and Network Technology (ICCNT), *2010 Second International Conference on*, IEEE, pp. 262–266, 2010.
9. Paliwal, S. and Gupta, R., Denial-of-service, probing and remote to user attack detection using genetic algorithm. *Int. J. Comput. Appl.*, 60, 19, 57–62, 2012.
10. Lin, W.-C., Ke, S.-W., Tsai, C.-F., CANN: An intrusion detection system based on combining cluster centers and nearest neighbors. *Knowl.-Based Syst.*, 78, 13–21, 2015.
11. Elhag, S., Fernandez, A., Bawakid, A., Alshomrani, S., Herrera, F., On the combination of genetic fuzzy systems and pairwise learning for improving detection rates on intrusion detection systems. *Expert Syst. Appl.*, 42, 22, 193–202, 2015.
12. Javaid, A., Niyaz, Q., Sun, W., & Alam, M. A deep learning approach for network intrusion detection system. In Proceedings of the 9th *EAI International Conference on Bio-inspired Information and Communications Technologies (formerly BIONETICS).* ICST Institute for Computer Sciences, Social-Informatics and Telecommunications Engineering, pp. 21-26, 2016
13. Wang, G. *et al.*, A new approach to intrusion detection using Artificial Neural Networks and fuzzy clustering. *Expert Syst. Appl.*, 37, 9, 6225–6232, 2010.
14. Hosseinpour, F. *et al.*, Survey on Artificial Immune System as a Bio-Inspired Technique for Anomaly Based Intrusion Detection Systems. *International Conference on Intelligent Networking and Collaborative Systems*, 2010.
15. Kolias, C., Kambourakis, G., Maragoudakis, M., Swarm intelligence in intrusion detection: A survey. *Comput. Secur.*, 30, 8, 625–642, 2011.
16. Chen, Y.S., Qin, Y.S., Xiang, Y.G., Zhong, J.X., Jiao, X.L., Intrusion detection system based on immune algorithm and support vector machine in wireless sensor network. In Information and Automation, pp. 372–376, Springer, Berlin, Heidelberg, 2011.

17. Alomari, O. and Othman, Z., Bees algorithm for feature selection in network anomaly detection. *J. Appl. Sci. Res.*, 8, 3, 1748–1756, 2012.
18. Chung, Y.Y. and Wahid, N., A hybrid network intrusion detection system using simplified swarm optimization (SSO). *Appl. Soft Comput.*, 12, 9, 3014–3022, 2012.
19. Gong, M., Zhang, J., Ma, J., Jiao, L., An efficient negative selection algorithm with further training for anomaly detection. *Knowl.-Based Syst.*, 30, 185–191, 2012.
20. Nishanthi, S., Intrusion Detection in Wireless Sensor Networks Using Watchdog Based Clonal Selection Algorithm. *IJREAT Int. J. Res. Eng. Adv. Technol.*, 1, 1, 1–5, 2013.
21. Soliman, O.S. and Rassem, A., A Network Intrusions Detection System based on a Quantum Bio Inspired Algorithm. *Int. J. Eng. Trends Technol. (IJETT)*, 10, 8, 371–379, Apr 2014.

9

The Socio-Behavioral Cipher Technique

Harshit Bhatia[1*], Rahul Johari[2†] and Kalpana Gupta[3‡]

[1]Reval India Private Limited, Gurugram, India
[2]USICT, GGSIPU, Delhi, India
[3]C-DAC, Sector-62, Noida, India

Abstract
The primitive and the traditional symmetric key cryptographic systems made use of a limited number of input keys with single encryption function for securing the data before the data can be transmitted over unsecure network. Such limited key cryptographic functions did not withstand the test of time and have become obsolete over time. With the advent of social networking era, the network traffic has also increased rapidly and this increase in unsupervised and unsecure traffic demands a strong and a secure symmetric key technique. This chapter presents a secure and an efficient symmetric key technique that harnesses the readily available social profiling information of the sender for encryption and decryption of the data blending the social behavior of the sender along with the cryptography.

Keywords: Cryptography, symmetric-key, encryption, social, behavioral, profiling

9.1 Introduction

With the increase in human footprint on the internet, there has been a rapid increase in the network traffic too. Much of the data that flows through the internet via the network highway enters and leaves from social network as the social networking has seen an exponential growth over the past years. This expansive data circulates across various nodes through the

**Corresponding author*: droid.harshit@gmail.com
†*Corresponding author*: rahul.johari.in@ieee.org
‡*Corresponding author*: kalpanagupta@ieee.org

Dinesh Goyal, S. Balamurugan, Sheng-Lung Peng and O.P. Verma (eds.) Design and Analysis of Security Protocol for Communication, (183–210) © 2020 Scrivener Publishing LLC

interconnected web present between the actual source and the destination. This information, often, travels unhindered and in plain-text form without any form of secure jacket encompassing around it. With the increase in social information of individuals arising from various social networking websites, the sensitivity of the data has also increased. Ever-increasing social data along with sensitive information poses serious need for advancing security tools that may cater to the social networks too.

There are several symmetric and asymmetric cryptography techniques available that cater to providing security of data [1, 2]. However with the increased social footprint of humans, there has been a need to find new and better cryptographic technique that can factor in the social profiling information of humans too within the encryption function. This unique collaboration of social profiling information of the user along with the encryption keys being fed to the encryption function will account for a technique that would be less penetrable to several attacks. The proposed technique is an approach that makes judicious use of the social footprint of the user and makes use of this social footprint on user on the internet to do social profiling of user. This social profiling information is further bundled together with an encryption function to generate the cipher text. The technique has been created to be able to provide an increased level of security of data for the social networking websites traffic, however just not limited to the social network.

9.2 Existing Technology

In [3], author(s) have discussed the need for cryptography in network security and various cryptographic algorithms used for network security. A discussion has been done on the advantages, disadvantages, and usage of various algorithms.

Cryptography is used for the purpose of security on web. However, like everything, this has its pros and cons too. Similarly, there are uses and misuses. So, in [4], author(s) have discussed the misuses of cryptography in web security. The experiments were conducted on ASP .NET to show how cryptographic algorithms were compromised in ASP .NET web applications. Author(s) have also suggested some measures to curb attacks on web security.

With the evolution of big data, the amount of data being produced is being increasing at incredible rates. With data being processed digitally, the attacks on data are very common these days. So, it is important to secure it. In [5], author(s) have discussed cryptography and security in relation with digital signatures. Digital signatures are used for binding identity to the information and making it secure with encryption. Still, attacks are possible on digital signatures. Author(s) have also discussed the attacks on digital signatures.

In [6], author(s) have presented a tool called SHAVisual for visualization of cryptographic algorithm: SHA (Secure Hash Algorithms) 512 algorithm.

In [7], author(s) have proposed a new cryptography algorithm. Then, comparison of the same has been made with the existing cryptography techniques in terms of throughput of key generation, to generate encryption text and to generate decryption text. Analysis has also been taken into consideration regarding how much prone it is to brute force attacks, in other words, how secure it is. The algorithm involves arithmetic and logical mathematical operations. According to the results presented, this algorithm has better performance in comparison to existing algorithms. The algorithm shows high throughput and high security features.

Visual cryptography came into existence to overcome the challenges of traditional cryptography algorithms, that is, they have larger computational times. Comparatively, visual cryptography involves less computing power. Although visual cryptography has easy encryption and decryption methods and other benefits, but it is still not a success due to its implementation features. It requires a new key every time. If same key used, then, one must compromise with the security. There are numerous applications of visual cryptography. In [8], author(s) have discussed one of the features of visual cryptography, that is, user authentication. Traditional visual cryptography techniques have vulnerabilities, so, author(s) have proposed a new system protocol based on visual cryptography technique for user authentication to server. This protocol can be used for the creation of secured channel between two parties.

In [9], author(s) have presented a visualization tool called VIGvisual for learning of cryptography algorithm vignere cipher. The tool involves both encryption and decryption techniques. In author(s) opinion, tool is versatile, efficient and user friendly.

In [10] author(s) have attempted to develop a bi-lingual machine translation tool for sentences in simple present and past sentences. The translation of the user interface of a knowledge-based system has been automated. The project executes the transformation process of well-structured simple present and past sentences written in Arabic language to a well-structured English sentence by using dictionary as a means for translation. The methodology which has been adopted is dependent on the basic structural components such as the parts of speech of a language that are necessary for translations.

Elliptic Curve Cryptography is replacing cryptographic techniques because of its high level of security. In [11], author(s) have further improvised ECC algorithm by replacing the mapping the characters to affine points in the elliptic curve with the pairing up of ASCII values of the text.

First, this change reduces the overall cost of the algorithm by removing the mapping operation. Second, with this change there is no longer any need to share the lookup tables between sender and receiver. Further this algorithm can encrypt and decrypt any text of ASCII values.

In [12] author(s) have used already existing affine cipher technique to be implemented at the encryption phase of the storage part where a confidential data such as credit card detail is to be stored. The cipher technique has been achieved along with the mapping of plain text characters to cipher text being generated in Hindi language characters.

In [13], author(s) have focused on cryptography, its goals, terms of cryptography, algorithms, attacks. A review has been presented on cryptography, mainly focusing on security and time constraints. In author(s) opinion, depending upon the security level, cryptography algorithm must be chosen.

Visual cryptography refers to encryption of visual information in which decryption is not anymore, a digital process but a mechanical one. In [14], author(s) have focused on the application area of visual cryptography such as data hiding, securing images, color imaging, multimedia, *et al.* Encryption of data in visual cryptography has been explained.

In [15], author(s) have discussed the data hiding techniques and cryptographic algorithms. The reasons for evolution from early stage cryptographic algorithms to present cryptographic techniques have been explained. Their advantages and disadvantages have also been taken care in the discussion. Cryptography and steganography are also explained. Both aim at data security but with different approaches. In cryptography, data is encrypted as well as hidden from the attackers but in steganography, data is also encrypted but not hidden from anyone. Its real meaning is hidden.

Dynamic nature and the limited resources of sensor nodes pose a challenge in implementation of secure wireless sensor networks. Clustering of the sensor networks is a solution for this, but security is an issue in this. In [16], ECC algorithm has been used for the generation of unique 176-bit encryption binary strings for each sensor. This algorithm is robust to brute-force attack, HELLO flood attack, selective forwarding attack, and compromised cluster head attack.

9.3 Methodology

The author[s] have proposed a lightweight cryptographic technique in the literature that is aimed at increasing the security of the data by harnessing the social profiling information of the end user. The proposed system is a symmetric key cryptographic technique which employs the same domain of keys for the process of encryption as well as decryption. The technique uses a series of mathematical operations on the plain-text input and returns an encrypted cipher text by performing the operations in a pre-defined order.

By symmetric key cryptography, we refer to the class of cryptosystems which use the same set of keys for both encryption of the data at the sender's end, as well as for decryption of cipher text received on receiver's end to obtain the original plain text that was meant to be transmitted. Both sender and receiver share their set of keys by means of a secure channel. The keys must always be kept secret between the sender and receiver and this forms as one of the necessary conditions for the symmetric key ciphers to work. The method by which the keys are shared between the sender and receiver via a secure channel is out of the scope of this technique and the literature here makes no comment on how the keys must be shared. The technique proposes the cryptosystem wherein the keys are being used by the technique to encrypt and decrypt the transmitted text.

The increase in the social data has brought into the picture the need to harness the readily available social information to protect the same unsecure information that is being transmitted out. The proposed technique makes use of the fact that social information of the sender is readily available and should be made use of, to secure the data that sender is transmitting out to the receiver and hide it from unauthorized sniffer or attacker to gain access to information. For the same purpose, the social profiling information of the sender is made use of. The social profiling process points to the building of the identity of the user based on several social network activities and social network data that is readily available with the consent of the user from the user's local machine itself.

9.3.1 Key Arrangement

The primary candidate for building a secure symmetric cryptographic technique is the choice of the keys that ascertain the invulnerability of the technique to various threats. The good choices of strong keys, like good passwords, need to be hard to guess as well as must be bigger in size to counter the traditional attacks on them. The choice of the keys is critical to the security of the key and therefore the keys must be carefully handpicked. It is often noticed that a bad and small encryption key falls prey to attacks when used even on secure algorithms. To counter this problem of how to determine good candidates for secure encryption keys, a good technique must make that choice on the parameters and variables available to it. Often the most serious threat to an encryption technique is from the end user itself. To elaborate upon this statement, if the user chooses an easy to guess and a simple encryption key then it opens up the technique to a series of attacks. Therefore, reducing the human interaction element from the input domain and automating the process could also add to the security of the technique.

Keeping the above picture in perspective, the proposed technique makes use of an automated key selection procedure where the technique takes the keys from encryption environment itself without asking for the input from the end user. The cipher technique is focused on bringing the social aspect of end user into the cryptographic methodology and hence the social profiling information of the end user/sender makes for one of the primary keys in the technique.

The technique has a domain of five encryption keys that are kept secure and secret. The keys are not provided by the sender to the technique, hence, it adds to the security of the encryption technique and also makes it automated to be run. The sender only provides the plain text to the technique, and the cryptosystem encrypts the text before sending it to the receiver.

9.3.2 Key Selection

The first key is derived from the social profiling information of the user. The social profile, as explained above, is the social identity of the user which is derived from the data obtained from social networking information of the user. This technique makes use of the user's social browsing habits to identify the social interests of the user and hence, ascertain the field that patronizes the user's browsing. The browsing habits of user are analyzed over a period of 24-h window to predict the behavioral pattern of internet browsing by making use of the available browsing habits of user.

The cookies that are stored on the machine running the cryptographic technique (sender's system) are used to serve the purpose of the web profiling of the user. Data from the cookies are read by the technique and the websites browsed by the user over a period of 24-h is analyzed. These websites are then matched against a table of stored websites and the type of category that website belongs to. For instance, there are a set of pre-defined categories available with a list of sets belonging to each category, like Sports, Movies, Education, Music, Games, News, Finance, etc. The websites are matched against these categories and the category with the greatest number of matched websites is chosen. This predicts the user's interest area and this interest area has a predefined encryption defined against it which is then used as one of the encryption keys. The key-category pair value changes periodically over a period of time so as to exempt any kind of pattern to be formed by making use of same keys. For the websites that do not match any of the pre-defined categories a counter for miscellaneous category is incremented and if the miscellaneous category is maximum then the key is picked up from the miscellaneous key-category pair and that is used as the first encryption key.

The second key is selected by using the physical address of the machine (MAC address) that is running the cryptographic technique and from which the first key was selected. The alphanumeric MAC address is converted into a numerical key and the colon separators are removed from between. The alphabets are mapped into a corresponding number where A is mapped to 1, B to 2, and so on till Z is mapped to 26. The obtained number serves as the second key of cryptographic system.

The third key is chosen to be the current timestamp when the user starts the execution of the encryption mechanism. The current timestamp in milliseconds is used as the key and ensures every round of execution of cryptographic technique ensures a new key and hence makes it difficult for the attacker to sniff around and obtain the flowing encrypted data out of the system as plain text. The third key needs to be co-prime with the number of characters in the encoding standard being used. For instance, the illustration uses the ASCII character set, hence the third key needs to be co-prime with 256. If that is not the case, then the nearest upper bound co-prime of current timestamp with 256 is used as the third key.

The geographical coordinates of the user also form a basis of the social profile of the user. The demographic information is therefore used as the last two keys of the crypto system. The latitude and longitude serve as the fourth and the fifth key respectively and they are easily calculated with the user's current location.

The set of five chosen keys is selected in such a manner that they are always unique to every user, every machine and every encryption round. This setup is similar to the rotational key setup where the keys are changed periodically. The advantage of such a unique keyset is that they are always hard to guess or be obtained easily by the attacker and thus, this increases the overall security of the encryption cryptosystem by manifolds.

9.3.3 Mathematical Operations

Another candidate that decides the effectiveness as well as the security of the technique is the operations that are being performed on the text using the keys to encrypt the data. The symmetric key cypher technique uses the same set of keys for both the encryption as well as decryption of the data. Along with the same set of keys, the symmetric cipher technique also uses the same set of mathematical operations for encryption and the counter mathematical operations for decryption of the data. By counter mathematical operation, we refer to the family of mathematical operation where the use of an operation with a key would map the characters to a different set of characters, and the use of a different operation with same keys on the new character set gives back the original text. This second operation is referred to as the counter operation to the first operation. A very primitive example of this is the operation Addition and counter operation is Subtraction. If we add 5 (mapped as key) to a number 10 (original text), we get 15 (cipher text). If we subtract the same key, 5, from the cipher text, 15, we get the original text back which was 10.

The proposed cryptographic system has introduced a lightweight cryptography technique that makes use of primitive mathematical operation which makes the technique fast without making any compromise on the security of the data being transmitted. A good technique must be secure as well as be quick to avoid any kind of notable delays in transmitting data between sender and receiver. The operations that are being used by any technique must also be easy to implement in the hardware system. Often using heavier mathematical operations requires more expensive hardware implementations and therefore adds to the overall cost of transmitting data. The proposed technique makes use of cheaper mathematical operations which are both cost-effective as well as faster in terms of processing speeds.

The technique makes use of the following mathematical operations to encrypt the data in a predefined order (discussed in next two sections):

1. Addition
2. Subtraction
3. XOR
4. Multiplication
5. Bit dispersion

The bit dispersion mathematical operation garbles the length of the text by varying the plaintext length to that of the final cipher text length. This makes it harder for the attacker to map the length of the plain text to that of the cipher text thereby decreasing the probability of linear attacks on the technique. The use of multiple mathematical operations along with the use of multiple keys to encrypt and decrypt the data makes it harder to decipher the cipher text.

9.3.4 Algorithm

This section presents the algorithm of the socio-behavioral cipher technique. First algorithm deals with the selection of the first key from the social web profiling of the user and loading of other four keys:

Step 1: Start
Step 2: read cookies <= 24 hours
Step 3: store website name from cookies → website[n]
Step 4: initialize i → 1
Step 5: load category database containing pre-defined websites
Step 6: if website[i] = db(category, website)
Step 7: increment category count
Step 8: increment i
Step 9: Repeat steps 7 through 9 till i > n
Step 10: choose max_count(category)
Step 11: choose key against max_count(category) → K1
Step 12: fetch MAC address
Step 13: convert(MAC) to ASCII → K2
Step 14: get current timestamp in milliseconds → K3
Step 15: if coprime(K3, 256) is false
Step 16: nearest_coprime(K3, 256) → K3
Step 17: fetch current location latitude → K4
Step 18: fetch current location longitude → K5
Step 19: end

The above algorithm shows how the five keys are loaded into the system and are made available for the cryptographic technique to be used. Second algorithm depicts the encryption process performed on these keys:

Step 1: start
Step 2: accept plaintext from user → PT
Step 3: load keys K1, K2, K3, K4, K5
Step 4: convert PT to ASCII decimal → P
Step 5: XOR(P, K1) → E1
Step 6: Subtract(E1, K2) → E2
Step 7: Multiply(E2, K3) → E3
Step 8: Addition(E3, K4) → E4
Step 9: Dispersion(E4, K5) → C
Step 10: return final Cipher Text as ASCII character → CT
Step 11: end

Similarly, the decryption algorithm works with encryption steps performed in a counter fashion. The decryption process is intuitive and therefore the algorithm has not been presented in this text.

9.3.5 Encryption Operation

This section brings forward a conjectural adoption of the discussed cryptographic technique in the previous sections on a sample plaintext and input keys. The example illustration uses the ASCII character set to work on for the technique; however, the actual implementation of the technique is not limited to the ASCII character set and can easily work on the Unicode characters too.

The ASCII characters are first encoded into the decimal number notation to perform the mathematical operations on them. The bit dispersion method accepts an ASCII character in binary form of 8 bits each and then groups the binary bits of the entire plaintext together, and then groups them into buckets of 7 bits each and then converts these 7 bits of binary bits into the corresponding ASCII character which is forwarded as the final cipher text. If the last bucket has bits less than 7 then the last bucket is appended with trailing zeroes as the padding bits.

The example illustrates the process of encryption and the section that follows talks about the decryption process in detail on the sample plaintext and an input of five keys. The actual keys that the technique uses have been defined in the previous section but have been briefed below:

1. Key 1: Social Profiling key based on category
2. Key 2: Physical MAC address
3. Key 3: Current timestamp in milliseconds
4. Key 4: Latitude of current location
5. Key 5: Longitude of current location

The example below illustrates a sample plaintext as well as it assumes simpler values of the five private keys that are always kept private between the sender and receiver and are not shared with the outside world.

- Plaintext- PROFILE

Let the private keys be (assumption: The example mentioned below uses smaller values of the five encryption keys for making the mathematical calculations easy and simple for demonstration purposes).

- $K_1 = 17$,
- $K_2 = 29$,
- $K_3 = 37$,
- $K_4 = 47$,
- $K_5 = 30$

The technique makes use of following sequential mathematical operations to obtain a cipher text which is then transmitted to the receiver over an unsecure channel:

$$E_1 = (PT\ XOR\ K_1)$$
$$E_2 = (E_1 - K_2) \bmod 256$$
$$E_3 = (E_2 * K_3) \bmod 256$$
$$E_4 = (E_3 + K_4) \bmod 256$$
$$E_5 = (E_4\ XOR\ K_5)$$
$$C.T. = \text{bit dispersion } (E_5)$$

Table 9.1 describes the process with the help of an example and briefs the working of the technique and Figure 9.1 shows the encryption through a flowchart.

9.3.6 Decryption Operation

The process of the decryption is used to obtain the plain text from the cipher text at the receiver's end. The secret keys have already been shared between the sender and the receiver. The final cipher text was obtained from the bit dispersion method, so the decryption process must begin with the reverse bit-dispersion method. This process takes the Cipher text and converts the ASCII values into binary bits which are then grouped together as character stream. This character stream is then converted back by regrouping into the 8-bit binary bits and discarding the additional padding (if any). The 8-bits are converted back into the ASCII numbers which become the input for the further mathematical operations of the decryption process. Mathematically, the process is carried out as follows:

- Cipher text, C is **>lq(}!b<**
- $K_1 = 17$,
- $K_2 = 29$,
- $K_3 = 37$,
- $K_4 = 47$,

- $K_5 = 30$.
- The modulo multiplicative inverse to be used for the decryption process is depicted below:

$K_3 = 37$ and $K_3^{-1} = 173$ (K_3 must be co-prime with 256 for inverse to exist.)

The resultant final message which is the Plain-Text can be formulated by the receiver by employing the use of following specified mathematical steps:

$$D_c = \text{reverse bit dispersion } (C)$$
$$D_1 = (D_c \text{ XOR } K_5)$$
$$D_2 = (D_1 - K_4) \bmod 256$$
$$D_3 = (D_1 * K_3^{-1}) \bmod 256$$
$$D_4 = (D_3 + K_2) \bmod 256$$
$$P.T = (D_4 \text{ XOR } K_1)$$

D_1, D_2, D_3, and D_4 are intermediate decryption step texts obtained and C is the input cipher text to the decryption algorithm along with five keys. D_c is the output of the reverse bit dispersion function.

The final plain text is denoted as D_5 and can easily be derived as it is received at the receiver's end. In order to ensure the security of the crypto-system, the sender and receiver must keep both the private keys as well as the order in which the mathematical operations are being performed as secret between the two of them and must be only shared over a secure channel (The key transmission and sharing is out of scope of the literature here). The length of cipher text and plain text are different thus avoiding the linear mapping of characters.

The above example has been simulated in Java with the same keys and plaintext as above. The actual implementation, also made in Java, only accepts the plaintext from the user and computes the keys as described in the previous sections.

Tables 9.1, 9.2, 9.3, and 9.4 list out the illustrative example along with each of the steps that have been performed on the plaintext along with the assumed set of keys. The entire process that has been briefed in the previous two sections has been illustrated in a tabular form for better understanding. Further, Table 9.5 lists out a sample database of websites along with categories, which are used for the computation of the Key 1. Table 9.6 has a sample list of websites that have been obtained from the user cookies which are cross-referenced against the websites sample list

Table 9.1 Encryption table.

P.T.	E_1 = (P.T. XOR K_1)	$E_2 = (E_1 - K_2)$ mod 256	$E_3 = (E_2 * K_3)$ mod 256	$E_4 = (E_3 + K_4)$ mod 256	$E_5 = (E_4$ XOR $K_1)$
P(80)	(80 XOR 17) = 65 (A)	(65 – 29) mod 256 = 36 ($)	(36 * 37) mod 256 = 52 (4)	(52 + 47) mod 256 = 99 (c)	(99 XOR 30) = 125 (})
R(82)	(82 XOR 17) = 67 (C)	(67 – 29) mod 256 = 38 (&)	(38 * 37) mod 256 = 126 (~)	(126 + 47) mod 256 = 173 (¡)	(173 XOR 30) = 179 (|)
O(79)	(79 XOR 17) = 94 (^)	(94 – 29) mod 256 = 65 (A)	(65 * 37) mod 256 = 101 (e)	(101 + 47) mod 256 = 148 (ö)	(148 XOR 30) = 138 (è)
F(70)	(70 XOR 17) = 87 (W)	(87 – 29) mod 256 = 58 (:)	(58 * 37) mod 256 = 98 (b)	(98 + 47) mod 256 = 145 (æ)	(145 XOR 30) = 143 (Å)
I(73)	(73 XOR 17) = 88 (X)	(88 – 29) mod 256 = 59 (;)	(59 * 37) mod 256 = 135 (ç)	(135 + 47) mod 256 = 182 (╢)	(182 XOR 30) = 168 (¿)
L(76)	(76 XOR 17) = 93 (])	(93 – 29) mod 256 = 64 (@)	(64 * 37) mod 256 = 64 (@)	(64 + 47) mod 256 = 111 (o)	(111 XOR 30) = 113 (q)
E(69)	(69 XOR 17) = 84 (T)	(84 – 29) mod 256 = 55 (7)	(55 * 37) mod 256 = 243 (≤)	(243 + 47) mod 256 = 34 (“)	(34 XOR 30) = 60 (<)

Table 9.2 Bit dispersion operation.

Obtained E_5	125	179	138	143	168	113	60	
E_5 ***binary***	01111101	10110011	10001010	10001111	10101000	01110001	00111100	
Cipher	0111110	1101100	1110001	0101000	1111101	0100001	1100010	0111100
Cipher Text	62	108	113	40	125	33	98	60

Final transmitted cipher text for CRYPTO plaintext is >**lq(}!b<.**

Table 9.3 Reverse bit dispersion operation.

Obtained C	62	108	113	40	125	33	98	60
C in binary	0111110	1101100	1110001	0101000	1111101	0100001	1100010	0111100
Re-Dispersed	01111101	10110011	10001010	10001111	10101000	01110001	00111100	
Dispersed ASCII	12	17	138	14	16	113	60	

Table 9.4 Decryption table.

D_c	$D_1 = (C \text{ XOR } K_5)$	$D_2 = (D_1 - K_4) \bmod 256$	$D_3 = (D_2 * K_3^{-1}) \bmod 256$	$D_4 = (D_3 + K_2) \bmod 256$	$D_5 = (D_4 \text{ XOR } K_1)$
} (125)	(125 XOR 30) = 99 (c)	(99 – 47) mod 256 = 52 (4)	(52 * 173) mod 256 = 36 ($)	(36 + 29) mod 256 = 65 (A)	(65 XOR 17) = 80 (P)
| (179)	(179 XOR 30) = 173 (¡)	(173 – 47) mod 256 = 126 (~)	(126 * 173) mod 256 = 38 (&)	(38 + 29) mod 256 = 67 (C)	(67 XOR 17) = 82 (R)
è (138)	(138 XOR 30) = 148 (ö)	(148 – 47) mod 256 = 101 (e)	(101 * 173) mod 256 = 65 (A)	(65 + 29) mod 256 = 94 (^)	(94 XOR 17) = 79 (O)
Å (143)	(143 XOR 30) = 145 (æ)	(145 – 47) mod 256 = 98 (b)	(98 * 173) mod 256 = 58 (:)	(58 + 29) mod 256 = 87 (W)	(87 XOR 17) = 70 (F)
¿ (168)	(168 XOR 30) = 182 (╢)	(182 – 47) mod 256 = 135 (ç)	(135 * 173) mod 256 = 59 (;)	(59 + 29) mod 256 = 88 (X)	(88 XOR 17) = 73 (I)
q (113)	(113 XOR 30) = 111 (o)	(111 – 47) mod 256 = 64 (@)	(64 * 173) mod 256 = 64 (@)	(64 + 29) mod 256 = 93 (])	(93 XOR 17) = 76 (L)
< (60)	(60 XOR 30) = 34 (“)	(34 – 47) mod 256 = 243 (≤)	(243 * 173) mod 256 = 55 (7)	(55 + 29) mod 256 = 84 (T)	(84 XOR 17) = 69 (E)

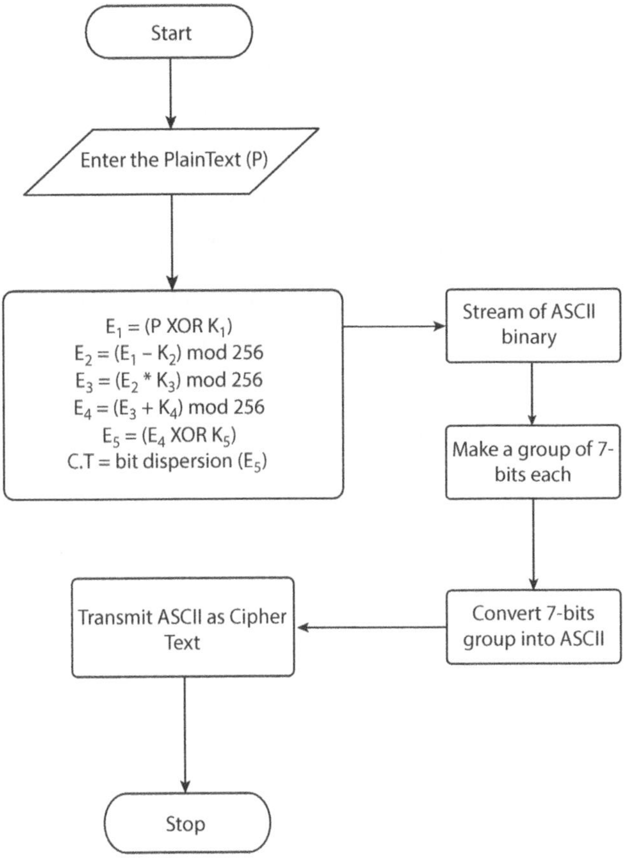

Figure 9.1 Flowchart for encryption.

in Table 9.5. The matching websites against each category increment the value of counter for that category. The category with maximum value at the end of the cookie list is picked up from the pool and the key associated with the chosen category is used as Key 1. The categories that are to be used as listed below:

1. News
2. Music
3. Movies
4. Games

The Tables 9.5 and 9.6 indicate the list of websites (the links of each website used here have been added to the references section at the end

Table 9.5 List of sample websites [17–47].

News	Music	Movies	Games
The Hindu	SoundCloud	The Internet Archive	Miniclip
Times of India	YouTube	Retrovision	Armor Games
NDTV News	SoundClick	Roku Channel	Kongregate
India Today	AudioMack	Sony Crackle	NewGrounds
Deccan Chronicle	Jamendo	Pluto TV	Steam
The Indian Express	Amazon Music	PopCornFlix	Nitrome
The Financial Express	CCTrax	Hulu	AddictingGames

Table 9.6 List of websites obtained from cookies.

Cookies
The Hindu
YouTube
SoundClick
Hulu
Steam
Amazon Music
NDTV News
Roku Channel
YouTube

of the chapter). The website list in the user's cookie database shows the usage of the list of websites, which the user has accessed over the past 24 h. The count of the matches of websites with the category names is listed below:

1. News: 2
2. Music: 4
3. Movies: 2
4. Games: 1

This list clearly indicates that based on browsing habits of the user over a period of 24 h, the user has a preference of music over other three categories. Hence, the key associated to the category music is picked and is chosen as the key 1.

9.3.7 Mathematical Modeling

The Socio-Behavioral Cipher Technique employs the use of several mathematical operations for the purpose of the Encryption as well as Decryption operation. These mathematical operations have been revisited in this section to be depicted as mathematical equations. As a widely known fact, the encryption operation can be thought of a s a mathematical operation that takes in a series of mathematical operation(s) and a domain of plain- text and outputs a cipher text. This cipher text can be mathematically depicted to be obtained by a cipher function, C(q) parsed through mathematical operations. This function can be used in reverse to obtain the initial plain-text and this operation is known as the decryption operation.

$C(q) = BitDispersion\ (E_5(q))$ *where,* $E_5(q) = (E_4(q)\ XOR\ K_5(q))$,
and, $E_4(q) = (E_3(q) + K_4(q))\ mod\ 256$,
and, $E_3(q) = (E_2(q) * K_3(q))\ mod\ 256$,
and, $E_2(q) = (E_1(q) - K_2(q))\ mod\ 256$,
and, $E_1(q) = ((P(q)\ XOR\ K_1(q))$
where $P(q)$ is plaintext length of size N_n,
$E(q)$ is the encryption function set which is composed of the five Encryption steps $E_1(q)$, $E_2(q)$, $E_3(q)$, $E_4(q)$, and $E_5(q)$,
and $K(q)$ is the private key set comprised of five keys $K_1(q)$, $K_2(q)$, $K_3(q)$, $K_4(q)$, and $K_5(q)$, which are being used by the encryption function set, each encryption function consuming

individual keys on each single character of plain-text of size Nn. However, the bit dispersion operation that is being used here scrambles the obtained text and it is impossible to have on-to-one-character mapping between the cipher text and plain text, hence the cipher text length is different from that of plain text and length of cipher text C(q) can be denoted as m*

1. The results of each encryption operation have been denoted as intermediary steps by E1…E5 and the result obtained is encoded as a numerical value which needs to be converted into the corresponding ASCII value. This value is finally transmitted as the cipher text from sender to the receiver end. The process of decoding the values of a cipher text of length "n" is performed by taking each functional integral value and then individually converting the integer to its corresponding ASCII character set, where the number is a "Real Whole number" and is in the range $0 < C_x(q) < 255$, *where* $C_x(q)$ *represents the individual character from the set of Cipher text C, comprised of* $\{C_0(q), C_1(q), C_2(q),\ldots C_n(q)\}$.

2. The text obtained as a result of applying the Encryption function at step $E_5(q)$ is fed to the method 'Bit Dispersion' where it groups the set of input bits and scrambles them into a new group of bits that constitute the final cipher text. The method takes in a set of numerical values in Base10 Decimal form and then converts them to Base2 Binary format. The Base10 to Base2 (Decimal to Binary) conversion is done for every individual number which is a part of the input set of 'Bit Dispersion' method. The conversion rule for each bit q_i can be summarized as:

   $Q_1 = q_i/2$ where q_i denotes the decimal bit and operation returns a remainder y_0,
   $Q_2 = y_0 2$ where the operation returns a remainder as y_1, until the quotient Q_x is 0.
   The final Binary number that is obtained has x number of bits where this x denotes the step where Quotient was 0 and x will always belong to a set of Natural Integer. The number of bits will be in the range $0 < x < 9$, since the

mathematical operations are using the MOD operation with 256, hence the number of bits can never be greater than 8. The final binary text for each individual decimal number can be denoted as $y_0\ y_1\ y_2\ y_3\ y_4\ y_5\ y_6\ y_7$ where the "y" denotes the remainders at every step.

3. The "Bit Dispersion" method is aimed at accepting a number, converting the Integer number to a binary number and then perform bit scrambling operation to return a new Binary number which is then converted back to the Integer number which is the final output. The Decimal to Binary conversion returns an 8-bit binary number for every single decimal number, as explained above. All the binary values are then clubbed together and a group of 7 bit each is formed from these. The group of 7 binary bits is converted back to Decimal number and this forms the Cipher Text. The $E_5(q)$ is composed of "n" number of numbers where 'n' is the length of plain-text and can be denoted as:

   $E_5(q) = R_1\ R_2\ R_3\ \ldots..\ R_n$
   Each R_i *can be denoted as Binary number of 8 bits each as* $y_0 y_1 y_2 y_3 y_4 y_5 y_6 y_7$
   Thus, $E_5(q) = y_{0R1} y_{1R1} y_{2R1} y_{3R1} y_{4R1}\ y_{5R1}\ y_{6R1}\ y_{7R1}\ y_{0R2}\ y_{1R2}\ y_{2R2}\ y_{3R2}\ y_{4R2}\ y_{5R2}\ y_{6R2}\ y_{7R2} \ldots..\ y_{0Rn}\ y_{1Rn}\ y_{2Rn}\ y_{3Rn}\ y_{4Rn}\ y_{5Rn}\ y_{6Rn}\ y_{7Rn}$
   $C(q) = y_{0R1}\ y_{1R1}\ y_{2R1}\ y_{3R1}\ y_{4R1}\ y_{5R1}\ y_{6R1}\ y_{7R1}\ y_{0R2}\ y_{1R2}\ y_{2R2}\ y_{3R2}\ y_{4R2}\ y_{5R2}\ y_{6R2}\ y_{7R2}\ y_{0R3}\ y_{1R3}\ y_{2R3}\ y_{3R3}\ y_{4R3} \ldots\ldots.$

   Converting the group of 7 Binary bits into the Decimal bits will return a set with a different length than "n" since the text has been scrambled. The new length of cipher text is denoted as "m*" and the final cipher text which is the result of the "Bit Dispersion" method is shown:
   $C(q) = C_1\ C_2\ C_3 \ldots\ldots.\ C_{m*}$

4. The Binary to Decimal operation is also required where the transformation occurs when converting the Base2 binary value to a Base10 Decimal number. This operation is important to obtain the final Cipher Text number. The transformation takes in an 8-bit binary number which is represented as $y_7\ y_6\ y_5\ y_4\ y_3\ y_2\ y_1\ y_0$ which is then converted into a

Table 9.7 Time calculation.

S. no.	Operations	Time taken
1.	First encryption $E_1(q)$	ΔT_0
2.	Second encryption $E_2(q)$	ΔT_1
3.	Third encryption $E_3(q)$	ΔT_2
4.	Fourth encryption $E_4(q)$	ΔT_3
5.	Fifth encryption $E_5(q)$	ΔT_4
6.	Final cipher text C(q)	ΔT_5
7.	Computing social key	ΔT_6
8.	Decimal to binary conversion	ΔT_7
9.	Bit dispersion operation	ΔT_8
10.	Binary to decimal conversion	ΔT_9
11.	ASCII to character mapping	ΔT_{10}
12.	Character to ASCII mapping	ΔT_{11}

single Base10 Decimal denoted as 'R' and can be computed as shown below:

$$R = (y_0 \times 2^0) + (y_1 \times 2^1) + (y_2 \times 2^2) + (y_3 \times 2^3) + (y_4 \times 2^4) + (y_5 \times 2^5) + (y_6 \times 2^6) + (y_7 \times 2^7)$$

5. The decimal numbers must be mapped into a corresponding ASCII character before it can be transmitted. The process of encoding the Decimal number to ASCII character and decoding the ASCII character to the decimal number will not alter the length of the input and will always return an output of same length as that of the input. The encoding operation is useful to compute the final encrypted cipher text which will be transmitted to the receiver and is also used to obtain the final plain-text on the receiver's end. However, the decoding operation is used by the sender to convert the

plain-text into the decimal numbers to perform mathematical operations on to it and is also used by the receiver to change the received cipher text into decimal numbers to be able to perform decryption operations on to it.

6. The execution time can be broken into 12 parts as specified by Table 9.7 and average execution time, T, can be denoted as, $T = (\Delta T_0 + \Delta T_1 + \Delta T_2 + \Delta T_3 + \Delta T_4 + \Delta T_5 + \Delta T_6 + \Delta T_7 + \Delta T_8 + \Delta T_9 + \Delta T_{10} + \Delta T_{11})/12$.
7. The Socio-Behavioral Cipher Technique has an O (n) time complexity (denoted in Big-Oh notation) where n is the total characters in the input plain-text.

9.4 Conclusion: Future Scope and Limitations

The Socio-Behavioral cipher technique is a light-weight and a robust crypto technique which has a minimalistic execution time of encrypting the data. The technique is fast but is also secure by making use of multiple keys and multiple operations. The technique does not require heavy computations and have any additional hardware requirements to implement the crypto-system. The use of cost-effective mathematical operations along with the automatic selection of keys by the crypto-system, make it a secure technique. The cipher technique's unique key selection mechanism and its use of the social browsing habits of the sender have blended the field of cryptography with the web profiling of user's browsing behavior. This unique blend of social networking with cryptography makes the technique accurate to be used in the world where social data marks the majority of every day's network traffic flowing via the internet.

The Socio-Behavioral Cipher Technique has been compared with its predecessor Triplicative Cipher Technique [19], where the running time has been compared of the two techniques. The results draw a clear picture toward the more advanced Socio-Behavioral technique which is both faster as well as stronger of the two cipher techniques as is depicted in the Figure 9.2. The cryptographic technique was simulated on a Java based simulation environment whose specifications are listed in Table 9.3. The output of the simulation is depicted by Figure 9.3.

The proposed innovative Socio-Behavioral technique is a symmetric key cryptographic technique; however, in the future, efforts would be made

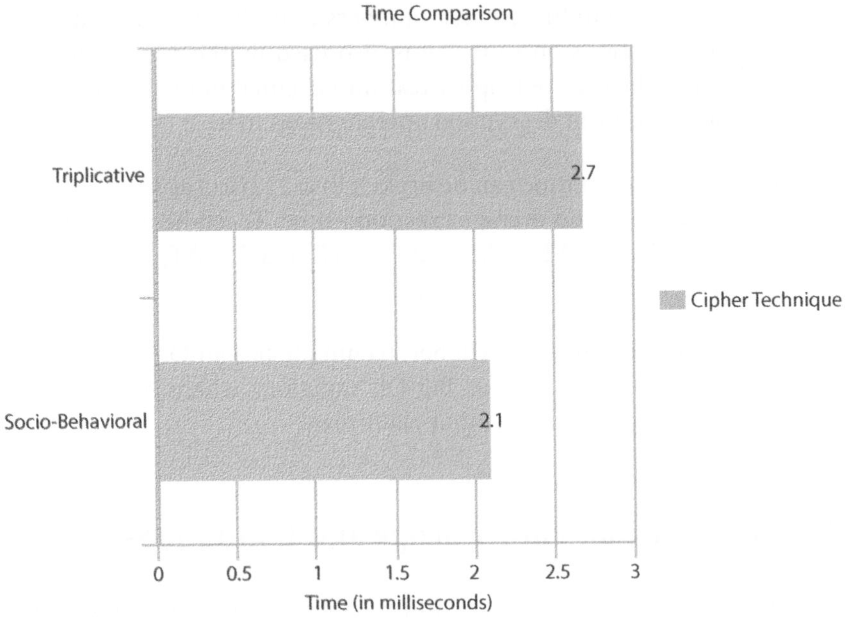

Figure 9.2 Comparison of the results of triplicative and socio-behavioral cipher technique [19].

to extend it to be an asymmetric key cryptographic technique. The asymmetric cryptographic technique instead of a single key domain which is used for both encryption and decryption, a pair of public and private key is used, which is turn is helpful to enhance the prevailing level of security. Currently, the Socio-Behavioral technique uses a series of concrete yet simple mathematical operations on the user's plain-text input and returns an encrypted cipher text by performing the operations in a pre-defined order. However, in future, the current work would be extended to pick the mathematical operations from a pool of operations in a random order that would change with every cycle of encryption. After such an implementation, a comparison of the two techniques would be carried out and the results would be compared. Currently, the proposed technique makes use of an automated key selection procedure. Similarly, in future it is proposed to come up new and innovative ways and means as to how the technique would take more keys from encryption environment itself without prompting for the input from the end user creating a perfect socially compatible cryptographic environment. Not only this, though the current cipher technique is focused on bringing the social aspect of end user into the cryptographic

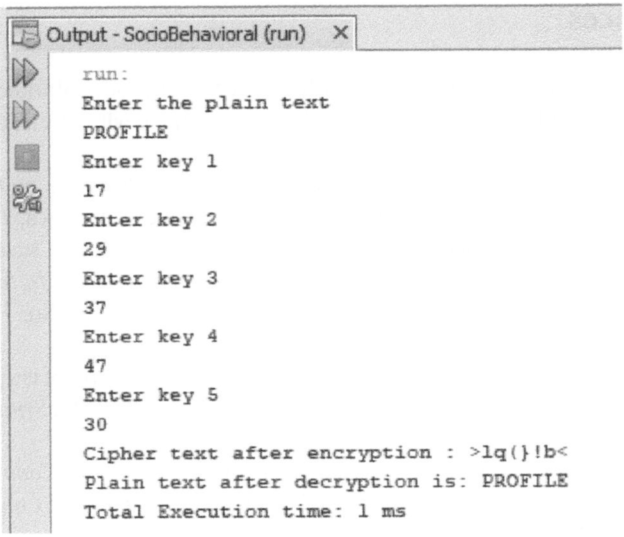
Output - SocioBehavioral (run)
run:
Enter the plain text
PROFILE
Enter key 1
17
Enter key 2
29
Enter key 3
37
Enter key 4
47
Enter key 5
30
Cipher text after encryption : >lq(}!b<
Plain text after decryption is: PROFILE
Total Execution time: 1 ms

Figure 9.3 Output for socio-behavioral technique simulation as example illustration.

Table 9.8 Simulation table.

Simulation environment	
O.S. used	Windows 10 Pro 64 bit
Processor	Intel Core i5 3230M
RAM	8 GB
Simulation Env	NetBeans IDE
IDE version	8.2.0 build 201403101706
Development Lang	Java
Build Version	1.8.0 build 25.25-b02

methodology but in future more social profiling information like Caching of Facebook and Instagram details of the end user/sender would be taken into consideration. The newly proposed technique is currently using only five keys, but the new and improved version of this technique would use more keys and the results would be compared in order to achieve efficient and socio secure encryption technique.

References

1. Forouzan, B.A., *Cryptography and Network Security*, Special Indian Edition, McGraw-Hill, published in India by arrangement with the McGraw-Hill Companies, Inc., New York, 2007.
2. Stallings, W., *Cryptography and Network Security-Principles and Practices*, fourth Edition, Pearson, printed in the United State of America, 2007.
3. Preneel, B., Cryptography for network security: Failures, successes and challenges, *International Conference on Mathematical Methods, Models, and Architectures for Computer Network Security*, Springer, Berlin, Heidelberg, 2010.
4. Duong, T. and Rizzo, J., Cryptography in the web: The case of cryptographic design flaws in asp. net, *Security and Privacy (SP), 2011 IEEE Symposium on. IEEE*, 2011.
5. Devi, T.R., Importance of cryptography in network security, *Communication Systems and Network Technologies (CSNT), 2013 International Conference on. IEEE*, 2013.
6. Ma, J. *et al.*, SHAvisual: A secure hash algorithm visualization tool, *Proceedings of the 2014 conference on Innovation and technology in computer science education*, ACM, 2014.
7. Nilesh, D. and Nagle, M., The new cryptography algorithm with high throughput, *Computer Communication and Informatics (ICCCI), 2014 International Conference on. IEEE*, 2014.
8. Sabitha, S., User authentication using visual cryptography, *Control Communication and Computing India (ICCC), 2015 International Conference on. IEEE*, 2015.
9. Li, C. *et al.*, Vigvisual: A visualization tool for the vigenere cipher, *Proceedings of the 2015 ACM Conference on Innovation and Technology in Computer Science Education*, ACM, 2015.
10. Singh, L. and Johari, R., CLCT: Cross Language Cipher Technique, *International Symposium on Security in Computing and Communication*, Springer International Publishing, pp. 217–227, 2015.
11. Singh, L.D. and Singh, K.M., Implementation of text encryption using elliptic curve cryptography. *Procedia Comput. Sci.*, Jan 1, 54, 73–82, 2015.
12. Gupta, A., Semwal, S., Johari, R., METHS: Mapping from English Language to Hindi Language for Secure Commercial Transactions, *IEEE International Conference on Computing Communication and Automation 2.*
13. Kumar, M.G.V. and Ragupathy, U.S., A Survey on current key issues and status in cryptography, *Wireless Communications, Signal Processing and Networking (WiSPNET), International Conference on IEEE*, 2016.
14. Pandey, A. and Som, S., Applications and usage of visual cryptography: A review, *Reliability, Infocom Technologies and Optimization (Trends and Future Directions) (ICRITO), 2016 5th International Conference on. IEEE*, 2016.

15. Bhardwaj, A. and Som, S., Study of different cryptographic technique and challenges in future, *Innovation and Challenges in Cyber Security (ICICCS-INBUSH), 2016 International Conference on IEEE*, 2016.
16. Elhoseny, M., Yuan, X., El-Minir, H.K., Riad, A.M., An energy efficient encryption method for secure dynamic WSN. *Secur. Commun. Netw.*, Sep 10, 9, 13, 2024–31, 2016.
17. Singh, L. and Johari, R., CLCT: Cross Language Cipher Technique, *International Symposium on Security in Computing and Communication*, Springer International Publishing, pp. 217–227, 2015.
18. Jain, I., Johari, R., Ujjwal, R.L., CAVEAT: Credit Card Vulnerability Exhibition and Authentication Tool, *Second International Symposium on Security in Computing and Communications (SSCC"14)*, Springer, pp. 391–399, 2014.
19. Johari, R., Bhatia, H., Singh, S., Chauhan, M., Triplicative Cipher Technique. *Procedia Comput. Sci.*, 78, 217–223, 2016.
20. https://timesofindia.indiatimes.com/
21. https://www.thehindu.com/
22. https://www.ndtv.com/
23. https://www.indiatoday.in/
24. https://www.deccanchronicle.com/
25. https://indianexpress.com/
26. https://www.financialexpress.com/
27. https://soundcloud.com/
28. https://www.youtube.com/
29. https://www.soundclick.com/
30. https://audiomack.com/
31. https://www.jamendo.com/
32. https://music.amazon.com/
33. https://cctrax.com/
34. https://archive.org/details/movies
35. http://retrovision.tv/
36. https://channelstore.roku.com/browse/movies-and-tv
37. https://www.sonycrackle.com/
38. https://pluto.tv/
39. https://www.popcornflix.com/
40. https://www.hulu.com/
41. https://www.miniclip.com/games/en/
42. https://armorgames.com/
43. https://www.kongregate.com/
44. https://www.newgrounds.com/
45. https://store.steampowered.com/
46. http://www.nitrome.com/
47. http://www.addictinggames.com/

10

Intrusion Detection Strategies in Smart Grid

P. Ponmurugan[1]*, C. Venkatesh[2], M. Divya Priyadharshini[1] and S. Balamurugan[4]

[1]Department of Electrical and Electronics Engineering
Sri Krishna College of Technology, Kovaipudur, Coimbatore, India
[2]Engineering College, Tiruchengode, Namakkal, India
[3]Research & Development, QUANTS IS & CS, Coimbatore, India

Abstract

Cyber security turns vulnerable as a society becomes dependent on automated systems progressively for industrial applications, medicinal applications, and financial applications, etc. This chapter instigate with introduction to smart grid and the significance of detecting intrusion in it. This also addresses the various threats in security and detection of intrusion frameworks in smart grid. Cyber security can be improved by utilizing detection of intrusion to look for unseen attack patterns and actions. Intrusion detection has extensive roles in autonomous forensics systems to identify successful breaches. The earlier cyber-physical system is considered safe but due to vast diversity domain of cyber-physical system and everything are fastened to the internet makes cyber-physical system unsafe. There are various attacks successfully launched against cyber physical systems. Hackers launched many spiteful attacks on power networks. Several security weaknesses exist in all kind of cyber-physical systems. It is a cyber-physical system that includes hardware, software and physical components appropriately integrated, interacting and interrelating to sense the fluctuating state of the substantial world. Smart grid provides electricity on-demand to customers from both centralized and also distributed generation stations, using information and communication technologies. Ample of researches are on-going about intelligent grid system implementation. Most of these researches do not focus on the security requirement for it. Reliability is a key issue in its system development.

Corresponding author: murugan.pmsm@gmail.com

Dinesh Goyal, S. Balamurugan, Sheng-Lung Peng and O.P. Verma (eds.) Design and Analysis of Security Protocol for Communication, (211–234) © 2020 Scrivener Publishing LLC

IDS have engrossed importance in it. Detection and prevention of attacks in it is complicated when compared to Internet attacks. Hackers can use multiple stages to evade and access it.

Keywords: Smart grid, cyber security, intrusion detection systems, types of IDS, security issues

10.1 Introduction

The electrical grid that supplies power for our industrial and commercial needs is commonly referred as "The grid". It is a web of electrical machines like transformers, substations, and transmission lines and this network is exploited to its capacity. To extend it further we need to engineer a new one which is futuristic, automated, and well-grounded, which can handle the needs of this century. The automated connection established among transmission lines—for fault sensing, utility, and the customers defines the smart grid. It has controlling systems, computing systems, automated equipment with state of the art techniques, which are working together and responding for our changing demands, like Internet. Figure 10.1 shows the general architecture of the conventional smart grid.

10.2 Role of Smart Grid

The smart grid provides a remarkable future to the energy industry in terms economy and ecosystem by providing reliable and efficiency power system [1–4]. The benefits of Smart Grid include:

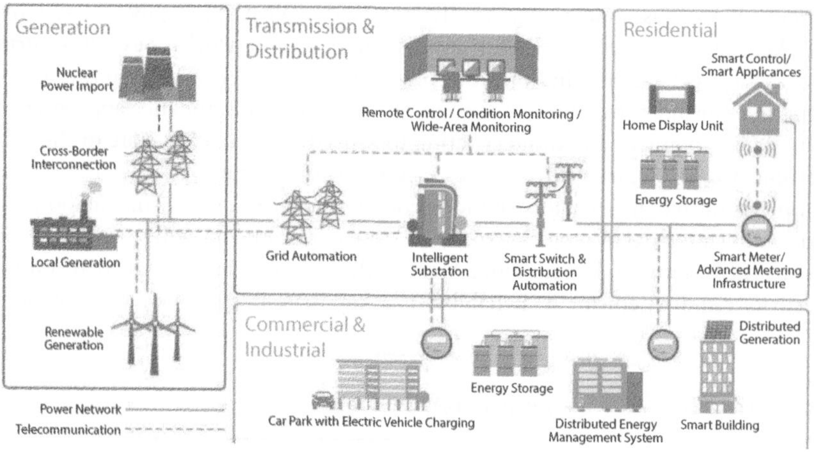

Figure 10.1 Smart grid architecture.

- ✓ Efficient electricity transmission than conventional systems
- ✓ Restoration after faults are quick
- ✓ Cost reduction for operations and management eventually reducing cost for consumer
- ✓ Low tariff as an effect of reduced demands
- ✓ Micro girds and sustainable grids are integrated better
- ✓ More secure

A blackout today can cost as much as space shuttle by affecting all industries such as banking, communications, traffic, security, and domestic needs especially on a hot summer day. If the gird is smart it will be more resilient and makes better decisions at the time of calamities both natural and manmade. A smarter grid has the capacity of automatic rerouting during faults because of its interactive ability. This two-way interaction also reduces the effects aftermath. During outages, smart grid identifies and isolates the fault before they become large scale. The newer smart grid technologies ensure a faster and strategic recovery after an emergency.

The Smart Grid takes greater benefits of customer-owned power generators in addition to power production when it is unavailable from utilities. By having "distributed generation" resources combined in a grid, health centre, police department, traffic lights, phone System, and grocery store keeps operating even during emergencies. Added to emergency operations it upgrades the older gird and replaces an intelligent grid. It increases awareness about interlink in energy use and environment and more energy efficient and brings improved national security to our energy system by consuming more sustainable energy which is available even during disasters.

10.3 Technical Challenges Involved in Smart Grid

With broader scope the potential standards and landscape of smart grid is also huge and complex. The basic issue in organizing and prioritizing smart grid is to make it interoperable and secure.

(i) Cyber security

A grid connected to the network is vulnerable and has various cyber-attacks in which most of them are unnoticed. It is essential to recognize and eliminate these threats in the system. Availability—reliable and timely access to database, Integrity—improper modification of system and confidentiality—secured from unauthorized access are the three main objectives of a secure smart grid. Security is an important issue to be addressed because any threat can cause damage to the grid. Some of the known attacks are hackers, DDoS, Malwares, etc [5–9]. Any such security provided should be able to tackle the eve growing cyber threats faced at all levels of smart grid.

(ii) Storage concerns

Smart Grid involves sustainable power resources for mass power generation in addition to distributed power generation. Power generated from renewable sources is ununiformed—they are infrequent, fluctuating, and requires storage. Battery which is most commonly used storage device has meager life span of 4 or 5 years and other technologies including flywheels, thermal storage, hydrogen storage, etc., have their own drawbacks whereas pumped storage techniques is 70–85% efficient. The setback in pumped storage techniques is that, it requires enormous areas as reservoirs, available only in hill side. Flywheels are competent in absorbing energy in fewer seconds and delivers quickly. Researches have proved that Flywheels are found useful in maintaining grid frequency for few seconds but unstable at long run [10–12]. The prevailing technique in electricity storage is batteries and lead-acid batteries are famous because of portability but has low energy density, weight, and size are also drawbacks in addition to shortage of raw material. Researches are done on increasing battery efficiency and reducing cost of storage but still they are expensive.

(iii) Data management

Smart Grid impregnate the grid with myriad meters, sensors and controllers to collect and enhance data to the operator's capability, like weather forecast, security cameras, etc. Meticulous analysis of data avoids a breakdown or damage well in prior and also this big data is used for system operation, alarms, forecasting demand, generation, price, etc. Affluent data collected from these devices are not only burdensome but also poses vital challenges in retrieval and handling. Database management is a significant affair in Smart Grid with voluminous data, process of data collection, analysis, and report generation are slowed down. Developing technology is important and necessary to manage the data, defining standards and protocols. Cloud technologies and IoT technology aid in analysis of big data and handling the processed data.

(iv) Communication issues

Having a broad ranges of communication technologies for implementation in Smart Grid but they all have their own setbacks. If a technology has bandwidth limitation while the other operates with range limitations, third has increased data loss and few others have limited success in underground installations. Smart grid lacks fool proof solution despite of the numerous benefits because the communication protocols for smart grid are not properly defined. Some of the known technologies under this category are GSM and GPRS with coverage of 10 km and poor data rate, PLCC, 3G with costlier spectrum, ZigBee has only a range of 30–50 m, Broad band over PLC, etc. Wired communication like power line communication has drawbacks of interferences yet it overcomes the issues of wireless communication. Optical fiber is known fast way of communication and also secure, but is uneconomical. Router based Radio Frequency technology with a canopy answers some problems, while it lacks the history of proven existing performance problems besides the economy issues.

(v) Stability concerns

Smart Grid incorporates various distributed generation (Renewables/sustainable energy sources) and micro grids (MGs) on a huge network. The distributed generation causes bidirectional flow of power. Renewable energy sources have various benefits over non-renewable/conventional source of energy and nuclear energy sources but have the advantages of high penetration. This penetration of renewables and MGs would increase the stability concerns like:

✓ Lower overall system inertia, which causes angular stability
✓ Lower power sharing support which effects voltage stability
✓ Low-frequency power oscillation.
✓ Transients of Smart grids during the islanding of micro grids.
✓ Inability to serve as system reserve

(vi) Energy management and electric vehicle
Using EV (electric vehicle) as storage element is a prospective proposal. Researches on electric vehicles for efficient utilization even during peak hour are under study. EV batteries can be charged in off peak period and used as source during peak periods. Few basic controls in managing energy through EV include:

- ✓ Flow of power from
  - ➢ V2G—vehicle to grid
  - ➢ G2V—grid to vehicle
  - ➢ V2V—Vehicle to vehicle
- ✓ Reactive power control.
- ✓ DC link voltage control.
- ✓ Grid voltage support.

All the above said controls are defined properly yet but they are still evolving. Development of such standards for electric vehicle battery connected to smart grid is undergoing.

10.4 Intrusion Detection System

Monitoring the network traffic for any suspicious activity or attacks and alerting the discovery of such activity is the duty of an intrusion detection system (IDS). While abnormality is detected, reporting of the anomaly is the primary function. Few intrusion detection systems have the capability to take actions when such malicious activities or anomalous traffic is found. The plausible solutions include blocking of traffic sent from malicious IP addresses.

Although IDS (intrusion detection systems) watches over the networks carefully for potentially malicious activity, they are also liable to false alarms (false positives). Eventually, organizations require fine-tuning their IDS products when it is installed which means correctly configuring their IDS (intrusion detection systems) to identify what normal traffic on their network looks like compared to potentially suspicious activity.

The IDS systems when implemented are usually attacked by malicious attacks by themselves and thus cautious steps should have to be made in securing those IDS systems appropriately. To employ a successful functional IDS system, multiple types of technologies must be used and information achieved must be comprehensive and cost benefit. Accurate identification of malicious activity and also economical at the same time justifies the deployment of the IDS.

10.5 General Architecture of Intrusion Detection System

Any intrusion detection system comprises of the following components in general. These components interacts with each other through a suitable input and output communication messages in order to collect, store, process, and analyze the data. Then the IDS draw the conclusions about the attacks. Figure 10.2 depicts the components present in an Intrusion Detection System. These components perform the below said functions.

Collector provides an interface for accessing data in the detection process. Network tap is commonly used as data collector. It accesses every raw network packets that can cross a certain position in a network. External databases or interfaces to host-based data are also used as collectors.

Detector carries out the actual detection process and acts as a core part of the system. It can access data given by collector, stores it, and decides what must be triggered as an alert signal.*User Interface* is used for reporting the collected results to the user, enabling the user to control the IDS and simultaneously accessing the storage, detector and responder.

Storage stores constant data for the detector or required to the user interface. These collected data are either copied by the detector directly or can be given as external input. Storage has the control to database system.

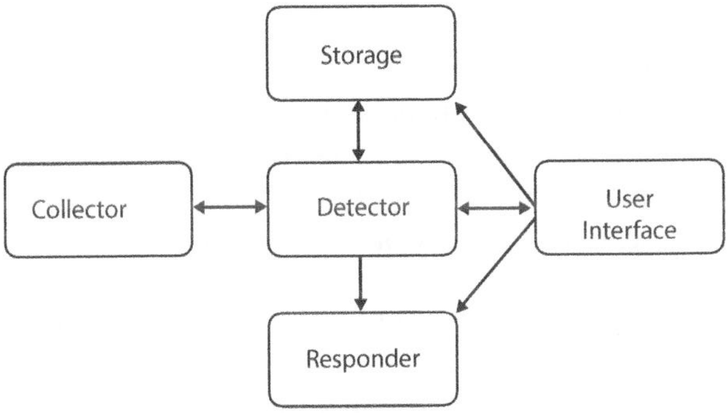

Figure 10.2 General components of an intrusion detection system.

Responder reacts to identify intrusions and regulated it to prevent further damage to the system's security. A response will be triggered automatically or manually through the user interface.

10.6 Basic Terms in IDS

Attack is the action manifested by one party, the intruder, against another party the victim system. The intruder or attacker stages an attack with certain predefined objective in plan. It is either a group events or a single event that may cause one or more security troubles over the system. Formulation to fulfill a predefined goal for intruder is called as attack.

Intrusion is a synonym for the word "attack" and it may also be called as victorious attack.

Intruder is someone who attacks the systems with or without true intentions and attacker is a synonym for intruder.

Incident is data collectively acknowledging one or more related attacks.

True Positive is the genuine attack which alerts produces an alert in IDS.

True Negative is when no alert is sent when no actual intrusion has taken place.

False negative is when the IDS has not detected or failed to detect an attack on the event of an actual attack.

False positive is when IDS mistakes an event as an attack but it is not truly an attack.

Confidence value is a pre-set value determined by the organization through analysis of previous events. This value is used for identification of future attacks.

Alarm filtering is identifying and differentiating the false positives and true attacks.

Burglar Alert/Alarm is an alert which is set out when the system is under attack.

Detection Rate is the ratio between the numbers of attacks detected to the total number of attacks available in the set value.

Vulnerability is a measure of weakness of systems and identification of weak point which are prone to attacks.

Exploit is using a vulnerability of a system to cause an attack against a security policy.

Trust is the degree of the confidence in which the system behaves as expected well as IDS.

Threat is any event with the potential to harm any essential element of the system.

Site policies are the policies about the IDS of an organization and its rules.

Site policy awareness is the ability to upgrade the organization site policy according to the changes in the environment for better performance.

10.7 Capabilities of IDS

Intrusion detection system monitors the network traffic to detect when an attack is through an unauthorized entity. Intrusion detection system does it by providing few or all of these functions to security professionals:

- ✓ Monitors the security control files (firewalls, routers, key management servers) which are easily targeted by the hackers
- ✓ A path for creating, adjusting, and analyzing the operation is providing to the administrator. These logs are usually offensive.
- ✓ A new user friendly environment is created for the armatures working in the system.
- ✓ Includes an enormous attack signature database against which information from the system can be matched.
- ✓ Recognizes and reports when the IDS identifies that data files have been changed or altered.
- ✓ Generates an alert and notifies that security is breached.
- ✓ Reacts to intruders by blocking them or blocking the server.

IDS are be implemented as: a) a software application running on customer hardware b) a network security appliance c) Cloud-based intrusion detection systems to protect data and systems in cloud deployments.

10.8 Benefits of Intrusion Detection Systems

Intrusion detection systems give organizations numerous advantages, starting with the ability to identify security incidents. It can be used in analyzing the quantity or the types of attacks. Organizations can use this data provided by the intrusion detection system to change their existing security systems or deploy more effective control systems. An intrusion detection system helps companies in identifying the bugs or problems associated with their network device configurations. These metrics given by the IDS can then be applied to assess future risks.

Intrusion detection systems help the enterprise to attain regulatory compliance and give companies a greater visibility over their networks by making it easier to define security regulations. In addition to this, businesses can apply their IDS logs as part of the documentation to prove that they are meeting certain compliance requirements.

Intrusion detection systems improve the security response because IDS sensors can identify the network hosts and devices. They can also be implemented to inspect data within the network packets, and also identify the operating systems of services which are being used. Using an IDS to gather such information can be a lot efficient that a manual censuses of connected systems.

10.9 Types of IDS

The different Intrusion Detection Systems which are categorized based on

(i) Detection Methods [13–15]

✓ Anomaly [16–18]

The anomaly-based IDS correlate the definition of activity which is considered as usual against identified events with the goal of implementing significant deviations. It has a benefit of being very efficient at identifying already known attacks but has drawbacks of recklessly including deviations from statistically normal behavior of the system within a profile (malicious activity).

Anomaly detection algorithms are grouped into supervised or unsupervised. Supervised algorithms are no training data is applied to derive the model (inferring) based on supervised learning, and the model is then applied to test data. This has a set of labeled data as input. One important point worth mentioning is the presence of unknown intrusions in the data applied as inputs to the supervised detection algorithm negatively affects the correctness of the classification. Examples of supervised algorithms are K-nearest neighbor, support vector mechanism (SVM), and decision trees, etc.

Unsupervised anomaly detection algorithms, on the other hand, are based on unsupervised learning where training data is used to derive the model by reasoning (inferring) and the model application just like the inference relies exclusively on test data. This takes a set of unlabeled data as input and attempts to find an intrusion in this data. The presence or absence of unknown attacks in the dataset does not affect the accuracy or performance of this classification. Examples of this category of algorithms are clustering algorithms which can be further subdivided into partition based, e.g., K-means, hierarchical-based and density-based.

✓ SPA (Stateful Protocol Analysis)

SPA process involves comparing the previously identified profiles of agreed definitions of agreed protocol activity for every observed events against each protocol state and tries to detect deviations [19, 20]. The analysis examines a single request or response at a time and as such has a drawback of not being able to detect any attacks that do not violate acceptable protocol behavior, such as denial of service (DOS) [21]. Intrusion detection that is specification-based which essentially compares an input with some specified protocol specifications is an example of SPA [22, 23].

(ii) Type of events they monitor and mode of deployment

✓ Network-based IDS

Network-based IDS watched over the network traffic for certain network segments or elements and compares the network and uses it protocol activities with the goal of detecting malicious activity [24]. This in most cases implemented at a boundary between networks, example is a closer border firewalls or routers, VPN (virtual private network) servers, wireless networks and remote access servers.

✓ Wireless IDS

Wireless IDS, as the name suggests, typically monitor wireless network traffic and analyses its wireless networking protocols to identify suspicious activity involving the protocols themselves. However, it cannot identify suspicious activity in the application layer or higher-layer network protocols such as transmission control protocol (TCP), and user datagram protocol (UDP) within the traffic transferred by the wireless network.

✓ Network behavior analysis IDS

Network behavior analysis IDS performs analysis of network traffic mainly to identify threats that generate unusual traffic flows, for example, distributed denial of service (DDoS) attacks and other existing policy violations.

✓ Host-based IDS
Host-based IDS looks at the characteristics of a single host and the events occurring within that host in search of the presence of any suspicious activity [25, 26].

10.10 IDS in a Smart Grid Environment

Smart grid is the combination of the communication network and power system. Malicious activity should be detected in either the communication network or the physical power system or both. The incorporation of the communication network and power system refers to the cyber-physical aspect of the smart grid. The Intrusion Detection Framework for the Smart Grid is shown in Figure 10.3.

Smart grid network is proposed for Home Area Network (HAN), Neighborhood Area Network (NAN), and Wide Area Network (WAN).

(i) Intrusion Detection in Home Area Network
Home area network is the first layer of the smart grid comprises of the service component and metering component. Service module provides energy consumption and cost. The metering module provides consumer home energy consumption. There will be one IDS for every HAN. IDS will track inbound and outbound communication to home area network to identify security breaches. At the time of security breaches, IDS will notify home area network and send this

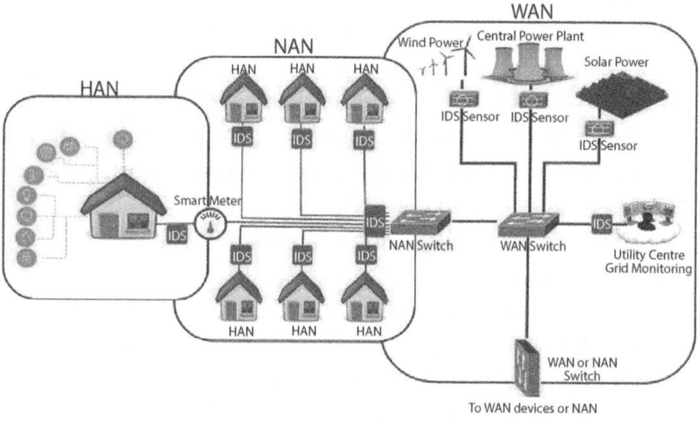

Figure 10.3 Intrusion detection framework architecture for the smart grid.

information to central operational network administrator of smart grid for further processing and necessary action.

A HAN (Home Area Network) can be any individual user of Smart Grid. These HAN networks consists of state of the art meters called smart meters which are implemented in the Smart Grid architecture and AMI (Advanced Metering Infrastructure) for enabling automatic two way communication between the utility provider and the utility meter.

10.10.1 Smart Meter

A smart meter is a common electronic device which records electric energy consumption in intervals (an hour or less) and communicates that information daily back and forth to the utility for billing and monitoring purposes. Three-phase meters are used in residential and commercial metering applications.

10.10.2 Metering Module

Metering module is used for measuring and transmitting fine-grained usage information of electric power and information on the power quality of electricity to the utility. This information is used for generating customer bills and also automatic control of the consumption of electricity through load control messages delivered to the smart meters.

(i) Intrusion Detection in Neighborhood Area Network
Neighborhood area network (NAN) is the second layer of the smart grid. The neighborhood area network is a large network, which collects service and metering information of multiple HANs that are geologically adjacent each other. The neighborhood area network consists of the smart meter data collector (SMDC) and a central access controller (CAC). There will be one IDS for every NAN. CAC act as an interface among HANs and energy supplier communication. The SMDC control all metering record for the entire HANs in neighborhood area network. All incoming and outgoing data will be passed through the neighborhood area network IDS for possible security threats. At the time of security breaches, IDS will send a notification to central operational network administrator of smart grid for supplementary handling and essential action.

One or more HAN Networks that are grouped and counted with interfaced with higher layer in the smart grid is called a NAN network. It is advanced level of metering and controlling network, which is used to collect metering and service information from the various HANs that are geographically situated close to each other. The utility provider will be able to watch the amount of power is being distributed to a certain neighborhood through a NAN by the distribution substation, respectively.

10.10.3 Central Access Control

The target of central access control is to ensure the sensor network services to be available to authorized users on time, even in presence of an internal or external attack. To reach this target, additional communication among nodes system may be adopted for successful delivery of every message to its recipient.

10.10.4 Smart Data Collector

Smart Data Collector is a communication gateway that coordinates communication within the NAN. It operates as the intermediary data concentrators, collecting and filtering data from groups of mesh-enabled meters, and economically sharing wide area network resources making communication more affordable while ensuring high performance.

(i) Intrusion Detection in Wide Area Network
Wide area network provides wireless and wired communication among distributed network devices, substation, NANs. This layer also contains SCADA controller, energy distributed system (EDS). There will be many IDS sensors at various location in the wide area network which are part of smart grid but not included in NANs. EDS regulate metering data and energy distribution. SCADA provides control to manage distribution grid elements. Data collected from IDS sensors in WAN will be correlated for possible malicious activity or violation of any security policy. The network administrator of the smart grid will be informed accordingly for additional processing and necessary action.

Broadband wired and wireless communication are provided in the WAN layer among the NAN, substations, other distributed grid devices, and the utility. This WAN layer must have similar characteristics to a foundation network, collecting information from the users and conveying it to the control centers of the Smart Grid.

10.10.5 Energy Distribution System

Energy distribution system possess of a wide range of fewer in scale and modular devices modeled to give electricity, and various other times also thermal energy, in locations situated near by consumers. They contain fossil and renewable energy technologies, storage devices for storing energy, and combination of heat and power systems.

10.10.6 SCADA Controller

SCADA (Supervisory Control and Data Acquisition) systems are PCS (Process Control Systems) which are used in monitoring, collecting, and comparing real-time environmental data simply from an office building or a nuclear power plant which is complex.

10.11 Security Issues of Cyber-Physical Smart Grid

The physical power system in a smart grid, and the information cyber system and technologies used for communication are highly coupled which introduced new security concerns. Smart grid security problems require addressing new challenges for available, safe, efficient, and stability of the grid. It is vital to observe that available security approaches are either not applicable to the system, not feasible, scalability is not sufficient, not compatible, or simply not enough and it must be replaced by new and complex techniques to make sure the enormous and complicated dynamic smart grid environment is safe [27]. Combinations of software, hardware, and communication protocols, which are components of power systems and they are integrated physically comprises a smart grid [28].

The islanding of physical power system cannot be captured as a complete profile because in a smart grid both physical system and cyber security system are important and any issues regarding security is not well recorded. The problems associated with the cyber physical smart gird are:

1. Faults in the physical power system components of the smart grid
2. Issues in the control system centers and control applications
3. Stability issues, reliability issues, and efficiency of operation for the cyber infrastructure planning.
4. The aftermath of the cyber-attack and its comparison with physical impacts.
5. Protection against such cyber threats.

A smart grid is considered as the backbone of physical power system. Recently, many such loads are being included in the grid, including plug-in hybrid EVs (electric vehicles). Rapidly increasing power demand and grid is becoming more complicated due to the inclusion of new technologies. Green technologies are improvingly used to make the grid more sustainable, with new ideas and technologies, which are making the grid more complicated to analyze. A complex smart grid will have all of it resources compiled as one with the cyber physical grid and this will be considered as the center. A bidirectional interconnection is established for the network for software, hardware, and the communication protocols. Implementing newer technologies daily makes the gird more vulnerable for these attacks and eventually degrades the system performance. It may also cause grid failure and the potential risk accompanied will be [29]:

1. Implementation of more complex structures increases the complexity of bridging the new technologies which are included.
2. Failures in including both random and targeted domains increase the risk in cascading failure of smart grids. The systems are closely packed and the risk of attack in any one domain may cause damage to the other too.
3. Increase in number of nodes in the network increase the point of attacks in the increase thus increasing the number of adversaries. Risks are increased and that is the main reason behind the increase in malwares and other malicious codes related issues in smart grid.
4. Privacy issues concerning the data in the smart grid is most common and IED (Intelligent Electronic Devices) are used for the detection, data gathering and two way extensive information flows in the grid. This new information flow has

increased the vulnerability of privacy issues like data confidentiality and intrusions.

10.12 Protecting Smart Grid From Cyber Vulnerabilities

The vulnerabilities in the smart grid have hiked often recently many times because of wide usage of communication network under different levels of operation and planning of a power grid. To protect this smart grid, it is crucial to protect the physical grid from three broad varieties of cyber-attacks [31] as mentioned below:

(i) Protection from component-wise cyber attack
A security agent based model is developed at the device or component level is proposed in [30–32] for smart grid protection. These security agents must be placed in the IED or field devices an also at substation level (RTUs). Few function of the security agents are [30]:

- ✓ Pattern of network traffic and data traffic are collected.
- ✓ Data log and report maintenance.
- ✓ Compilation of security patches and IDS algorithms.
- ✓ Maintaining end-to-end security.
- ✓ Alert management.

Protection of such a grid control system and its anomaly detection techniques are discussed in [33, 34]. In these researches, Rough Classification Algorithms is the techniques used in anomaly detection for security of power system control systems to be improved in the Electric Power System Critical Infrastructure. Normal and the abnormal modes of operations are the two modes considered during security analysis of smart grid. A compact set of knowledge based rules are used to enhance the performance of anomaly detection and to reduce the data associated in the rough classification algorithm. A comprehensive model is developed in [35] to protect the critical power system infrastructure. In the above said work monitoring in real time, detection of anomaly, implementation of mitigation strategies and impact analysis are designed under SCADA security. Protection of relay from false attacks, a probabilistic neural network based approach was proposed in [36].

Researches have proven that smart meters and PMUs are too weak for the cyber-attacks and several other researches are underway to study the security of the smart meters and PMUs. To place the PMUs at optimal place a strategic placement of component has been proposed by [37]. Specification based IDS are used for the design of IDS of smart meters and [38] discusses the architectural directions and requirements. The advantages over the signature based detection techniques and anomaly based detection techniques in case of AMI security are due to:

- ✓ In AMI application a greater accuracy of specifications are based on IDS.
- ✓ Digital signature based identifies activities to black list approaches which need an attack data set. In terms of AMI, it is difficult to prepare an empirical attack data set.
- ✓ The development of specification based IDS for AMI is cost effective.

(ii) Protection from Protocol-wise Cyber Attack

Commonly used power system infrastructure is SCADA. When multiple stakeholders are considered large networks of SCADA may fail to attend security issues based on encryption, authentication, and firewalls [39]. Considering SCADA as a single entity and focusing the security issues does not solve the problems and hence it is vital to make sure each individual device connected in the network is secured form cyber-attacks [39]. For automation and operation of smart grid various communication protocols are used among the SCADA devices. In early 1980s the evolution of proprietary and industrial SCADA protocols started when Modbus, Modbus Plus, and proprietary and vendor specific protocols were first developed [40]. The Distributed Networking Protocol (DNP) was first developed in 1990 by Westronic, Inc as an open protocol. DNP3 protocol is based on the IEC 60870-5 protocol and this protocol was mainly designed for better reliability in data communication but it is still weak to cyber-attacks. Hence a DNP3 which is rule based devices is proposed in [39] to cover the smart grid from cyber terrorists. A SCADA based simulation framework was developed in [41] a Modbus protocol for illustrating simulation based attacks. Guidelines and the best practices for the development of smart grid protocols considering design principles are discussed in [42].

(iii) Protection from Topology-wise Cyber Attacks
Smart grid is too prone to topology wise cyber-attacks. Examples are based on the knowledge of the power system topologies; an attacker may intrude the bad data detection algorithms of the current state estimators [43]. Another topology based cyber-attack is applied in [44], where attack on the CB (electric circuit breaker) will cause the islanding of the generation sources from the power grid. In [45], it is proposed that a cyber-attack on confidentiality with proper topological knowledge can lead to an integrity and availability attack. Therefore, a flow of information security-based design is proposed for reducing these security problems. In [46], an agreeable inter-link placement strategy opposing random attacks in the cyber-physical network is put forth which includes that the strategy is ensuring a better security compared to all other plausible strategies, which includes strategies using random allocation, unidirectional interlinks, in the model when topology of the cyber and physical network is unidentified to each other.

10.13 Security Issues for Future Smart Grid

For a grid smarter, remarkable initiatives has to be taken throughout the globe and these measures will not only rejuvenate the grid but also increase the overall system's efficiency, stability, and clearly the reliability but security problems should be maintained to make sure the uninterrupted power supply is given to the end users. Also the IDS have to protect the national electricity grid from terrorist attacks. It is vital to acknowledge that a neatly farmed defense design against cyber-attack should solve all aspects related to the cyber-crime in a complicated cyber-physical electricity grid infrastructure which means, not only available cyber-attack should be considered but also, unintentional ICT based attacks should be addressed such as human operator errors, software errors, equipment failures, and natural disaster related issues. During the process of building the power grid smarter, even more automated controls will be introduced in the grid. The risks of cyber-attacks will hike as the grid becomes more automatic. Especially control centers are the vital focus by the cyber terrorists. Energy utilities are applying advanced techniques and cyber security plans to avoid cyber-attacks. Higher intrusion detection and prevention techniques can be deployed in different entry point of the smart grid. Security management systems are being deployed in different utilities. Energy providers will be adopting different risk management strategies and defense approach against cyber-attack. It is clear that smart grid provides more of benefits including smart home, which are energy-efficient, solar and wind sources, which are greener technology, demand-side management, which are cost-effective, smart charging stations for electric cars and so on. To ensure these advantages, smart grid security measures must be maintained.

10.14 Conclusion

Smart grid is a complex entity which has various power system components included in it. Cyber threats are enormous in smart grid security. If the security threats discussed in the chapter are not taken care of then it might lead to catastrophic ends in energy eco system. An intrusion detection system should be intelligent enough to handle all the above said threats like topology based attacks, component based attacks and protocol based attacks in a futuristic grid. Further researches will be on advanced intrusion detection system which can even detect the minor faults in the components like smart meters, transmission line, substations which are inherent in the component.

References

1. Shalhoub, Z.K. and Al Qasimi, S.L., "Cyber Law and Cyber Security in Developing and Emerging Economies. *Security and Trust in Cyber Space,* Edward Elgar Publishing, 2019. https://www.elgaronline.com/view/9781845428716.00005.xml.
2. Jokar, P., Nicanfar, H., Leung, V.C., Specification-based Intrusion Detection for home area networks in smart grids, *2011 IEEE International Conference on Smart Grid Communications*, 2011.
3. Salman, S.K., *Introduction to the Smart Grid Concept.* IET Digital Library , 2017, https://digital-library.theiet.org/content/books/10.1049/pbpo094e_ch1.

4. Sato, T., Kammen, D.M., Duan B., Macuha, M., Zhou, Z., Wu, J., Tariq, M., Asfaw, S.A., Security and Safety for Standardized Smart Grid Networks, in: Smart Grid Standard, T. Sato, D.M. Kammen, B. Duan, M. Macuha, Z. Zhou, J. Wu, M. Tariq and S.A. Asfaw (eds.), 2015.
5. Enose, N., Advanced Technologies Implementation Framework for a Smart Grid. *J. Clean Energy Technol.*, 2, 1, 88–94, 2014.
6. Falk, R. and Fries, S., Smart Grid Cyber Security—An Overview of Selected Scenarios and Their Security Implications. *Energyo*, 34, 168–175, 2018
7. Giani, A. and Bent, R., Addressing smart grid cyber security, *Proceedings of the Eighth Annual Cyber Security and Information Intelligence Research Workshop on - CSIIRW 13*, 2013.
8. Hu, J., Framework of Smart grid, *2010 International Conference on Power System Technology*, 2010.
9. Metke, A.R. and Ekl, R.L., Smart Grid security technology, *2010 Innovative Smart Grid Technologies (ISGT)*, 2010.
10. Ullah, I. and Mahmoud, Q.H., An intrusion detection framework for the smart grid, *2017 IEEE 30th Canadian Conference on Electrical and Computer Engineering (CCECE)*, 2017.
11. Wagner, M., Kuba, M., Oeder, A., Smart grid cyber security: A German perspective, *2012 International Conference on Smart Grid Technology, Economics and Policies (SG-TEP)*, 2012.
12. Zhang, Y., Wang, L., Sun, W., Ii, R.C., Alam, M., Distributed Intrusion Detection System in a Multi-Layer Network Architecture of Smart Grids. *IEEE Trans. Smart Grid*, 2, 4, 796–808, 2011.
13. Han, W., Xiong, W., Xiao, Y., Ellabidy, M., Vasilakos, A.V., Xiong, N., A class of non-statistical traffic anomaly detection in complex network systems, *International Workshop on Network Forensics, Security and Privacy (NFSP'12) in conjunction with ICDCS'12*, Macau, China, June, pp. 640–646, 2012.
14. Ahmim, A. and Ghoualmi-Zine, N., A new adaptive intrusion detection system based on the intersection of two different classifiers. *Int. J. Secur. Netw.*, 9, 3, 125–132, 2014.
15. Sun, B., Shan, X., Wu, K., Xiao, Y., Anomaly detection based secure in-network aggregation for wireless sensor networks. *IEEE Syst. J.*, 7, 1, pp. 13–25, 2013.
16. Zheng, H., Hou, M., Wang, Y., An efficient hybrid clustering-PSO algorithm for anomaly intrusion detection. *J. Softw.*, 6, 12, 2350–2360, 2011.
17. Zhou, M., Hui, H., Qian, W., A graph-based clustering algorithm for anomaly intrusion detection, *7th IEEE International Conference on Computer Science and Education (ICCSE)*, Melbourne, Australia, 14–17 July, pp. 1311–1314, 2012.
18. Fang, X., Li, J., Li, L., Restudying the artificial immune model for network intrusion detection, *2009 IEEE International Workshop on Intelligent Systems and Applications (ISA 2009)*, Wuhan, China, 23–24 May, pp. 1–6, 2009.

19. Fu, B. and Xiao, Y., Accountability and Q-Accountable logging in wireless networks. *Wireless Pers. Commun.*, 75, 3, 1715–1746, 2014.
20. Gogoi, P., Bhattacharyya, D.K., Kalita, J.K., A rough set-based effective rule generation method for classification with an application in intrusion detection. *Int. J. Secur. Netw.*, 8, 2, 61–71, 2013.
21. Scarfone, K.A. and Mell, P.M., Guide to Intrusion Detection and Prevention Systems (IDPS). Special Publication, 800–94, 2007.
22. Berthier, R., Sanders, W.H., Khurana, H., Intrusion detection for advanced metering infrastructures: Requirements and architectural directions, *First IEEE International Conference on Smart Grid Communications*, 2–6 October, NIST, MD, USA, pp. 350–355, 2010.
23. Jokar, P., Nicanfar, H., Leung, V.C.M., Specification based intrusion detection for home area networks in smart grids, *The Proceeding of The Second IEEE International Conference on Smart Grid Communications (IEEE SmartGridComm)*, Brussels, Belgium, 17–20 October, pp. 208–213, 2011.
24. Ozdemir, S. and Xiao, Y., FTDA: Outlier detection-based fault-tolerant data aggregation for wireless sensor networks. *J. Secur. Commun. Netw.*, 6, 6, 702–710, 2013.
25. Han, W. and Xiao, Y., IP2DM for V2G networks in smart grid, *Proceedings of the 2015 International Conference on Communications (ICC'15)*, London, UK, June 2015, pp. 782–787, 2015.
26. Han, W. and Xiao, Y., IP2DM: Integrated privacy preserving data management architecture for smart grid V2G networks. *Wireless Comm. Mobile Comput. (WCMC) J.*, John Wiley & Sons, 16, 17, 10 December, pp. 2775–3186, 2016.
27. Mo, Y., Kim, T.H.-H., Brancik, K., Dickinson, D., Lee, H., Perrig, A., Sinopoli, B., Cyber–Physical Security of a Smart Grid Infrastructure. *Proc. IEEE*, 100, 1, 195–209, Jan. 2012.
28. Sridhar, S., Hahn, A., Govindarasu, M., Cyber–Physical System Security for the Electric Power Grid. *Proc. IEEE*, 100, 1, 210–224, Jan. 2012.
29. S. Clements and H. Kirkham, *Cyber-security considerations for the smart grid*, IEEE PES General Meeting, Providence, RI, 1–5, 2010.
30. Dolezilek, D. and Hussey, L., Requirements or recommendations? Sorting out NERC CIP, NIST, and DOE cybersecurity, *Proc. 2011 64th Annu. Conf. Protective Relay Engineers*, 2011.
31. Wei, D., Lu, Y., Jafari, M., Skare, P.M., Rohde, K., Protecting Smart Grid Automation Systems Against Cyberattacks. *IEEE Trans. Smart Grid*, 2, 4, 782–795, Dec. 2011.
32. Dong, W., Jafari, M., Yan, L., On Protecting Industrial Automation and Control Systems against Electronic Attacks, *IEEE International Conference on Automation Science and Engineering*, 176–181, 22–25 Sept. 2007.
33. Coutinho, M.P., Lambert-Torres, G., da Silva, L.E.B., Martins, H.G., Lazarek, H., Neto, J.C., Anomaly detection in power system control center critical infrastructures using rough classification algorithm, *3rd IEEE International*

Conference on Digital Ecosystems and Technologies, 2009, 1–3 June 2009, vol., no., pp. 733–738.
34. Coutinho, M.P., Lambert-Torres, G., da Silva, L.E.B., Lazarek, H., Improving Detection Attacks in Electric Power System Critical Infrastructure Using Rough Classification Algorithm, *Proceedings of the Second International Conference on Forensic Computer Science*, Brazil, no. 1, vol. 2, pp. 18–23, 2007.
35. Ten, C.-W., Manimaran, G., Liu, C.-C., Cybersecurity for Critical Infrastructures: Attack and Defense Modeling. *IEEE Trans. Syst. Man Cybern. Part A Syst. Humans*, 40, 4, 853–865, July 2010.
36. Sheng, S., Chan, W.L., Li, K.K., Xianzhong, D., Xiangjun, Z., Context Information-Based Cyber Security Defense of Protection System. *IEEE Trans. Power Deliver.*, 22, 3, 1477–1481, July 2007.
37. Huang, Y., *et al.* Bad data injection in smart grid: Attack and defense mechanism. *IEEE Commun. Mag.*, 51, 1, 27–33, 2013.
38. Berthier, R., Sanders, W.H., Khurana, H., Intrusion Detection for Advanced Metering Infrastructures: Requirements and Architectural Directions, *2010 First IEEE International Conference on Smart Grid Communications (SmartGridComm)*, p. 350–355, 4–6 Oct., 2010.
39. Mander, T., Cheung, R., Nabhani, F., Power system DNP3 data object security using data sets. *Comput. Secur.*, 29, 4, 487–500, 2010.
40. Ten, C.-W., Manimaran, G., Liu, C.-C., Cybersecurity for electric power control and automation systems, *Proc. eNetworks Cyberengineering Workshop, IEEE-SMC*, pp. 29–34, 2007.
41. Queiroz, C., Mahmood, A., Tari, Z., SCADASim—A Framework for Building SCADA Simulations. *IEEE Trans. Smart Grid*, 2, 4, 589–597, Dec. 2011.
42. Khurana, H., Bobba, R., Yardley, T., Agarwal, P., Heine, E., Design Principles for Power Grid Cyber-Infrastructure Authentication Protocols, *43rd Hawaii International Conference on System Sciences (HICSS)*, 5–8 Jan. 2010, vol., no., p. 1, 10.
43. Xie, L., Mo, Y., Sinopoli, B., Integrity Data Attacks in Power Market Operations. *IEEE Trans. Smart Grid*, 2, 4, 659–666, Dec. 2011.
44. Srivastava, A., Morris, T., Ernster, T., Vellaithurai, C., Pan, S., Adhikari, U., Modeling Cyber-Physical Vulnerability of the Smart Grid With Incomplete Information. *IEEE Trans. Smart Grid*, 4, 1, 235–244, March 2013.
45. Gamage, T.T., *et al.* Mitigating Event Confidentiality Violations in Smart Grids: An Information Flow Security-Based Approach. *IEEE Transactions on Smart Grid*, 4, 3, 1227–1234, 2013.
46. Yagan, O., Qian, D., Zhang, J., Cochran, D., Optimal Allocation of Interconnecting Links in Cyber-Physical Systems: Interdependence, Cascading Failures, and Robustness. *IEEE Trans. Parallel Distrib. Syst.*, 23, 9, 1708–1720, Sept. 2012.

11

Security Protocol for Cloud-Based Communication

R. Suganya[1*] **and S. Sujatha**[2†]

[1]*Department of Information Technology, Thiagarajar College of Engineering, Madurai India*
[2]*Department of Computer Applications, Anna University, Trichy, India*

Abstract

Cloud technology and its services lessens the requirement to spend more in modern technology infrastructure, by providing access to infrastructure and services on a "pay per use" model, which severely diminishes the cost and make things easier to accept the current technology. But security concern has become the biggest hindrance to adoption of cloud because all information and data are completely under the control of cloud service providers. Security problems have pierced into the most layers of cloud computing, from system to framework administration. It is classified as two broad categories: security issues faced by cloud providers and security issues faced by their clients. Lot of security issues in system and information supply are additionally relevant to cloud computing because of the interconnections between the specialized applications like virtual machine. Hence flexible distributed storage integrity auditing mechanism has provided a secure and dependable services in cloud computing. Newly designed framework is called as privacy and integrity preserving dynamic auditing protocol for data storage security in cloud computing. This framework has been utilized the homomorphic authenticator and random masking which guaranteed that Third Party Authenticator cannot learn any knowledge about the data content stored on the cloud server during the auditing process.

Keywords: Cloud computing, dynamic auditing protocol, homomorphic authenticator, policy monitoring system, data storage security, third party authenticator, authentication and authorization, enhance cloud protection system

**Corresponding author*: rsuganya@tce.edu
†*Corresponding author*: sujathaaut@gmail.com

Dinesh Goyal, S. Balamurugan, Sheng-Lung Peng and O.P. Verma (eds.) Design and Analysis of Security Protocol for Communication, (235–242) © 2020 Scrivener Publishing LLC

11.1 Introduction

Cloud computing is emerging buzz word from recent advances in technologies such as hardware virtualization, web services, distributed computing, utility computing, and system automation. It is continuously evolving and showing constant growth in the field of computing. As more businesses move toward integrated communications in the cloud, securing sensitive information confidential data becomes a primary concern. Several security threats exist including call fraud, phreaking, malware, and denial of service attacks to name a few [1]. Though the cloud communication service provider offers security protection as part of its services, enterprises must also take measures to ensure data and information is secure. The fundamental factor defining the success of any new information computing technology is the level of security it provides. The three basic requirements of security: confidentiality, integrity/veracity, and availability are required to protect data throughout its lifecycle. Information must be safe guarded during the different stages of creation, sharing, archiving, processing, etc. However, situations become more complicated in case of a public cloud where we do not have any control over the service provider's security practices. Lot of security issues in system and information supply are additionally relevant to cloud computing because of the interconnections between the specialized applications like virtual machine [2]. Hence flexible distributed storage integrity auditing mechanism has provided a secure and dependable services in cloud computing.

With virtualization, one or more physical servers can be arranged and partitioned into multiple independent "virtual" servers, all working independently and appearing to the user to be a single physical device. Those virtual servers are separated from their physical server, and scaled up or down on the fly without affecting the end user. With multiple users from different organizations contributing to data in the Cloud, the time and cost will be much less compared to having to manually exchange data and hence creating a clutter of redundant and possibly out-of-date documents. With social networking services such as Facebook, the benefits of sharing data are numerous such as the ability to share photos, videos, information, and events [3, 4]. Google Docs provides data sharing capabilities as groups of students or teams working on a project can share documents and can collaborate with each other effectively. This allows higher productivity compared to previous methods of continually sending updated versions of a document to members of the group via email attachments. The

Global Outbreak Alert and Response Network of WHO rely on web-based sources for the purpose of daily surveillance. Also in modern healthcare environments, healthcare providers are willing to store and share electronic medical records via the Cloud and hence remove the geographical dependence between healthcare provider and patient. The need of Cloud Mining and security over web is gaining popularity in recent days. The infrastructures under the cloud are much more powerful and reliable than personal computing devices; they are still facing the broad range of both internal and external threats for data integrity. Although outsourcing data to the cloud is economically attractive for long-term large-scale data storage, it does not immediately offer any assurance on data integrity and availability.

11.2 Existing Technology and Its Review

Considering the large size of the outsourced data and the user's constrained resource ability, the tasks of auditing the data correctness in a cloud environment can be difficult and expensive for the cloud users [5]. The public auditing system of data storage security in Cloud Computing and provide a privacy-preserving auditing protocol, i.e., our method enables an external auditor to audit user's outsourced data in the cloud without learning the data content [6]. In this method support scalable and efficient public auditing in the Cloud Computing achieves batch auditing where multiple delegated auditing tasks from different users can be performed simultaneously by the TPA.

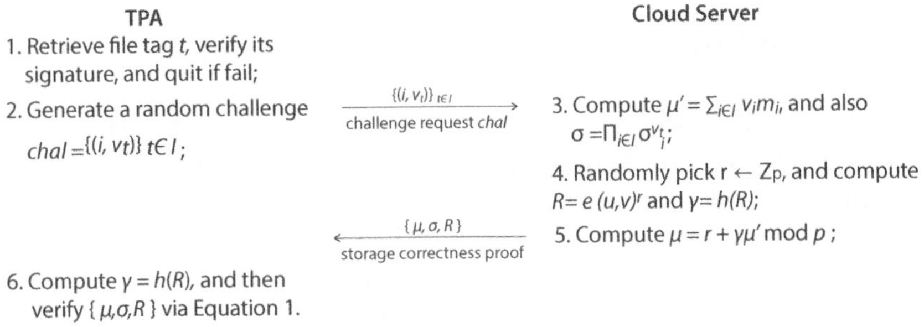

Enhanced secure cloud computing has achieved through service level agreements and policy monitoring Techniques.

11.3 Methodology (To Overcome the Drawbacks of Existing Protocols)

This chapter emphasize on achieving Secure Cloud Computing Services using Virtualization and Service Policy Monitoring Techniques. Policy Monitoring is a continuous process based on narrow compliance, information risk, based on service and cloud business requirement. The newly designed architecture namely "Cloud Security Module" has two key components such as Policy Monitoring module (PM) and Security Auditing Module (SAM) [7]. The Policy Monitoring Module contains the access control policy and enhanced message protection policy algorithm called Merkle–Hash algorithm. In this algorithm, hash computational function has produced signature and sent along with the encrypted data to the Cloud. The Security Auditor Module explores the Network Mapper (NMap) tool. This data communication network traffic tool, which provides the vulnerability analysis, and risks have identified periodically to estimate the assessment of risks [8]. This method assures the security either by isolating the intruded virtual machine or by reconstructing the virtual machine images from the snapshots using hypervisor. Results exhibits that our techniques generated a Merkley digest for the data integrity and also checks for the checks for the vulnerability of virtual machines if necessary intruded virtual machine.

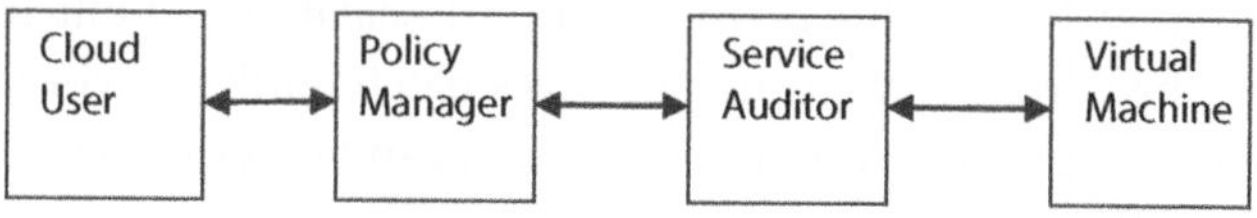

Major Components of CSM

11.4 Findings: Policy Monitoring Techniques

Cloud Services are services provided to the end user/subscriber. Here there will be a Service Level Agreement (SLA) between the Cloud Provider and the user. In General, security and compliances are applicable to all the layers. Each layer level has its own security. When it comes to the topmost layer where applications are deployed and accessed will be coming under much security policy besides with firewall and service vulnerability monitoring, risk assessment and control management. By using Java Authentication and Authorization Service (JAAS) can check who is accessing the service and whether they have authorized to access as per SLA. Enhanced

Cloud Protection System (ECPS) model has provides policy-monitoring technique.

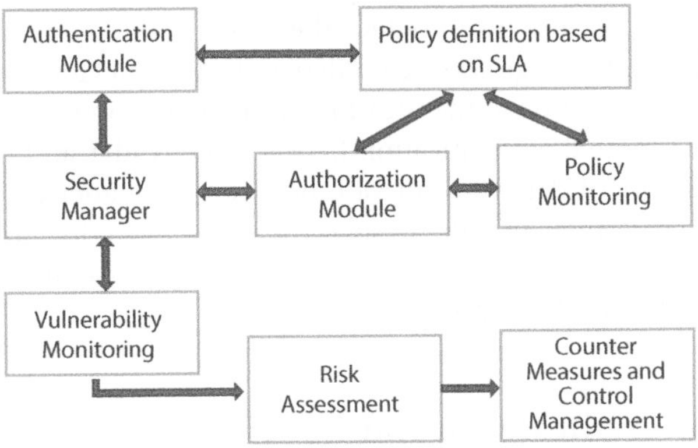

In this Authentication module, it checks for who is accessing the service regardless of the service type and nature. Authorization module checks for whether the user has authorized to access the service based on Service Level Agreement. Policy has generated based on the Service Level Agreement between the user and the provider. Hence policy can be influenced by cost. Security manager will monitor for any vulnerability, risk assessment is made and based on the risk assessment, countermeasure steps are taken to overcome the security problem. Consider the following scenario, based an end user's requirement, whether it is a IaaS, PaaS, SaaS type of service, a single virtual machine is allotted for the user. Creation of Virtual Machine and its images are taken based on their policy requirement. Suppose our monitoring report system indicates some vulnerability, then appropriate steps can be taken. Isolating Virtual Machines of each user is important which is done by the second layer with the help of a hypervisor. Snapshots can be taken. If it is intruded, necessary steps are taken to recover by forwarding request to the next VM which will be created with the help of images taken already. At worst case, the entire virtual machine can be destroyed and can be reconstructed immediately with the help of the images without affecting the regular workload of the user. Many Virtual Machines can be run on a single host machine itself [9]. Proper updating of VMs Operating system, installing, and updating the firewalls in VMs like the physical machine are important to ensure the security of the service. Based on the policy based risk assessment report generated, Virtual Machine maintenance is easy to achieve the enhanced security of the Cloud [10].

Development of the Internet of things and cloud storage, a large number of objects access to the Internet through radio frequency identification technology, cloud-based radio frequency identification system attracts more attention because it can reduce the costs of system maintenance by renting the cloud storage service on demand. Hence a cloud-based radio frequency identification authentication protocol is proposed. It considers not only the mutual authentication between the reader and the tag, but also the security of data transmission between the reader and the cloud database. In particular, in order to solve the reader's location privacy problem, the proposed scheme introduces MIPv6 network framework without adding additional infrastructure.

11.5 Future Research and Conclusion

Our Proposed work Policy Monitoring Techniques assure Enhanced and Secure Cloud Computing Services in communication protocol. Encryption techniques generated a Homomorphic Merkley Digest for the data integrity and also checks for the vulnerability of virtual machines if necessary intruded virtual machine is reconstructed from the snapshots taken, which assures enhanced secure cloud services to the user.

In addition to this vulnerability analysis is also represented in a topology format. By monitoring the resource utilization, such as CPU, memory, network, and port at a specific interval, intruded Virtual Machines are isolated. By monitoring specific port as well as services, threats can be identified. Based on risk assessment, neither CSM reacts by preventing further running of these machines or by reconstructing virtual machine images from the snapshots using hypervisor. Vulnerabilities of the Cloud are dynamically detected and corrective measures are taken by the system, which assures two fold securities to the cloud services with CSM.

In future, more emphasis is going to be in the area of cloud security by defining new cryptographic methods and key management techniques. One of the major concerns in future is computing with less power. With virtualization, apart from flexibility, scalability, security, utilizing underutilized resources/idle resources, manageability, cost effective cloud computing with virtualization technology takes less power since more than one virtual machines can be run on a single physical machine. In future like IaaS, PaaS, and SaaS, anything as a Service (XaaS) is going to be possible and can be achieved through Virtualization.

Reference

1. Chang, V. and Ramachandran, M., Towards Achieving Data Security with the Cloud Computing Adoption Framework. *IEEE Trans. Serv. Comput.*, 9, 1, 138–151, 2016.
2. Malensek, M., Pallickara, S., Pallickara, S., MINERVA: Proactive Disk Scheduling for Qos in Multi-tier, Multi-tenant Cloud Environments. *IEEE Trans. Internet Comput.*, 20, 3, 19–27, 2016.
3. Wu, Z., Li, Y., Plaza, A., Li, J., Xiao, F., Wei, Z., Parallel and Distributed Dimensionality Reduction of Hyperspectral Data on Cloud Computing Architectures. *IEEE J. Sel. Top. Appl. Earth Obs. Remote Sens.*, 9, 6, 2270–2278, 2016.
4. Xu, X. and Tu, Q., Data Deduplication Mechanism for Cloud Storage Systems, in: *Proceedings of International Conference on Cyber-Enabled Distributed Computing and Knowledge Discovery (CyberC)*, pp. 286–294, 2015.
5. Wu, L., Garg, S.K., Versteeg, S., Buyya, R., SLA-Based Resource Provisioning for Hosted Software-as-a-Service Applications in Cloud Computing Environments. *IEEE Trans. Serv. Comput.*, 7, 3, 465–485, 2014.
6. Hashizume, K., Rosado, D.G., Fernndez-Medina, E., Fernandez, E.B., An Analysis of Security Issues for Cloud Computing. *J. Internet Serv. Appl.*, 4, 1, 1–13, 2013.
7. Chintada, S.R. and Chinta, C., Dynamic Massive Data Storage Security Challenges in Cloud Computing Environments. *Int. J. Inno. Res. Comp. Comm. Eng.*, 2, 3, 3609–3616, 2014.
8. Wang, C., Wang, Q., Ren, K., Cao, N., Lou, W., Toward Secure and Dependable Storage Services in Cloud Computing. *IEEE Trans. Serv. Comput.*, 5, 2, 220–232, 2012.
9. Satoh, F. and Tokuda, T., Security Policy Composition for Composite Web Services. *IEEE Trans. Serv. Comput.*, 4, 4, 314–327, 2011.
10. Takabi, H., Joshi, J.B.D., Ahn, G.-J., Security and Privacy Challenges in Cloud Computing Environments. *IEEE Secur. Priv.*, 8, 6, 24–31, 2010.

12

Security Protocols for Mobile Communications

Divya Priyadharshini M.[1]*, Divya R.[1], Ponmurugan P.[1] and Balamurugan S.[2]

[1]*Department of Electrical and Electronics Engineering, Sri Krishna College of Technology, Kovaipudur, Coimbatore, India*
[2]*Department of Research and Development, Quantis IS and CS Technologies, Coimbatore, India*

Abstract
Internet of Things is the bread and butter for the future wireless network communications. The advancement in these technologies is also demanding advanced security. The chapter begins with the introduction to communication networks and importance of the security of network. It has also summarized the various available mobile communication technologies, the threats faced by them and the measures undertaken for avoiding those threats. In the proposed method section an approach for integrating LoRaWAN and 5G has been discussed with security challenges faced by the system. By integrating the systems low power, low latency and higher efficient system is achieved. RFID along with PLS is used to address the security issues discussed along with result and performance measures. Further the chapter concludes by summarizing the proposed method and its analysis.

Privacy and data confidentiality will be a severe problem in 5G networks PLS provides data security, asymmetric cryptographic algorithm provides location security. In the proposed system a LoRa connected 5G system, RFID authentication along with PLS is used, which will address most of the 5G security problems. By this, eavesdropping, jamming and data piracy are avoided by using PLS and by using RFID for authentication security issues are avoided.

Keywords: Mobile communications, security protocols, 5G network, Lora security, security threats, wireless communications, 5G security, network security

**Corresponding author*: mdivyapriyadharshini@gmail.com

Dinesh Goyal, S. Balamurugan, Sheng-Lung Peng and O.P. Verma (eds.) Design and Analysis of Security Protocol for Communication, (243–264)

12.1 Introduction

In affluent communication devices connected environment, a secure communication and key exchange are indispensable security issues. Mobile communications has poor user interface, limited processing capability, and complex network protocol. Also the security is laborious and demanding than other communication systems [1]. To design a successful mobile communication device, mobile applications and operating conditions plays integral roles, since some hardware aspects make the security design hard. The arena of mechanisms has the following eight players, such as:

a) Authentication management
b) Identity and confidentiality management
c) Protection of the privacy of users
d) Security between the terminals and the network
e) Security on network interfaces
f) Security visibility and configurability
g) Cryptographic algorithms
h) Protection against DoS attacks [2].

Mobile communication security is defined in terms of confidentiality, authentication, integrity, and non-repudiation of the data which is transmitted. These demands are fulfilled using various cryptographic techniques which are strong and cannot be easily breached; but they may cause complications while designing [3]. Data confidentiality is ensured by end-to-end encryption between the two communicating parties. The mechanism used for encryption depends upon the technology in which it is used. Data authentication is an asymmetric service and it depends on the security protocol used. The solutions for authentication and data privacy can be achieved by running additional protocols at the data link layer. User identification for sensitive applications has to run an additional protocol with server database. Like authentication non-repudiation is also asymmetric unlike the fact that the recipient will know the origin of the message. Example: Digital Signature [4].

Mobile communication security is difficult because of its complex architecture. It has been developing exponentially and is used by almost every sapiens on the planet earth. Network architecture depends on the communication protocol layer. It is an abstract way to represent the data communication model and implementation [5]. It has five layers namely physical, data link, network, transport, and application as shown in Figure 12.1.

The physical, data link, and network layers are node to node layers whereas the transport and application layers are end to end layers and a gateway between them. Authentication and non-repudiation can be implemented on application layer since they need end to end protection and confidentiality can be implemented in any of the layers. The security protocols which we have in use can be said metaphorically as infant steps toward a long journey [6]. The user should not be naive about the security concerns and the operations but at the same time the evidence provided should be intellect and intuitive. Security protocols are set of defined rules which concentrate on the security of the communication device. Mobile communication has reached its fifth generation of mobile devices, its security issues and protection techniques will be discussed later in this chapter.

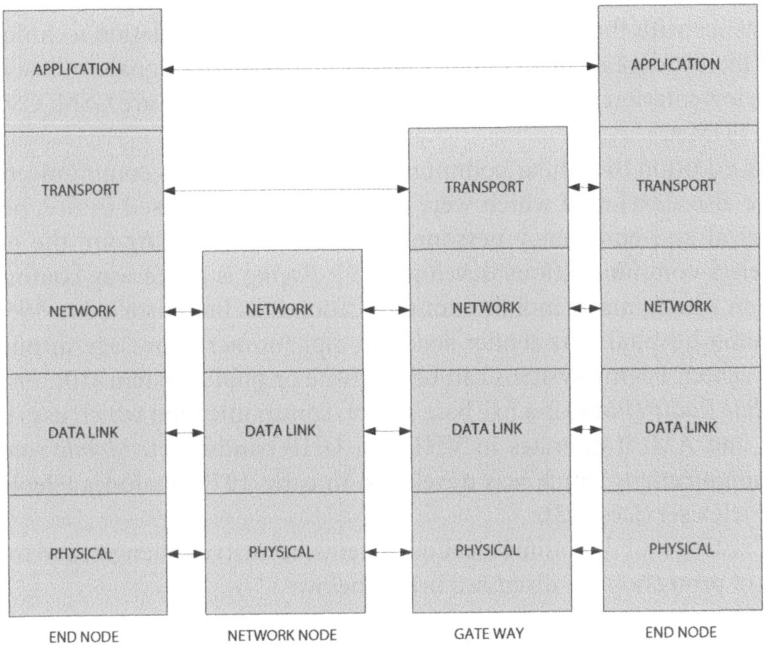

Figure 12.1 Communication protocol layers.

12.2 Evolution of Mobile Communications

Communication is an art which differentiates us from other beings in the planet. Mobile communication has grown drastically from the year 1987 when Guglielmo Marconi demonstrated his first radio communication [7]. Mobile communication evolution can be divided into three phases: pointer phase, commercial phase, and wireless communication. The pioneer phase includes the early experiments carried out from 1927 to 1947. The mobile communication came to reality during the Second World War. The commercial phase includes the commercialization of radio and television from 1946 to 1968.

The wireless era from 1947 is a remarkable growth phase in history of mankind which paved way for various developments in our society. The basic architecture of a mobile cellular phone was designed with the following principles: Low power transmitters, small coverage, reuse of frequency, increasing capability of computing by cell splitting, off hands and central control modes. The first commercial mobile was introduced in 1983 [8]. The first analog cellular systems were developed in Japan and Europe which faced severe downfall. Then the digital cellular systems came into existence with the advantages of advanced digital modulation techniques, low bit rate digital voice coding, reduction of overhead signals, robust control, less interference and improved efficiency. Examples are GSM, CSMA, and FDMA.

In addition to cellular communication other wireless communications were also developed which were application specific used in fire, police medical and emergency personnel circuit. The following are the other wireless communications developed [9]: *Paging* is a one way communication which mimic mobile communication it as first installed in 1956 in London hospital. The sender sends an alphanumeric message through a call center. Paging systems can be a private or public system [10]. *Private Mobile Radio (PMR)* is a fixe base station communication which uses both FM and AM. It operates in VHF and UHF bands [11]. *Mobile satellite communications* which was developed in early 1970s includes telephone and telex services [12].

Existing mobile communication systems, security challenges, and methods of protection are discussed briefly below:

Global System for Mobile Communications is commonly called as GSM which is a second generation mobile communication technology (2G). It is a massive commercial hit despite its weaknesses which includes weak cryptographic algorithms, meager protection against attacks and weak architecture [13]. These insufficient security issues led to new security goals such as confidential user identity, authentication, data concealment and signal information privacy. 2G uses circuit switched scheduling for transmission. The above said security issues can be overcome using authenticated key agreement (AKA) protocol with aid of Subscriber Identity Module (SIM) [14].

Universal Mobile Telecommunications System (UMTS) or the widely called 3G (third generation) systems have demanding data transfers. Here the security is provided with mutual authentications and enhanced encryption algorithms [15]. 3GSM has enhanced protection in the network layer but still faces attacks like denial of service (DoS) and capture of identity. To counterattack these problems integrity protection for critical signaling messages and temporary identity are used [16].

Long Term Evolution (LTE) also the fourth generation of mobile communication uses an IP-based packet-switched architecture and improved radio layer. It offers Voice and Small messaging services (SMS) as IP-based services rather network services [17]. Threats in 4G system includes physical threats, attacks on the privacy of the user, unauthorized access of IMS, lack of privacy and data loss, DoS, and DDoS. These many threats can be overcome by introducing industrial standards to provide physical safety, usage of IPS Intrusion Prevention System, usage of secured gateways, virtual private network and enhanced encrypting algorithms and antivirus software [18].

GSM opened new mechanism for enhanced security for user anonymity and privacy, halting weaknesses in security was succeeded by altered network security in UMTS. UMTS can be characterized as malleable architecture for solving flaws in the security. It still had susceptibility which was overcome by LTE [19]. LTE responded by using well-founded cryptographic algorithms, security in its embedded architecture which was IP based and mutual authentication mechanisms. It was laid bare to new issues like spamming, espionage, malware distribution, IP spoofing, data and services theft, Distributed Denial of Service (DDoS), etc. [20].

12.3 Global System for Mobiles (GSM)

The GSM idea was formed in 1982 and it was implemented in the year 1991 in Europe. The architecture of GSM comprises of three subsystems namely Mobile station (MS), Base Station Subsystem (BSS), and Network Subsystem (NSS). Mobile Station (MS) will have the mobile phone (ME) and the SIM (Subscriber Identity Module) which stores the IMSI (International Mobile Subscriber Identity Module) and the secret Key that is used in the authentication processes [21]. Figure 12.2 shows the components in a GSM architecture and they are:

- Base Station Controller (BSC)
- Base Station (BS)
- Mobile services Switching Center (MSC)

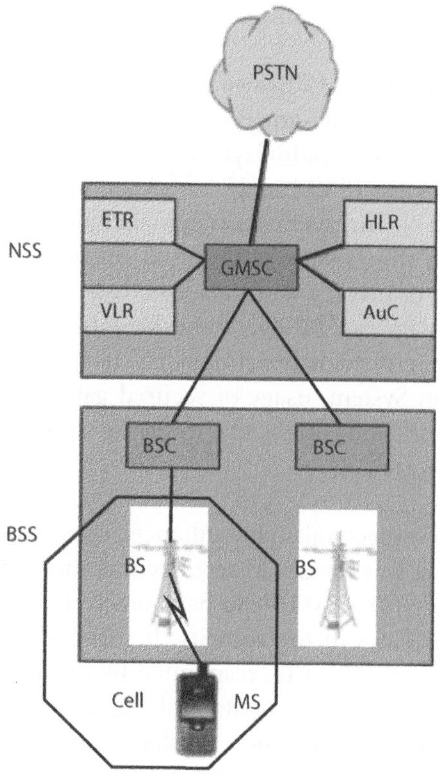

Figure 12.2 Components of GSM.

- Core Network (CN)
- Visitor Location Register (VLR)
- Public Switched Telephone Network (PSTN)
- Equipment Identity Register (EIR) [22]

The remarkable innovation in GSM is the SIM and the secret key (Ki) associated [23]. It has a step by step process in authentication and as show in Figure 12.3.

Step 1: Network sends 128 bit random (RAND) challenge to the ME
Step 2: Algorithm A3 (The MS Authentication Algorithm) for the secret key (Ki) to respond, SRES
Step 3: If SRES matches then it proceeds to the next step
Step 4: Algorithm A8 (The Ciphering Key Generation Algorithm) to challenge session key (Kc)
Step 5: Algorithm A5 (The Stream-Ciphering Algorithm) sends encrypted data to BS

Vulnerabilities in GSM include Masquerading or ID Spoofing in which the attacker disguise as authorized personnel and accesses unauthorized resources, discloses unauthorized information and information flow, alters the resources and information without authorization, repudiation of actions, and DoS (denial-of-service) [24]. Some of the other vulnerabilities in GSM are:

- Use of false BS to interpret communication
- Encryption in only on the crust and so cipher keys and authentication are exposed

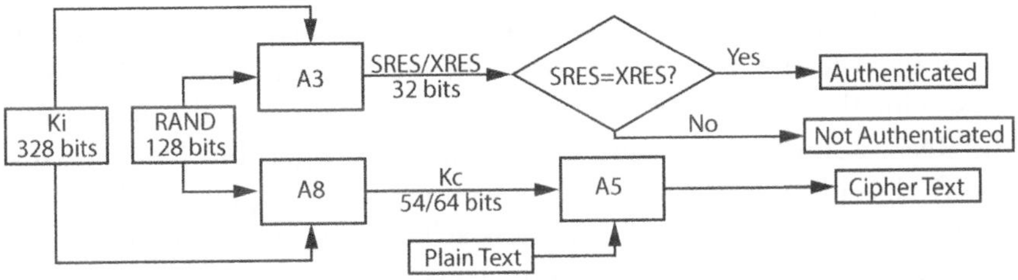

Figure 12.3 Flowchart of GSM operations.

- Data integrity is at stake
- Less flexible for security upgrade
- Lack of user visibility

12.4 Universal Mobile Telecommunications System (UMTS)

UMTS was first established in A USIM is used for the authentication processes. UMTS security systems have to be built on the existing 2G systems which have the following advantages: Identity confidentiality, network authentication, radio interference encryption, removable SIM with a hardware module security without assistance, SIM authentication by subscriber. The additional features of security in UMTS include a) Integrity Protection of Signaling Information b) Integrity Protection of Signaling Information c) Ciphering/Integrity Protection d) Trust and Confidence by Published Algorithms d) Authentication Failure Indication e) Enhanced UMTS Authentication and Key Agreement Mechanism f) USIM Control of Cipher/Integrity Key Usage. The following diagram Figure 12.4 explains the UMTS system Architecture [25].

Authentication and Key agreement (AKA) in UMTS consists of two phases in operation phase one is Generation of Authentication Vectors and the other phase is Authentication and Key Agreement. After receiving the request for data from the service network, the authentication center creates "n" number of authentication vectors namely [26]:

- RAND—A random number
- XRES—an expected response
- CK—A cipher key
- IK—an integrity key
- AUTN—an authentication token

For the security architecture of UMTS we need various 3G standard security algorithms. These security algorithms are used in the process of integrity protection and encryption of the message transmitted [27]. Thus preserving the security of the message transferred between the mobile and the RNC. KASUMI algorithm comprising of f8 algorithm for ciphering and f9 algorithm for the integrity protection is used. Ciphering algorithm is used for encryption and integrity is achieved by calculating the cryptographic checksums for the signaling messages.

In spite of the complex security and complex algorithms in 3G, security breaches happen in this system. Any security threat faced by the fixed

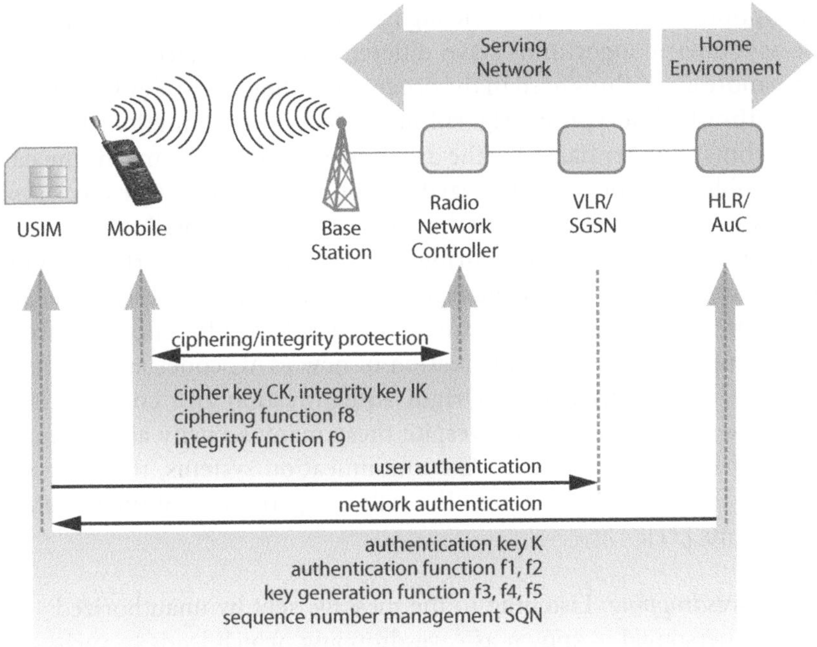

Figure 12.4 UMTS security architecture.

host connected to the Internet is also faced by the 3G terminal. When a new user is registering for the first time a clear text is sent to the IMSI acknowledging the user. A false base station (BS) can be created and the user is out of reach from the SN thus an active attack is possible. The authentication key Authentication and Key Agreement (AKA) protocol is unidirectional. Calls connected to the network can be easily hijacked and the eavesdropper disables the encryption [28]. This intruder disguised attack is called man-in-the-middle attack. Thus the same attack can be replayed. Data integrity and user authentication are under stake due to weak encryption.

12.5 Long Term Evolution (LTE)

Overcoming the security drawbacks of the third generation the fourth generation LTE has better cryptographic algorithms than UTMS. The authentication is done by AKE (Authentication Key Exchange) Protocol which includes Key Establishment Protocols and Entity Authentication Protocols. Both symmetric and asymmetric protocols are used for the encryption [29]. The symmetric algorithms have the same key whereas the asymmetric algorithms have different keys. Furthermore there are three more algorithms used in the process and they are: a) Key Generation Algorithm b) Encryption Algorithm c) Decryption Function. By these algorithms confidentiality for the data is preserved, which means the data is available only for the authorized personnel. *Cryptographic algorithms* are defined by two main properties security and non-malleability. *Hash functions* are also used in securing 4G systems, the properties include: collision resistance, pre-image resistance, 2nd-preimage resistance [30]. *MAC (Message Authentication Codes)* or keyed hash functions assure us with computational ease and creation of new MAC codes any input. By using MACs Integrity, Data Origin authentication and confidentiality of the message is preserved. Despite these many security algorithms to secure the messages sin the 4G communication systems, there are still possible threats to the systems. The following are some of the threats to 4G systems [31]:

Eavesdropping: Listening to the message sent by unauthorized personnel is known as eavesdropping, which leads to various other severe threats to the system.

Modification of messages: when messages are eavesdropped there are good chances of modification of messages sent.

Replay: when the attacker has modified the message and injects it in the line at that moment or latter such attacks are replay. These attacks are overcome by preplay adversaries.

Denial of Service: These attacks are those which prevent the authorized access when host is trying to communicate with many clients. DoS is of two types namely, resource depletion attacks and connection depletion attack. DoS cannot be completed avoided but the frequency attacks can be minimized [32].

Typing attacks: these attacks replace the protocols of message form one field to the other field. MAC cryptographic action avoids these typing attacks.

Cryptographic Attacks: These are simple encryption techniques based attacks to decipher the key. It is impossible to find such attacks and also a counter measure for the attack.

Protocol Interaction: These attacks run a new protocol within a known protocols and malicious of long term keys are used.

Hijacking and Spoofing: inserting affective packets in the line, substituting traffic, and breaching firewalls include hijacking

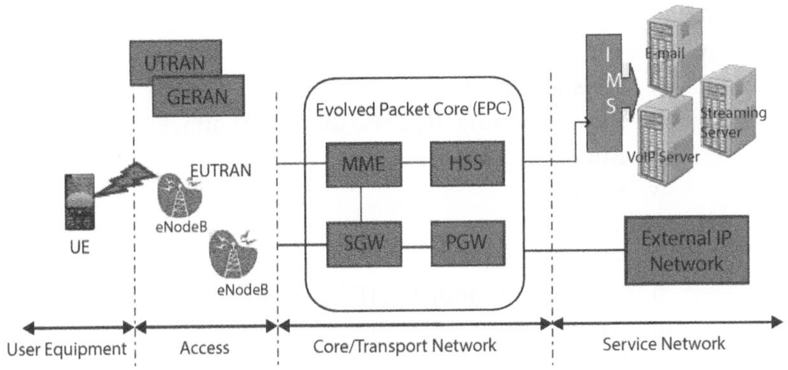

Figure 12.5 LTE security architecture.

and network snoop. These can be avoided by having strong authentication methods; Figure 12.5 shows the LTE security architecture [33].

Generally every attack and their possible solutions can be classified as:

1. General architecture
   a. Threats
      i. Distributed network and open architecture
      ii. Decentralized accountability for security
      iii. Complex business models (IS/Service sharing)
      iv. Minimizing security spend
   b. Solutions
      i. Interoperability standards
      ii. Security audits with remediation commitments
      iii. Strong partner agreement
      iv. Security Budget
2. User equipment (UE)
   a. Threats
      i. Physical attacks
      ii. Lack of security standards and controls on UEs
      iii. Risk of data loss, privacy
      iv. Application layer: virus, malware, phishing
   b. Solutions
      i. Subscriber education
      ii. Industry security standards and controls on UE
      iii. Antivirus
      iv. Strong authentication, authorization, OS encryption

3. Access
    a. Threats
        i. Physical attacks
        ii. Eavesdropping, Redirection, MitM attacks, DoS
        iii. Rogue eNodeBs
        iv. Privacy
    b. Solutions
        i. Physical security
        ii. Network monitoring, IPS systems
        iii. Authentication, authorization, encryption
        iv. Security Architecture
4. Evolved Packet Core (EPC)/Transport and Service
    a. Threats
        i. Unauthorized access
        ii. DoS and DDoS attacks
        iii. Overbilling attacks (IP address hijacking, IP spoofing)
    b. Solutions
        i. Security Architecture: VPNs, VLANs
        ii. Encryption, IKE/IPSec
        iii. Network monitoring, management and load balancing
5. Service network
    a. Threats
        i. Security Architecture: VPNs, VLANs
        ii. Encryption, IKE/IPSec
        iii. Network monitoring, management and load balancing
    b. Solutions
        i. Security Architecture: VPNs, VLANs
        ii. Encryption, IKE/IPSec
        iii. Network monitoring, management and load balancing

12.6 5G Wireless Systems

Fifth generation of communication systems are beyond 4G with the legacy of it and also added features of radio communications and Internet of Things. The advancements include: increased density of users of broadband, device to device communications and machine type communications. It has goals of lower errors is communication thus decreasing latency, low energy consumption and better communication with Internet of Things, increased bandwidth, increased number of connected devices, reliability, coverage, increased battery life and reduction of energy usage. Figure 12.6 shows the architecture of 5G wireless communication systems [34].

The security requirements of 5G include [35]:

- It requires improved resiliency and availability against signal based threats
- Special design for decreased latency
- Compliance with exiting 3G and 4G networks
- Provides public safety and mission critical communications
- Robust and can withstand jamming attacks
- Improved security for small cell nodes

Like other systems here also authentication, confidentiality, integrity, and availability are the four main security goals to be achieved. There are mainly four attacks which interrupt services in the 5G communication network and they are [36]: eavesdropping, jamming, DoS and DDoS, MITM. Eavesdropping and traffic analysis are both passive attacks. Eavesdropping has an intruder in between the sender and the receiver and listens to the messages sent. Traffic analysis includes the information theft such as identity, location and communication parties. Due to sudden increase in technology improvement eavesdroppers have taken advantage of information theft. Jamming is disrupting the communication between the two users it may also prevent the users from using the radio communications [37]. Jamming is an active attack and resource allocation strategy is used between the jammer and the fusion center.

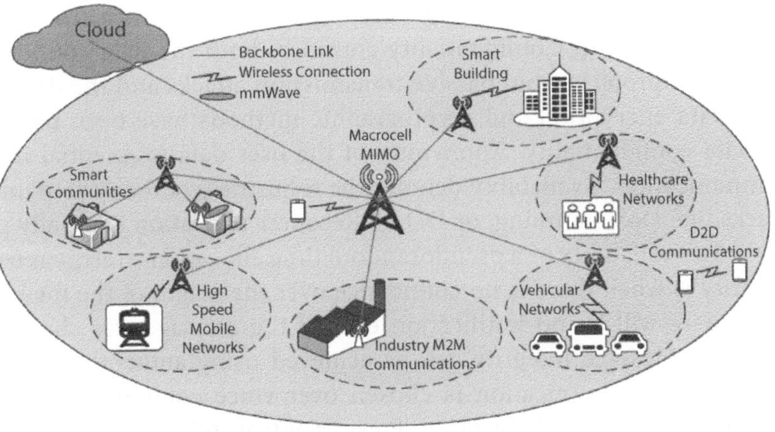

Figure 12.6 5G security architecture.

A DoS attack is an active attack which violates the availability of resources for the authorized user. Jamming techniques can be used for launching a DoS attack. DoS expand as Denial of Service attack. DoS and DDoS are potential threats for the service providers. DoS attack the physical components and the network infrastructure. Based on the attack it can be found whether the attack was for the device or for the network infrastructure. In a MITM attack the intruder takes control of the Communication channel between the users or the legitimate parties. Authentication between the mobile device and the base station can avoid the false base station attacks. It is active attack, which can be implemented on any layer [38]. It is a very common attack which forces the user to communicate with the false base station.

Many researches are still under progress for a stronger security mechanism, as discussed earlier any security mechanism developed should have entity authentication, message authentication, data confidentiality, privacy, availability, and integrity. Several technologies are used for the security mechanism like, HetNet, Network Functions Virtualization (NFV), massive MIMO, Software Defined Network (SDN), D2D, Software Defined Radio (SDR), Cloud Radio Access Network (C-RAN), and IoT [39]. These technologies are used for the extensive use for the spectrum flexibly, storage, computing, and technology access.

When authentication is considered 5G requires complex authentication methodologies since authentication among, service provider, user, and the mobile management entity. Cyclic redundancy check based authentication is suggested since authentication between the user device and the service provider is necessary because of the amount of information communicated regularly. It can be implemented as network only, service provider only or authentication by both the network and service provider only [40]. Confidentiality considers both the data confidentiality which protects from passive transmission attacks and the data privacy. Data encryption and cryptographic methods have been used for the data confidentiality. Anonymity of the user data is essential in 5G communication. Availability denotes the robustness of the system under attacks like DoS, jamming, or DDoS. Resource allocation is usually preferred for availability or a pseudorandom time allocation strategy is used. Integrity is when there is no confidence over the origin of the messages [41]. There will be no notification even if the message was change or modified. Message integrity can be achieved using authentication systems. Data communication is chosen over voice communication hen integrity attack are taking place. Power control, relays, artificial noise, signal processing are various methods used in the security of the more modern 5G communication systems.

12.7 LoRA

There are various wireless transmission systems like Bluetooth Low Energy (BLE), LoRaWAN, ZigBee, and Z-Wave based on energy level, coverage range, and usage. Low power wide area networks (LPWAN) are used in low power consumption based applications; LoRAWAN is an application of LPWAN [42]. We are just taking only infant step toward LoRA and researches under the progress for the security of LoRAWAN. AES is used in two step levels for the security of the data transmitted. One is between the device and the gateways, whereas the other is on the application level. Figure 12.7 shows the architecture of LoRA.

The advantages of LoRa include: a) increased batter life because of asynchronous nodes and communicates only when needed, b) high network capacity because of adaptive data rate and multi modem transceiver in the gateways, c) different device classes because of downlink communication latencies, d) security because of two layered security is achieved. Security is achieved in both network and the application layers. AES128 secret key is used for secret key exchange and authentication, these key changes every session for making communication more secure [43–45].

Threats for the LoRA are the same as in 5G system and the security measures are still under study. Various studies have proposed various security protocols and these protocols are validated every day.

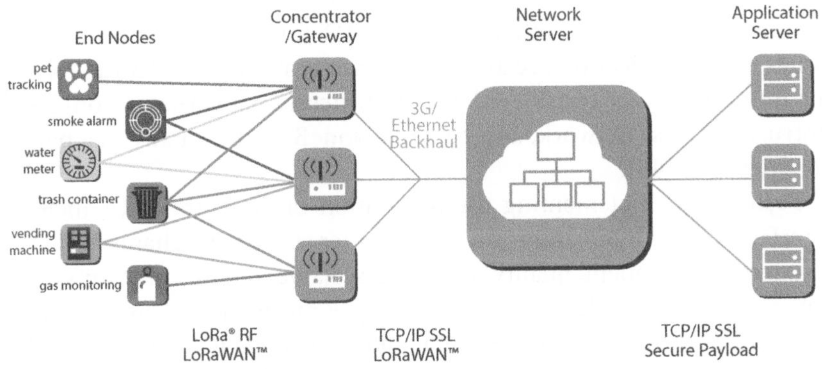

Figure 12.7 Architecture of LoRA.

12.8 5G Integrated With LoRA

LoRaWAN (Low Range Wide Area Network) is a low power network which can connect to billions of devices. With IoT (internet of Things) reaching its pinnacle, researches have begun in the integration of 5G (fifth generation of mobile communications) with LoRa [46]. By the integration of LoRa and 5G networks low power consumption and low latency can be achieved. 5G will have numerous sensors which are IoT and can handle affluent mobile devices at a single time. All the connected devices can be monitored and controlled in the cloud with IoT.

With myriad devices interconnected in a network having 5G and IoT under consideration security is a big issue. Threats and breach of 5G network added to the problems like viruses, wormholes which are faced in internet has to be addressed. 5G network faces threats like eavesdropping, jamming, Dos and DDoS, Man in the middle (MITM) attacks. LoRa also faces security issues like wormhole attack, replay attack and jamming. For authentication issues authentication and key agreement (AKA) protocol based entity authentication is implemented and for the message authentication cyclic redundancy check authentication is implemented [47]. Encryption avoids eavesdropping incase the eavesdropper is strong or multiple leaks cryptographic algorithm, physical layer security is used. Resource allocation strategy detects jamming in 5G networks. Privacy and data confidentiality will be a severe problem in 5G networks PLS provides data security, asymmetric cryptographic algorithm provides location security.

In the proposed system a LoRa connected 5G system, RFID authentication along with PLS is sued, which will address most of the 5G security problems. By this, eavesdropping, jamming, and data piracy are avoided by using PLS and by using RFID for authentication security issues in authentication are avoided. To integrate with LoRA the following four options are considered: via 3GPP access network, via non-3GPP untrusted access network, as a part of eNodeB, and virtually as a part of core network [48].

Features of implementing the integration of 5G with LoRA includes interface of communication and traffic, better security mechanism, instant resource management, quality of service, scalable, support in today's available commercial products, and complexity of mechanism. This integration has enabled the user for cost efficient and energy efficient communication portal. The cloud stores all the collected data and transmission logs. The cloud has to be secure as well. Security threats include [49]:

Replay attacks: It is so commonly possible and can be achieved using any LoRA transceiver. Once the intruder gets hold of a user he can totally block the user for the network form constant replaying the message.

Eavesdropping: Crib dragging methods can be easily used to receiver or encrypt the message transmitted in the air. LoRA implements the channel confidentiality through AES in counter mode.

Bit Flipping Attack: A non-readable bit flipped message is used for the authentication as an integrity check. LoRA avoids the integrity check which in turn opens the gates for the attack.

ACK Spoofing: Where a captured message is delayed and it can be used in acknowledging selectively the receipt of an unrelated message successfully even it is not available in the backend.

Identification and connection of the messages are also considered as the vulnerabilities in the LoRA; hardware itself is simple and unprotected, which could be dangerous. The system is always at is weakness at its link [50].

12.9 Physical Layer Security and RFID Authentication

PLS (Physical layer security) is the new way to secure the 5G integrated with LoRA environment. Typical active attacks in this system is anticipated as man-in-the-middle attack (MITM), replay attack, denial of service (DoS) attack, and distributed denial of service (DDoS) attack. Having RFID for the authentication will avoid the unauthorized join in the network problems. Thus the problem of replay, ACK spoofing, bit flipped attacks can be avoided since the messages will be already authenticated using RFID and hence the communicating device in under the control. Having PLS will avoid the common problems like eavesdropping, jamming, and spoofing. The implementation of this security mechanism is done as such in the 4G and 5G systems.

12.10 Conclusion

5G mobile communication network will have affluent wireless devices connected and the issues faced on security front will be enormous. The evolution of mobile communication and its generations are discussed along with the security measures taken in each generation. The future is in the hands of wireless communication. A novel security method for the LoRa integrated 5G network is introduced. The security protocol includes PLS and RFID securing. The results and performance analysis have proven well suited for the futuristic communication systems. The future of the proposed work extends unto securing the system from wormholes.

References

1. Ahmad, I., Liyanage, M., Shahabuddin, S. *et al.*, Design Principles for 5G Security, in: *A Comprehensive Guide to 5G Security*, pp. 75–98, 2018.
2. Ali, M., Khan, S.U., Vasilakos, A.V., Security in cloud computing: Opportunities and challenges. *Inf. Sci.*, 305, 357–383, 2015.
3. Amraoui, H., Habbani, A., Hajami, A., Bilal, E., Security & cooperation mechanisms over mobile ad hoc networks: A survey and challenges. *2017 International Conference on Electrical and Information Technologies (ICEIT)*, 2017.
4. Apoorv, R. and Mathur, P., Smart attendance management using Bluetooth Low Energy and Android. *2016 IEEE Region 10 Conference (TENCON)*, 2016.
5. Aras, E., Ramachandran, G.S., Lawrence, P., Hughes, D., Exploring the Security Vulnerabilities of LoRa. *2017 3rd IEEE International Conference on Cybernetics (CYBCONF)*, 2017.
6. Bluetooth Low Energy Mesh Networks: A Survey. *Sensors*, 17, 7, 1467, 2017.
7. Brauer, S., Zubow, A., Zehl, S. *et al.*, On practical selective jamming of Bluetooth Low Energy advertising. *2016 IEEE Conference on Standards for Communications and Networking (CSCN)*, 2016.
8. Cao, J., Ma, M., Li, H. *et al.*, A Survey on Security Aspects for LTE and LTE-A Networks. *IEEE Commun. Surv. Tutorials*, 16, 1, 283–302, 2014.
9. Dabbagh, M., Hamdaoui, B., Guizani, M., Rayes, A., Software-defined networking security: Pros and cons. *IEEE Commun. Mag.*, 53, 6, 73–79, 2015.
10. Dohler, M. and Nakamura, T., *5G Mobile and Wireless Communications Technology*, 1st edition, Cambridge University Press, 2016.
11. Foster, G., Vahid, S., Tafazolli, R., SON Evolution for 5G Mobile Networks, in: *Fundamentals of 5G Mobile Networks*, pp. 221–240, 2015.
12. Hrri, J. and Bonnet, C., Security in Next Generation Mobile Networks, in: *Wireless and Mobile Network Security*, pp. 409–435.
13. LTE Advanced Networks-Secure Data Sharing Strategy for D2D Communication technique. *Int. J. Mod. Trends Eng. Res.*, 4, 4, 187–196, 2017.
14. Markelj, B. and Zgaga, S., Mobile Security: Two Generations of Potential Victims, in: *Advances in Cybersecurity 2017*, pp. 65–76, 2017.

15. Monshizadeh, M. and Yan, Z., Security Related Data Mining. *2014 IEEE International Conference on Computer and Information Technology*, 2014.
16. Monshizadeh, M., Khatri, V., Gurtov, A., NFV security considerations for cloud-based mobile virtual network operators. *2016 24th International Conference on Software, Telecommunications and Computer Networks (SoftCOM)*, 2016.
17. Nguyen, H. and Iacono, L.L., RESTful IoT Authentication Protocols, in: *Mobile Security and Privacy*, pp. 217–234, 2017.
18. Oca, E.M.D. and Mallouli, W., Security Aspects of SDMN, in: *Software Defined Mobile Networks (SDMN)*, pp. 331–357, 2015.
19. Padgette, J., Scarfone, K., Chen, L., *Guide to bluetooth security*. NIST Special Publication 800, 121, 25, 2012.
20. Pavia, J., Lopes, D., Cristovao, P. *et al.*, The evolution and future perspective of security in mobile communications networks. *2017 9th International Congress on Ultra Modern Telecommunications and Control Systems and Workshops (ICUMT)*, 2017.
21. Perez, A., Security Mobile Network, in: *Implementing IP and Ethernet on the 4G Mobile Network*, pp. 193–203, 2017.
22. Powering the Internet of Things With 5G Networks, in: *Advances in Wireless Technologies and Telecommunication*, 2018.
23. Qiao, J., Shen, X., Mark, J. *et al.*, Enabling device-to-device communications in millimeter-wave 5G cellular networks. *IEEE Commun. Mag.*, 53, 1, 209–215, 2015.
24. Sharma, V., You, I., Leu, F.-Y., Atiquzzaman, M., Secure and efficient protocol for fast handover in 5G mobile Xhaul networks. *J. Netw. Comput. Appl.*, 102, 38–57, 2018.
25. Shim, K., Do, T.N., An, B., A physical layer security-based routing protocol in mobile ad-hoc wireless networks. *2018 20th International Conference on Advanced Communication Technology (ICACT)*, 2018.
26. Spectral coexistence for next generation wireless backhaul networks, in: *Access, Fronthaul and Backhaul Networks for 5G & Beyond*, pp. 307–335.
27. Doelitzscher, F., *et al.*, Understanding cloud audits, in: *Privacy and Security for Cloud Computing*, Springer, London, 125–163, 2013.
28. Wang, M., Yan, Z., Niemi, V., UAKA-D2D: Universal Authentication and Key Agreement Protocol in D2D Communications. *Mobile Netw. Appl.*, 22, 3, 510–525, 2017.
29. Wang, W. and Hu, L., A Secure and Efficient Handover Authentication Protocol for Wireless Networks. *Sensors*, 14, 7, 11379–11394, 2014.
30. Wang, Y. and Alshboul, Y., Mobile security testing approaches and challenges. *2015 First Conference on Mobile and Secure Services (MOBISECSERV)*, 2015.
31. Wei, L., Hu, R.Q., Qian, Y., Wu, G., Energy Efficiency and Spectrum Efficiency of Multihop Device-to-Device Communications Underlaying Cellular Networks. *IEEE Trans. Veh. Technol.*, 65, 1, 367–380, 2016.

32. Yasmin, R., Petajajarvi, J., Mikhaylov, K., Pouttu, A., On the integration of LoRaWAN with the 5G test network. *2017 IEEE 28th Annual International Symposium on Personal, Indoor, and Mobile Radio Communications (PIMRC)*, 2017.
33. Yrjo, R. and Rushil, D., Cloud computing in mobile networks—Case MVNO. *2011 15th International Conference on Intelligence in Next Generation Networks*, 2011.
34. Zhang, J., Xie, W., Yang, F., An Architecture for 5G Mobile Network Based on SDN and NFV. *6th International Conference on Wireless, Mobile and Multi-Media (ICWMMN 2015)*, 2015.
35. Dolezilek, D. and Hussey, L., Requirements or recommendations? Sorting out NERC CIP, NIST, and DOE cybersecurity. *2011 64th Annual Conference for Protective Relay Engineers*, 2011.
36. Wei, D., Jafari, M., Lu, Y., On Protecting Industrial Automation and Control Systems against Electronic Attacks. *2007 IEEE International Conference on Automation Science and Engineering*, 2007.
37. Wei, D., Lu, Y., Jafari, M. *et al.*, Protecting Smart Grid Automation Systems Against Cyberattacks. *IEEE Trans. Smart Grid*, 2, 4, 782–795, 2011.
38. Coutinho, M., Lambert-Torres, G., Silva, L.D. *et al.*, Anomaly detection in power system control center critical infrastructures using rough classification algorithm. *2009 3rd IEEE International Conference on Digital Ecosystems and Technologies*, 2009.
39. Coutinho, M., Lambert-Torres, G., Silva, L., Lazarek, H., Improving Detection Attacks in Electric Power System Critical Infrastructure Using Rough Classification Algorithm. *Proceedings of The Second International Conference on Forensic Computer Science*, 2007.
40. Ten, C.-W., Manimaran, G., Liu, C.-C., Cybersecurity for Critical Infrastructures: Attack and Defense Modeling. *IEEE Trans. Syst. Man Cybern. Part A Syst. Humans*, 40, 4, 853–865, 2010.
41. Su, S., Duan, X., Zeng, X. *et al.*, Context Information based Cyber Security Defense of Protection System. *2007 IEEE Power Engineering Society General Meeting*, 2007.
42. Huang, Y., Esmalifalak, M., Nguyen, H. *et al.*, Bad data injection in smart grid: Attack and defense mechanisms. *IEEE Commun. Mag.*, 51, 1, 27–33, 2013.
43. Berthier, R., Sanders, W.H., Khurana, H., Intrusion Detection for Advanced Metering Infrastructures: Requirements and Architectural Directions. *2010 First IEEE International Conference on Smart Grid Communications*, 2010.
44. Mander, T., Cheung, R., Nabhani, F., Power system DNP3 data object security using data sets. *Comput. Secur.*, 29, 4, 487–500, 2010.
45. Ten, C.-W., Govindarasu, M., Liu, C.-C., Cybersecurity for electric power control and automation systems. *2007 IEEE International Conference on Systems, Man and Cybernetics*, 2007.

46. Queiroz, C., Mahmood, A., Tari, Z., SCADASim—A Framework for Building SCADA Simulations. *IEEE Trans. Smart Grid*, 2, 4, 589–597, 2011.
47. Khurana, H., Bobba, R., Yardley, T. *et al.*, Design Principles for Power Grid Cyber-Infrastructure Authentication Protocols. *2010 43rd Hawaii International Conference on System Sciences*, 2010.
48. Xie, L., Mo, Y., Sinopoli, B., Integrity Data Attacks in Power Market Operations. *IEEE Trans. Smart Grid*, 2, 4, 659–666, 2011.
49. Srivastava, A., Morris, T., Ernster, T. *et al.*, Modeling Cyber-Physical Vulnerability of the Smart Grid With Incomplete Information. *IEEE Trans. Smart Grid*, 4, 1, 235–244, 2013.
50. Gamage, T.T., Roth, T.P., Mcmillin, B.M., Crow, M.L., Mitigating Event Confidentiality Violations in Smart Grids: An Information Flow Security-Based Approach. *IEEE Trans. Smart Grid*, 4, 3, 1227–1234, 2013.

13

Use of Machine Learning in Design of Security Protocols

M. Sundaresan[1]* and D. Boopathy[2]†

[1]*Department of Information Technology, Bharathiar University, Coimbatore, Tamilnadu, India*
[2]*Department of Information Technology, Bharathiar University, Coimbatore, Tamilnadu, India*

Abstract
Machine learning is an application of artificial intelligence that provides systems with the capacity to learn automatically and improve them from previously acquired experience without being explicitly programmed. Network security protocol is a type of network-related protocol that ensures the protection and integrity of data while transmission over a network connection. Network security protocols describe the processes and methodology to protect the network data from any unlawful attempt to evaluate or extract the contents of data. The growth of network communications creates the cloud services as major breakthrough to change the resource utilization and it provides all types of services to the end users. The security breaches and data-security-related threats are together creating a major issue in cloud services. The user's data are targeted as prey by the offenders and the active attacks or passive attacks were initialized to analyze the weakness in the cloud services. The identified weakness will be used as a loophole by attackers to execute their attacks on the cloud service. Moreover, the cloud services are designed to maintain and provide the data security to their users. In particular, most of cloud concerns are depending on the third party service providers to protect them from the data security related threats. These types of dependency need to be eradicated, and in addition, the cloud concerns need to be designed and thus create the cloud services with self-defending protocols against different attacks. The JOKER (Joint and Offensive Kinetic Execution Resolver) technique is a self-defending security methodology, and it can avoid

**Corresponding author*: bu.sundaresan@gmail.com
†*Corresponding author*: ndboopathy@gmail.com

Dinesh Goyal, S. Balamurugan, Sheng-Lung Peng and O.P. Verma (eds.) Design and Analysis of Security Protocol for Communication, (265–286) © 2020 Scrivener Publishing LLC

the attacks and be able to protect the data by itself from passive attacks and data security related threats.

Keywords: Self-defending protocol, security protocol, data protection, privacy, active attacks, passive attacks

13.1 Introduction

The system invaders and security hackers generally concentrate on the user's data. Data is the key point which contains general and confidential information of users. Hence the data will meet different attacks on three states, and they are data at transmission, data at process, and data at rest [1]. Based on the states of data, the offenders will choose different attack types, and they are - active attacks and passive attacks [2]. Figure 13.1 illustrates the active attack, and passive attack is illustrated in Figure 13.2. The active attack is used to change the system resources, make some modification on data, cause damage to the user's system, and create threat to integrity and availability [2]. The passive attack is used to utilize the information from the system, and provide threat to confidentiality [2]. The most important need for avoiding the active attack is detection of the attacks earlier and for avoiding the user from passive attack is preventing that user's data. From the awareness point of view,

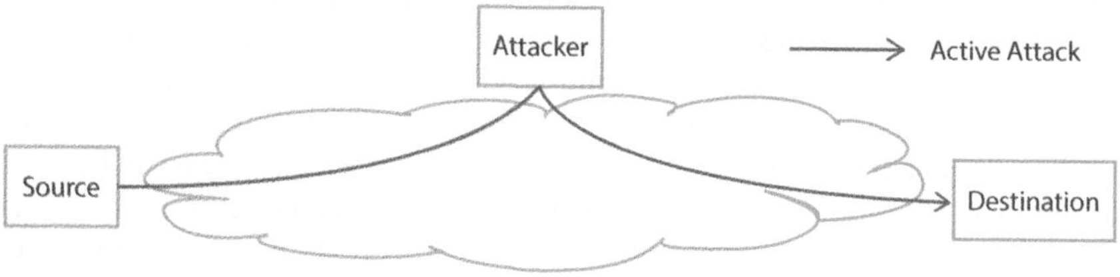

Figure 13.1 Active attack.

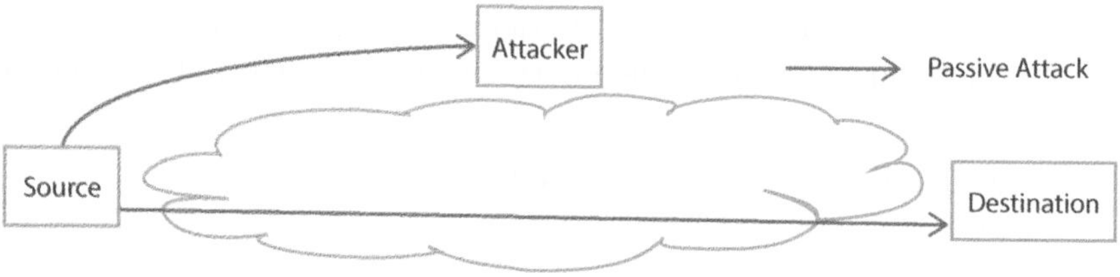

Figure 13.2 Passive attack.

it must be noted that with reference to the active attack the victim can get informed about the attack, but in passive attack the victim is not at all aware of the attack.

The data security has three key points, and they are as follows: Confidentiality, Integrity, and Availability (i.e., CIA) [3]; and they can be broken by using both active and passive attacks. It shows that the data in transmission from source to destination are at risk, and further the data retrieval from cloud storage and processing the retrieved data in cloud applications are also at risk, and finally data at storage, i.e., at rest, are under risk too. The growth of digital industry makes the users by default to depend on the cloud storage for many services; in those services the cloud related data storage is obligatory. The cloud storage provides the data access at "on-demand method" and easy usage of data by different online processes when required. By default, each and every technology has its negative part too, in the cloud data storage the negative part is—data related attacks and related threats. The present scenario shows that the users cannot avoid the cloud data storage but they need to protect their data from unauthorized persons and its related threats. These things must be taken care of by the cloud service providers, but up-to now they are trying hard to safeguard the user's data from security related threats. But apart from the common users, last year (2017) some companies including Deep Root Analysis, UK National Health Services, Verizon Communications, Yahoo, Uber, TIO Networks faced the security breaches, and data thefts [4].

In practice, the data are stored in public resource or private resource and made them available for usage by connecting that resource into the internet, and then the connected resources will surely meet the data related threats. The defenders need to enrich the defense methods rapidly to defend the attacks and prevent the data to be available from unauthorized persons. The above discussed contents from different perspectives are taken into consideration and are applied to design the JOKER Self-defending Protocol.

The Figure 13.3 illustrates the Secured Cloud Data Storage Prototype Model (SCDSPM) [5–8] which was already designed and tested to create the secured cloud storage environment. The results which were obtained from that SCDSPM achieved the objectives of the design. But SCDSPM was designed for storage of data in safer manner and also to avoid the user's files from data mishandling-related problems. In this chapter, the JOKER protocol is concentrating on transferring of data to the destination securely without being affected by any one of the passive attacks (i.e., tapping attack).

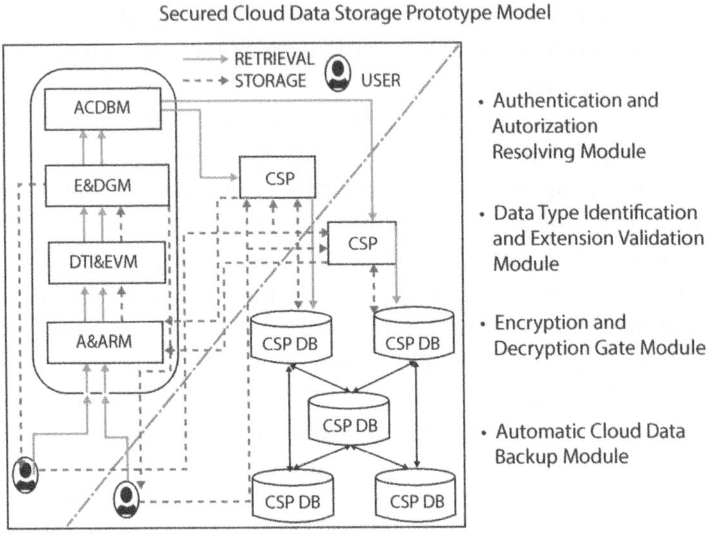

Figure 13.3 Secured cloud data storage prototype model (SCDSPM).

The security protocol is used to analyze, prevent, and defend the security threats. The cyber war is already going on between countries and some incidents happening around the world provide evidence for it. Those cyber attacks were done at destination successfully from the located source somewhere. Nowadays systems and gadgets are connected to the internet and those things are treated as our third eye. That third eye is always keeping us on surveillance and tracks all our activities through internet. This information shows that most of the gadgets are getting vulnerable and making us a prey to the hackers. Sometimes the attack may target shutting down resources or taking the information away from systems.

In this technological era, the weapon of the enemy will be either cyber terrorism or cyber warfare. Some years ago, one of the top 10 countries made a cyber attack on a south Asian country's nuclear plant. Whether the system resources were connected to the internet or not, the attack will reach the target system in any mode like malware, man-in-middle attack, and infected hardware. The government and industries are learning some lessons from each and every cyber attack experienced in the past.

The security protocols are basically core—designed at the introduction of internet—related security issues. Later, some modifications and improvements took place on the existing security protocols and were made available for public use. The international standards, country jurisdictions, government regulations, and standards are prepared to confirm the users' safety in communications. The attacks can be either active or passive attacks. In active attacks the system resources can be altered and will affect the specific operation. The passive attacks are done to learn something or make the use of information from the target systems without affecting the system resources.

The security protocols, which are used in communication sector, need to be redesigned to defend the upcoming attacks. The worms, viruses, security breaches and security attacks are then changing attacking strategies every new and then, and moreover, the existing defense methods are not able to figure out those attacks and made the resources a prey. So the new type of security protocol is in need and that too one which concentrates on the machine learning. Once the security protocol is designed with machine learning, then it can get the capability of defending the upcoming attacks automatically. This kind of security protocol can be adapted by any kind of online applications, which need security from the future attacks.

Machine learning concept is taken into consideration in the JOKER protocol. The machine learning is defined as "*Machine learning is an application of artificial intelligence (AI) that provides systems the ability to automatically learn and improve from experience without being explicitly programmed. Machine learning focuses on the development of computer programs that can access data and use it learn for themselves.* [9]"

The security protocol is defined as "*Network security protocols are a type network protocol that ensures the security and integrity of data in transit over a network connection. Network security protocols define the processes and methodology to secure network data from any illegitimate attempt to review or extract the contents of data*". [10]

Section 13.2 reviews the related works concerning the existing self-defending security protocol methods and its related works. Section 13.3 deliberates the JOKER protocol; JOKER protocol's working methodology, JOKER protocol's procedure, and JOKER protocol's Pseudo code. Section 13.4 analyses the simulation of experimental results, features of the JOKER protocol and the comparison of the JOKER protocol. Section 13.5 presents the conclusion derived from the findings, and the advantages of the JOKER protocol, and finally its related future enhancements.

13.2 Review of Related Literature

Sung-Ju *et al.* proposed an on-demand routing scheme identified as "Split Multipath Routing" that creates and uses various paths of maximally disjoint paths. Route recovery process and control message overhead will be minimized by the provision of the multiple routes. The proposed protocol uses a per-packet allocation method to allocate data packets into various routes of active sessions. This traffic distribution efficiently utilizes available network resources and prevents nodes of the route from being congested in heavily loaded traffic situations [11].

Rob *et al.* proposed a formal model for a fragmentation and a reassembly protocol running on top of the consistent Controller Area Network bus, which is broadly used in automotive and aerospace applications. Even though, the Controller Area Network bus comes with an in-built mechanism for prioritization, the authors argue that this is not sufficient and so want to provide another protocol to overcome the shortcoming [12].

Yan *et al.* introduced a new R-tree node-splitting algorithm. R-tree is widely used in geographical information systems, Computer Aided Design systems, and spatial databases. Linear node-splitting algorithm could construct an R-tree fast and efficiently, by partitioning the minimum bounding rectangle of the node. Then the authors found that this node-splitting algorithm would generate uneven nodes. After that they also developed an algorithm to balance those uneven splitting results to meet the demands of the R-tree definition. Finally they improved the node-splitting algorithm by considering the siblings of the splitting node [13].

Kiran *et al.* designed a Multi-radio Hybrid node that performs traffic splitting over a Multi-Hop Ad-hoc wireless network. The multi radio nodes have a WiMAX and a WiFi Radio that are used in transmitting data traffic over two different radio channels. In this proposed work the mobility aspect of the network was considered. The implementation was executed by using the AODV Routing protocol and the Bee Hive Routing algorithm on these nodes, which compared the Throughput and End-to-End delay for data transmission in the network [14].

Jatinder *et al.* explained how we can detect passive attack and then detailed on how to develop prevention from passive attacks. The detection of passive attacks was done by using the concept of key loggers and the registry files concept. Here preventive methods from passive attacks used the concept of virtual keyboards and the Network Access Control concept during online transmission of data. The authors explained the network security and unethical hacking. The major benefit of combining these concepts is that it helps to check the behavior of the network whether it is secure or not secure during data transmission from source to destination [15].

Katharina *et al.* proposed and presented an analysis of mixing strategies as a counter measure to trace analysis attacks in Tor [16].

Fan *et al.* proposed a traffic reshaping technique to thwart traffic analysis. The proposed technique creates multiple virtual Media Access Control interfaces over a single wireless card, and then it dynamically schedules the data packets over these interfaces, thereby reshaping the packet features on each virtual interface. The features of original traffic are obscured and unavailable for the adversary to infer the users' online activities. The proposed technique evaluates the performance of traffic reshaping through trace-based experiments. The acquired results showed that the traffic reshaping was effective and efficient in defending against the traffic analysis related attacks [17].

Xinwen *et al.* suggested statistical pattern recognition as a primary technology to evaluate the effectiveness of active traffic analysis attacks and the equivalent counter measures. The evaluation shows that the sample entropy of ping packets' round trip time is an effective feature of statistics to discover the payload traffic rate. Also the Xinwen and others proposed the simple counter measures that can significantly reduce the effectiveness of ping-based active traffic analysis attacks. The experiments discussed here validate the effectiveness of the proposed scheme, which can be used in other scenarios too [18].

13.3 Joint and Offensive Kinetic Execution Resolver

The data in cloud storage needs protection with minimum of three layers. The First layer is encryption layer where the data need to be encrypted with the international encryption standards along with the user's country level data regulations. The Second layer is authorization layer where the persons who are authorized to use the data must be defined in this layer and moreover, their identity needs to be verified within this layer. The third layer is data authentication layer, from where the data are getting authenticated and the data-transferred destination must be verified, whether the data transmission to the destination is legally permitted by the country's regulations or not. These things must be covered in the data protection. Figure 13.4 illustrates the data covered with all the three layers.

Communication between two nodes will transfer the data from source to destination and this transmission needs to be taken care of by cloud service provider. The literature study defined some issues related to the network attacks and its measures to solve the problems. But in reality the growth of information industry creates a chance to make the existing data handling and transmission methods vulnerable.

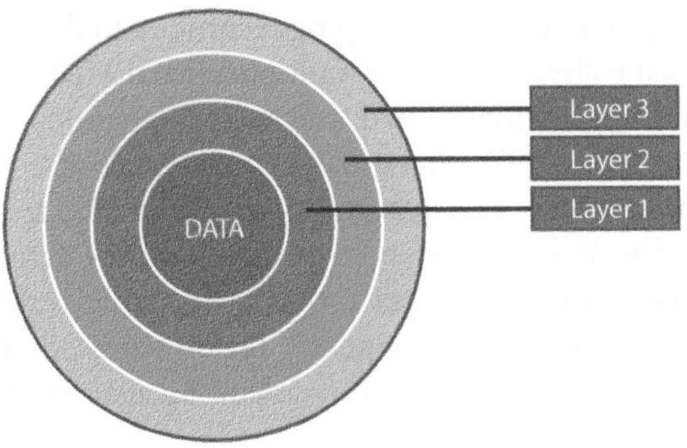

Figure 13.4 Data protected with the three layers.

The JOKER protocol includes finding the availability of nodes, creating the different routes to reach the destination, finding the shortest path routes among the created routes to transfer the data in different routes, encrypting the data, splitting the encrypted data into packets, and jumbling the data packets. Finally it will send the jumbled data packets to the destination. The JOKER protocol is illustrated in Figure 13.3 as design methodology and its related working model as illustrated in Figure 13.4 and the JOKER protocol process are defined in procedure and pseudo code sections. The JOKER protocol is able to self-defend itself by using the non-uniform packets transmission. By default most of the users are linked with more than one application at-a-time. While transferring the data packets under the JOKER protocol, all other applications packet transmissions also take place simultaneously between the user's ends to different service provider's end. So, it is difficult to figure out what other routes are used to transfer the data packets, and also it is unpredictable whether in passive attack all the data were captured by attackers from user end, then merging of those captured packets are not possible because of split and jumble process. The total number of data packets is not predictable by attackers and moreover, to complete the non-complete data packets into complete data packets is also impossible.

For example, the data are divided into 50 data packets and those data packets are transferred to the destination through different routes. An attacker captures one route's data packets and tries to know the information from that captured data packets is not possible, because it is only a part of the transferred data packets. Even if all the data packets were captured by attacker, then merging the data packets into the correct data packets is again not at all possible. The "self-defend" is defined here as "not to provide the information to the attacker even though all the data packets were captured by the attacker". It must be remembered that the passive attack will affect the confidential nature of the user data and as a result, the cloud service users will lose their trust on their cloud service providers. While designing this JOKER protocol, the SCDSPM model was kept under consideration. The SCDSPM was designed to create and maintain the security to the user's data in cloud storage; however, it is unavoidable that the data might be captured during the time of transmission. To overcome the data capturing at the time of data transmission will be partly avoidable by this JOKER protocol. In fact the JOKER protocol will add more efficiency to the SCDSPM.

13.3.1 Design of JOKER Protocol

The Joker method has been explained in the following diagrams. The diagram illustrates both the Source to destination and destination to source flow.

Figure 13.5 shows the design of the JOKER protocol, Figure 13.6 to Figure 13.8 explain the step by step working model of single source to

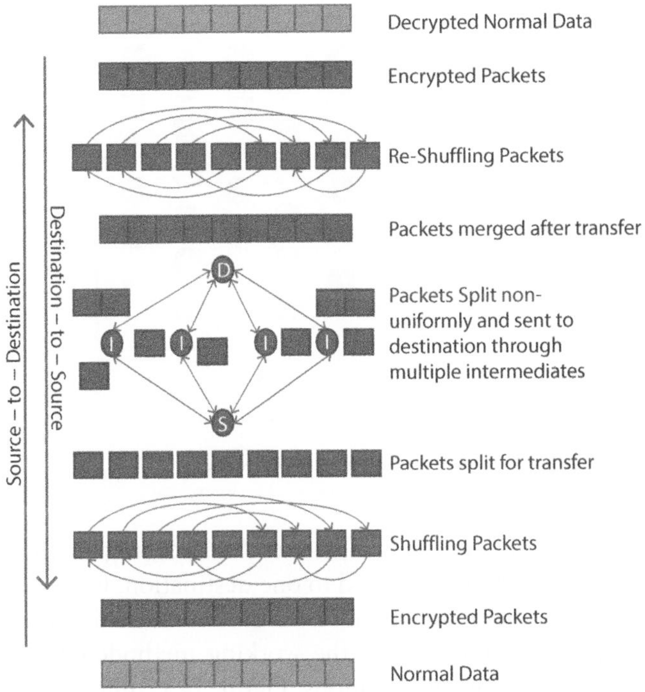

Figure 13.5 Design of the JOKER protocol.

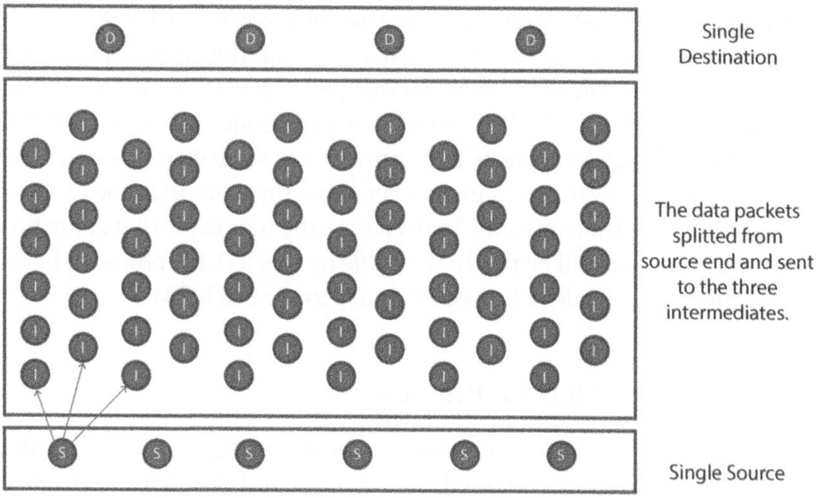

Figure 13.6 Design of the JOKER protocol—first step.

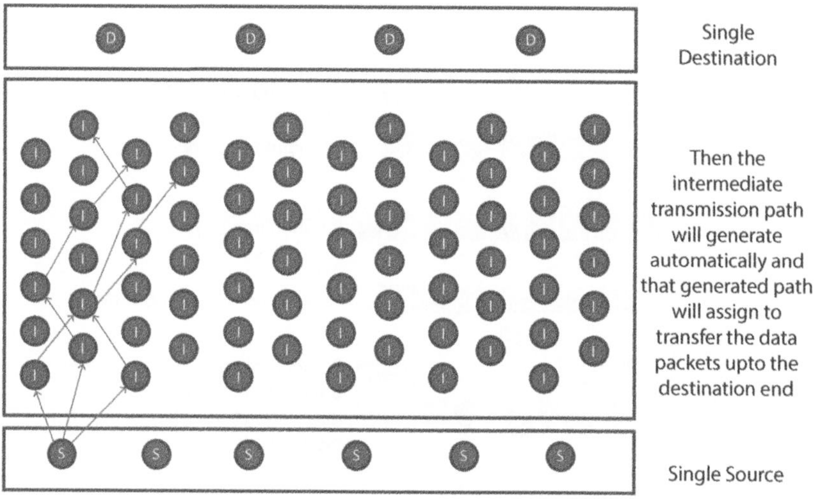

Figure 13.7 Design of the JOKER protocol—second step.

single destination. Figure 13.9 illustrates the working methodology of more than one resources connected to one destination, Figure 13.10 illustrates the working methodology of one source connected to multiple destinations. Figure 13.11 illustrates the working methodology of multiple sources connected to two destinations; Figure 13.12 illustrates the working methodology of multiple sources connected to multiple destinations.

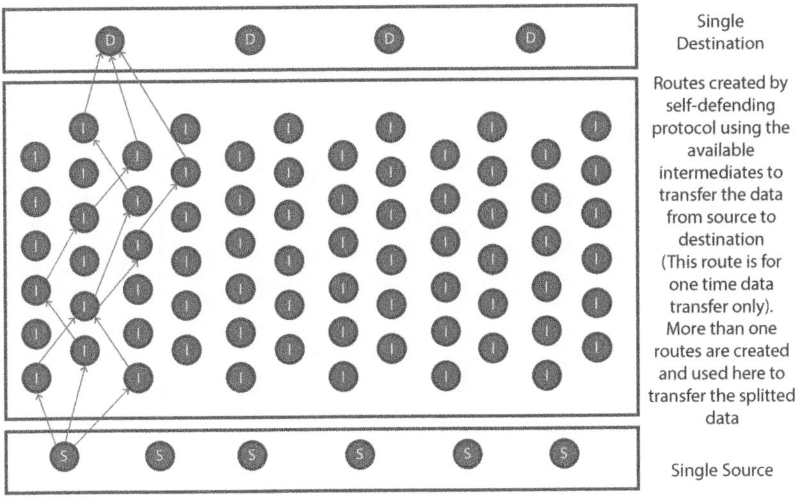
Single
Destination
Routes created by self-defending protocol using the available intermediates to transfer the data from source to destination (This route is for one time data transfer only). More than one routes are created and used here to transfer the splitted data
Single Source

Figure 13.8 Design of the JOKER protocol—third step.

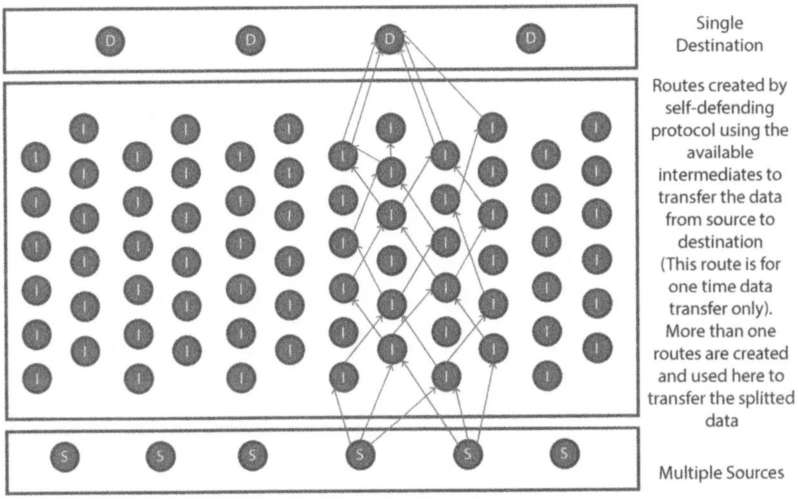
Single
Destination
Routes created by self-defending protocol using the available intermediates to transfer the data from source to destination (This route is for one time data transfer only). More than one routes are created and used here to transfer the splitted data
Multiple Sources

Figure 13.9 Design of the JOKER protocol—more than one sources.

The short forms shown in Figure 13.5 to Figure 13.12 are S = Source, D = Destination, and I = Intermediate.

The Node availability and Classification, Route Identification, Route Allocation, Re-Routing, while the data transmission from source to destination will be automatically taken cared by JOKER protocol. The Methodology and design show the possibility of JOKER protocol implementation.

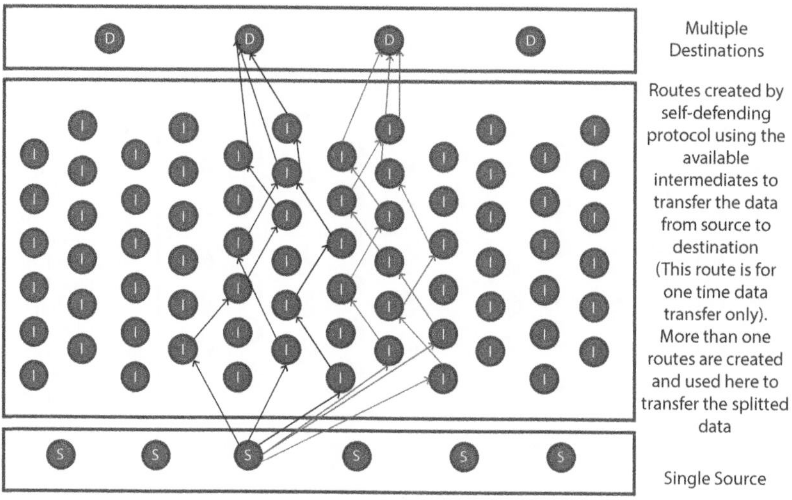
D
D
D
D
Multiple Destinations
Routes created by self-defending protocol using the available intermediates to transfer the data from source to destination (This route is for one time data transfer only). More than one routes are created and used here to transfer the splitted data
S
S
S
S
S
S
Single Source

Figure 13.10 Design of the JOKER protocol—more than one destination.

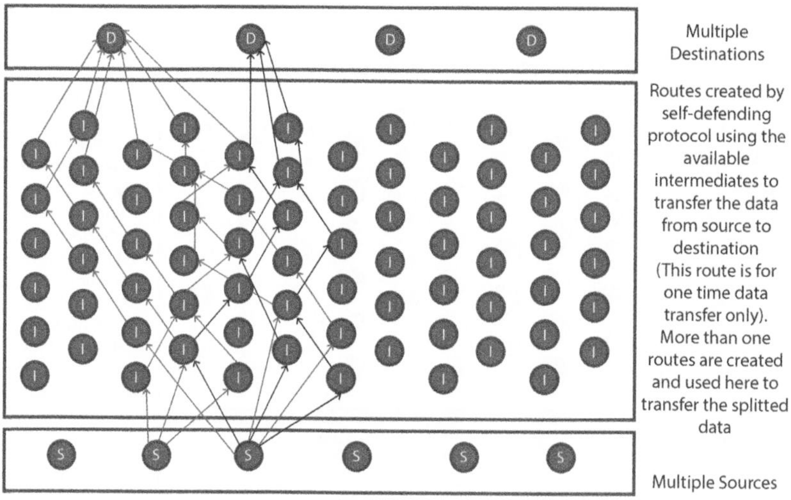
D
D
D
D
Multiple Destinations
Routes created by self-defending protocol using the available intermediates to transfer the data from source to destination (This route is for one time data transfer only). More than one routes are created and used here to transfer the splitted data
S
S
S
S
S
S
Multiple Sources

Figure 13.11 Design of the JOKER protocol—more than one sources and destinations.

13.3.2 Procedure

The procedure for the JOKER protocol:

Step 01: Start the process
Step 02: Select the data to transfer from source to destination
Step 03: Analyze the selected data to apply the encryption process

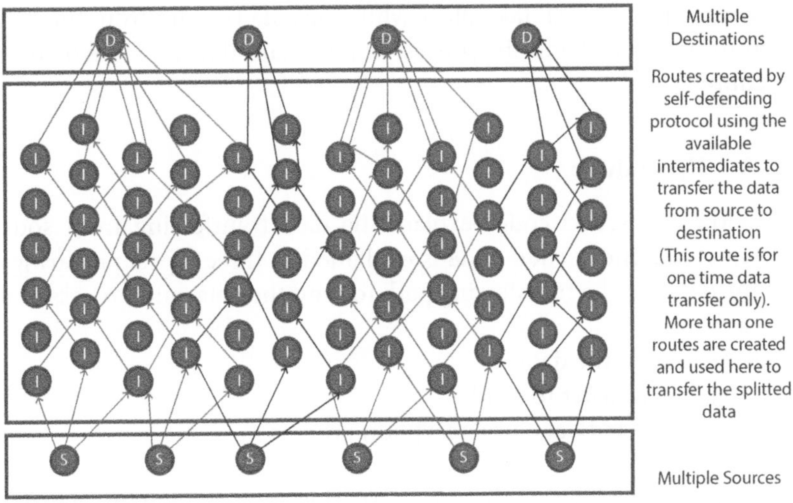
Multiple Destinations
Routes created by self-defending protocol using the available intermediates to transfer the data from source to destination (This route is for one time data transfer only). More than one routes are created and used here to transfer the splitted data
Multiple Sources

Figure 13.12 Data transmission method in JOKER protocol—all sources and all destinations.

Step 04: Apply the encryption process when the analyzing process has finished
Step 05: Analyze the encrypted data to split into packets
Step 06: Split the packets and prepare those packets for jumbling process
Step 07: Jumble the data packets and make them prepared to send in non-uniform method
Step 08: Need to set the transferring path from source to destination through automatic path selection method
Step 09: Send the jumbled data packets from source to destination through selected path
Step 10: Once the data packets received at the destination end; merge those data packets
Step 11: Re-jumble the data packets to get the actual data packets in-order
Step 12: Analyze the re-jumbled data packets to verify whether the data are in order
Step 13: Apply the Decryption process on to the received and analyzed data packets
Step 14: Final output of Data received after the decryption process
Step 15: Stop the process

The same process will take place while the data transfer from the destination to source end and the process will be started from STEP 01 of the procedure.

13.3.3 Procedure

The following pseudo codes explain the data transferring from source to destination. The pseudo code is explained as three types: preparing to send the data, set the transferring path to send the data, and process at the destination.

Preparing to send the data:
Select the data transfer to send
Analyze the selected data for encryption process
If
  Selected data are appropriate for encryption process Then forward them to next step
Else
  Intimate that selected data are not appropriate for encryption process
Apply the Encryption process on the analyzed data
Split the data into data packets
Apply the jumble process on those data packets
Make them ready to transfer
Set the transferring path to send the data:
Get the Source Details
Get the Destination Details
Analyze the intermediates availability
Fix the different Routes to reach the destination from available intermediates
Analyze and Select the Shortest route from the different routes
If
  Destination is reachable by selected intermediates Then forward to next process
Else
  Destination is not reachable again Analyze the shortest route from different routes
Verify the destination to send the packets
Send the split data packets with non-uniform manner through the selected route
Procedure at the Destination:
Merge the received split data packets from different intermediates
Apply the Re-jumble process

Verify the re-jumbled process to confirm whether all the packets are received
Apply the decryption process which was applied for transmission process
Store the decrypted data in storage

13.3.4 Simulation Details and Parameters

The Network Simulator 2 (NS2) was used to simulate the JOKER protocol. It is an open-source event-driven simulator designed specifically for research in computer communication networks [19].

13.3.4.1 Packet Delivering Ratio Calculation

The packet delivery ratio is used to measure the ratio of data packets received by the destinations to those which were generated and transferred by the sources.

$$PDR = \frac{S1}{S2} \tag{13.1}$$

Equation (13.1) shows the packet delivery ratio calculation formula. PDR = Packet Delivery Ratio, S1 = Number of packets received by the each destination, and S2 = Number of packets generated by the each source [20].

13.3.4.2 Packet Loss Ratio Calculation

The packet loss ratio is used to calculate the ratio of data packets loss during the data being transferred from the source to destination [21].

$$PLR = \frac{L1}{L2} \tag{13.2}$$

Equation (13.2) shows the packet loss ratio calculation formula. PLR = Packet Loss Ratio, L1 = Number of lost packets, and L2 = Number of sent packets.

13.3.4.3 Latency (Delay) Calculation

Latency is a measure of delay. In a network, latency measures the time it takes for some data to get to its destination across the network [22].

It is usually measured as a round trip delay—the time taken for information to get to its destination and back again [22].

$$FST = \frac{S}{R} \tag{13.3}$$

Equation (13.3) shows the delay calculation formula where FST = Frame Serialization Time, S = Packet size (bits), and R = Transmission Rate Packet size (bits per second).

13.3.4.4 *Throughput Calculation*

The "throughput" in network refers to the average data rate of successful data or message delivery over a specific communications link.

Network throughput is measured in bits per second (bps) [23].

$$\text{Througput} = \frac{\text{TCPmaximumReceiveWindowSize}}{\text{RTT}} \tag{13.4}$$

Equation (13.4) shows the throughput calculation formula where TCP = Transmission Control Protocol, RTT = Round Trip Time. This calculation considers only when transmission is done without packet loss.

13.4 Results and Discussion

The obtained testing results were verified to calculate the parameters which include Packet Delivering Ratio Calculation, Packet Loss Ratio Calculation, Latency (Delay) Calculation and Throughput Calculation to identify whether the JOKER protocol is able to achieve the data transmission from source to destination or not.

The JOKER protocol in this chapter is a combination of multiple techniques, which is combined to achieve the particular objective, i.e., to defend the passive attack in transmission of data.

The results of the JOKER protocol were analyzed with these parameters to verify whether this technique achieves its objective or not.

The JOKER protocol is designed to add more security to the SCDSPM, so the results of this JOKER protocol were partly compared with the parameters of existing models.

The number of packets generated and sent by the source to the destination was received as it is, i.e., Packet Delivery Ration is achieved 100%. While the users were transferring the data from source to destination, the packet loss did not occur, i.e., Packet Loss Ratio is 0%. The comparison of latency calculation of the JOKER protocol with existing TCP method is shown in Table 13.1 and Figure 13.13.

Table 13.1 Latency parameter details.

Parameters File Size	Latency (in s)	
	Existing	**JOKER**
1 MB	08	09
3 MB	25	24
6 MB	51	48
10 MB	95	89
20 MB	182	171

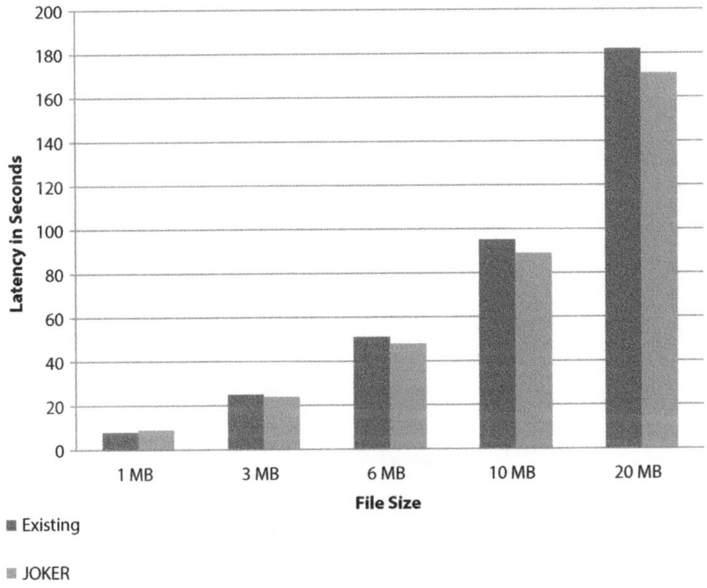

Figure 13.13 Latency parameter analysis.

The comparison of throughput of the JOKER protocol with existing TCP method is shown in Table 13.2 and Figure 13.14. The comparison shows that the JOKER protocol is better in latency and throughput parameters than the already existing method.

The JOKER protocol tries to transmit the data from source to the destination without giving a chance for the tapping attack which is considered as one of the passive attacks.

Table 13.2 Throughput parameter details.

Parameters Number of Nodes	Throughput (Kbit/s)	
	Existing	**JOKER**
10 Nodes	8192	8100
15 Nodes	12288	12589
20 Nodes	16384	16852
30 Nodes	32485	32245
50 Nodes	48758	48587

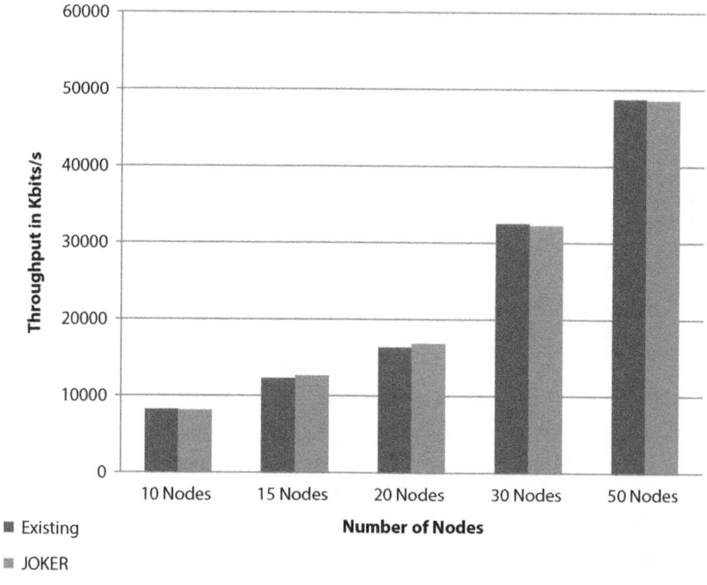

Figure 13.14 Throughput parameter analysis.

13.5 Conclusion and Future Scope

The tapping is one of the passive attacks which are not known by the victims. The confidential nature of the user's data becomes questionable under this attack. The main purpose of this attack is to surveillance the user's data without their knowledge and also to collect their information to know about their activities. This is also affecting the user's privacy in online. The JOKER protocol is one of the ways to split and send the data to the destination through multiple intermediates. Those available intermediate nodes are not permanent. This technique will use different routes at each and every time, when the user tries to send the data from the source to the destination. The JOKER protocol was simulated and the results turned out in positive manner.

The JOKER protocol has some limitations and, they are the JOKER protocol was simulated by using the simulator and results were compared with existing, based on simulator scenario results. While implementing the JOKER protocol into the real time scenario, that time the result may vary while comparing to existing methods. But whatever it may be, the JOKER protocol is using machine learning technique to select and send the data packets from the source to the destination. The Machine learning concepts and their methodologies were not fully discussed in this chapter, because the research of this JOKER protocol is still under enrichment to provide the better performance than its own results, i.e., which results were produced and acquired from the simulator work by using the JOKER protocol. In future this JOKER protocol will be extended to test in the real time scenario and then based on the results and refinements, the JOKER protocol will come to real time usage.

References

1. https://www.ed.ac.uk/arts-humanities-soc-sci/about-us/information-security-and-governance/what-information-do-i-have-to-protect/the-three-states-of-information. Accessed on 01/08/2018.
2. https://techdifferences.com/difference-between-active-and-passive-attacks.html. Accessed on 01/08/2018.
3. https://developer.mozilla.org/en-US/docs/Web/Security/Information_Security_Basics/Confidentiality,_Integrity,_and_Availability. Accessed on 01/08/2018.
4. https://www.trendmicro.com/vinfo/us/security/news/cybercrime-and-digital-threats/year-in-review-notable-data-breaches-for-2017. Accessed on 01/08/2018.

5. Boopathy, D. and Sundaresan, M., Securing Public Data Storage in Cloud Environment. *ICT and Critical Infrastructure: 48th Annual Convention of Computer Society of India*, Visakhapatnam, India, December 2013, pp. 555–562.
6. Boopathy, D. and Sundaresan, M., Secured Cloud Data Storage—Prototype Trust Model for Public Cloud Storage. *International Conference on Information and Communication Technology for Sustainable Development*, Ahmadabad, India, July 2015, pp. 329–337.
7. Boopathy, D. and Sundaresan, M., A Framework for User Authentication and Authorization using Request based One Time Passkey and User Active Session Identification. *Int. J. Comput. Appl.*, 172, 10, 18–23, August 2017.
8. Boopathy, D. and Sundaresan, M., IDOCA and ODOCA - Enhanced Technique for Secured Cloud Data Storage. *Int. J. Intell. Eng. Syst.*, 10, 06, 49–59, December 2017.
9. https://www.expertsystem.com/machine-learning-definition/. Access on 22/09/2018.
10. https://www.techopedia.com/definition/29036/network-security-protocols. Access on 22/09/18.
11. Lee, S.-J. and Gerla, M., Split Multipath Routing with Maximally Disjoint Paths in Ad hoc Networks. *IEEE International Conference on Communications*, Finland, 2001.
12. van Glabbeek, R. and Hofner, P., Split, Send, Reassemble: A Formal Specification of a CAN Bus Protocol Stack. *Models for Formal Analysis of Real Systems (MARS 2017), EPTCS 244*, June 2017, pp. 14–52.
13. Liu, Y., Fang, J., Han, C., A New R-tree Node Splitting Algorithm Using MBR Partition Policy. *17th International Conference on Geoinformatics*, USA, 2009.
14. Kiran, K., Shivapriya, T., Singh, A.A., DeepaShenoy, P., Venugopal, K.R., Patnaik, L.M., Traffic Splitting in a Mobile Ad-hoc Multi-radio Network. *2013 Annual IEEE India Conference (INDICON)*, Mumbai, 2013.
15. Teji, J., Chuchra, R., Mahajan, S., Gill, M.K., Dandi, M., Detection and Prevention of Passive Attacks in Network Security. *Int. J. Eng. Sci. Innov. Technol.*, 02, 06, 247–250, 2013.
16. Kohls, K. and Pöpper, C., Traffic Analysis Attacks in Anonymity Networks. *ASIA CCS 2017*, Abu Dhabi, pp. 01–03, 2017.
17. Zhang, F., He, W., Liu, X., Defending Against Traffic Analysis in Wireless Networks Through Traffic Reshaping. *31st International Conference on Distributed Computing Systems*, USA, pp. 593–602, 2011..
18. Fu, X., Graham, B., Bettati, R., Zhao, W., Active Traffic Analysis Attacks and Countermeasures. *Proceedings of the 2003 International Conference on Computer Networks and Mobile Computing*, China, pp. 1–9, 2003.
19. https://www.isi.edu/nsnam/ns/. Accessed on 01/08/2018.
20. https://www.igi-global.com/dictionary/packet-delivery-ratio/21749. Accessed on 01/08/2018.

21. https://en.wikipedia.org/wiki/Packet_loss. Accessed on 01/08/2018.
22. https://www.sas.co.uk/blog/what-is-network-latency-how-do-you-use-a-latency-calculator-to-calculate-throughput. Accessed on 01/08/2018.
23. https://en.wikipedia.org/wiki/Throughput. Accessed on 01/08/2018.

14

Privacy and Authentication on Security Protocol for Mobile Communications

Brajesh Kumar Gupta "Mewadev"

Eklavya P. G. College, Banda, Bundelkhand University, Jhansi, U.P., India

Abstract

For effective speaker identity authentication, a new protocol is proposed, the nature of mobile communication, characterized for example by terminals having good user interface and limited processing capacity concerned with the design of authentication protocols for a mobile computing environment. Communication security is often described in terms of confidentiality, integrity, authentication and non-repudiation of transmitted data and these protocols enable mutual authentication and establish a shared secret key between mobile users. On the other hand, a good identity authentication the system can guarantee that no unauthorized user fraudulently gets the required services from the home system, therefore, future systems will be characterized by a horizontal communication model. Authentication mechanisms may vary depending on the security technologies and policies used by different networks, based on pointer forwarding to reduce the HLR update cost and traffic load for the MS authentication protocol. Currently, there are no structured mobility management schemes for these heterogeneous multi-hop networks, if handover happens during an active session of service, especially between different networks, various issues arise such as how to maintain the integrity and consistency of accounting records, or how to implement non-repudiation (e.g., protection against a false denial by the customer that he or she has used the service).

Keywords: Mobile communications, security protocols, authentication, next generation networking

Email: dr.mewadevrain@gmail.com

Dinesh Goyal, S. Balamurugan, Sheng-Lung Peng and O.P. Verma (eds.) Design and Analysis of Security Protocol for Communication, (287–304) © 2020 Scrivener Publishing LLC

14.1 Introduction

Mobile phones are often used as a second factor in authentication and a first reason is the growth of both business and military communications as a consequence of this technology, which allowed for global communications in seconds rather than weeks. This is particularly evident from the surprisingly large number of published protocols which have later been found to contain various flaws, the authentication protocol to be proposed in the following uses part of the capacity of the broadcast channel for a base station to propagate to mobile users the certificate associated with its public key. One can expect that in the next generation of smart phones, users will install software with this capability, for high-security services it is not sufficient to only trust in the security offered by the mobile network, as happens with the use of transaction numbers sent over SMS. Mutual authentication and session key exchange protocols based on certificates for the wireless mobile communication/computing system are proposed so we explain how to set up secure mobile communication, including how to encrypt mobile laptop, PDA and Smartphone transactions using tools that can enforce the same over-the-air security, independent of device or network type.

Normally it is hard for an attacker to obtain prolonged physical access to the other end-point of the wireless connection, cell towers and the mobile terminal wants to make sure that it is connected to a legitimate access point and in designing the security protocols proposed, the low computational power of the mobile stations and the low bandwidth of the wireless networks are considered. The main architectural decision is at which layer to implement security besides using cell phones for voice communication, we are now able to access the Internet, conduct monetary transactions, send text messages, etc., using our cell phones, and new services continue to be added. Some applications may offer security in the application itself; this has an advantage that the security is connected to the end user but this approach requires a different solution for every application for preventing an attacker from doing too much damage once he gains full control of a femtocell, providers should place as little trust as possible in these devices, by treating them essentially as a relay to an actual cell tower and never sending them any confidential information. The only security service offered by the first generation systems was a secret user the identifier that was sent in clear over the network, similar to username and password in a computer system so this improvement makes it impossible to track a user's location based on his permanent identity in the mobile network, by replacing the permanent identities with temporary identities, which get renewed in secret.

14.2 Mobile Communications

Cellular Networks have been around since the 1980s and GSM was the first mass consumer communication system with cryptography; it was well ahead of its time, but it was probably not planned that the system would be still widely used 20 years after its introduction and each year their subscribers increase at a very fast rate so this kind of functionality requires installed client software, however, so it is critical to select a product that can support all device operating systems used by your mobile workforce with these strengths, if we keep producing and providing highly advanced services using four generation mobile communication technologies, our country can make a firm foundation to lead worldwide market in four generation mobile communication. However, complementary measures are needed to harden mobile devices against network-borne attack, endpoint compromise, and user error.

By the end of 2018, the number of mobile phone subscribers has doubled, there were 6.8 billion mobile cellular subscriptions in 2018 and is nearly 8.1 billion in world population. In order to better understand supply and demand-side factors in connecting the unconnected, the GSMA's Mobile Connectivity Index measures the performance of 163 countries – representing 99% of the global population – against the key enablers of mobile internet adoption: infrastructure, affordability, consumer readiness, and content and services. Furthermore, GSMA, 2018 [9] report mentioned that in 2020 there will be 9.2 billion mobile cellular subscribers in the world because communication is at the heart of human activity in all domains, the advent of this technology, allowing multimodal communication from anywhere to anywhere where there is the appropriate infrastructure, is supposed to have profound social effects. The scope covers all types of wireless networks: cellular, ad hoc, content-driven, delay-tolerant, mesh, metropolitan, sensor, cognitive, vehicular, robotic, Internet of Things, virtualized, etc., while there are examples of friendships and "communities" that have been fostered and developed exclusively via mediated interaction dating all the way back to telegraphy (Stand age 1998), for all practical purposes social interaction needs co present interaction in order to coalesce into a cohesive form, this process can be aided through the use of mediated interaction. Cellular telephony uses the base/mobile configuration to give mobile users access to the public switched telephone network even though mobile/wireless technologies can transmit voice and data by means of radio waves, infrared rays, microwaves, and electromagnetic waves, although people have integrated mobile phones into their everyday lives, we argue that unless there is a substantial change in social practices the much heralded "m-government" will take a significant amount of time to become a reality.

The mobile phone with NFC (Near Field Communication)-enabled can be used for mobile payment, e-ticketing, intelligent media browsing, and data transmission and exchange, we remark that although using a more advanced authenticated key exchange protocol for the leaves is a relatively small change, the resulting security property does not follow trivially. The analysis results of security and performance show that the improved protocol can provide user anonymity, session key security, resist against the modification attacks, withstand replay attacks, and withstand impersonation attack and even transacted data in an unencrypted form (clear text), allowing packet sniffing of the network traffic to read these values, which may then be used for unauthorized access to the server.

Next and future generations of mobile telecommunication technologies bring increased transmission speed and more versatile services, it seems somewhat pleasure for this industry since all terrestrial networks like phone lines and fiber optics, as well as land-based wireless infrastructure, have spread into almost all urbanized parts of the world leaving only a few abandoned places where there is the low density of population to utilize the bandwidth. Typical applications will include homeland defense sensors, monitoring flow and pressure of petroleum production, meter readings, and field communications. In cellular networks, physical resources are always limited, especially when shared among different contributors such as mobile network operator (MNO) or mobile virtual network operators (MVNO) etc. and being able to characterize the patterns of communications between individuals across different time scales is of great importance in understanding people's social interactions. Look for in-car telemetric to include GPS, data storage, docking for multiple types of handheld devices, hard-copy output, and so on, and the nodes in these networks represent geographical locations, and the link strength is proportional to the volume of calls between the corresponding cells. The goal to attain globalization of the mobile communications industry would be achievable if strong long-term partnerships are developed that give equal benefits to all partners, after all, there are numerous challenges to face due to disconnectivity within the network but one of the key challenges is that which intermediate node will be selected as custody transfer and till how much time custodian node can carry messages as it will have storage constraints until a destination node is found.

In the mobile architecture, mutual authentication with key-agreement protocol affords the authentication between the user and foreign agent via home agent and enables both to generate a communal session-key to encrypt the further conversation through insecure networks and networks depends on the levels of physical security provided for these networks and also on the nature of the cryptographic security, if any, provided for these networks. New security challenges are also mounting in conjunction with the evolution of mobile computing technologies and protocols suffer if the single server is compromised by the adversaries and in more than one server the protocols find high complexity in design and integration of keys so client authentication process uses a unique per-client, per-session token to confirm the identity of each participant attempting to join a meeting. Initially, we generate keys to the multiple servers by the protocol scheme and these servers validate the each user node to provide the information. In mobile networks, the possibility of spoofing is also high; however, the attacker is required to know the authenticating information of the user.

To do so, we create an aggregate network for each day over the period covered by our data, and perform community detection on each of them as described above, which in turn is driven by factors such as competition in mobile radio infrastructure.

14.3 Security Protocols

Nowadays, roaming in mobile communication became extremely famous, which we view as a specification language and proof system and also as a "protocol programming language". The protocol is designed to ensure that no one except the authorized user is allowed to communicate to each other and current research in security protocols has largely focused on the security of protocols, and there is the very little published discussion on the issue of protocol efficiency (notable exceptions are Boyd & Mathuria and Gong). The Global System for Mobile communication (GSM) network is proposed to mitigate the security problems and vulnerabilities observed in the mobile telecommunication system so the rapid growth of mobile telecommunications industry has been influencing the tremendous technological diffusion offering lower access cost, mobility, and convenience based communication as compared to wired telecom. Security protocols are an operating phase ensures the security and integrity of data sent through the connection of the computer network while we are enjoying the various services brought by mobile computing, we have to realize that it comes with a price: security vulnerabilities.

The universal mobile telecommunication system (UMTS), and the long-term evolution (LTE) system are based on the GSM system, the proposed protocol provides a realistic solution which guarantees reasonable computational cost. The use of wireless communication typically implies a lower bandwidth than that of traditional wired networks and extensive research on the GSM network exploits the issues of the challenge-response scheme such as the mutual authentication of communication entities, high bandwidth consumption, and storage overhead. Mobile communication networks are made possible by the convergence of several different technologies specifically computer networking protocols, wireless/mobile communication systems, distributed computing, and the Internet so to support mobility and portability, mobile devices generally obtain their energy through batteries or other exhaustive means, hence they are considered as energy constrained mobile hosts and it also can be developed further with the making of protocols and the application to connect to more than one domain. In addition, redundant components (where the same components are included twice or more in one message) have also been removed where authentication is necessary to ensure that the network services will not be accessed fraudulently.

Security comparison and performance analysis show that the proposed scheme is resistant against all possible attacks and it has very efficient performance making it suitable for the practical environment, the search will terminate without producing a protocol or produce a protocol that only satisfies some of the goals and it is a methodology of logical verification of authentication protocol that formally states the knowledge of information and mobile computing can offer sensing and monitoring capabilities to smart homes equipped with security, identification, personalization systems, intelligent assembly systems, and so forth. The security has been increased in the developed protocol for varying definitions of vulnerability define risk as related to demographic characteristics, interpersonal relationships, access to resources, individual capacity, and the availability of support, with the consideration of race and poverty as central factors in such a network, the information transfer is implemented in a multi-hop fashion, i.e., each node acts not only as a host but also as a router, forwarding packets for those nodes that are not in direct transmission range with each other. The nonce verification rule illustrates that the proposed protocol maintains the freshness of the timestamp values between the communication entities so domains of interest include formal relationships between models of cryptographic protocols, translations, expressive power; comparison between verification methods, accuracy, efficiency; fragments of first-order logic or extensions corresponding to various problems of interest in cryptographic protocol verification; decidability and complexity of cryptographic verification problems, reach ability, decidable sub cases; new logics and calculi for verifying cryptographic protocols;

new approaches to reduce state spaces from infinite to finite; logical characterizations of confidentiality/secrecy, authentication/integrity, non-duplication, non-repudiation, etc.

The authentication efficiency means the execution of the authentication process by reducing the number of cryptographic functions executed and also minimizing the overhead from the communication entities without compromising the security and There are no dedicated service nodes, which can work as a trusted authority to generate and distribute the network keys or provide certificates to the nodes, as the certificate authority (CA), does in the traditional public key infrastructure (PKI) supported approaches in order to effectively describe and present such artifacts and issues, selection of a suitable management methodology becomes crucial as a driver and to conduct the risk assessment based performance management. There is more than 75% improvement in the communication overhead required for the authentication process using the proposed protocol. The idea of intrusion detection is to characterize the user normal behavior within the network in terms of a set of relevant system features. So, what is important here is the verification of whether such features are being effectively used in terms of data transfer or not. It can be done by interacting with the user to verify if the user is really interested in enabling those features for regular use and indeed, some active attacks can be efficiently detected because of a large deviation of attackers' behavior from the normal user behavior. It is not realistic to assume that a protocol is running alone in the network and in the real world, such protocols must be tested for their functional correctness before they are used in practice. The effort to improve wireless network security is linked with many technical challenges including compatibility with legacy wireless networks, complexity in implementation, and practical values in the real market so simple things like making sure that default usernames and passwords are changed during initial setup help greatly. This paper covers a broad sweep of security issues that MNOs should consider when operating 4G LTE networks and proposes directional preventative measures with the objective of highlighting the critical role MNOs have to play in securing 4G LTE operations and the security aspects of a registration protocol in a mobile satellite communication system. Security is a very important requirement in any system, especially in wireless communication systems with such a large inter meshed growing milieu, and considering that cyber-attackers are poised to target mobile networks, security management in 4G LTE operations is a critical and complex challenge for MNOs.

Protocols such as Simple Network Management Protocol (SNMP) and Domain Name Service (DNS) that were developed a long time ago and have been widely deployed can pose security risks, the online exchanges in these protocols are due to, at least in part, the requirement for agents to know the public keys on their co-path. It provides a solution for intra-domain mobility without assuming the existence or use of any global mobility management protocol with high calculation speed; the proposed method can eliminate vulnerabilities of impersonations attacks and save the storage space of NFC devices. Domain Name Service (DNS) was originally designed as an open protocol so this allows them to have the commitment, verification, and secret-sharing rounds, after which the trust requirements upon all participants are the same.

In the following sections, an analysis of the most three famous schemes for mobile satellite authentication protocols is presented in vehicular communication networks that are hardened by public cryptographic systems, security modules including secret keys can be exposed to wrong hands due to the weakness of physical security than those that can be enforced. Devices should be regularly updated so that any problems discovered after their release can be corrected, but the patching mechanism itself can be a way for malicious actors to get into a device and our future work is to see how we can integrate our algorithm for automatically merging two networking files into the tools in order to facilitate the life of networking users.

14.4 Authentication

A set of goals for such a protocol are identified, as are a number of generic attacks; these goals and attacks are then used to evaluate the suitability of seven candidate third-generation user-to-network authentication protocols for mobile users include: (A) the authentication of the mobile user and Visitor Location Register/Home Location Register; (B) the data confidentiality between mobile station and Visitor Location Register, and the data confidentiality between Visitor Location Register and Visitor Location Register/Home Location Register (VLR/HLR); (C) the location privacy of mobile user. Security analysis and simulation experiment indicate that the proposed protocol has many excellent security properties when compared with other recent similar handover schemes, such as mutual authentication and resistance to known network threats, as well as requiring lower computation and communication cost through roaming technology, mobile users can access the services provided by a foreign network. A privacy and authentication protocol (PAP) requires a tag to perform four simple operations in mobile communications: a good identity authentication system means that no unauthorized user gets the required services from the home system.

Many authentication protocols have been developed to improve the original authentication protocol of mobile communication, but mostly cannot solve the problems without modifying the architecture of mobile communication. The strength of a protocol is in the encryption technique that it uses. Hence, stronger encryption techniques result in better security of the protocol. The speed of protocol is another important parameter to improve the security without losing the desirable features, we present a new handover authentication protocol that overcomes the security weakness of the original Pair Hand and achieves the same level of high efficiency. The ubiquitous computing environment has become important, which allows users to connect to the network regardless of their location and energy constraints, node variability, error rate, and information measure limitations mandate the design and use of adaptative routing and security mechanisms, for any sort of devices and eventualities. The network management is additionally distributed, which allows the network to possess a distributed name service but intermediate nodes may cause several problems like it can extract useful information packets, can deny to forward packets or may modify the contents of packets during the data transmission session. A protocol should have high reliability if it is to be used in handling critical data, an authentication based secure routing control protocols are dependent upon an underlying key management protocol. The only differences between the two versions appear at the selection of the group order in the system initialization phase and the computation of the hash value of the authentication message in the handover authentication phase, and our attack is exactly to address these two phases and instead of working on already proposed protocols and solve their vulnerabilities and strengthening them researchers are proposing new protocols without testing them properly for vulnerabilities which are later exploited by malicious users.

The prototype demonstrates, however, major standard, flexibility, dependability, efficiency, and transparency, affect the design and services of a dynamic network of devices to securely discover an authenticated route to the destination using either aggregated message authentication codes (MACs) or multi-signatures. Protocols use symmetric key cryptography for authenticating routing control packets and the response times obtained area unit appropriate to be used in real environments, even once devices have restricted resources. As this is a very vast area we have only surveyed and summarized different authentication based secure routing protocol and intrusion detection secure routing protocol and authentication process is one-way since the user is being authenticated first to the phone through the PIN number and then the operator though their SIM

(Subscriber identity module) based AAA (Authentication, Authorization, and Accounting) mechanism.

It is observed that the new proxy re-encryption scheme is better than the earlier one on the basis of the privacy; security and authentication and reduce overheads while roaming networks to the authentication token, in addition, includes a sequence number which is enlarged in both the network and the mobile after every victorious authentication. The main security models, parameters, modules and protocols are presented, also a detailed description of privacy and its related arguments, dimensions and factors is given where the security protocols deliver on its mission through training, research, publications, industry outreach, and open forums for end users and industry stakeholders in payments, mobile, healthcare, identity and access, transportation, and the IoT in the whole world, and these deployed mechanisms utilize the authentication procedure, since authentication is required for the signaling to perform integrity. The requirement originates in the early days of computing, when systems needed a digital means to authenticate a user, and has now proliferated into every virtual relationship so authentication mechanisms validate the user's identity. Authorization validates the privileges, services, permissions, and resources assigned to the user, which is by default authenticated and the need for higher levels of security is at odds with users' desire for convenience when accessing their digital services. In the telecommunication systems, the authentication procedure is performed along with the integrity and the ciphering procedures, furthermore, security issues in these systems include attacks, malicious node detection, access control, authentication, intrusion detection, privacy and anonymity, security architectures and protocols, security theory and tools, secrecy and integrity, and trust models.

Authentication relies on a number of technologies that leverage both hardware and software techniques to reliably identify a user and that user's mobile device for security purposes and the only implemented measures for non-repudiation are through the logs information within the home network; however, in case of roaming non-repudiation is not protected. In addition, a taxonomy and comparison of authentication protocols that are developed for the IoT in terms of the network model, specific security goals, main processes, computation complexity, and communication overhead are provided which combines scanning, security, and block chain technology for authentication with a set of APIs such as IBM's Soft Layer cloud infrastructure. The aim of the current survey paper is to provide a comprehensive and systematic review of recent studies on published authentication protocols for the new security mechanisms performed in the new service area should be kept minimal to assure seamless transfer between the areas. Feasible solutions for the problem of establishing a session key between a client and a server in the context of the Internet of Things were surveyed in, and support for ubiquitous computing through station mobility. One of the authentication factors in our protocol is biometrics, and the other factor can be either knowledge-based or possession-based and generalizes the paradigm of imperative functional programming in an elegant way that allows for recursive, remote function calls, and it provides a clear mechanism for the interaction between host and mobile code.

Therefore, the authentication mechanisms are required to support these security services and to be resilient to distinct attacks and we show how techniques for specifying the operational semantics of imperative functional programs (syntax-based semantics) and for formalizing variable binding constructs and mobile environments are used in combination with the natural representation of concurrency. The authentication is provided to the data that can be sent or accessed by any node in the network; therefore, their conclusion was that in order to ensure highly efficient and secure wireless communication systems cryptographic techniques that incorporate the SS features must be used. On the other hand, with the protocol, when the keys generated at the mobile router and the relay router for authentication are based on the concept of symmetric polynomials, an adversary cannot identify a shared key between two legitimate users making it impossible for him to impersonate a mobile router or a relay router, an exhaustive survey on the available protocols for authentication in the wireless sensor networks and their applications is provided. In order to satisfy the authentication model to secure IoT, namely, mutual authentication, perfect forward secrecy, anonymity, and un-traceability, the authentication protocols use both cryptosystems and non-cryptosystems countermeasures and various protocols might try to check the route quality with end-to-end acknowledgements comprising the information of reliability or latency. We also present an executable specification of the may testing equivalence on non-recursive asynchronous π-calculus processes, where the nodes can be convinced by the adversary to trust that the adversary is its nearby neighbor. As biometric authentication is becoming more popular and ubiquitous, protecting and ensuring the privacy of biometric templates is of utmost importance, in order to prove the performance of an authentication protocol in terms of security, researchers use formal security verification techniques. Authentication is a process by which the identity of a node in a network is verified and guarantees that the data or the control messages originate from an authenticated source, it preserves the privacy of the biometric templates, password and password-derived key against malicious and colluding service provider and database; and also offers identity privacy and unlink ability against malicious database, due to the database anonymization and the use of authentication. We implement both the usual transition semantics and the weak transition semantics where internal actions are not observed, authentication protocols should counteract these issues since the nodes are easily traceable. Specifically, the security of the system is significantly increased, making attacks much more difficult to the typical adversaries, and the privacy concerns posed by the use of biometrics are minimized by using the additional authentication factor for binding the binary biometric information, it possesses several benefits, comprising resistance to both replay and forgery attacks, decreasing the risk of user's password leakage, improved efficiency, and ability of changeable password. Therefore, we focus on the authentication phase in our analysis, when phase takes place during the deployment of the network in which every node discovers its neighbors within the range of communication and sets up the security of the network by proposing the idea of deploying a fault tolerance architecture to execute the authentication approach without any additional configuration or setup. Consequently, it necessitates an efficient and scalable protocol for establishing and updating the keys between nodes for secure communication and our protocol paves the way towards a secure and privacy-preserving authentication cloud service business model. It permits every single node to make its own decision on whether to transfer a message first or check it first, in this approach, the problem of original message broadcast authentication is minimized to the problem of public key distribution.

14.5 Next Generation Networking

The next generation mobile communication systems will need to support multiple services ubiquitously in different types of environments, different levels of data rates, and different mobility and traffic management techniques and The new Technologies are pivoted around building an advanced infrastructure that can cope with the technical specs and requirements needed by cutting-edge new applications like IOT, Virtual and Augmented Reality, Autonomous Vehicles, Distributed Computing, etc., including the history and service evolution of mobile communications and environments. The 4G development started when several standardization bodies and industry alliances such as 3GPP, NGMN and IMT-2020 started setting up a vision of how 5G should look like so ISG NGP laid the foundations, identifying requirements, scenarios, and example next-generation technologies.

The Next-Generation Telematics Protocol (NGTP) is a telematics protocol that is used in automobiles to provide connectivity and integrated services to drivers and passengers as well as to vehicles and some of the pitfalls of the current Internet Protocol (IPv4) as well as what is in the proposed design for its successor...Internet Protocol Next Generation (IPng or IPv6). Although broadcasting services are available in LTE and LTE-A networks, new improvements are needed in some areas to handle the demands expected in the near future but Philip Hammond also announced £200 million to support local "full-fiber" broadband network and £270 million to put the UK "at the forefront" of technology, including robotics, biotech, and driverless cars.

Resource allocation techniques for broadcast/multicast services, integration with new waveforms in fifth generation mobile communications (5G), initiatives for spectrum sharing and aggregation, or the deployment of small cells placed together with the existing macrocells, are some enhancements that are examined in detail, providing directions for further development but there can likewise be millions of people in this situation, scattered among millions of organizations, with an added wrinkle: by simply signing a service contract and installing some network hardware, they can all be made part of the Internet community instantly. A next-generation firewall (NGFW) is a part of the third generation of firewall technology that is implemented in either hardware or software and is capable of detecting and blocking sophisticated attacks by enforcing security policies at the application, port and protocol levels but the Wi-Fi Alliance—a consortium of tech giants that includes companies like Apple, Microsoft, Cisco and Intel—said in a statement timed for the opening of the annual Consumer Electronics Show that the new generation of the Wi-Fi Protected Access encryption protocol, called WPA3, would harden the connection between users' devices and Wi-Fi routers. Companies are also looking towards telecommuting as a way to reduce expenses to enable various players to provide diverse application services and achieve an open network that ensures mutual connectivity with other operator's IP networks, NTT plans to disclose interface specifications. This technology will speed the development of the next generation of network protocols, improve their security, and therefore increase the public acceptance of advanced, distributed IT applications based on them. A distributed network security architecture, comprising a hybrid firewall, intrusion detection, virtual honey net projects, and connectivity and interactivity between these three components, it always remains a challenge to provide a fully dependable secure NFV environment and hence next-generation mobile networks should have security controls in place to address the vulnerabilities imposed by NFV environment. Today traditional network provides hop by hop security by providing a secure communication path between the communicating parties which may not be efficient in a 5G environment which requires an end to end security to serve these new forms of specialized networks because core technologies being developed for the transport network include technologies for optical access systems, service edge systems, Ethernet edge systems, large-capacity routers, gateway systems for interconnecting to other operators, and various transmission systems.

The application of fast fault recovery technologies and traffic engineering technologies is also being studied with the aim of making the network even more reliable and efficient but the confidentiality of the data is also an important security requirement, which can be achieved by using existing security protocols such as IPSec or TLS or there is a need to design new crypto algorithms as per specialized network and the Internet Protocol Next Generation (IPng) is the successor designed to replace the current the version of the Internet Protocol (IPv4). At the same time, the real-time control of network equipment for achieving end-to-end quality control and other essential functions is becoming increasingly important to network services and more network virtualization will be adopted in the Telco clouds and the security architecture must address the issues related to virtualization such as to achieve a high degree of isolation in a shared virtualized environment. It is the purpose of this introductory article to briefly mention a larger cross-section of the fresh ideas and proposals for solutions of the problems raised by mobile networking, the programmatic improvements, adoption of standards and best practices include the need for increased government participation in standards development, vulnerabilities in mobile networks, and creation of a set of standards and security best practices for mobile application security tailored to government. However, the security and the privacy protection of communicating users in Wireless Mobile Communications (WMN) are challenging, and it is possible to connect to an open public network where anyone who knows where to look can intercept your information, or you can be on a password-protected wireless network with high-level encryption and other protective measures. It just depends on the Wi-Fi network. The new wireless media becoming available are among the primary drivers for the interest in mobile computing and its compared to the stability and advanced security solutions available for traditional desktops, networks, and servers, the mobile ecosystem continues to evolve, making it more difficult to secure.

It is imperative that you understand how to properly implement services and protocols, especially if the network has been in existence for some period of time and some services are no longer needed or have been forgotten furthermore one reason for this discrepancy in security guarantees, despite the large body of work on group key agreement is that most existing protocol designs are fundamentally synchronous, and thus cannot be used in the asynchronous world of mobile communications. The Internet of Things (IoT) may be disrupting the world economy, but security remains a sticking point. Low-power wide-area (LPWA) networks carrying IoT data from devices such as water meters and smoke detectors are particularly challenged by the heavy processing that security typically entails and you may not know a phone has been hacked until an employee reports an odd occurrence, such as a saved voicemail message that has been deleted or forwarded to an unusual number. The typical security process, though, involves overhead-heavy, certificate-based mutual authentication and complicated Public Key Infrastructure (PKI) management, security vulnerabilities that can be found in hybrid apps, by which important data are downloaded from a web server, were analyzed and HIGHT algorithm based on OTP delimiter modification and bit slicing was proposed to enhance the security of hybrid apps and this chapter discusses these concepts to help you understand how to use the proper network implementation of protocols and services as a tool to protect and mitigate threats against network infrastructure based on organizational needs. This setup saves battery power because you do not need to run authentication and encryption algorithms on IoT devices directly, centralize administration and use domain restrictions and two-factor authentication for administrative access, including to credentials, signaling data, and configuration files. The Internet Protocol Security (IPsec) authentication and encapsulation standard are widely used to establish secure VPN communications and all of these protocols are intrinsically synchronous: they require all parties to come online at the same time for the initial key exchange.

You can take advantage of BEST to differentiate your service offerings, create additional revenue streams, and mitigate risk and evaluate services such as VLAN configuration, user authentication, and encryption, as well as the security of configuring and signaling methods. The Internet Protocol Security (IPsec) authentication and encapsulation standard are widely used to establish secure VPN communications for depending on your goals (including compliance requirements), users' applications and locations, and the IP phone system you are using, whether onsite or hosted when counting exponentiations the pair wise cost depends on how many people have ratcheted since the sender's last update.

14.6 Conclusion

In this chapter, we perform an automated analysis of multi-protocols in security analysis to authentication protocols for mobile satellite communication systems and we believe that this special issue is a good snapshot of current research and development of wireless network security and is an important reference for researchers, practitioners, and students. Many telecommunication companies still use the old standard of a Pan-European digital cellular system (GSM) or integrate the GSM system with their 3G/4G systems and encryption should always be used in the update process so that the patch is not readable by someone with a hex editor. To keep track of the whereabouts of a mobile user, the HLR must get the location updated frequently so the traffic can move on the software that comes with your router needs occasional updates. Before you set up a new router and periodically thereafter, visit the manufacturer's website to see if there is a new version of the software available for download.

Whereas, the proposed protocol offers perfect mutual authentication, user anonymity with untraceable, pre-authentication in the smartcard, mutual authentication with key-agreement, efficient password changing phase, and withstands all the familiar security threats and the physical limitations of the intended devices such as mobile phones, made it necessary to develop a protocol which would make minimal use of computing resources. The informal and formal security analyses demonstrate the resistance of the proposed protocol against all sorts of security attacks as the number and diversity of connected services that interact with vehicles continue to increase, cyber threats also evolve and grow.

To overcome the issue of limited resources that can be allocated to users, the resource constraint hardware, specialized software, low energy devices, and hostile environment makes the security in wireless sensor networks a challenging task as and when compared to the traditional computer networks. The execution of the protocol may sometimes incomplete caused by some unexpected modeling errors, furthermore, the algorithms within the systems chosen should enhance the system's security and efficiency, with security being given at a higher priority than efficiency. Simulation results verify the validity of the proposed security model and these encrypt both commands and data, preventing passwords and sensitive information from being transmitted in the clear over the network. I expect this to lead to many more alternative designs in future works and this paper proposes an improved light-weight authentication protocol for mobile services using elliptic curve cryptography.

References

1. Redli, S.M., Weber, M.K., Oliphant, M.W., *GSM and Personal Communications Handbook*, Artech House, Inc., Boston, London, 1998.
2. Wang, J. and Ng, T.-S., *Advances in 3G Enhanced Technologies for Wireless Communications*, Artech House, (U.K.), *IEEE Journal*, 2002.
3. Chen, T.Z., Lee, W.B., Chen H.B., Chen, A self-verification authentication mechanism for mobile satellite communication systems, *Computer and Electrical Science* Eng., 35 (1) 41–48, 2009.
4. Mottishaw, P., *Policy control and charging for LTE networks*, Analysis Mason U.S.A., 2009.
5. Escudero-Andreu, G., Phan R.C-W., Parish, D.J., *Analysis and Design of Security for Next Generation 4G Cellular Networks*, PGNet, Loughborough, U.K., 2012.
6. Belmekki, E., Bouaouda, N., Raouyane, B., Bellafkih, M., IP Multimedia Subsystem: Security Evaluation, *Journal of Theoretical and Applied Information Technology*, 51, page no. 1-6, 2013.
7. Balamurali B.T., Nair, Esam, Alzqhou, A. S., Guillemin, B. J., *International Journal of Sensor Networks and Data Communications*, 131-135, 2015.
8. Jorge Granjal, J.S.S., Edmundo Monteiro, Security for the internet of things: A survey of existing protocols and open research issues, *IEEE Commun. Surv. Tutorials*, 17, no. 3, 1294-1312, 2015.

15

Cloud Communication: Different Security Measures and Cryptographic Protocols for Secure Cloud Computing

Anjana Sangwan

Swami Keshvanand Institute of Technology, Gramothan and Management, Jaipur, India

Abstract
In this chapter, cloud communication and the various platforms used for it are introduced. Also discussed, are the security measures provided by the cloud and as well as some well-known protocols for encryption of data that establish a secure communication for clouds. Some of these protocols like Secure Shell Protocol (SSP), Internet Protocol Security (IPSec), Kerberos, Wired Equivalent Privacy (WEP), and WiFi Protected Access (WPA) are outlined and shown how these have been effective in the cloud for secure communication.

Keywords: Cloud communication, platform, security, encryption, communication, protocol

15.1 Introduction

Cloud communications is the mix char of multiple communication modalities. These cover methods such as voice, email, chat, and video, in an integrated fashion to trim or eliminate communication lag. Cloud communications is originally internet-based communication. The technology has taken the world to a new level and has made it into a global village. Internet has reduced the distances to an extent that people in the different country of the world can now see and talk with each other through Cloud communications. This internet based communication application combined the

Email: sangwan.anjana@gmail.com

Dinesh Goyal, S. Balamurugan, Sheng-Lung Peng and O.P. Verma (eds.) Design and Analysis of Security Protocol for Communication, (305–332) © 2020 Scrivener Publishing LLC

different communication modalities like voice, video, email, and chat to reduce communication lag.

This has originated with the introduction of Voice Over Internet Protocol (VOIP). A branch of cloud communication is cloud telephony, which refers specifically to voice communications.

The storage, applications and switching are directed and hosted by a third party through the cloud. Cloud services are a broader expression of cloud communication. These services act as the initial data center for enterprises, and cloud communications is one of the services offered by cloud service providers. Hence we can conclude that cloud communications provides a variety of communication resources, from servers and storage to enterprise applications such as data security, email Backup and data recovery, and voice, which are all delivered over the internet. The cloud provides a hosting environment that is elastic, critical, scalable, secure, and readily available.

Cloud communications [1] providers provide communication services through servers owned and maintained by them. These services are then pervaded by the user, through the cloud. The users can just pay for the services used by them. The service providers also offer disparate communication resources from the storage and the servers to enterprise applications like email, data recovery, backup, voice, and security. The present status provided by the cloud is easily available, adaptable, flexible, prompt, and secure.

Some of the application and communication issues that can be used by an enterprise and are applicable, covered by cloud communications that include Private branch exchange, call center, text messaging, SIP Trunking, Voice broadcast, Call tracking software, contact center telephony, interactive voice response, and fax services. All these benefit build different communication necessary of an enterprise. These contain of intra- and inter-branch communication, customer relations, inter-department memos, call forwarding, conference, and tracking services and operations center.

Cloud communications is foremost for the enterprises as it is the center for all communications, which are managed, hosted, and maintained by the third-party service providers. The enterprise has to pay the fees for these services provide to them.

15.2 Need for Cloud Communication

Many organizations today agree that the cloud is not only a powerful, flexible, and reliable platform for office richness applications, but also an equally compelling platform for business communications solutions along with phone, fax, voice, short message service (SMS) text, and video conferencing. Add the ability to integrate business communications solutions directly into Office 365, Salesforce, Service Now, and other cloud-based Software as a Service (SaaS) solutions, and the business benefits are enormous. However, there is a gap between the capabilities of communications systems that support human and machine conversation, and the demands of modern commerce as enabled by cloud technology. Bridging this gap offers a substantial business opportunity. These are some points that show why many organizations moving towards the clouds [2]:

1. Cost—Expected monthly costs. This may seem like old news, but many companies do not admit just how much they can recover by moving their communications to the cloud. By introduce a phone system over the Internet, businesses are on credit on an "as needed" basis, paying only for what they use. That makes cloud-based communication systems completely cost-effective for limited businesses—wipe-out the need to pay for the installation and maintenance of a traditional phone system.
2. Management—Outsource IT support to the provider. The management of an on-premise solution can be very big-ticket. Because of the complexity of today's communications systems, it can often take an entire IT department to manage. Cloud-based communications can help lighten the burden by drop maintenance, IT work load, and some of the more costly internal infrastructure, including servers and storage systems.
3. Scalability—Scale up or down based on users. Anyone who has moved or expanded an on-premise phone system knows just how difficult it can be. Whether a business is growing, moving or sizing down, the cloud provides the flexibility and scalability the business needs now and in the future. With cloud-based systems, businesses can access and add new features without any new hardware requirements.
4. Vendor management—One vendor for everything. With cloud communications, a vendor manages communication systems off-site, and IT departments are freed up to focus on other high-priority issues.
5. Technology—Quick updates. With cloud communications, service is outsourced, and upgrades are set out through

automatic software updates. This allows organizations to stay join on their business and leave the upgrades to the cloud communications vendor.

6. Quality of service—Maximize uptime and downtime scope. For many businesses, uptime is crucial. To keep things running, they rely on the ability to scale and leverage remote work teams or serve customers from anywhere. For these kinds of businesses, cloud communications maximizes uptime and coverage through multiple, remotely hosted data centers, helping them hold off costly interruptions and downtime.
7. Affordable Redundancy—Leverage shared resources. With an on-premise communication system, hardware and software geographic redundancy can be challenging to deliver. But when multiple businesses share resources in a cloud environment, they get access to a level of redundancy that would be too expensive to procure with an on-premises solution.
8. Disaster recovery—Business continuity made easy. Businesses are using the cloud to protect themselves from the affects of disasters. With cloud communications, they can get up and running quickly after a disaster, or in some cases, continue running the entire time. Some reroute calls to remote locations and cell phones. Others rely on remote access to voicemail or use cloud-based auto attendants continue taking calls and providing information. It is a hard-to-resist combination of reliability, resiliency, and redundancy.
9. Simplicity—Easy to use interface. With a cloud-based interface, it is easy for employees to talk, chat, collaborate, and connect anytime through a single platform.
10. Mobility—Feature-rich mobile integration. Many businesses need to keep their teams connected and communicating efficiently even when they are miles, states, or even countries apart. With cloud-based unified communications, remote workers have access to the full feature set from their mobile devices anywhere they go, just as if they were sitting at their desks. It opens up a whole new world of productivity and possibilities.

15.3 Application

"Cloud computing" takes hold as 69% of all internet users have either stored data online or used a web-based software applications.

Customers that use webmail services, store data online, or account software programs such as word processing applications whose service is located on the web. In that process, these customers are making use of "cloud computing," an emerging architecture by which required data and applications store in cyberspace, with authorization that users can access them through any web-connected device. Cloud telephony services were predominantly used for business processes, such as advertising, e-commerce, human resources, and payments processing.

With the advancement of remote computing technology, clear lines between cloud and web applications have blurred. The term *cloud application* has gained great cachet, sometimes leading application vendors with any online aspect to brand them as cloud applications.

Cloud and web applications approach data residing on distant storage. Both use server processing power that may be located on premises or in a distant data center [3].

A key difference between cloud and web applications is architecture. A web application or web-based application must have an unbroken internet connection to function. Conversely, a cloud application or cloud-based application performs processing tasks on a local computer or workstation. An internet connection is required primarily for downloading or uploading data.

A web application is unusable if the remote server is inaccessible. If the remote server becomes unavailable in a cloud application, the software installed on the local user device can still operate, although it cannot upload and download data until service at the remote server is restored.

The difference between cloud and web applications can be illustrated with two common productivity tools, email and word processing. Gmail, for example, is a web application that requires only a browser and internet connection. Through the browser, it is possible to open, write, and organize messages using search and sort capabilities. All processing logic occurs on the servers of the service provider (Google, in this example) via either the internet's HTTP or HTTPS protocols.

A CRM application accessed through a browser under a fee-based software as a service (SaaS) arrangement is a web application. Online banking and daily crossword puzzles are also considered web applications that do not install software locally.

15.4 Cloud Communication Platform

Cloud communication platform is the platform that provides information technology services and products to the users on demand. This system provides all data and voice communication services through a third-party foreign the organization and is accessed over the public internet infrastructure.

CPaaS stands for Communications Platform as a Service. A CPaaS is a cloud-based platform that enables developers to add real-time communications features (voice, video, and messaging) in their own applications without needing to build backend infrastructure and interfaces.

Traditionally, real-time communications (RTC) have taken place in applications built specifically for these functions. For example, you might use your native mobile phone app to dial your bank, but have you ever wondered why you cannot video chat a representative right in your banking app?

These dedicated RTC applications—the traditional phone, Skype, FaceTime, WhatsApp, etc.—have been the paradigm for a long time because it is costly to build and operate a communications stack, from the real-time network infrastructure to the interfaces to common programming languages.

CPaaS offers a complete development framework for building real-time communications features without having to build your own. This typically includes software tools, standards-based application programming interfaces (APIs), sample code, and pre-built applications. CPaaS providers also provide support and product documentation to help developers throughout the development process. Some companies also offer software development kits (SDKs) and libraries for building applications on different desktop and mobile platforms [4].

Communications platform as a service (CPaaS) is a cloud-based delivery model that allows organizations to add real time communication capabilities such as voice, video, and messaging to business applications by deploying application program interfaces (APIs). The communication capabilities delivered by APIs include Short Message Service, Multimedia Messaging Service, telephonic communication, and video.

15.5 Security Measures Provided by the Cloud

Cloud communication provider will offer security allocation such as data encryption authentication protocols to help protected communication in the cloud.

Some factors that ensure cloud security:

- Cloud Protection is Not a Network Protection
  A common confusion is that cloud-based service providers action complete security degree for cloud communications. While this may be true for the applications residing in the cloud, it does not cover the network used, call flows, media, or endpoints not in the cloud. When implementing cloud communications, the company must regulate what is assured by the service provider and what must be assured on the business end.
- Real-Time Security for Your Network
  Most companies expand firewalls to care for their data; however, this is not in real time. IP-based Session Initiation Protocol (SIP), which is used on VoIP based communication, operates in real-time passing both voice and video among the cloud and the network. Not implementing security amount to hold your unsecured SIP communications boost the risk of real-time VoIP based attacks, such as Denial of Service (DoS) and eavesdropping. While your firewall will protect data flow, it is not acceptable to look after VoIP communication because you may have to turn off firewall features to get your voice and video communications to work; thus, opening your network up to potential attacks [5].

  Adding a session border controller (SBC) to the servers that come in tap with the cloud will no doubt increase your cloud communication security on the network member end. The SBC is a SIP firewall that protects and encrypts real-time communication by:
- Protecting Denial of Service Rush
  DoS rush overwhelm the network with uncool traffic in an attempt to look for deficiency in the VoIP system. An SBC will protect your network by divide VoIP traffic from malicious activity and protecting it from any degradation in quality that frequently occurs during a DOS attack.
- Encryption
  SBCs use secure real-time encryption, making communication unseen to hackers.
- IP Traffic Management
  An SBC can mitigate voice traffic on a network; thus, limiting the number of allowable sessions that can take place at

the same time. This is similar to DoS protection, and it helps establish Quality of Service.

- Toll Fraud Protection
  Many hackers only break into a VoIP system just to make person toll calls, but an SBC can deny secondary dial tones and prevent this type of attack.

15.6 Achieving Security With Cloud Communications

When using a cloud communications service provider, you should establish a security plan and determine your responsibilities versus the cloud communication provider's responsibilities. Also, use and restore your virus protection and make aware software locally as well as updating your softphones and other endpoints. Finally, adding SBCs at all sites that connect to the cloud will not only protect the SIP call flow but establish high-quality voice and video is delivered.

It is important to function that a secure transmission is not the only component in IP-based communications. While your cloud communications partner can hit secure transmissions, you must also protect your endpoints and network to earn entire security.

Cloud communications is changing the way business communicates. From cloud PBX being a more adjustable back-up to on-premise legacy PBX systems, to achieving true unified communications by being able to integrate different channels like voice, fax, conferencing, SMS, and team messaging into one cloud-based service, thus the birth of Unified Communications-as-a-Service (UCaaS).

With all the improvements in cloud communications, Gartner is predicting that unified communications spending will grow at 3.1% CAGR through 2020. There is just a lot of optimism regarding the rise of cloud in terms of business communications.

One of the possible concerns is, of course, security. It is not that enterprises are not recognizing the interest of moving to the cloud, it is just that the idea of having your conversations and other sensitive data pass through the public Internet is quite scary, and if you also own a business, big or small, it should concern you as well [6].

That is why if you plan to move your communications to the cloud, you should realize that you are putting an enormous amount of trust to your UCaaS provider because they will be the ones responsible in safeguarding your data as it passes through your end, through their data centers, and the public Internet. So before choosing your next provider, be sure that you are well-versed about cloud security and multi-layered defense. For more info on this topic, read our guide article on the most useful SaaS solutions for small businesses.

Here are some of the things your next UCaaS provider should give you details about when it comes to cloud security:

1. Safe and secure data center. The UCaaS providers should have the ideal a strong physical location with redundant power and reliable disaster recovery procedures. It would not hurt if they have multiple data centers from different locations to maximize redundancy so that when one data center goes down, another can take over. Security and reliability should also be backed by independent certifications.
2. Encrypted data including voice. All data that passes through the provider's network should be encrypted in transit and at rest. This, of course, includes voice data. Voice traffic should be encrypted to prevent eavesdropping or any form of hacking during the flow of any data.
3. User access control and account administration. Providers should also be able to give you a way to control user access. This includes defining user roles and permissions. The company or the administrators should also be able to demote and revoke these accesses in certain situations like when a user leaves the company. Vendor should also implement a strong password policy and, if possible, two-factor authentication. A nice plus would be a single sign-on feature to prevent employees or users' log-in fatigue.
4. Fraud prevention measures. The UCaaS provider should have protections against possible fraud risks like toll fraud and credentials theft. Continuous monitoring against anomalies and other fraud indicators should be a must. Provider should also promote best practices against fraud to all their clients. This is not to dissuade anyone from moving to cloud communications. This is just to make companies aware that while there are a lot of benefits, moving to the cloud has its own security risks and their provider of choice should not only be aware of these risks but are also implementing countermeasures to protect their subscribers.

15.7 Cryptographic Protocols for Secure Cloud Computing

Cryptography in the cloud employs encryption techniques to protected data that will be used or stored in the cloud. It allows users to conveniently and securely access shared cloud services, as any data that is hosted by cloud providers is protected with encryption. Cryptography in the cloud protects sensitive data without delaying information exchange.

Cryptography in the cloud allows for securing critical data beyond your corporate IT environment, where that data is no longer under your control. Cryptography expert Ralph Spencer Poore explains that "information in motion and information at rest are best protected by cryptographic security measures. In the cloud, we don't have the luxury of having actual, physical control over the storage of information, so the only way we can ensure that the information is protected is for it to be stored cryptographically, with us maintaining control of the cryptographic key."

The application of cryptography in cloud computing has four basic security requirement such as non-repudiation, authentication, integrity and confidentiality. Cloud computing provides what industry experts call a computing environment that is distributed and consisting of a series of heterogeneous components. The components here include firmware, networking, software, and hardware [7].

The benefits of cloud computing are being realized by more companies and organizations every day. Cloud computing gives clients a virtual computing infrastructure on which they can store data and run applications. But, cloud computing has introduced security challenges because cloud operators store and handle client data outside of the reach of clients' existing security measures. Various companies are designing cryptographic protocols tailored to cloud computing in an attempt to effectively balance security and performance.

Most cloud computing infrastructures do not provide security against untrusted cloud operators, which poses a challenge for companies and organizations that need to store sensitive, confidential information such as medical records, financial records, or high-impact business data. As cloud computing continues to grow in popularity, there are many cloud computing companies and researchers who are pursuing cloud cryptography projects in order to address the business demands and challenges relating to cloud security and data protection.

There are various approaches to extending cryptography to cloud data. Many companies choose to encrypt data prior to uploading it to the cloud altogether. This approach is beneficial because data is encrypted before it leaves the company's environment, and data can only be decrypted by authorized parties that have access to the appropriate decryption keys. Other cloud services are capable of encrypting data upon receipt, ensuring that any data they are storing or transmitting is protected by encryption by default. Some cloud services may not offer encryption capabilities, but at the very least should use encrypted connections such as HTTPS or SSL to ensure that data is secured in transit.

15.8 Security Layer for the Transport Protocol

The TLS or the Security Layer for the Transport Protocol in the cloud computing purposes refers to a protocol with a built in capability that allows the client server applications in the virtual mode to carry out communication across the network.

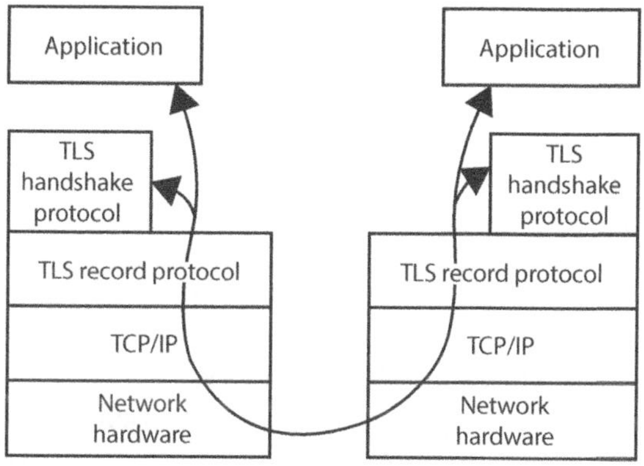

We discuss following protocols in brief:

- Secure Shell Protocol
  The SSH protocol (also referred to as Secure Shell) is a method for secure remote login from one computer to another. It provides several substitute options for strong authentication, and it care for the communications security and integrity with strong encryption. It is a secure alternative to the non-protected login protocols (such as telnet, rlogin) and insecure file transfer methods (such as FTP).

- Typical Uses of the SSH Protocol
  The protocol is used in corporate networks for:
  - providing secure access for users and automated processes
  - interactive and automated file transfers
  - issuing remote commands
  - managing network infrastructure and other mission-critical system components.

- How Does the SSH Protocol Work
  The protocol works in the client-server model, which means that the connection is established by the SSH client connecting to the SSH server. The SSH client drives the connection setup process and uses public key cryptography to verify the identity of the SSH server. After the setup phase the SSH protocol uses stable symmetric encryption and hashing algorithms to ensure the privacy and integrity of the data that is exchanged between the client and server.

  The figure below presents a simplified setup flow of a secure shell connection.

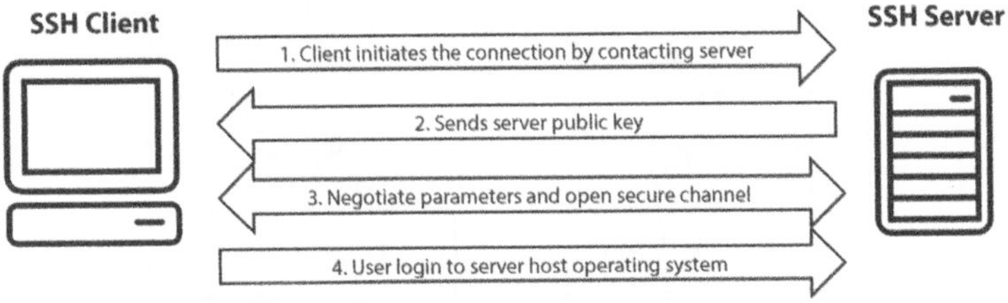

- Strong Authentication With SSH Keys
  There are several options that can be passed down for user authentication. The most common ones are passwords and public key authentication.

  The public key authentication method is primarily used for automation and sometimes by system administrators for single sign-on. It has turned out to be much more widely used than we ever anticipated. The idea is to have a cryptographic key pair—public key and private key—and configure the public key on a server to authorize access and grant anyone who has a copy of the private key access to the server. The keys used for authentication are called SSH keys. Public key authentication is also used with smartcards, such as the CAC and PIV cards used by US government.

The main use of key-based authentication is to set up secure automation. Automated secure shell file transfers are used to seamlessly integrate applications and also for automated systems and configuration management [8].

We have found that large organizations have way more SSH keys than they imagine, and managing SSH keys has become very relevant. SSH keys grant access as user names and passwords do. They require a similar provisioning and termination processes.

In some cases we have found several million SSH keys authorizing access into production servers in customer environments, with 90% of the keys actually being unused and representing access that was provisioned but never terminated. Ensuring proper protocols, processes, and review also for SSH usage is critical for proper identity and access management. Traditional identity management projects have overlooked as much as 90% of all credentials by ignoring SSH keys. We provide services and tools for implementing SSH key management.

15.9 Internet Protocol Security (IPSec)

IPsec is determined for use with both current versions of the Internet Protocol, IPv4, and IPv6. IPsec protocol headers are included in the IP header, where they appear as IP header extensions when a system is using IPsec.

The most important protocols considered a part of IPsec include:

- The IP Authentication Header (AH), specified in RFC 4302, defines an optional packet header to be used to guarantee connectionless integrity and data origin authentication for IP packets, and to protect against replays.
- The IP Encapsulating Security Payload (ESP), specified in RFC 4303, defines an optional packet header that can be used to provide confidentiality through encryption of the packet, as well as integrity protection, data origin authentication, access control and optional protection against replays or traffic analysis.
- Internet Key Exchange (IKE), defined in RFC 7296, "Internet Key Exchange Protocol Version 2 (IKEv2)," is a protocol

defined to allow hosts to specify which services are to be incorporated in packets, which cryptographic algorithms will be used to provide those services, and a system for sharing the keys used with those cryptographic algorithms.

- Previously defined on its own, the Internet Security Association and Key Management Protocol (ISAKMP) is now specified as part of the IKE protocol specification. ISAKMP defines how Security Associations (SAs) are set up and used to define direct connections between two hosts that are using IPsec. Each SA defines a connection, in one direction, from one host to another; a pair of hosts would be defined by two SAs. The SA includes all relevant attributes of the connection, including the cryptographic algorithm being used, the IPsec mode being used, encryption key and any other parameters related to the transmission of data over the connection.

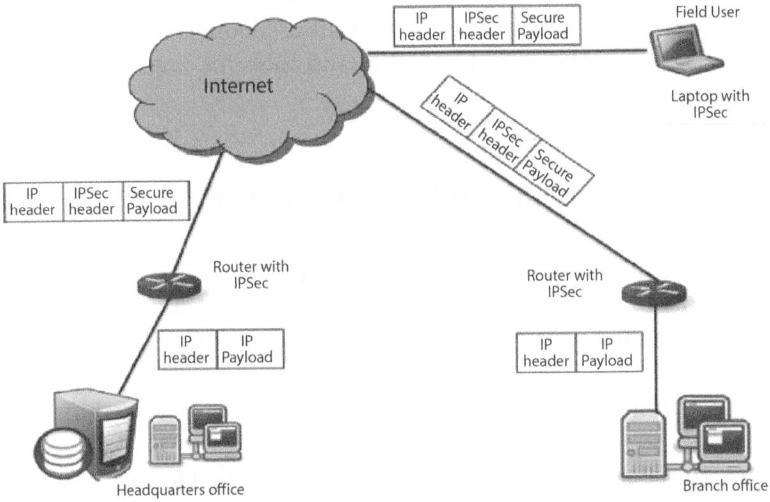

Numerous other protocols and algorithms use or are used by IPsec, including encryption and digital signature algorithms, and most related protocols are described in RFC 6071, "IP Security (IPsec) and Internet Key Exchange (IKE) Document Roadmap."

15.9.1 How IPsec Works

The first step in the process of using IPsec occurs when a host verify that a packet should be transmitted using IPsec. This may be done by checking the IP address of the source or destination against policy configurations to determine whether the traffic should be considered "interesting" for IPsec purposes. Interesting traffic triggers the security policy for the packets, which means that the system sending the packet applies the appropriate encryption and/or authentication to the packet. When an incoming packet is determined to be "interesting," the host verifies that the inbound packet has been encrypted and/or authenticated properly.

The second step in the IPsec process, called IKE Phase grants the two hosts using IPsec to negotiate the policy sets they use for the secured circuit, authenticate themselves to each other, and initiate a secure channel between the two hosts.

IKE Phase 1 sets up an initial secure channel between hosts using IPsec; that secure channel is then used to securely negotiate the way the IPsec circuit will encrypt and/or authenticate data sent across the IPsec circuit.

There are two options during IKE Phase 1: Main mode or Aggressive mode. Main mode provides greater security because it sets up a secure tunnel for exchanging session algorithms and keys, while Aggressive mode grants some of the session configuration data to be passed as plaintext but enables hosts to establish an IPsec circuit more quickly [9].

Under Main mode, the host initiating the session sends one or more proposals for the session, indicating the encryption and authentication algorithms it prefers to use, as well as other aspects of the connection; the responding host continues the negotiation until the two hosts agree and establish an IKE Security Association (SA), which defines the IPsec circuit.

When Aggressive mode is in use, the host initiating the circuit specifies the IKE security association data unilaterally and in the clear, with the responding host responding by authenticating the session.

The third step in setting up an IPsec circuit is the IKE Phase 2, which itself is conducted over the secure channel setup in IKE Phase 1. It depends upon the two hosts to negotiate and initiate the security association for the IPsec circuit carrying actual network data. In the second phase, the two hosts negotiate the type of cryptographic algorithms to use on the session, as well as agreeing on secret keying material to be used with those algorithms. Nonces, randomly selected numbers used only once to provide session authentication and replay protection, are exchanged in this phase. The hosts may also negotiate to enforce perfect forward secrecy on the exchange in this phase.

Step four of the IPsec connection is the actual exchange of data across the newly created IPsec encrypted tunnel. From this point, packets are encrypted and decrypted by the two endpoints using the IPsec SAs setup in the previous three steps.

The last step is termination of the IPsec tunnel, usually when the communication between the hosts is complete, when the session times out, or when a previously specified number of bytes has been passed through the IPsec tunnel. When the IPsec tunnel is terminated, the hosts discard keys used over that security association.

15.10 Kerberos

Kerberos is a computer network authentication protocol that works on the basis of *tickets* town nodes communicating over a non-secure network to prove their status to one another in a protected way. The protocol was named after the character *Kerberos* (or *Cerberus*) from Greek mythology, the ferocious three-headed guard dog of Hades. Its designers marked it mainly at a client–server model and it bring mutual authentication—both the user and the server verify each other's identity. Kerberos protocol messages are protected across eavesdropping and replay attacks.

That is, the same key is used to encrypt and decrypt messages. Microsoft's implementation of the Kerberos protocol can also make defined use of asymmetric encryption. A private/public key combination can be used to encrypt or decrypt fundamental authentication messages from a network client or a network service.

- What Is Kerberos Authentication?
  In this section
  - Kerberos Authentication Benefits
  - Kerberos V5 Protocol Standards
  - Supported Extensions to the Kerberos V5 Protocol
  - Technologies Related to Kerberos Authentication
  - Kerberos Authentication Dependencies

The Kerberos version 5 authentication protocol provides a mechanism for authentication—and mutual authentication—between a client and a server, or between one server and another server.

Windows Server 2003 implements the Kerberos V5 protocol as a security support provider (SSP), which can be accessed through the Security Support Provider Interface (SSPI). In addition, Windows Server 2003 implements extensions to the protocol that permit initial authentication by using public key certificates on smart cards.

The Kerberos Key Distribution Center (KDC) uses the domain's Active Directory directory service database as its security account database. Active Directory is required for default NTLM and Kerberos implementations.

The Kerberos V5 protocol considers that initial transactions between clients and servers take place on an open network in which packets transmitted along the network can be monitored and modified at will. The assumed environment, in other words, is very much like today's Internet, where an attacker can easily stand as either a client or a server, and can readily eavesdrop on or tamper with communications between legitimate clients and servers.

- Kerberos Authentication Benefits
  The Kerberos V5 protocol is more secure, more elastic, and more dynamic than NTLM. The benefits gained by using Kerberos authentication are:
  - Delegated authentication
    Windows services impersonate a client when accessing resources on the client's behalf. In many cases, a service can outright its work for the client by accessing resources on the local computer. Both NTLM and the Kerberos V5 protocol provide the information that a service needs to impersonate its client locally. However, some distributed applications are designed so that a front-end service must impersonate clients when connecting to back-end services on other computers. The Kerberos V5 protocol introduces a proxy mechanism that enables a service to impersonate its client when connecting to other services. No equivalent is available with NTLM.
  - Interoperability
    Microsoft's implementation of the Kerberos V5 protocol is based on standards-track specifications that are supported to the Internet Engineering Task Force (IETF). As a result, the implementation of the Kerberos V5 protocol in Windows Server 2003 lays a foundation for interoperability with other networks in which the Kerberos V5 protocol is used for authentication.
  - More efficient authentication to servers
    With NTLM authentication, an application server must connect to a domain controller in order to authenticate each client. With the Kerberos V5 authentication protocol, on the other hand, the server is not required to go

to a domain controller. Instead, the server can authenticate the client by examining credentials presented by the client. Clients can obtain credentials for a particular server once and then repeat those credentials throughout a network logon session. Renewable session tickets replace pass-through authentication. For more information about what renewable session tickets are and how they work, please see "How the Kerberos Version 5 Authentication Protocol Works."

- Mutual authentication

  By using the Kerberos protocol, a party at either end of a network connection can verify that the party on the other end is the entity it claims to be. Although NTLM enables servers to verify the identities of their clients, NTLM does not enable clients to verify a server's identity, nor does NTLM enable one server to verify the identity of another. NTLM authentication was designed for a network environment in which servers were assumed to be genuine. The Kerberos V5 protocol makes no such assumption.

- Kerberos V5 Protocol Standards

  The Kerberos authentication protocol originated at MIT more than a decade ago, where it was developed by engineers working on Project Athena. The first public turnout was the Kerberos version 4 authentication protocol. After board industry analysis of that protocol, the protocol's authors developed and released the Kerberos version 5 authentication protocol.

  The Kerberos V5 protocol is now on a standards track with the IETF. The implementation of the protocol in Windows Server 2003 closely follows the specification defined in Internet RFC 1510. In addition, the mechanism and format for passing security tokens in Kerberos messages follows the specification defined in Internet RFC 1964.

  The Kerberos V5 protocol specifies mechanisms to:

  - Authenticate user status. When a user wants to gain access to a server, the server needs to verify the user's identity. Consider a situation in which the user claims to be, for example, Alisha@trisha.com. Because access to resources are based on identity and associated permissions, the server must be sure the user really has the identity it claims.

- Securely package the user's name. The user's name—that is, the User Principal Name (UPN): Alisha@trisha.com, for example—and the user's credentials are packaged in a data structure called a ticket.
- Securely deliver user credentials. After the ticket is encrypted, messages are used to transport user credentials along the network.

➢ Kerberos Authentication Dependencies

This section reviews dependencies and summarizes how each dependency relates to Kerberos authentication.

- Operating System

  Kerberos authentication relies on client performance that is built in to the Windows Server 2003 operating system, the Microsoft Windows XP operating system, and the Windows 2000 operating system. If a client, domain controller, or target server is running an earlier operating system, it cannot natively use Kerberos authentication.
- TCP/IP Network Connectivity

  For Kerberos authentication to occur, TCP/IP network connectivity must exist between the client, the domain controller, and the target server.
  - *Domain Name System*

    The client uses the fully qualified domain name (FQDN) to access the domain controller. DNS must be functioning for the client to obtain the FQDN.

    For best completion, do not use Hosts files with DNS. For more information about DNS, see "DNS Technical Reference."
  - *Active Directory Domain*

    Kerberos authentication is not supported in previous operating systems, such as the Microsoft Windows NT 4.0 operating system. You must be using user and computer accounts in the Active Directory directory service to use Kerberos authentication. Local accounts and Windows NT domain accounts cannot be used for Kerberos authentication.
  - *Time Service*

    For Kerberos authentication to function correctly, all domains and forests in a network should use the same time source so that the time on all network computers is synchronized. An Active Directory domain controller acts as an authoritative source of time for its domain, which guarantees that an entire domain has the same time. For more information, see "Windows Time Service Technical Reference."

- Service Principal Names
  Service principal names (SPNs) are one and only identifiers for services running on servers. Every service that uses Kerberos authentication needs to have an SPN set for it so that clients can identify the service on the network. If an SPN is not set for a service, clients have no way of locating that service. Without correctly set SPNs, Kerberos authentication is not possible. For more information about user-to-user authentication, see "How the Kerberos Version 5 Authentication Protocol Works," and search for "The User-to-User Authentication Process."

➢ Overview/Main Points
Weaknesses/Limitations (version 4 and 5)

- Biggest lose: assumption of secure time system, and resolution of synchronization required. Could be fixed by challenge-response protocol during auth handshake.
- Password guessing: no authentication is required to request a ticket, hence attacker can gather equivalent of/ etc/passwd by requesting many tickets. Could be fixed by D-H key exchange.
- Chosen plaintext: in CBC, prefix of an encryption is encryption of a prefix, so attacker can disassemble messages and use just part of a message. (Is this true for PCBC?) Does not work in Kerberos IV, since the data block begins with a length byte and a string, destroying the prefix attack?
- Limitation: Not a host-to-host protocol. (Kerberos 5 is user-to-user; Kerberos 4 is only user-to-server).

Weaknesses in proposed version 5 additions

- Inter-realm authentication is allowed by forwarding, but no way to derive the complete "chain of trust", nor any way to do "authentication routing" within the hierarchy of authentication servers.

- ENC_TKT_IN_SKEY of Kerberos 5 allows trivial cut and paste attack that prevents mutual authentication
- Kerberos 5 CRC-32 checksum is not collision proof (as MD4 is thought to be).
- K5 still uses timestamps to authentication KRB_SAFE and KRB_PRIV messages; should use sequence numbers.

Recommendations

- Add challenge/response as alternative to time-based authentication
- Use a typical encoding for credentials (ASN.1), to avoid message ambiguity; prevents having to re-analyze each change in light of the redundancy in the binary encodings of various messages as a possible attack point (like prefix attack above)
- Explicitly allow for handheld authenticators that answer a challenge using Kc, rather than just using Kc to decrypt a ticket.
- Multi-session keys should be used to negotiate true one-time session keys
- Support for special hardware (e.g., keystone)
- Don't distribute tickets without some minimal authentication
- No point in including IP address in credentials, since network is assumed to be evil

1. Relevance
   Kerberos IV is widely disseminated, so even the limitations/weaknesses fixed in version 5 are worth addressing. Also, important to note that, just as for software correctness, any nontrivial change to the system results in a whole new system whose security properties must be re-derived "from first principles", or risk introducing security holes.
2. Flaws
   Some of the constraints in Kerberos IV stem from its initial assumptions in the MIT Athena environment, and some of the formal techniques for security verification that lead to the discovery of certain attacks were not widely known when it was designed. The attacks described on Kerberos 5 suggest that a thorough verification using formal methods would be wise.

15.11 Wired Equivalent Privacy (WEP)

- WEP is a security protocol for Wi-Fi networks. Since wireless networks transmit data over radio waves, it is easy to intercept data or "eavesdrop" on wireless data transmissions. The goal of WEP is to make wireless networks as secure as wired networks, such as those connected by Ethernet cables.
- The wired equivalent privacy protocol adds security to a wireless network by encrypting the data. If the data is intercepted, it will be unrecognizable to system that intercepted the data, since it is encrypted. However, authorized systems on the network will be able to recognize the data because they all use the same encryption algorithm. Systems on a WEP-secured network can typically be authorized by entering a network password.

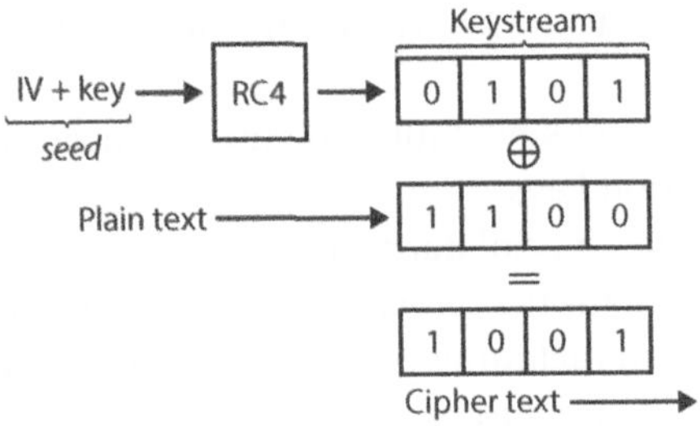

15.11.1 Authentication

Two methods of authentication can be used with WEP: Open System authentication and Shared Key authentication.

In Open System authentication, the WLAN client need not provide its credentials to the Access Point during authentication. Any client can authenticate with the Access Point and then attempt to associate. In effect, no authentication occurs. Subsequently, WEP keys can be used for encrypting data frames. At this point, the client must have the correct keys.

In Shared Key authentication, the WEP key is used for authentication in a four-step challenge-response handshake:

1. The client sends an authentication request to the Access Point.
2. The Access Point replies with a clear-text challenge.

3. The client encrypts the challenge-text using the configured WEP key and sends it back in another authentication request.
4. The Access Point decrypts the response. If this matches the challenge text, the Access Point sends back a positive reply.

After the authentication and association, the pre-shared WEP key is also used for encrypting the data frames using RC4.

At first glance, it might seem as though Shared Key authentication is more secure than Open System authentication, since the latter offers no real authentication. However, it is quite the reverse. It is possible to derive the keystream used for the handshake by capturing the challenge frames in Shared Key authentication. Therefore, data can be more easily intercepted and decrypted with Shared Key authentication than with Open System authentication. If privacy is a primary concern, it is more advisable to use Open System authentication for WEP authentication, rather than Shared Key authenticati on; however, this also means that any WLAN client can connect to the AP. (Both authentication mechanisms are weak; Shared Key WEP is deprecated in favor of WPA/WPA2.)

15.12 WiFi Protected Access (WPA)

- WPA is a security protocol designed to invent secure wireless (Wi-Fi) networks. It is similar to the WEP protocol, but offers improvements in the way it handles security keys and the way users are authorized.
- For an encrypted data transfer to work, both systems on the outset and end of a data transfer must use the same encryption/decryption key. While WEP provides each authorized system with the same key, WPA uses the temporal key integrity protocol (TKIP), which dynamically changes the key that the systems use. This prevents intruders from creating their own encryption key to match the one used by the secure network.
- WPA also implements something called the Extensible Authentication Protocol (EAP) for authorizing users. Instead of authorizing computers based soley on their MAC address, WPA can use several other methods to verify each computer's identity. This makes it more challenging for unauthorized systems to gain access to the wireless network.

Wi-Fi Protected Access (WPA) is a security standard for users of computing devices equipped with wireless internet connections. WPA was developed by the Wi-Fi Alliance to provide more sophisticated data encryption and better user authentication than Wired Equivalent Privacy (WEP), the original Wi-Fi security standard. The new standard, which was ratified by the IEEE in 2004 as 802.11i, was designed to be backward-compatible with WEP to encourage quick, easy adoption. Network security professionals were able to support WPA on many WEP-based devices with a simple firmware update.

WPA has discrete modes for enterprise users and for personal use. The enterprise mode, WPA-EAP, uses more stringent 802.1x authentication with the Extensible Authentication Protocol (EAP). The personal mode, WPA-PSK, uses preshared keys for simpler implementation and management among consumers and small offices. Enterprise mode requires the use of an authentication server. WPA's encryption method is the Temporal Key Integrity Protocol (TKIP). TKIP includes a per-packet mixing function, a message integrity check, an extended initialization vector and a re-keying mechanism. WPA provides strong user authentication based on 802.1x and the Extensible Authentication Protocol (EAP). WPA depends on a central authentication server, such as RADIUS, to authenticate each user.

Software renew that allows both server and client computers to implement WPA became available during 2003. Access points (see hot spots) can operate in mixed WEP/WPA mode to support both WEP and WPA clients. However, mixed mode effectively provides only WEP-level security for all users. Home users of access points that use only WPA can operate in a special home mode in which the user need only enter a password to be connected to the access point. The password will trigger authentication and TKIP encryption.

15.13 Wi-Fi Protected Access II and the Most Current Security Protocols

WPA2 superseded WPA in 2004. WPA2 uses the Counter Mode Cipher Block Chaining Message Authentication Code Protocol (CCMP). It is based on the applicable obligatory Advanced Encryption Standard algorithm, which organizes message authenticity and integrity verification, and it is much secure and more reliable than the original TKIP protocol for WPA.

WPA2 still has vulnerabilities; primary among those is unauthorized access to the enterprise wireless network, where there is an invasion of attack vector of certain Wi-Fi Protected Setup (WPS) access points. This can take the invader several hours of concerted effort with state-of-the-art computer technology, but the threat of system compact should not be deduced. It is approved the WPS be disabled for each attack vector access point in WPA2 to discourage such threats.

15.13.1 Wi-Fi Protected Access

Though these threats have traditionally, and virtually completely, been directed at business wireless systems, even home wireless systems can be exposed by weak passwords or passphrases that can make it accessible for an attacker to deal those systems. Privileged accounts (such as administrator accounts) should always be supported by stronger, longer passwords and all passwords should be changed frequently.

15.13.2 Difference between WEP, WPA: Wi-Fi Security Through the Ages

Since the late 1990s, Wi-Fi security protocols have supported multiple upgrades, with outright deprecation of older protocols and significant correction to newer protocols. A stroll through the history of Wi-Fi security serves to focus both what's out there right now and why you should avoid older model.

15.14 Wired Equivalent Privacy (WEP)

Wired Equivalent Privacy (WEP) is the most abroad used Wi-Fi security protocol in the world. This is a function of age, backwards compatibility, and the fact that it comes out first in the protocol selection menus in many router control panels.

WEP was ratified as a Wi-Fi security standard in September of 1999. The first versions of WEP weren't particularly strong, even for the time they were free, because U.S. restrictions on the export of separate cryptographic technology led to manufacturers enclose their devices to only 64-bit encryption. When the restrictions were lifted, it was increased to 128-bit. Despite the introduction of 256-bit WEP, 128-bit remains one of the most common implementations.

Despite modification to the protocol and an increased key size, over time numerous security bloom were discovered in the WEP standard. As computing power increased, it became easier and easier to effort those bugs. As early as 2001, proof-of-concept effort were floating around, and by 2005, the FBI gave a public demonstration (in an effort to boost awareness of WEP's flaws) where they cracked WEP passwords in minutes using freely available software.

Despite various enhancements, work-around, and other experiments to shore up the WEP system, it remains highly vulnerable. Systems that rely on WEP should be upgraded or, if security upgrades are not a choice, replaced. The Wi-Fi Alliance officially retired WEP in 2004.

15.15 Wi-Fi Protected Access (WPA)

Wi-Fi Protected Access (WPA) was the Wi-Fi Alliance's express response and replacement to the increasingly possible burden of the WEP standard. WPA was formally approve in 2003, a year before WEP was officially retired. The most familiar WPA configuration is WPA-PSK (Pre-Shared Key). The keys used by WPA are 256-bit, a significant development over the 64-bit and 128-bit keys used in the WEP system.

Some of the significant changes implemented with WPA admitted message integrity checks (to terminate if an attacker had captured or altered packets passed between the access point and client) and the Temporal Key Integrity Protocol (TKIP). TKIP employs a per-packet key system that was entirely more secure than the fixed key system used by WEP. The TKIP encryption standard was later superseded by Advanced Encryption Standard (AES).

Although what a powerful improvement WPA was over WEP, the ghost of WEP haunted WPA. TKIP, a basic component of WPA, was designed to be easily rolled out via firmware upgrades onto existing WEP-enabled devices. As such, it had to recover certain elements used in the WEP system which, ultimately, were also exploited.

WPA, like its predecessor WEP, has been shown via both proof-of-concept and applied public demonstrations to be vulnerable to intrusion. Interestingly, the process by which WPA is usually breached is not a direct attack on the WPA protocol (although such attacks have been successfully demonstrated), but by attacks on a supplementary system that was rolled out with WPA—Wi-Fi Protected Setup (WPS)—which was designed to make it easy to link devices to modern access points.

15.16 Conclusions

Secure cloud communication is still a leading challenge due to the huge number of attacks made on the cloud. In addition, the amount of resources in the cloud and the various functions, it carries out means that eventually, hackers and others penetrate the system and determine how the various security functions work. Although use of different security protocol play an meaningful role to protect the cloud.

References

1. Armbrust, M., Fox, A., Griffith, R., Joseph, A.D., Katz, R.H., Kon-winski, A., Lee, G., Patterson, D.A., Rabkin, A., Stoica, I., Zaharia, M., Above the clouds: A Berkeley view of cloud computing, Berkeley Tech. Rep. UCB-EECS-2009-28, 2009.
2. Cloud Services—Cloud Computing Solutions, Accenture, Accenture White paper. Retrieved on 2014-01-29.
3. www.sersc.org/journals/IJSIA/vol10_no2_2016
4. https://beacontelecom.com
5. Bala Chandar, R., Kavitha, M.S., Seenivasan, K., A proficient model for high end security in cloud computing. *Int. J. Emerg. Res. Manag. Technol.*, 5, 10 697–702, 2014.
6. https://technet.microsoft.com/pt-pt/library.
7. http://www.netgear.com/docs/refdocs/Wireless/wirelessBasics.htm.
8. http://www.wi-fiplanet.com/tutorials/article.php.
9. http://www.computerbits.com/archive/2003/0200/hotspotsecurity.html.

Index

Printed and bound by CPI Group (UK) Ltd, Croydon, CR0 4YY
27/10/2024
14580467-0001